The food resource

THEMES IN RESOURCE MANAGEMENT
Edited by Professor Bruce Mitchell, University of Waterloo

Already published:
John Blunden: Mineral Resources and their Management (Out of Print)
John Chapman: Geography and Energy
Paul Eagles: The Planning and Management of Environmentally Sensitive Areas (Out of Print)
R. L. Heathcote: Arid Lands: their use and abuse
Adrian McDonald and David Kay: Water Resources: issues and strategies
Peter H. Omara-Ojungu: Resource Management in Developing Countries
Francis Sandbach: Principles of Pollution Control (Out of Print)
Stephen Smith: Recreation Geography

Forthcoming:
L. G. Smith: Impact Assessment and Sustainable Resource Management
D. S. Slocombe: Managing Resources for Sustainability

John T Pierce

The Food Resource

Longman
Scientific &
Technical

Copublished in the United States
with John Wiley & Sons Inc., New York

Longman Scientific & Technical
Longman Group UK Ltd.
Longman House, Burnt Mill, Harlow,
Essex CM20 2JE, England
and Associated Companies throughout the world.

Copublished in the United States with
John Wiley & Sons, Inc., 605 Third Avenue, New York, NY 10158

© Longman Group UK Limited 1990

First published 1990
Reprinted 1992

British Library Cataloguing in Publication Data
Pierce, John T.
  The food resource.- (Themes in resource management).
  1. Food resources
  I. Title   II. Series
  338.1'9

ISBN 0-582-30537-3

Library of Congress Cataloging-in-Publication Data
Pierce, John T.
  The food resource/John T. Pierce
    p. cm. – (Themes in resource management)
  Bibliography: p.
  Includes index.
  ISBN 0-470-21512-7 (USA only)
  1. Agriculture. 2. Food supply. 3. Food crops. I. Title.
II. Series.
S493.P65   1990
338.1'9–dc20   89-12327
                                                                         CIP

Set in 10/12 Times

Printed in Hong Kong
WC/02

Contents

Contents

List of figures

List of tables

Acknowledgements

We are grateful to the following for permission to reproduce copyright material:

Academic Press Inc. and the authors A. Rao & I. Singh for table 9.3 adapted from table 1 (Rao & Singh, 1977b); American Dairy Science Association for part of table 9.2 from table 1 by D. M. Graham on pp. 103–5 of *Journal of Dairy Science*, Vol 53, 1970 (Rao & Singh, 1977a); The Annals of Regional Science and the author, Prof. Pearce for fig. 10.3 from fig. 1 (Pearce & Markandya, 1987); Butterworth Scientific Ltd. for figs 9.1 from fig. 1 (Bhatia, 1985), 9.2 & 9.3 from figs 8.2 & 8.3 (Leach *et al.*, 1986); Deere Company Publications for fig. 9.5 from a figure (Stickler *et al.*, 1975); Elsevier Applied Science Publishers Ltd. for fig. 2.1 adapted from fig. 2 (Bunting *et al.*, 1982) and table 8.1 from table IV (Oram, 1982); Elsevier Science Publishers (Physical Sciences & Engineering Div.) and the author, H. Linnemann for table 4.7 from tables 2.5/A2.7 and Appendix 10A (Linnemann, 1979); The Foundation for Environmental Conservation for tables 7.7 & 7.8 from tables I & II (Mabbutt, 1984); International Institute for Applied Systems Analysis for fig. 8.14 from fig. 1.15 (Parry & Carter, 1987); Journal of Soil & Water Conservation for figs 7.6 from figs 7 & 8 (Pierce *et al.*, 1983), 7.11 from fig. 1 (Dregne, 1978); the author, Dr. W. Kellogg for figs 8.12 & 8.15 from figs 11.3 & 11.2 (Kellogg & Schware, 1981); Longman Group UK Ltd. for figs 6.2a & 6.2b from fig. 13.1 (Heathcote, 1983); Macmillan Magazines Ltd. and the author, P. Jones for figs 8.11 from fig. 5 (Jones *et al.*, 1986), 8.13a & 8.13b from figs 1 & 2 (Wigley *et al.*, 1980) copyright (c) 1980 & 1986 Macmillan Magazines Ltd.; Minister of Supply and Services, Canada and the author, D. Coote for fig. 9.9 from map 3 and table 9.6 from table 3 (Coote, 1983); The MIT Press for figs 4.4, 4.5 & 4.6 from figs 4.9, 4.70 & 4.90 (Meadows, 1974); National Research Council of Canada for figs 8.9 & 8.10 from figs 3 & 4 (Sinclair & Fryxell, 1985); Organisation for Economic Co-Operation & Development for fig. 5.6 from fig. 2.1 (OECD, 1985);

Oxford University Press Inc. for figs 3.3 from fig. 1.4 (World Bank, 1986), 5.2 from fig. 4.2 (World Bank, 1984) (c) 1984 & 1986 The International Bank for Reconstruction & Development/The Third World Bank and table 4.3 from table 22 (Leontieff, 1977) (c) 1977 United Nations, all redrafted by permission; Pergamon Press PLC. for figs 2.2 & 2.7 from figs 2.3 & 2.11 and tables 2.6 & 2.7 from tables 2.2 & 2.3 (Falkenmark, 1980), 6.10 from table 7 (Ehlers, 1977) copyright (c) 1977 & 1980 Pergamon Press PLC.; Resources for the Future Inc. for fig. 6.6 from fig. 3.1 and table 6.7 from table 3.2 (Frederick & Hanson, 1982); Scientific American Inc. for figs 2.8 & 6.7 adapted from figures on pp. 102 & 116 (Ambroggi, 1980), 5.3 from a figure on p. 198 (Deevey, 1960); Texas A & M University Press and the respective authors for figs 6.8 from fig. 2 (Ahmad, 1987), 6.9 from fig. 1 (Bhuiyan, 1987) and tables 2.2 from table 2 (Boyer, 1987), 6.1 & 6.2 from tables 1 & 2 (Rangeley, 1987), 6.9 from a table (Silliman & Lenton, 1987), 7.5 from a table (Aston, 1987), 7.6 from table 4 (Aceves-Navarro, 1987), 9.1 adapted from tables 1, 2 & 3 (Faidley, 1987), 9.8 from table 1 (Smerdon & Hiler, 1987); Westview Press for table 9.7 from table 11.2 (Altiera, *et al.*, 1984); John Wiley & Sons Inc. for fig. 2.5 from fig. 7.1 (Butler, 1980) and tables 2.1 from table 7 (Mitchell, 1984), 6.5 from tables 3.8 & 3.9 (Lindh, 1979), part of table 9.2 from table 2, p. 4 of *Dairy Cattle Feeding & Management*, 5th ed. by P. N. Reaves, Wiley 1963 (Rao & Singh, 1977a); Worldwatch Institute for table 5.1 from table 8.2 (Brown, 1978).

Foreword

The Themes in Resource Management Series has several objectives. One is to identify and to examine substantive and enduring resource management and development problems. Attention will range from local to international scales, from developed to developing nations, from the public to the private sector, and from biophysical to political considerations.

A second objective is to assess responses to these management and development problems in a variety of world regions. Several responses are of particular interest but especially *research* and *action programmes*. The former involves the different types of analysis which have been generated by natural resource problems. The series will assess the kinds of problems being defined by investigators, the nature and adequacy of evidence being assembled, the kinds of interpretations and arguments being presented, the contributions to improving theoretical understanding as well as resolving pressing problems, and the areas in which progress and frustration are being experienced. The latter response involves the policies, programmes and projects being conceived and implemented to tackle complex and difficult problems. The series is concerned with reviewing their adequacy and effectiveness.

A third objective is to explore the way in which resource analysis, management and development might be made more complementary to one another. Too often analysts and managers go their separate ways. A good part of the blame for this situation must lie with the analysts who too frequently ignore or neglect the concerns of managers, unduly emphasize method and technique, and exclude explicit consideration of the managerial implications of their research. It is hoped that this series will demonstrate that research and analysis can contribute both to the development of theory and to the resolution of important societal problems.

John Pierce's book is the eighth in the Themes in Resource Management Series. As with the seventh book which focused upon commercial energy systems and national policies, the primary focus is upon the global scale, creating significant problems regarding data. Within that context, John Pierce has identified major themes and issues and then examines the resources for and constraints upon food production. In turn, he considers the impacts of population, water, land degradation, climate and energy on the production of food in the developed and developing nations. His analysis stresses that we live very much in an interdependent world, and that the interrelationships among food, land and people are among the most fundamental with which societies must deal.

John Pierce has been analysing agricultural and rural problems for over 15 years. He completed his PhD at the London School of Economics and Political Science and has published numerous articles focused upon agriculture and food production. In this book, he provides a synoptic study of the role of resource and environmental factors which influence the productive capacity of food production in a variety of countries. In a world in which starving children in drought-prone and war-devastated countries have becomes a regular but discomforting item in newspapers and television, such a book is timely and needed. The production and distribution of food on a global scale are fundamental problems for which considerable progress is still required.

Bruce Mitchell
University of Waterloo
Waterloo, Ontario

May 1989

Preface

The Food Resource has its genesis in research that I was conducting in the early 1980s with Owen Furuseth at the University of North Carolina and Bob Stathers at the University of British Columbia into some of the major natural and environmental resource constraints affecting expanded food production in North America. While the problem at the time was one of abundance and not scarcity, there was a growing body of evidence in North America and worldwide indicating that our present practices were not sustainable over the long-term. While science is important to the future of agriculture it must be emphasized that agriculture is still an overwhelmingly resource-based activity. In an attempt to appraise the changing environment for food production the book out of necessity became a global assessment, retrospectively and prospectively. It purposely emphasizes the supply side of the food equation, as opposed to the equally important demand side, and attempts to assess critically human intervention in the environment and the implications for agriculture. It was thought at the beginning of this project, as now, that to do justice to the topic and, to be of any use to the serious student, the issues must reflect a healthy balance between the physical and social sciences and be thoroughly documented. To that end considerable time and effort have been dedicated.

I am indebted to a large number of individuals for their research and assistance in the preparation of the Food Resource. Bruce Mitchell, the series editor acted as a very constructive critic whose frequent message was the need for clarity of expression. Dave Ellenwood, my research assistant for the last three years, lent his consummate analytical, research and drafting skills in a most dedicated way. His good humour and ability to persevere were qualities that were greatly appreciated. Ray Squirrell and Margaret Wheat provided drafting for many of the figures often at short notice and with limited resources. Word processing, often a thankless task but not in this case, was done by Moyna Gick, Gwen Fernandes, Barb

Martin, Mary Ward and Dave Ellenwood. Many colleagues and former geography professors directly or indirectly influenced my approach to the Food Resource – among these are Barry Smit, Mike Brklacich, Chris Bryant, Mike Troughton, Mike Bunce and Owen Furuseth. Lastly, I would like to thank my wife Jan for her invaluable advice and assistance in the preparation of the manuscript and my two sons, Emmet and Lewis, for the welcome diversions from the weightier issues of the world. Needless to say all errors of omissions and commission are mine alone.

This book is dedicated to my parents Ron and Beryl Pierce – *per ardua ad astra*!

CHAPTER 1

Themes and Issues

The rise in productive capacity

During the last 200 years humans have increasingly expanded their control over the bio-physical environment. With the cumulative growth in knowledge and its scientific, technical and social applications, the role of environmental resources in affecting human welfare has changed critically. The quantity and type of food produced were once rigidly tied to given environmental parameters of light, heat, moisture and nutrients. Now the application of knowledge from the industrial and scientific revolutions has loosened that tie and made humans the prime agent of change in the biosphere and much more the master than the servant of those resources. The development of artificial fertilizers, herbicides and a wide variety of plant hybrids, together with new storage and transportation facilities, has greatly extended market areas and increased the supply, variety and nutritional content of food.

Thus, technology has given humans power over nature and with that the Baconian view of 'the effecting of all things possible' (Medawar, 1969). Yet this control of resources is very much a double-edged sword. In addition to promoting abundance and pushing back the frontiers of scarcity, it also places extremely heavy demands on the resource base itself. This occurs not only in terms of basic inputs to the production process but also in terms of the delicate physical and biological balances which sustain life systems and make agricultural production possible. Conflicts between human goals and natural processes are becoming increasingly common.

In Western industrialized countries, the growth of food supply has been distinguished by rates of production far in excess of additions to the population base. Productivity growth has been of pivotal importance here as technological inputs expanded and energy use intensified. Not surprisingly, the importance of land has declined relative to other inputs since

1

the 1940s. This growth in production capacity has also been distinguished by enormous gains in the level of certainty and security with which food is produced. The phenomenal growth of world transport and communications has greatly reduced the risks associated with isolated food production. Together, increasing productivity and security of supply have been instrumental in facilitating the shift in the structure and function of society from rural–agricultural to urban–industrial, and in contributing to the confidence with which Western society can plan for growth and change through both market and non-market means.

In numerous developing countries, a similar pattern of growth in the agricultural sector has been apparent for two decades. The tremendous expansion in food output, along with growth in demand, is a direct result of a push to industrialize, an increase in resource inputs relative to land inputs and a trend toward a more science-based agricultural system. For example, the adoption of Green Revolution technology in India saw the introduction of energy intensive inputs (fertilizers, pesticides, irrigation) with high-yielding varieties of grain, all of which contributed to food production (since the 1960s) keeping pace with population growth.

However, many developing countries remain in other parts of Asia and in Africa which have been unable to balance, much less increase, food output in relation to population growth. The decline in food self-sufficiency in the Sahel is perhaps the most dramatic example of this. For those few developing countries with high rates of economic growth, food consumption has not suffered, but for those less successful economically this has not been the case. This is a reminder of the basic divergence between economic and physiological demands for food. The lack of ability to pay for needed foodstuffs represents one of the fundamental stumbling blocks to the achievement of proper nutrition in many of these countries. It also highlights the increasing population pressures on environmental resources (given available capital/technology) and the need to better understand the relationship between agriculture and the environment.

The regional dimensions of hunger and inadequate food supply are clear, as are to a lesser degree a number of environmental impacts of extensification and intensification of the food system. The solutions to the problems and the implications for world political, economic and environmental stability are not. The expected growth in world population and national incomes during the next twenty years will increase the demand for food and fibre at an unprecedented scale. To sustain growth in productive capacity of the worldwide food system, large increases in resource productivity and resource inputs will be required. The relative scarcity of these resources, the growth in technological innovation and the environmental impact of increased resource demands (including the land-use needs of a growing population) will determine the economic and environmental costs of growth in demand and ultimately the sustainability of our practices.

Visions of the future

A number of researchers have already questioned the sustainability of our present agricultural practices and our reliance on technological fixes, adding their voices to the 'limits to growth' chorus and the need for a 'conserver' society. Borgstrom (1980) has pointed to the growing divergence between crop and livestock production as having profound ecological repercussions. Eckholm (1976) and Brown (1981) have argued that soil erosion and other forms of land degradation represent major ecological hazards facing civilization. The carrying capacity of the land is either being reduced or exceeded in many instances. And Georgescu-Roegen (1981) has criticized conventional economic thinking for its failure to recognize the limits to economic growth imposed by a finite supply of natural resources. He argues that since the earth represents a closed system the economic growth process is one in which matter and energy are irreversibly transformed from an available to an unavailable state. Entropy, or the second law of thermodynamics, ultimately prevents the recovery of all of the resources used. Waste, pollution and carbon dioxide, for example, are the necessary but unwanted, and generally unrecoverable, byproducts of resource use. He goes on to observe that the transition from non-renewable to renewable energy paths will be extremely difficult since it must be based upon the use of fossil fuels.

But the growth and maintenance of the food system are circumscribed by factors which transcend resource/ecological issues. In discussing the organizational problems inherent in the continuation of technological growth, Ophuls (1977: 119–20) observed:

> Something like the ecological 'law of minimum,' which states that the factor in least supply governs the rate of growth of a system as a whole, applies to social systems as well as eco-systems, so that technological fixes cannot run ahead of the human capacity to plan, construct, fund, and man them – a fact many technological optimists either overlook or assume away.

Implicit in these interpretations is the notion that if humans are to survive the future and/or if the human condition is to improve, the way we manage our resources will have to change, as will the nature of the demands made by humans on the bio-physical base. Exponential growth in demands for goods and services derived from the transformation of resources is not sustainable over the long-term.

Against the ecological neo-Malthusian view of the human prospect, stands a significant body of thought which sees the human condition as less the product of physical/ecological constraints and more the product of economic and technological forces, social relations, property rights and power differentials (Chambers, 1983). This highly diverse group, which is

3

well represented on the right and left of the political spectrum, is far more optimistic about resource availability and may, for want of a better term, be referred to as institutionalist.

Some feel that the future will either be a confirmation of our present approaches to the use of resources and the development of technology or a change to an even more favourable hyper-expansionist approach. Dahlberg (1986: 26-7) has noted in regard to the latter that 'It involves not only high technology approaches, but the expectation of major breakthroughs in such areas as energy (fusion reactors) and genetic engineering.' Orthodox economists such as Simon (1981: 68-69), believed that 'the supplies of land and other natural resources do not constrain the world's food supply, nor will they in the foreseeable future.' There are, in this view, no natural constraints which will foreclose the growth in production capacity of the food system. Market-generated technological change and factor substitution can be relied upon to expand the opportunities for growth. Similarly, Dubos (1981) argued that population growth is slowing, new technologies are less harmful to the environment than old technologies, and the environment is more resilient than was originally believed. Above all else, both Simon and Dubos believed that human resources are the ultimate resource and 'trend is not destiny' (Berry et al., 1987).

Marxists, like their rival neo-classical economists, tend to have a optimistic view of future food production possibilities, and of the ability of humans to triumph over nature (Warnoch, 1987). The Soviet Union, for example, places great store on the efficient use of modern science and technology to expand food supply at home and in the Third World countries. Limitations to growth are not the product of natural resource constraints but rather of economic and political constraints. Unlike the neo-classical economists, Marxists explain scarcity of food within the context of the profit motive, and inequities in access to resources and income as products of the capitalist mode of production. Economic imperialism fostered by Western countries, which is aided and abetted by ruling élite in Third World countries, is inimical to development. Population pressures and poverty are not seen as the cause of underdevelopment but the result.

How does one reconcile the pronounced dualism in the way in which 'expert opinion' views future growth prospects? First, the differences in outlook among ecological and market-oriented institutional groups can in part be traced to differences in their respective approaches to the data. The former tend to use technological forecasts, incorporating population growth and its estimated impact on existing reserves of land and other resources, to ascertain future scarcity and adequacy. The latter use historical data, particularly changes in price/cost relationships, to ascertain future scarcity and adequacy. Institutionalists (including Marxists) generally place great faith in the role of science and technical fixes in affecting resource potential.

Both positions are rife with assumptions about the size and quality of the arable land base and water supplies, about the growth in technology, about future price/cost relationships and about the resilience of the environment. Castle (1982: 812) has argued that 'the fundamental deficiency of both approaches is the same: no one can know or predict the state of future knowledge.' He also argued that what appears to be physical scarcity is often inadequate incentives and obsolete institutions. This observation could easily be extended to include political and economic systems which, according to Marxists, fail in deriving the maximum benefit inherent in the agricultural system irrespective of physical limits.

Important physical/biological limits exist in agricultural systems which affect local carrying capacity and the ability of societies to meet long-term food needs. There is also great scope for change in the way in which food is produced and ultimately in the capacity to provide for everyone's food needs. A distinction perhaps needs to be made between what is possible, given ideal circumstances of perfect information, the free flow of goods, technology, adequate capital, etc., and what is probable or most likely to occur, given inadequate information and capital and injurious terms of trade. As Ophuls (1977: 120) noted earlier 'technological fixes cannot run ahead of the human capacity to plan, construct and man them.' Capital is not freely available, income distributions are skewed, our knowledge of the sensitivity of tropical and sub-tropical agricultural systems is limited, and allocative mechanisms are highly imperfect – regardless of the political system. Regarding the developing countries, it has been argued that the traditional social and institutional structures are unable to respond effectively to the adoption of technology and the intensification of the food system required to meet the growth in production (Hrabovszky, 1985).

Since such things as capital, income, land tenure, research and price/cost relations define the scope and utility of resources, shortages/imbalances in one or more of these can seriously curtail the development of agricultural systems. Hence, while the ecologists place too much emphasis on physical limits, institutionalists can be faulted for their unquestioning belief in adaptability of humans, in a social/institutional sense, in technical fixes and in the resilience of ecosystems.

Concepts and approaches

Given the above factors, considerable uncertainty still surrounds the issues of food security and adequacy, both regionally and internationally. Figure 1.1 provides a hypothetical example of changes to adequacy through the treatment of demand/supply projections under two different scenarios. Smit and Flaherty (1984: 3) have argued that the 'analytical problem is to devise methods to measure the size of the gap between food needs and production capacity and to assess the sensitivity of this gap to changes in conditions'. An incomplete picture exists regarding 'the sensitivity of this gap' to natural and human-induced constraints in the food production system. Considering the potential limitations these constraints pose for viable agricultural development, this book has several goals: first, to analyse and evaluate the impact of resource and environmental factors upon the productive capacity of food-production systems with emphasis on croplands in both developed and developing countries; second, to discuss the implications of these findings for global food-producing potential; and third, to examine policies and approaches designed to sustain growth in output while balancing economic and environmental costs.

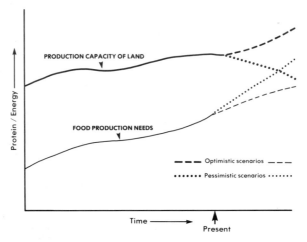

Fig. 1.1 Synoptic food supply and demand relations
Source after Smit and Flaherty (1984)

The focus of the book, therefore, is toward the supply side of the growth equation. While population and income growth (or demand factors) figure prominently in the analysis, the overriding concern here is to establish, conceptually and empirically, a better understanding of the major human-induced physical factors which affect the growth and adequacy of food-production systems. As a first step toward that better understanding of these factors it is helpful at this stage to try and sketch the conditions which shape and determine the long-term adequacy of the global food system.

Figure 1.2 illustrates one of many ways of conceptualizing long-term adequacy by emphasizing, in very general terms, the factors which affect supply potential. The question 'what is an adequate food supply?' cannot be given any definitive answer since adequacy is a subjective concept which can be measured along either economic or nutritional/physical lines. For simplicity, long-term adequacy is seen as a condition where at the very least supply potential must exceed demand potential in economic and/or

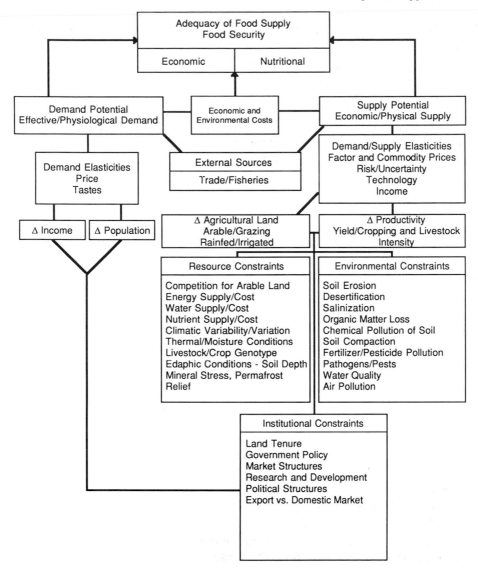

Fig. 1.2 Factors affecting supply and demand potential within the food system
Source adapted from Pierce and Furuseth (1986)

nutritional terms. Hence indications of a shortfall in supply relative to demand would be expressed in terms of rising economic and environmental costs in the production of food, physical shortages and nutritional deficiencies.

Demand potential for food is, like supply potential, an abstract concept. Nevertheless, growth and change in demand are most forcefully and directly affected by income and population growth. The exact expression of these factors will depend on demand elasticities, prices, GNP, tastes and other cultural factors. Although population growth is generally the more important factor affecting growth in demand, income growth can significantly shift the demand curve for cereals, as consumption increasingly favours animal and livestock products.

Supply potential, nationally or globally, is a product of the agricultural land base (arable and grazing) and its scope for expansion, and productivity growth which reflects changes in yields and cropping/livestock intensities. As in the case of demand, the actual supply at any given time is the product of relatively short-term circumstances that relate to supply elasticities, prices, technological change, weather, and risk and uncertainty. If adequacy is being defined in regional/national, as opposed to global terms, then trade in agricultural commodities becomes a critical factor affecting supply (and demand) potential. Although many countries may not have the physical resources to meet their food needs, earnings from exports of goods and services such as manufactured goods and cash crops provide the income to augment food consumption. Hence supply potential can be defined in terms of a country's comparative advantage in the production of non-food items. Moreover, countries may supplement domestic food production from fisheries. Borgstrom (1980) has referred to these offshore sources of food, whether from other countries or the sea, as ghost acreage. Food self-sufficiency levels for countries relying on external supplies of food must therefore be less than 100 per cent.

Since growth in crop production capacity is contingent upon growth in arable area, yield and cropping intensities, these components act as primary constraints. Associated with different land capability classes are different climatic resources. When these environmental factors are correctly combined with specific crop genotype and technological inputs, experimental or optimal yield levels can be established. In turn, when these are combined with the maximum arable land base, the ultimate production potential or supply potential of a region can be defined. Irrigation may, for example, allow for an extension in the arable land base, increase yields by improving the environment for crop production, and increase cropping intensities through an increase in harvested area. Just as all of these factors are required resources, they are also limiting factors to increased yield and production.

In studies of growth in crop yields, growth has been divided into a genetic portion and a technological portion (Jensen, 1978). Application of fertilizers, pesticides and other energy-intensive inputs improve and expand the environmental resources for food production, while the genotype determines the conversion and efficiency in the use of those resources. Reduction in yield growth and even the experience of yield ceilings occurs because of the existence of one or more limiting factors. It is possible to identify three different occasions when limiting factors occur (Pierce and Stathers, 1988):

(1) Ignorance of optimal combinations, unfavourable physico-chemical environments, pests and pathogens, increased costs of inputs or institutional barriers may contribute to slowing of yield growth and a failure to approach, much less achieve, experimental yield levels (Boyer, 1982).

(2) The interaction of climate resources and technology (genetic make-up, fertilizers, pests and disease control) determines yield growth. Hence when climate and technology continue to be compatible yield growth continues. However in numerous regions yield growth has slowed because of the incompatibility between these two factors (Kogan, 1985).

(3) Human intervention in the environment can diminish growth in yield. Numerous forms of land degradation, water pollution, consumption of prime agricultural land and climatic change can act as limiting factors to reduce yield growth and to reduce production potential.

While area, yield and cropping intensities ultimately determine supply potential of a crop system, these are but the final expressions of innumerable secondary constraints affecting quantity and quality of resources available for agriculture which set upper limits to growth and constrain growth potential. A number of natural constraints, such as solar radiation, thermal, moisture and nutrient conditions and genetic potential, set limits on the ultimate production potential, whereas many human-induced factors, such as soil erosion, urbanization of agricultural land, climatic change and narrowing of crop and livestock genetic base, can diminish the production potential inherent in the food system. Underlying both resource and environmental constraints and directly impacting productivity and the arable land base (and demand) are a variety of long-term institutional constraints. 'Institutional' is defined very broadly. Private and public decisions regarding allocation of the land resource base for export purposes as opposed to domestic use, government subsidies and investment strategies, research, land tenure policy, the pricing of goods, and political structures and stability all play a crucial role in affecting the opportunities for agricultural production on both the demand and supply sides of the food equation.

Hence while potential for expanding food production is present in many countries that require additional food, failure to achieve that potential is largely because of institutional and social reasons. Limits to the quality and quantity of those physical factors which affect adequacy have their origins not just in natural systems but also human systems.

Role of resource development and management

The world today possesses both the resources and the technology to meet

9

expected food requirements for the foreseeable future. The gap between the food needs of the future and what is now being produced, regionally and globally, can be narrowed by extended development of agricultural systems in conjunction with overall economic development. This can be accomplished through expansion of irrigation facilities and arable land, as well as by selective targeting of technology and other non-land inputs, improved pricing, markets and financing. But development alone without proper resource management (by knowing the economic, cultural and bio-physical characteristics of the system for sustained use) will only trade-off the future for the present. The maintenance and growth of agricultural systems are dependent upon adopting a far more comprehensive and positive approach to agriculture systems and their development. Implicit in this approach is the recognition that agriculture and food are renewable but at the same time based upon depletable resources. This requires a more careful accounting (environmentally, economically and socially) of the impact of inputs and outputs in agriculture in both on-site and off-site terms. Indeed, the delicate but essential balance that needs to be struck between development and management of agricultural resources is one of the great challenges facing humans.

Policies and resource management practices aimed at optimizing resource use and sustaining the productive qualities of land are to be favoured over those which do not. But rarely are those choices clear for reasons that transcend the multiplicity of goals which are at the heart of any society. For example, lack of information and associated uncertainty, the absence of clearly-defined property rights or institutional agreements in lieu of those rights, shortage of capital and technical expertise, the existence of imperfect markets, conflicts within agricultural policy, the preference for the present in consumption decisions, the increasing importance of equity issues in relation to efficiency and rapid population growth – all have a significant bearing upon the allocation of resources and environmental quality.

Numerous other resource and production issues require inter- and intra-sector comparisons of the economy. In many instances the agricultural sector of developing countries is competing with the industrial sector for capital, technical support and other resources. In this regard Mellor and Johnston (1984) wrote that the 'pronounced dualism in capital allocations' leads to a preference for the capital intensive industrial sector to the detriment of the majority of small-scale farm units. Also complicating optimal resource allocation is the competition for water from industrial and domestic uses. Moreover, for many Third World countries the need to earn foreign exchange and to finance their debt has led to agricultural development strategies favouring the production of cash crops. While successful in this objective, the strategies have limited access to land by small land-owners and the availability of food per person.

Any final assessment of the most appropriate strategy depends upon a careful weighing of total costs and benefits – all of which is a formidable task. Within this context the need to consider trade-offs is an important one. Decisions must be made about the most appropriate rate of discount to be applied to benefits from each strategy in order to set the weight or preference society is going to apply to present versus future interests. Trade-off decisions must also be made about acceptable levels of land degradation. On what basis should growth and development proceed and when do social costs of growth become prohibitive within a society? The importance of efficiency and equity concerns in resource allocations is unlikely to be resolved through simple numerical exercises. Here, ethical, moral and philosophical issues are closely intertwined with economic ones. Subsidiary concerns, such as the degree of energy intensity and technical sophistication, are linked to issues of scale and dependency on international assistance.

The prospects for optimal paths of growth in the food system under general conditions of uncertainty are poor for most developing countries. Moving closer to the development of an environmentally-sensitive agriculture that meets the future nutritional needs of the population is possible but dependent upon the successful combination of numerous institutional factors addressing legal, financial, economic and ecological concerns. More than ever it is imperative that we recognize that the present constraints have both human and natural origins, the current dimensions of which are dependent upon existing technical progress and resource management practices. By extension, there is nothing inevitable about the impact of these constraints (Pierce and Furuseth, 1986). This is not to suggest that there are no limits in the system, but rather to stress the scope for change in our current outlook and practices.

Volume organization

The organization of the material contained within the food resource is based largely on the conceptualization of food demand and supply relations introduced in Fig. 1.2. Given both the complexity and scale of these relations and the already voluminous literature on the 'food problem', the text purposely steers a course towards the supply side of the food equation. The major theme addressed within this sphere is the dependence of food production upon the bio-physical resource base and the effect on that base of human intervention in the environment.

To set the stage for this analysis of the changing environment for food production the text first introduces the reader in Chapter 2 to a review and evaluation of the bio-physical environment for food production. The spatial and physical characteristics of agro-ecosystems are described, as are the critical natural resources required for food production. In this regard particular attention is paid to the supply and distribution, globally, of two critical resources – arable land and fresh water. Against a consideration of the ecological relations of agriculture, Chapter 3 proceeds with a systematic look at the performance of the food system during the period following the Second World War, as well as the factors responsible for that performance. Drawing upon an extensive literature on the subject, the chapter concentrates on the imbalances in food production and consumption between developed and developing countries.

Having established a profile of the growth trends in food production during the recent past, Chapter 4 goes on to provide a critical review of studies devoted to exploring future food–population relationships. The main object of the chapter is to assess the prospects for change in the production and consumption of food, regionally and globally, using different assumptions about population growth rates, pollution, technological change, trade policy and the carrying capacity of the environment.

The core of the text deals with the principal resource and environmental constraints on expanded food production. Chapter 5 is devoted to a study of the changing demands for agricultural lands and changing population–land ratios. Declines in the quantity of the resource base for agriculture and implications for food production are examined within the context of the conversion of agricultural land to built-up uses.

Yet another critical resource, water, is the subject of Chapter 6. Water and not land is seen as a limiting factor to the growth in food production in many regions of the world. These limits, which have both quantitative and qualitative dimensions, are examined in both a physical and institutional/managerial context. Similarly, the theme of a qualitative decline in the resource base for agriculture is continued in Chapter 7. The regional variations and productivity effects of the two most serious forms of land degradation – soil erosion and salinization – are profiled. The chapter concludes with a consideration of the collective expression of the above two processes – desertification – and the consequences for human habitation.

Like land degradation, climate change is a human-induced process with the potential for far-reaching and long-lasting effects upon agriculture. Chapter 8 examines both climate variability and climate change. Although climatic variability is a natural phenomenon, numerous human activities magnify the risk of crop failure. Climate change in the form of CO_2-induced warming is examined according to probable changes in temperature/moisture conditions and their potential impact on the geography and viability of crop production.

Since the productivity of agricultural systems is predicated upon energy supply, it is fitting that the final thematic chapter (Chapter 9) should concentrate on this resource. The objective is to illustrate the importance of energy to the success of numerous agricultural systems (both modern and traditional), some of the environmental implication of energy use, and alternative and more efficient approaches to the use of energy in agriculture.

12

The concluding chapter (Chapter 10) provides a synthesis of the nature of demand and supply relations in food and agriculture and a discussion of the necessity for, and prospects of, sustainable agricultural development. The solution to most of the resource and environmental constraints lies in institutional and social change. An important ingredient underlying that change is the willingness and capacity of humans to relearn their approaches to the use of the environment.

CHAPTER 2

Resources available for agriculture

Agro-ecosystems

Agricultural systems are modified natural ecological systems. The modification of these natural systems and their subsequent success is due to three specific sets of factors: (1) transplanting of species to new environments (e.g., maize to Africa and cereals to North America); (2) recognizing and matching the natural resource needs of plants through environmental manipulation of thermal, nutrient and moisture conditions; and (3) improving the growth performance of plants and making them more disease resistant within specific environments through genetic manipulation (e.g. high-yielding varieties of wheat, rice and maize). Agro-ecosystems then are far simpler than natural ecosystems which have a natural tendency towards diversity and stability (Altieri et al., 1984). To maintain the specialized character of these systems requires not only large energy subsidies but also strategies to compensate for the lack of self-regulating mechanisms in pest control.

The growth and distribution of crops is a product of the interplay among ecological, cultural/social and economic conditions. It is through an appreciation of these relationships, particularly among the ecological dimensions, that we can understand the potential for growth in food systems and the natural constraints that impede that growth. This chapter begins with a discussion of the global distribution of major crops coupled with an explanation of the biophysical basis for this distribution. Following this is a survey of the availability of two critical resources in food production: arable land and fresh water.

Crop distribution

Relatively few cultivars provide either directly or indirectly the majority of dietary energy/protein for humans. Cereals, the most important cultivars in terms of area harvested, tonnage, caloric and protein contribution, dominate agricultural systems. Wheat, rice, maize, barley, millet, sorghum, oats and rye comprise over 98 per cent of cereal production on approximately 52 per cent of the arable land base. Worldwide, cereals account for approximately 50 per cent of total per capita calorie supply and 45 per cent of per capita protein supply.

During the two decades prior to 1980, traditional grains such as oats and rye experienced declines in area planted by 32 and 49 per cent respectively (McKey, 1981). Offsetting these declines were relatively strong gains in all of the other previously-mentioned cereals, particularly maize, barley and sorghum. Figure 2.1 provides a highly-generalized view of dominant cereal crops by region. Not surprisingly, regional specializations reflect suitable climatic and edaphic conditions. Wheat and maize are the two principal cereal crops of North and South America; rice and, to a lesser degree, wheat dominate the area devoted to cereals in Asia, whereas maize, sorghum and millet are important to Africa. Continental Europe and the USSR are primarily dedicated to wheat, barley and rye. The second major food source is roots and tubers such as yams, cassava, potatoes, sweet potatoes and aroids comprising, globally, 7 per cent of per capita caloric intake and 3.7 per cent of per capita protein intake. Where potatoes are the most significant tuber crop in continental Europe and the USSR, cassava is the most significant in Africa and sweet potatoes in China and South-East Asia. Tubers dominate local food consumption in some of these regions and in turn are the primary source of both calories and protein (Bunting et al., 1982).

The third and last significant plant group is pulses (legumes) and nuts. They contribute less to per capita caloric requirements (5 per cent) but more to protein (11 per cent) than tubers. They are particularly significant in Africa and other subsistence economies in the developing world.

Climate and crop production

The importance of climate in affecting crop distribution has already been alluded to. If climate is defined in terms of solar radiation, temperature and precipitation, then these are the keys which unlock soil nutrients and provide the basis for the accumulation of biomass within the food chain. Primary production and the process of photosynthesis occur when plants transform solar or radiant energy into chemical energy. Solar radiation received on the earth's surface is a function of latitude, time of year, cloudiness and day length. There are, therefore, significant variations in the availability/intensity of sunlight and in turn the capacity of plants to turn solar energy into chemical energy. Incoming solar radiation can be expressed in joules (1 J = 0.239 calories; 1000 J (KJ) = 239 calories). Comparisons of different climatic regions reveal significant differences in the availability of radiation (see Fig. 2.2). In temperate areas of North America, input ranges from 420 to 600 $KJ\,cm^{-2}\,y^{-1}$, whereas the humid

15

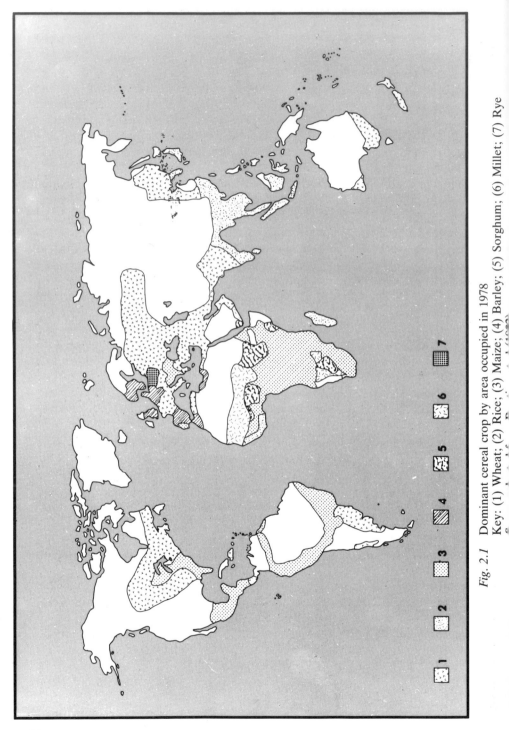

Fig. 2.1 Dominant cereal crop by area occupied in 1978
Key: (1) Wheat; (2) Rice; (3) Maize; (4) Barley; (5) Sorghum; (6) Millet; (7) Rye

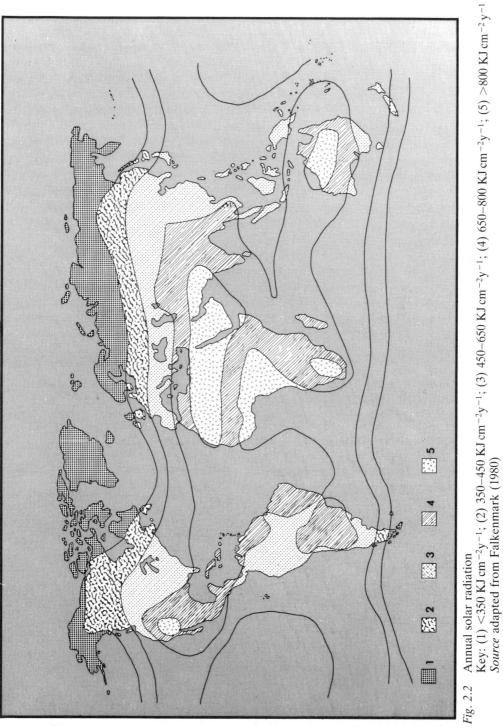

Fig. 2.2   Annual solar radiation
Key: (1) <350 KJ cm^{-2}y^{-1}; (2) 350–450 KJ cm^{-2}y^{-1}; (3) 450–650 KJ cm^{-2}y^{-1}; (4) 650–800 KJ cm^{-2}y^{-1}; (5) >800 KJ cm^{-2}y^{-1}
Source adapted from Falkenmark (1980)

and semi-humid tropics have values ranging from 650 to 800 $KJ\,cm^{-2}\,y^{-1}$. The highest values are to be found in the arid tropics and semi-tropics where total cloud cover is less than in the more moist regions (Bayliss-Smith, 1982).

Only a small amount of solar radiation is used for plant growth (from 0.7 to 3 per cent and averaging about 1 per cent). The efficiency by which this radiation is used varies with the leaf area index (the ratio of total leaf area to soil surface) and with the method or pathway by which plants convert carbon dioxide into dry matter. In the case of C_4 pathway plants, such as maize, sorghum and millet, they assimilate best under warm tropical conditions with high light intensity. Of the C_4 plants only maize performs well in mid-latitudes. C_3 class pathway crops, such as wheat, rice, soybean and sugar beet, commonly found in mid-latitude regions, show no improvement in assimilation in sub and tropical latitudes. Total production of dry matter (including roots and stems) is much higher for C_4 as opposed to C_3 plants, often by a margin of almost 2 to 1. Table 2.1 profiles above-ground annual net primary production for a combination of C_3 and C_4 plants using chemical and organic (traditional) farming methods. Wheat yields are approximately half those for maize – a consideration which no doubt has encouraged the replacement of wheat by maize as the principal grain crop in the United States.

The actual usable proportion of plants varies considerably. Leafy vegetables such as spinach and cabbage have the highest harvest index (ratio of edible material to total dry matter produced) and are therefore considered to be the most productive (efficient) method of using land (Pirie, 1976). Other agricultural crops have harvest indices ranging from 5 to 60 per cent.

Table 2.1 Productivity of upland seed crops

	Growth rate (gm^{-2} day^{-1})		ANP^a (tonne ha^{-1})		Harvest index
	Maximum	Average	Inputs Chemical	Organic	
Barley C$_3$	—	11.8	6–18	2.5	0.55
Maize C$_4$	52	18–23	20–30	8.3	0.43
Millet C$_4$	54	19.6	22	5.7	0.21
Oats C$_3$	—	7–15	3–6	4.9	0.41
Rye C$_3$	—	—	6–13	3.0	0.30
Sorghum C$_4$	51	12–18	10–15	3.6	0.41
Soybean C$_3$	27	6.7	8	3.1	0.32
Sunflower C$_3$	68	6.7	10	—	0.57
Wheat C$_3$	22	8–18	9–13	4.2	0.45

^{a}ANP = Above Ground Net Production

Source after Mitchell (1984)

Were solar radiation the only resource determining plant growth the volume of crop production would be significantly higher and more predictable than it actually is. However, limitations in temperature, moisture, soil structure and nutrients are important physico-chemical constraints also affecting plant growth. Table 2.2 indicates that while diseases, insects and weeds play an important role in reducing yields, by far the most important yield suppressants are physico-chemical constraints.

Most plants are able to germinate, mature and be harvested within a range of temperatures, with some exhibiting far more temperature adaptability than others. The majority of cereals in temperate regions will develop at average temperatures as low as 5°C and as high as 37°C, with optimal conditions around 25–31°C. The distribution of temperature is, of course, equally important. Winter wheat requires mean monthly temperatures at sowing of 8–16°C, spring wheat 6–12°C and Mediterranean wheat 12–20°C. Harvesting occurs at warmer temperatures than sowing: 16–24°C for winter wheat, 10–24°C for spring wheat and 18–26°C for Mediterranean wheat (Bunting et al., 1982). In contrast, C_4 plants can tolerate hotter temperatures but smaller ranges overall.

Temperature also plays a major role in affecting the humus content of soils. Where temperature falls below 20°C (as is the case in temperate regions), humus content of soil forms faster than the ability of microorganisms to break it down. However, above 20°C (as is the case in tropical regions) the reverse is true. Consequently, humus content and along with that nutrient levels of tropical and sub-tropical soils tend to be

Table 2.2 Record yields, average yields and yield losses resulting from disease, insects, weeds, and unfavourable physico-chemical environments for major US crops

Crop	Yields (t/ha) Record	Average	Average losses (t/ha) Diseases	Insects	Weeds	Physico-chemical[a]
Corn	19.3	4.6	0.9	0.9	0.7	12.2
Wheat	14.5	1.9	0.4	0.2	0.3	11.7
Soybeans	7.4	1.6	0.3	0.1	0.4	5.0
Sorghum	20.1	2.8	0.4	0.4	0.5	16.5
Oats	10.6	1.7	0.6	0.1	0.5	7.7
Barley	11.4	2.1	0.4	0.1	0.4	8.4
Potatoes	94.1	28.2	8.4	6.2	1.3	50.0
Sugar beets	121.0	42.6	10.7	8.0	5.3	54.4
Mean percentage of record yield	100.0	21.5	5.1	3.0	3.5	66.9

[a]Calculated as record yield–(average yield + disease loss + insect loss + weed loss)
Source after Boyer (1987)

lower than in temperate regions. The 20°C isotherm can therefore represent a formidable constraint to the development of continuously-cropped soils.

The influence of temperature upon plant growth is intricately tied to that of precipitation. Measures of seasonal precipitation generally provide only a broad brush indicator of the quantity of water available for plant growth. A more useful approach is to examine the ratio of actual precipitation to potential evapotranspiration (quantity of water evaporated from soil and plant surfaces when kept permanently moist). This provides a general indication of water balance and of the time and length of growing season. If the ratio is equal to 1 then a balance exists between the two. If less than 1 (e.g., 0.7 or 70 per cent of water requirements met), water shortages will occur. How critical this water shortage is for plant growth or the degree of moisture stress will depend upon the time of year. For wheat, moisture stress causes the greatest yield reduction during jointing and heading stages of plant growth (Desjarden and Ouellet, 1977). Generally a minimum value of 0.5 is required for germination and sustained growth. Figure 2.3 illustrates the relationship between precipitation and potential evapotranspiration (PET) for four climatic conditions. In case 3 precipitation always exceeds 100 per cent of PET, as would be the case in the humid tropics, whereas in case 4 precipitation is always less than 50 per cent (0.5) of PET in certain arid regions. In the two other scenarios precipitation is sufficiently high and prolonged to meet minimum plant requirements (50 per cent of PET). Case 2 is characteristic of dry savannah and case 1 of many humid temperate regions.

Soils for plant growth

All of the above factors of temperature, moisture and radiation interact with parent material and topographical conditions to determine soil development in its myriad forms of texture, structure, organic matter and rooting depth. Deficiencies in either physical and/or chemical properties weaken utility and flexibility of the soil for crop production. Most of the major world soil groups are deficient in one or more of these key attributes (see Table 2.3). A significant proportion of the cold climates of the northern hemisphere are covered by unproductive entisols, inceptisols, mountain soils and spodsols (see Fig. 2.4). Entisols, inceptisols and mountain soils are young soils with little profile development. They tend to be low in organic matter, high in acidity and offer limited rooting depth potential. Spodsols are also acid (and leached), poorly drained and boglike in places.

In the dry savannah, steppe and desert climates occupying most of North Africa, the Middle East, south-western United States, Central Asia and Australia are to be found aridisols. These too are low in humus content and also are saline and alkaline. Any potential for agricultural production

Table 2.3 World soils subject to environmental limitations

Environmental limitations	Percentage of world soils subject to limitations
Drought	27.2
Shallowness	24.2
Mineral	22.5
Excess water	12.2
Miscellaneous	3.1
None	10.1
Total	100.0
Temperature	14.8

Source after Dudal (1976)

1. Moderately long growing season

2. Short, predictable growing season

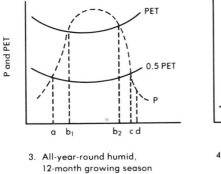

3. All-year-round humid, 12-month growing season

4. All-year-round dry, no predictable growing season

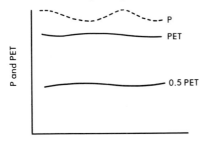
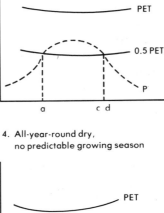

Key:

a	Beginning of rains and growing period	d	End of growing period
b₁ b₂	Start and end of humid period respectively	P	Precipitation
c	End of rains and rainy seasons	PET	Potential evapotranspiration

Fig. 2.3   Four examples of growing season length as determined by different rainfall levels and potential evapotranspiration
Source after FAO (1978a)

is contingent upon the development of irrigation, improving the water retention abilities of the soil and ensuring proper drainage to lower salinity content.

On either side of the equator in the humid tropics are to be found oxisols and ultisols. These cover approximately 66 per cent of the region and are well drained, deep and granular, but possess poor mineral properties. They are low in nutrient supply, showing major deficiencies in phosphorus, nitrogen, potassium, calcium, magnesium, sulphur and zinc, and high in acidity and aluminum toxicity. Although they have a reputation for becoming lateritic when cleared, only a small percentage of these two soil groups have plinthite in the subsoil that produces hardpan conditions.

Generally referred to as low base status soils, ultisols and oxisols have low cation-exchange capacities and a tendency to immobilize phosphorus. As a result, the ability of the soil to retain positively-charged cations such as calcium, magnesium and potassium is diminished. With base nutrients easily leached away, acidity of the soil remains high. If these soils are to be used for agriculture, as they are in China and south-eastern United States, they require fertilizer supplements such as nitrogen and phosphorus, lime to reduce acidity, as well as manures and careful land-management practices to control erosion. Most of the potential arable land base which is uncultivated is to be found in this tropical region of oxisols and ultisols.

Not all tropical soils are low base and hence inferior for agricultural purposes. High-base status soils such as alfisols, vertisols and mollisols have good physical and chemical properties for crop production. They cover about 18 per cent of tropical land and are the centres for the major concentrations of population living in the tropics (Sanchez and Buol, 1975). Relatively small investments in fertilizers, particularly nitrogen, during the Green Revolution made these soils highly productive for agricultural purposes.

These same soil categories are to be found in humid–warm and cool–temperate climates of central North America, Argentina, Australia, Central Europe and the Soviet Union and China. With the best soil and climatic resources for food production, it is not surprising that these regions are the major source of food production globally.

Despite the introductory nature of this survey of the biophysical basis for crop production, sufficient details have been provided to indicate the delicate physical and biological balance which sustains life systems, makes agricultural production possible and determines the physical limits of feasible production in the future. It is also possible to appreciate the common difficulties of examining resources in isolation in order to identify prospects for growth in the food systems. By the late 1980s, less than 13 per cent of the earth's land mass has been cultivated (with a possibility of extending it to 25 per cent), even though far larger areas may be suited climatically or edaphically.

Comparisons of environmental quality

Geographical distribution of optimal combinations of agricultural resources is concentrated in a few areas. Those countries or regions with superior combinations of resources (e.g., soil and climate) tend to be better producers of food. While this should come as no surprise, environmental quality is a potent force underlying many of the variations in food production among nations.

In a study of environmental quality and land productivity in Canada, the United States and the Soviet Union, Field (1968) cross-classified cropland by thermal conditions (measured in degree months) and moisture availability (measured by actual evapotranspiration as a percentage of potential evapotranspiration) for each of the three countries. Table 2.4 highlights the (in some cases) dramatic differences (particularly the vertical and horizontal totals) in environmental quality. In the United States, 81 per cent of the cropland base has 200 or more degree months compared to 2 per cent for Canada and 20 per cent for the Soviet Union. In terms of moisture classes, over half of US cropland receives 90 per cent or more of water required – double the proportion for either Canada or the Soviet Union. In fact over half the cropland in these last two countries suffers from moisture stress. Acknowledging that technological factors also contribute to productivity differences among the countries, Field (1968: 11) emphasized that 'environmental quality must be weighted heavily in assessing the relative productivity of the agricultural land resources of the Soviet Union and North America.'

Economic and technological factors can reduce the effect of limiting factors and enhance the environment for food production. As price/cost ratios change, technical advance proceeds and tastes change, the margin of crop production shifts as does the intensity and structure of production. Improvements in transportation, harvesting and irrigation technology during the last 100 years have had a profound effect upon the geography of crop production throughout the world. Advances in biological technology have made crops more disease resistant, more efficient in their use of nutrients and capable of ripening earlier. The great biological success stories of the twentieth century are the adaptation/extension of corn, wheat and other cereals to previously hostile environments, and the development of high-yielding variety grains capable, with the correct inputs, of producing two to three times more than traditional varieties.

Arable land and water resources

Land

In the late 1980s the world's cultivated arable land base was 1.4 billion hectares. If permanent crops are included, it equalled almost 1.5 billion hectares. Figure 2.5 shows a generalized distribution of the permanently

23

Table 2.4 Cropland classified by thermal and moisture zones (percentage distributions)

(AE/PE)ᵃ x100 (%)	Canada Degree-months				United States Degree-months				Canada and United States Degree-months				USSR Degree-months			
	100–199	200–299	300+	total	100–199	200–299	300+	total	100–199	200–299	300+	total	100–199	200–299	300+	total
90–100	22	2		24	8	30	19	57	10	25	15	50	26	0.1	0.3	26
80–89	10			10	2	5	2	9	4	4	2	10	14	1		15
65–79	48			48	5	7	3	15	13	5	3	21	18	6		24
0–64	18			18	4	7	8	19	7	5	7	19	22	9	4	35
Total	98	2		100	19	49	32	100	34	39	27	100	80	16	4	100

ᵃAE = Actual evapotranspiration; PE = potential evapotranspiration

Source after Field (1968)

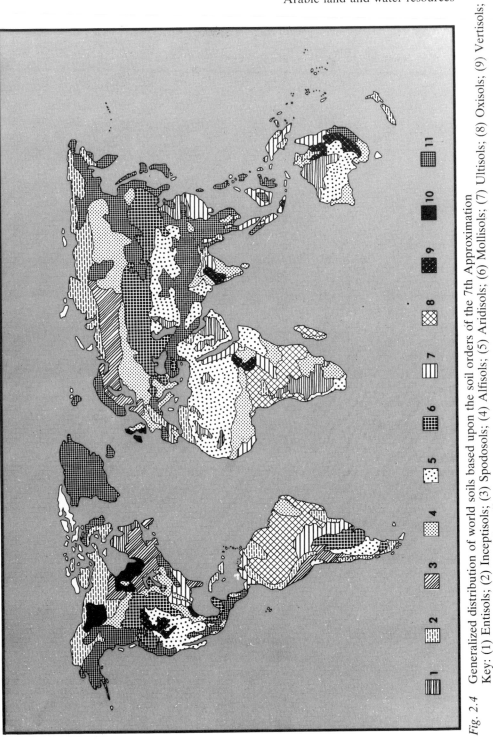

Fig. 2.4 Generalized distribution of world soils based upon the soil orders of the 7th Approximation
Key: (1) Entisols; (2) Inceptisols; (3) Spodosols; (4) Alfisols; (5) Aridisols; (6) Mollisols; (7) Ultisols; (8) Oxisols; (9) Vertisols;
(10) Histosols; (11) Mountain soils
Sources Espenshade (1978); Tarrant (1980)

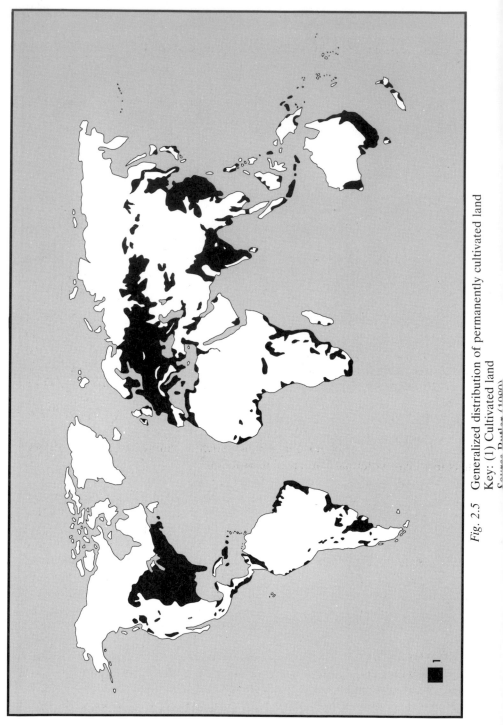

Fig. 2.5 Generalized distribution of permanently cultivated land
Key: (1) Cultivated land
Source: Butler (1980)

cultivated land base, the majority of which lies within a relatively narrow range of approximately 35° (20–55°N), demarcating the location of dominant food-producing regions of the world.

Cereals account for half of the total cultivated area: permanent crops, such as cotton, coffee, sugar cane, coconuts, account for 7 per cent of cultivated area; an equivalent area is given over to tubers and pulses. The remaining area is occupied by vegetables, oilseeds, fruit and hay, and by land devoted to fallow. As much as one-third of the earth's arable land is fallowed each year. Developed countries have been most successful at reducing the need for fallow through nutrient supplements (Grigg, 1985). Grazing land or permanent pasture, at an estimated area of 3.2 billion hectares, was more than double the size of the arable land base, but with a far lower biological carrying capacity.

The potential expansion of the cultivated arable land base for crop production is tied to a variety of bio-physical, economic, technological and cultural factors. Global estimates of (ultimate) potential arable land incorporating all of these factors are difficult to make. Studies which have been made on the world supply of agricultural land have generally pursued fairly simple approaches by emphasizing the importance of bio-physical factors to the detriment of other factors. Norse (1979) observed that estimates of the size of the potential arable land base reflects the use of three criteria: (1) length of growing season; (2) topography; and (3) soil type. Not surprisingly, the conclusions reached by these studies during the past three decades are similar. As part of a study entitled 'The World Food Problem' the United States President's Science Advisory Committee (1967) provided the first comprehensive estimate of the potential global arable land base (Buringh, 1977). By superimposing climate maps on soil maps, arable, non-arable and land with grazing potential were defined. It was determined that 24 per cent of the earth's land surface, or 3.2 billion hectares, has potential for crop production (see Table 2.5). This means that an additional 1.7 billion hectares of land, which is now used for grazing and/or forestry, has potential for agricultural production. It would appear, however, that the majority of this land has relatively low potential for agriculture. Buringh (1981), for example, has estimated the quality of the present cropland base of 1.5 billion hectares as follows: 400 million hectares representing high potential, 500 medium and 600 low. He defines high as having 60 per cent of potential production, medium 40–60 per cent and low 20–40 per cent. A similar exercise was completed for the (ultimate) potential cropland base in which high, medium and low productivity soils were estimated as 447 million hectares, 894 and 1937 respectively. Estimates of the quality of the land base available for cropland expansion are heavily weighted in favour of land of low productivity. Fully 78 per cent of the 1.7 billion hectares of land that is estimated to have agricultural potential has low productivity.

How much of this land is capable of active cultivation depends upon

Table 2.5 Total land area and arable land by continent

Continent	Total land area	Cultivated land	Percentage of land area cultivated	Potential arable land[a]	Ratio of cultivated to potential arable land
Africa	3,010	158	5.2	734	22
Asia	2,740	519	18.9	627	83
Australia and New Zealand	820	32	3.9	153	21
Europe	480	154	32.1	174	88
North America	2,110	239	11.3	465	51
South America	1,750	77	4.4	681	11
USSR	2,240	227	10.6	356	64
Total	13,150	1,406	10.6	3,190	44

[a]Areas are given in millions of hectares

Source after Buringh (1977), based upon US President's Advisory Committee, (1967)

assumptions about development costs, technology and the extent of deficiencies as limiting factors. In another estimate of potential arable area, Buringh et al. (1979) arrived at a value of 3.7 billion hectares. But this expanded estimate was soon deflated when correction factors were introduced for soil and water deficiencies (see Chapter 4, Table 4.1). It was assumed in this study that these estimates reflected the use of current technology. After the introduction of correction factors, less than 50 per cent of the 3.7 billion hectares was usable. When irrigation was added, the total potential area was 1.9 billion hectares. Development costs associated with expanding the cropland base are expected to be high. Norse (1979) estimated that less than 8 per cent of the potential cropland could be made available at low cost <$200/ha (1975 dollars). The majority (70 per cent) would require between $1500–$3000/ha to develop. Estimates for the clearing and draining of rainforests run as high as $10,000/ha (Norse, 1979).

In yet another study of the potential arable land base, Revelle (1976; 1984) accepted the President's Science Advisory Committee's estimates of 3.2 billion hectares, but took into consideration the potential for irrigated area and multiple cropping. He estimated (1984: 185) that:

Of the 3.2 billion net cultivatable hectares, one rain-fed crop could be grown on 2.17 billion hectares; two crops under rain-fed conditions on an additional 180 million hectares; and the equivalent of three four-month crops could be produced, if suitable technology could be developed, on 510 million hectares within the humid tropics, where precipitation exceeds potential evapotranspiration throughout the year. Irrigation is needed to grow even one crop on 350 million hectares.

When these figures are converted into gross cropped area (net cultivated area times the number of crops grown per year), then outside the tropics the equivalent of 3.6 billion rainfed and irrigated hectares are available; and within the tropics approximately 1.5 billion hectares (assuming the harvesting of three crops per year). But since technology is unavailable for high-yielding agriculture on a large scale in the humid tropics, much of the gross cropped area in the region could not be considered available for cultivation.

In all of the above studies South America and Africa stand out as possessing the greatest potential for expansion in the global cropland base. Together they contain between 50–60 per cent of the potential arable land which has yet to be cultivated. There is considerable controversy over the economic, technological and ecological constraints to the conversion of these areas to productive farmland. Critical questions which have been poorly investigated are: what proportion of these areas can sustain agricultural production indefinitely, at what cost and with what level technology? The environmental issues are least well understood, particularly within the context of deforestation and the hydrological balance in tropical regions.

These unknowns have prompted a number of researchers to discount heavily the potential for expansion in the arable land bases of these two continents. Mesarovic and Pestel (1974), in the second report to the Club of Rome, went so far as to argue that North America and Australia, and not the tropical regions of the world, hold the greatest promise for expansion in the arable land base. They, as well as others (Brown, 1981; Eckholm, 1976), argue that the highly-weathered, leached and lateritic character of tropical soils, the costs of development, lack of suitable technology and the transmission of diseases to human and animal populations from insects and water-borne parasites pose significant if not insurmountable obstacles to agricultural development. Some of these questions will be examined in more detail in Chapter 4.

Water

Like arable land, water is limited in supply, and that supply is variable over space, time and in quality. This variability impacts the maintenance and growth of both rainfed and irrigated forms of agriculture. Whereas the former system still dominates the global agricultural system, there is increasing dependence upon irrigated sources of water as attempts are made to increase yields and expand production in new regions.

Underlying both rainfed and irrigated agriculture is the hydrologic cycle. Although highly simplified, Fig. 2.6 provides the key components to understanding the flow characteristics of water and the phenomenon of

29

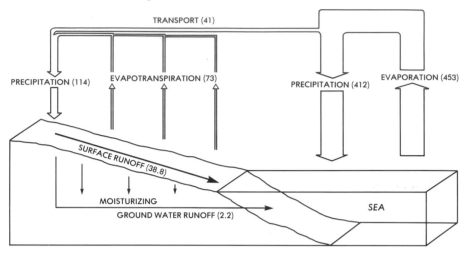

( ) '000s of km³/yr

Fig. 2.6 The global hydrologic cycle
Source L'vovich (1979)

water balance. The cycle is driven by solar radiation providing the necessary energy for evaporation and transpiration. The oceans serve as the main sink for the evaporation and precipitation of water. Approximately 10 per cent of the water evaporated from the ocean is transported to the continental land masses where it accounts for 36 per cent of the rainfed water resources. The remaining 64 per cent comes from evapotranspiration within the continental land masses themselves. To balance the equation, 36 per cent of total precipitation returns to oceans through surface and groundwater run-off.

Infiltration of water increases soil moisture storage and moistening of the soil in the root zone. The process of infiltration and run-off holds the keys to the availability of water for plant growth and human use. A number of variables affect the process of infiltration, including duration and intensity of rainfall, relief, vegetative cover and soil structure. Whether the moistening of the soil through infiltration is sufficient for plant growth depends to a large degree on potential evapotranspiration.

The conventional approach for calculating water surplus and deficit conditions for plant growth is to compare potential evapotranspiration with actual rainfall. Figure 2.7 provides a highly-generalized regionalization of water deficit and surplus conditions. The darkest areas of the map generally correspond with the areas of highest average solar radiation. The largest deficits occur in those areas with the lowest rainfall and highest radiation (or potential evapotranspiration). Large portions of the tropical and subtropical world have either large seasonal and/or yearly deficits making irrigation a necessity if agriculture is to have the potential to

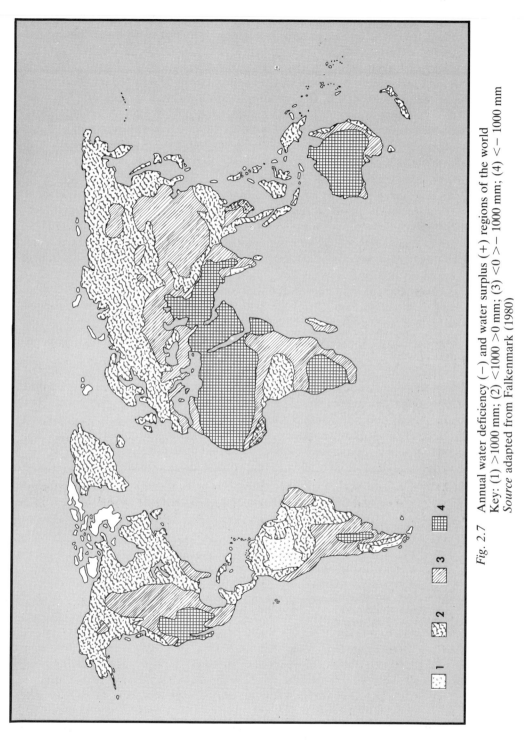

Fig. 2.7   Annual water deficiency (−) and water surplus (+) regions of the world
Key: (1) >1000 mm; (2) <1000 >0 mm; (3) <0 >− 1000 mm; (4) <− 1000 mm
Source adapted from Falkenmark (1980)

sustain indigenous populations.

More insight into the nature of regional water balances can be gained through a comparison of the moisture regimes in three different areas: Scandinavia, East Africa and India (Falkenmark, 1980). A comparison of precipitation values and potential evaporation indicates the magnitude of the water deficits in the dry savannah and savannah of desert type (see Table 2.6). Although a significant percentage of the precipitation enters the soil (moisturization) in the dry savannah and savannah desert type, practically all of it is evaporated with the residual forming the base flow or ground water segment. Relatively little therefore, is usable for plant growth. Run-off fed by base flow and surface flooding is also low.

On a global scale the large variations in precipitation and evapotranspiration produce large differences in run-off. Figure 2.8 highlights the distribution of water resources according to these three variables. The relative availability of fresh water resources (usable fresh water) is considerably below total run-off resources. Estimates of total run-off range between 38,000 and 44,000 km^3, excluding the freshwater reserves contained in Greenland, the Antarctic and Canadian Archipelago. Most estimates of stable run-off or base flow, usable for human purposes, ranges from 13,000 to 24,000 km^3. Given the fact that at least 5,000 km^3 of the resource are in uninhabited regions, these estimates should in theory be scaled down by an equivalent amount (Ambroggi, 1980).

In examining the distribution of world water resources and the expected need for those resources on a regional basis (see Table 2.7), Widstrand (1980) identified three major groups. In the first group, comprised of North Africa and the Middle East, the water requirement for all uses in the year 2000 is expected to be 97 per cent of the usable resource. The second group is comprised of Southern and Eastern Europe, North and Central Asia and South Asia. Here prospective utilization ratios range

Table 2.6 Type values for hydrological elements in different zones

	Taiga	Dry savannah	Savannah of desert type
Precipitation	700^a	1,000	300
River run-off			
– flood part	160	100	18
– base flow part	140	30	2
– total	300	130	20
Moisturization	540	900	282
Evaporation	400	870	280
Potential evaporation	500	1,300	1,300

^{a}mm/year

Source adapted from Falkenmark (1980)

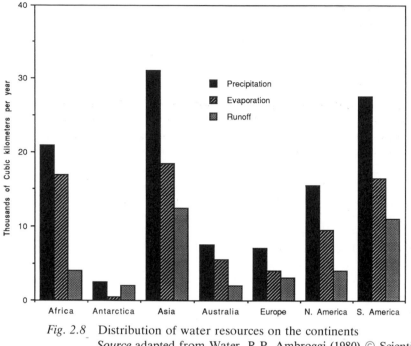

Fig. 2.8 Distribution of water resources on the continents
Source adapted from Water, R.P. Ambroggi (1980) © Scientific
American Inc. *All rights reserved.*

from 40 to 70 per cent. The semi-arid nature of these regions indicates
considerable need for water conservation and improved methods of storage. The last group, consisting of North America, North-West Europe,
Central and South America, Central Africa, East Africa and East
Asia/Oceania, have ratios below the global average of 25 per cent by the
year 2000. Management of water resources is still important in these
regions, particularly with respect to decline in water quality from industrial
contamination.

Since all of the above regions are large, significant internal variations
arise in the availability of water and in regional requirements. Moreover,
as White (1983) has stressed, generalizations about water supply and use
are only meaningful when viewed within the context of geographical
realities which determine the distribution and accessibility of the resource
and within the context of social, economic and technological conditions
which determine the uses made of the resources.

The consumption of fresh water is dominated by agriculture, industry
and domestic uses. 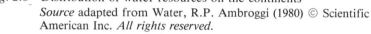Industrial and domestic demand for water are highest
relative to agriculture in the developed world, particularly Western
Europe. This reflects not only a larger industrial base and a more affluent
population, but also the significance of rainfed agriculture. In the United
States and the Soviet Union, agricultural and industrial uses of water

Table 2.7 Global usable water resources and requirements to the year 2000

	Surface area (1000 km²)	Population (millions)		Potential average resources			Ultimately usable resources		Need in 2000		Percentage need of readily available resources
		1985	2000	km³/yr	m³/person 1985	m³/person 2000	km³/yr	m³/person 2000	km³/yr	m³/person 2000	
North America	21,515	262.4	296.3	4,953	18,876	16,616	3,962	13,573	1,013	3,420	26
North-western Europe	2,568	245.1	362.1	1,392	5,679	5,311	1,253	4,780	195	745	16
Southern Europe	2,105	194.3	229.1	500	2,573	2,182	425	1,855	177	773	42
Eastern Europe	6,316	321.1	357.7	1,046	3,258	2,924	837	2,340	565	1,580	68
North and Central Asia	28,671	1,238.0	1,448.7	3,812	3,079	2,631	3,050	2,150	1,302	899	43
Central America	2,733	142.2	216.9	948	66,667	4,371	664	3,059	103	475	16
South America	17,820	283.2	402.7	10,978	38,764	27,261	4,940	12,267	191	475	4
North Africa and Middle East	21,114	314.3	469.0	425	1,352	906	340	725	331	705	97
Central Africa	7,448	177.1	275.4	2,257	12,744	8,195	1,354	4,917	175	635	13
East Africa	7,150	149.8	235.6	917	6,121	3,892	734	3,114	150	635	20
South Asia	4,986	1,038.2	1,434.1	3,786	3,647	2,640	2,272	1,584	1,197	835	53
East Asia and Oceania	12,573	448.0	623.0	6,709	14,975	10,769	4,025	6,461	549	881	14
World	135,159	4,813.8	6,250.6	37,723	7,836	6,035	23,856	3,817	5,948	950	25

Source adapted from Widstrand (1980)

34

dominate the picture, whereas in Mexico and India water for agriculture consumes more than 90 per cent of total water withdrawals. L'vovich (1979) estimates that globally industry uses 200 km^3/yr and domestic use 110 km^3 of water, but these and other uses, including livestock and irrigated agriculture, pollute approximately 5580 km^3. In per capita terms, average annual withdrawals of water (of which actual use is only a small percentage) in the United States, USSR, Mexico and UK are 2300, 1000, 930 and 200 cubic metres (UN, 1976).

Agriculture is the largest user and consumer of water. The rainfed system of agriculture, representing about 85 per cent of the earth's cultivated land, consumed about 11,500 km^3 of water, whereas irrigated agriculture, on the remaining land, consumed 2500 km^3. This consumption value for irrigated agriculture which is 6 per cent of total run-off (38,000 km^3) and 19 per cent of stable or usable water translated into an average consumption in 1970 of 12,000 to 14,000 m^3/ha. Water consumption per tonne of grain averages 3300 m^3, but with improvements in efficiency has the potential to be reduced to 1900 m^3 (L'vovich, 1979). Rice requires more than double the quantity of water for production compared to wheat.

In terms of the water required to support the nutritional needs of the population (at 3000 calories/day/person), along with domestic and industrial needs, water requirements would be no more than 350–450 m^3 per person, which in theoretical terms could support a population of 20–25 billion (Ambroggi, 1980). However, the uneven distribution of both the demand for and supply of water, along with deterioration in the quality of the resource from effluents, makes this support highly unlikely. The fact that "77 per cent of the world's population is concentrated in Europe and Asia but only 38 percent of the world reserves of perennially renewed fresh water occur in that area" (Voskresensky, 1978: 509) underlines some of these inequalities. As well, the question of possible scarcity is not so much a physical one as it is an economic one. Since agriculture is a low-value use of water, and since the competition for this water promises to intensify from industrial uses, the prospects of retaining or enhancing its share of the consumption of this resource are remote. It is to these and other issues concerning water–agriculture relations that we shall return in Chapter 6.

Summary

The great imbalance in the global distribution of environmental resources required for plant growth imposes significant natural limitations on the area, location, variety and yield of cereals grown and other important food sources. Only 11 per cent of the earth's surface is now devoted to crop production, most of which is concentrated along a relatively narrow band of land within a 35° latitude. Within this band there are large variations in the environments for crop production. By far the most important factor accounting for the difference between record or experimental yields and average yields is unfavourable physico-chemical environments. The superior thermal and moisture conditions within the United States, compared to either Canada or the USSR, are at the heart of US natural production advantages.

Natural constraints to the growth in food production will be determined largely by the future supplies of land and water. It is clear that parts of Asia and Europe are already approaching physical maxima in terms of arable land supply. And North Africa and the Middle East will by the turn of the century have exploited practically all of the usable water resource. Of course the environment for crop production is not determined exclusively by natural factors and conditions. Clearly plant breeding, the diffusion of irrigation and the use of fertilizers and other energy-intensive technology has removed a number of former limiting factors and expanded the range and yield of crops grown. Future supplies of land and water for crop production will also depend heavily upon changes in technology and favourable development costs. Despite the large potential for the expansion of rainfed and irrigated cultivated lands in equatorial regions of the world, enormous obstacles, both economic and environmental, will have to be overcome. The uncertainty over the feasibility of the conversion of these resources for agricultural purposes underlines the necessity to protect and enhance the existing agricultural resource base.

CHAPTER 3

Trends in world food production

Introduction

The balance between growth in population and food production has been a precarious one during the history of the human race. The recent dynamics of this balance are particularly complex and uneven, with the developed world achieving a consistently higher equilibrium between food supply and food demand than its developing counterpart. This division highlights three important features of the existing food system – the vastly uneven distribution in food purchasing power, in food production per person and in food consumption per person.

The growth of the world's food system and how that growth matches food requirements is the basic theme of this chapter. The guiding concern is to trace the changes, over space and time, in the production and consumption of food, as well as to identify the factors responsible for these changes.

Growth of population and food production

Change within the food system has manifested itself in two distinct forms. In addition to the physical increase in the volume of food produced, there has been considerable structural change and reorganization in the system itself. From either perspective, the growth in the productive capacity of the system in response to increasing population and demand pressures is without precedent. The thirty-year period beginning in 1950 witnessed a 76 per cent increase in world population. While the developed world experienced general declines in its rates of population growth, the majority of countries in the developing world sustained or increased their rates of growth. Average annual rates of growth for this period were 1.25 and 3.1 per cent for developed and developing countries respectively. Hence the developed world's share of global population fell from 34 per cent to 27 per cent; and by the year 2000 it is expected to be 22 per cent.

During the same period, food production (including cereals, roots/tubers, groundnuts, bananas and legumes) more than doubled, with developing countries registering the largest increase of 117 per cent (Barr, 1981). Given the large differential between the two groups in terms of population growth rates, however, per capita production increased only marginally in the developing world (0.4 per cent/year), but relatively rapidly in the developed world (1.4 per cent/year, compound annual rates). Figure 3.1 highlights the growth in food production globally, and by development level. During the 1970s 69 out of 128 developing countries experienced rates of population growth in excess of that for food production. Significant among the regions of poor per capita food production performance was Africa (excluding South Africa) which experienced about a 10 per cent decrease in output per person between 1972 and 1982. The USSR and parts of Oceania also experienced small declines. On the other hand, strong gains in output per person from the 1960s through to 1985 were made by China, Indonesia, Brazil, Argentina, Korea and Thailand. Much of this strong growth can be traced on the supply side to the adoption of new high-yielding grain varieties, in combination with energy-intensive inputs such as fertilizers, pesticides, irrigation and mechanical technology and, on the demand side, to growth in income coupled with declining growth in population. While all of these factors were present in

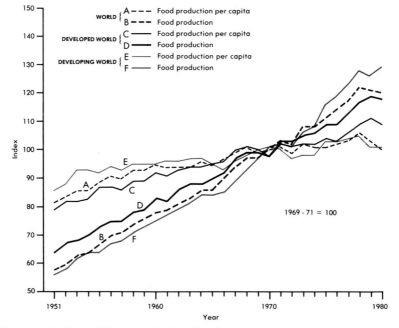

Fig. 3.1 Indices of food production for developed and developing countries. *Source* USDA (1981)

China throughout the 1970s it was not until the abandonment of communes and the introduction of greater incentives and choice of products grown, in the late 1970s, that the growth in cereals reached all time highs (around 6 per cent per year).

Shaping most of the growth of world food production has been the growth in world cereal production which increased by 149 per cent between 1950 and 1980 (see Fig. 3.2). Cereal production occurs on approximately 50 per cent of the world's cropland base and accounts for 75 per cent of world caloric production from crops. Cereals account for over half of the world's per capita calorie and protein intake consumed directly as food (FAO, 1978b). Indirectly, cereals are an important source of calories and protein through the consumption of animal products. In 1981, 47 per cent of world cereal production (exclusive of rice) was fed to animals (FAO, 1983b). This amounted to some 600 million metric tonnes which was sufficient in caloric terms to feed 2–2.5 billion persons. Whereas approximately 72 per cent of all grains consumed in the early 1980s in developed countries went to feed for animals, only 13 per cent was used for that purpose in developing countries. Livestock production accounts for at least half of the value of agricultural production in all developed countries (Grigg, 1985). To sustain growth in the consumption of animal

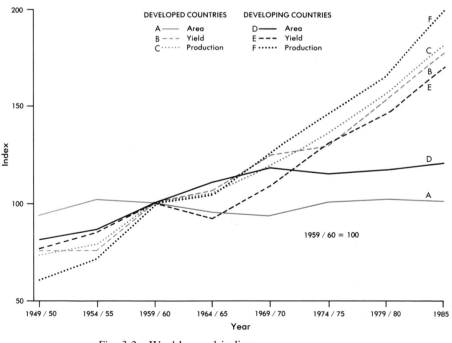

Fig. 3.2 World cereal indices
Sources FAO (1950–75); FAO (1986)

products an increasing proportion of cereal production will have to be devoted to that sector, particularly in developing countries. Although grazing land can be used as a substitute for grains grown on arable land, potential global meat output on all grazing land is only about one quarter of total global meat production.

World cereal production in 1982/83 was almost equally divided between developed (875 million metric tonnes) and developing countries (827 million metric tonnes). The cultivated land base of the former was 304 million hectares, compared to 411 million hectares for the latter. Figure 3.2 provides a profile of indexed production, area and yield for developed and developing nations. This information plus research by Barr (1981) for the period 1961–80, confirms a number of important trends. Growth in production for both groups is largely driven by high rates of growth in yield. Barr's data suggest that yield growth for developed countries during the 1970s (1 per cent per year) was slower than the previous decade (3.5 per cent per year), whereas for developing countries yield growth in the 1970s (2.5 per cent per year) was higher than the 1960s (2.3 per cent per year). Figure 3.2 suggests for the 1980s an even higher level of rate of growth for developing countries. A major difference, however, between the two groups of countries lies in the high degree of yield growth variability among developing regions. While China consistently achieved high-yield growth (4 per cent plus per year), West Asia was often less than 1 per cent per year. Individual developed countries are more homogeneous (either high or low) in their growth rates at any given time.

Additions to the arable land base have been extremely small in developed countries (<0.5 per cent per year). Although also modest, additions to the land base in developing countries grew at a faster overall rate in the 1970s and 1980s than their developed counterparts. This difference is due to a complex of factors. In Western countries demand for cereals has been more than met by annual increases in yields. The economic environment for farming in some of these countries (e.g. Canada and the United States) has induced an actual retrenchment in the cultivated land base. Developing countries, in contrast, have been less successful in meeting growth in demand through annual increases in yields. This factor, plus the greater relative availability of land in some countries (e.g. Brazil), accounts for the growth in cultivated area.

Changes in consumption, trade and nutrition

Changes in the production of food and cereals per capita provide approximate indications of the balance between demographic trends and the growth of food output. They do not provide, however, any indication of the effective demand for food and ultimate consumption patterns. Growth in demand can be traced to three key factors: (1) population growth; (2)

income growth; and (3) the income elasticity of demand. Population growth is by far the most important factor, over the long term, in shifting demand. How much food is actually consumed depends very much upon terms of trade, price of food, income, tastes, and a host of political/institutional and trade factors. Estimates of aggregate consumption are normally computed as national food (cereal) production plus imports minus exports. Changes in consumption regionally, nationally and globally provide important clues to shifts in nutritional levels as well as trade in food commodities.

Worldwide, between 1961–77 the consumption of food grew at a faster rate than population growth. Whereas consumption growth in developed countries was 137 per cent higher than population growth, it was only 11 per cent higher in developing countries excluding China (Mellor and Johnston, 1984). If consumption growth is compared with production growth we find that Latin America, North Africa and the Middle East, Sub-Saharan Africa and middle-income countries of South East Asia consumed more than they produced by significant margins. In Latin America, growth in food production exceeded growth in population by 18 per cent but growth in consumption exceeded growth in population by 32 per cent.

The end result of this imbalance between what is produced and what is consumed is a marked rise in food imports since the 1950s. Figure 3.3 provides a profile of the changing pattern of food trade. Developing countries have increased their food imports at a faster rate than food exports creating an unfavourable food trade balance. These changes reflect not only population growth but changing consumption patterns (a rise in the importance of wheat) and economic policies in developed and developing countries (World Bank, 1986).

A breakdown of the levels of imports and exports of cereals by region for 1950 to 1980 is provided in Fig. 3.4. The dramatic change in levels of self-sufficiency is evident. North America, in little over a quarter century, became the pre-eminent exporter of grains (including oilseeds), with the USSR, North Africa/Middle East and East Asia leading the way in imports. Despite the recent surplus supply of grains in Western Europe (about 15 million metric tonnes in 1984/85), there is little prospect of improving sufficiency levels over the near future for many other regions.

The reasons for this dramatic change in grain commodity flows are complex. A number of factors stand out above all others. First, as previously observed, population growth has exceeded production growth in a number of developing countries, particularly Sub-Saharan Africa. Second, increasing income in numerous areas of the world in part brought about by a larger and more profitable agricultural sector, combined with relatively high-income elasticities of demand have accelerated the demand for more and better quality foods, such as protein from animal production (Mellor and Johnston, 1984). Eastern Europe and the Soviet Union's

41

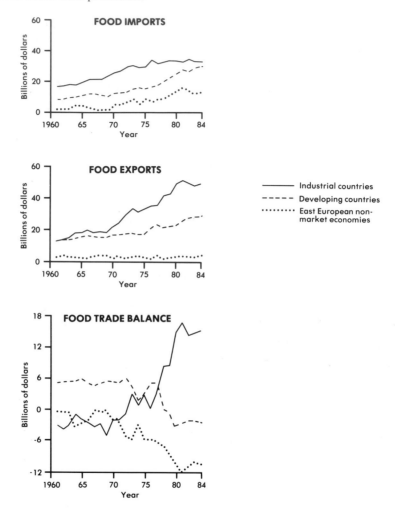

Fig. 3.3 Trends in food trade and trade balance 1961–84
Source after the World Bank (1986)

growth in consumption of cereals (particularly maize) derives from increasing consumption of animal products. Table 3.1 profiles income elasticities by region and product. In Asia and the Far East a 10 per cent increase in income will increase the consumption of calories of animal origin by 8.3 per cent; and in Africa the same increase will produce a change of 9.5 per cent. Compare these figures with North America or Oceania of 0.4 and 0.5 per cent increases and it becomes reasonably clear how income growth in developing countries translates into a far greater rate of increase in animal/livestock consumption.

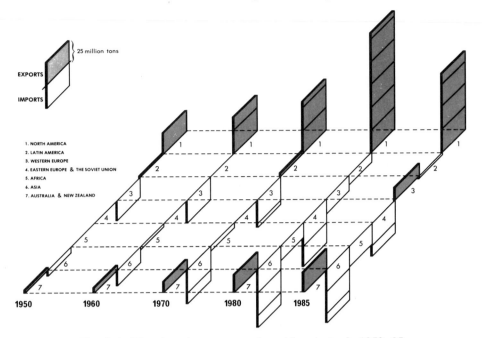

EXPORTS

IMPORTS

25 million tons

1. NORTH AMERICA
2. LATIN AMERICA
3. WESTERN EUROPE
4. EASTERN EUROPE & THE SOVIET UNION
5. AFRICA
6. ASIA
7. AUSTRALIA & NEW ZEALAND

1950   1960   1970   1980   1985

Fig. 3.4   The changing pattern of world grain trade 1950–85
Sources Brown (1984); FAO (1986)

Table 3.1 Income elasticity of demand for food in the main regions of the world (with market economies)

| Region | Income elasticity with respect to: | | |
	Total food calories	Calories of animal origin	Animal proteins
North America	0.01	0.04	0.02
Western Europe	0.07	0.29	0.37
Oceania	0.02	0.05	0.06
Others	0.14	0.47	0.42
Total developed countries	0.08	0.24	0.28
Africa	0.29	0.95	0.82
Latin America	0.20	0.42	0.41
Near East	0.15	0.52	0.51
Asia and Far East	0.34	0.83	0.83
Total developing countries	0.22	0.58	0.56

Source after Campbell (1979), based on OECD (1976)

War, famine and other natural disasters have seriously disadvantaged many countries' abilities to sustain production. Reliance on imports has

43

been the only means to prevent massive starvation. Equally important, those agricultural and trade policies of developed countries which support their agricultural sectors by encouraging exports and inhibiting imports have been injurious to the agricultural sectors of a number of developing countries. There is little incentive to produce grains if the price of imported grains from Europe or North America is below a country's cost of production.

Not unexpectedly, the worsening of food trade balances since the late 1970s correlates closely with the worsening of Third World debt. By the end of 1987 the seventeen most indebted countries owed Western banks $485 billion. Brazil and Mexico, the leading debtor nations, pay out one-third of their export earnings just to service their debts (*The Economist*, 1988a).

Having reviewed trade and consumption patterns, several questions remain. Are food supplies meeting nutritional requirements? Are individuals receiving sufficient caloric and protein intakes? The FAO (1977b) has shed some light on the issue of calorie supply by region. Throughout the 1960s and the first half of the 1970s, food consumption in developed countries exceeded basic requirements (2200 Calories per day) by increasing margins of 24 and 32 per cent. The nutritional situation in some parts of the developing world is much less sanguine. Whereas daily per capita calorie supply in Latin America and the Near East has shown modest improvements in exceeding requirements, largely because of increased imports, this has not been the case in the Far East and and Africa. Small increases in per capita food supply have taken place, but nutritional levels are still below basic requirements.

The FAO (1982) estimated that in 1966–68 there were as many as forty-one countries (62 per cent of total population of developing world) with average per capita food supplies of less than 2200 Calories. The proportion declined to thirty-one countries (48 per cent of total population) by 1977–79. Figure 3.5 demonstrates the low and deficient caloric intake in many tropical and subtropical regions of the world. The North–South division of the global economy takes on added meaning when viewed within the context of nutritional variations.

The averages conceal significant variations within countries. It could be argued that to be sure that the majority of the population is receiving minimum caloric levels, average per capita food supplies must be closer to 3000 calories. The data also give no clue to the level of diversity in diets. In Niger, Upper Volta and Bangladesh over 85 per cent of dietary energy is derived from cereals and other staple foods, compared to 25 to 30 per cent in developed countries. The body requires nine essential amino acids in combination before protein synthesis occurs. Cereal grains are deficient in the essential amino acid lysine, and legumes are deficient in methionine (Grigg, 1985). Animal products provide all essential amino acids, whereas no one cereal crop does. Since animal products represent such a small

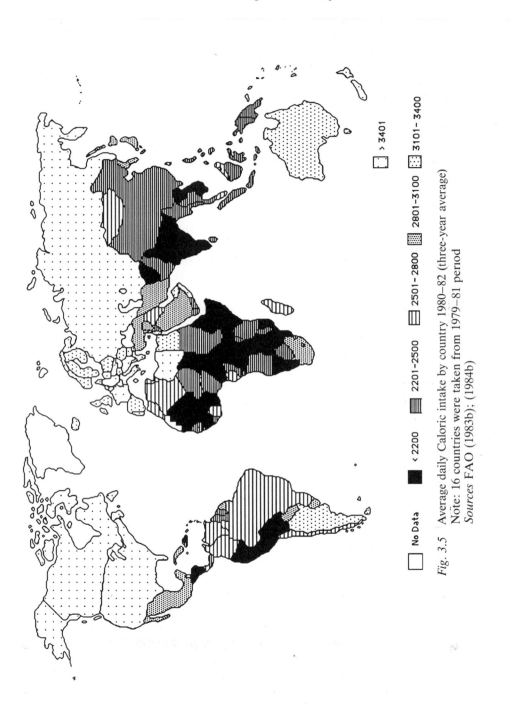

Fig. 3.5 Average daily Caloric intake by country 1980–82 (three-year average)
Note: 16 countries were taken from 1979–81 period
Sources FAO (1983b); (1984b)

Legend:
- No Data
- < 2200
- 2201–2500
- 2501–2800
- 2801–3100
- 3101–3400
- > 3401

percentage of food consumed in the developing world, the main source of protein is through vegetable products often combining cereals and legumes. Generally, an average daily protein intake of between 50–70 grams is a minimum requirement, but relatively few countries achieve that minimum range (see Fig. 3.6).

The actual levels of protein provided by cereals and staples varies by crop and ecological conditions. Cassava, a staple in much of the humid tropics, has only about 2 per cent protein. Durum wheat produced under very dry conditions will have 12 per cent protein content compared to highs of 20 per cent when grown under more moist conditions. And the protein level of all wheat tends to diminish as wheat yields increase. Hence reliance on vegetable protein for the main source of amino acids is often a prescription for malnutrition or undernutrition. Protein energy malnutrition can be found throughout the developing world. Typical examples are isolated districts in Kenya with poor soil and in north-east Brazil where the land is semi-arid and. relatively unproductive (FAO, 1978).

Components of growth in agricultural production

Models of agricultural development

Highly simplified explanations of growth in agricultural production tend to pursue the intensification/extensification theme. Production is enhanced by increasing yields, land area, cropping intensities or all three. Notwithstanding the usefulness of these categories, they lack the explanatory power of models of agricultural development. In reviewing the literature on agricultural development, Ruttan (1980) has identified six distinct models (see Table 3.2). The models should not be interpreted in terms of a sequence of conditions, nor does any one model sufficiently characterize agricultural development among countries over time. Collectively, however, they provide the underpinnings for understanding the variations in rate and structure of agricultural growth in different regions of the world at different times.

The frontier and urban-industrial models are useful for explaining changes in the agricultural sector of many developed countries during the last century and a half. The conservation, diffusion and high-payoff input models are more applicable to the experiences of the developing countries during the last forty years, particularly in their adoption of Green Revolution technology. Of all the models, the induced-innovation model offers the most comprehensive explanation of the behaviour of farm systems. There are two important features of this model. First, the development and adoption of technology (biological or mechanical) and the choice of inputs were guided by the scarcity of land, labour and capital. Hence, with the scarcity of land and relative abundance of labour in Japan, land-saving technologies were adopted through the use of

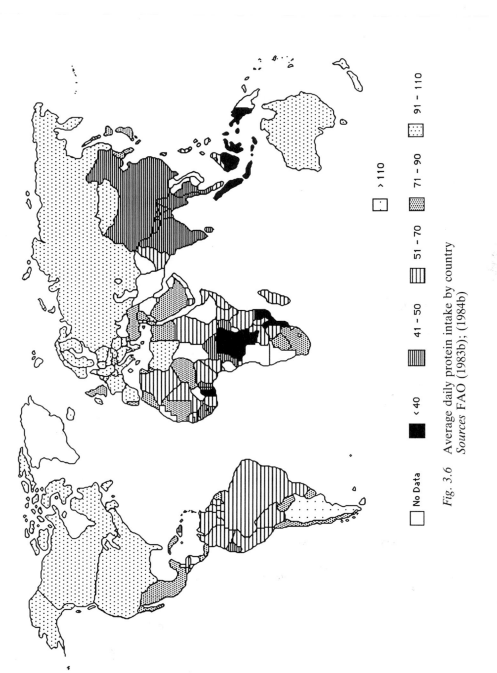

Fig. 3.6 Average daily protein intake by country
Sources FAO (1983b); (1984b)

Table 3.2 Models of agricultural development

Model	Features	Examples
Frontier	Expansion of cultivated and grazed areas	North and South America in eighteenth and nineteenth centuries
		South-east Asia by 1970
Conservation	Intensification through complex land- and labour-intensive cropping systems	Europe and Asia until twentieth century
	Most inputs supplied by farm sector	China and many poorer developing countries today
Urban–industrial impact	Agricultural development tied to growth in industrial development	Nineteenth-century Europe
	Surplus labour absorbed into urban-based industry	Twentieth-century North America
Diffusion	Spread of technology and knowledge from progressive areas to backward areas to increase productivity	North America in the nineteenth and early twentieth centuries
		Basis for rural development strategies in developing countries in 1950s
High-payoff input	Integration of peasant agriculture into agro-industrial system through the use of energy-intensive inputs and new plant varieties	Mexico in 1950s and India and the Philippines in 1960s
Induced innovation	Technical change is determined by a nation's resource endowment and different input combinations are location-specific	Developed economies and middle-income developing economies
	Hence technology enhances substitution of relatively abundant factors for relatively scarce	
	Convergence takes place over time in relative importance of input factors	

Source based upon information from Ruttan (1980)

fertilizers and high yielding crops to increase the productivity of the land. And, with scarcity of labour and relative abundance of land in the United

States, labour-saving technology was adopted through the use of machinery and other forms of mechanization to increase the productivity of the worker. Second, productivity growth (output in relation to input) is usually initiated by a single production factor (i.e., land or labour), but as development proceeds the contribution of other production factors increases. This eventually leads to a more balanced contribution of input factors to growth in output and to sustained growth in productivity.

All six models of agricultural development offer insight into the complex character by which society combines and transforms resources to enhance agricultural production possibilities. Identifying, categorizing and measuring the resources has proved historically to be a difficult and often arbitrary task. Here an attempt is made to identify the relative importance in the production process of such factors as arable land, irrigation, fertilizers, high-yielding grains and mechanical technology. To set the stage for this discussion we first discuss the issue of yields.

Yield growth and variability

Since the dawn of the first agricultural revolution, the expansion of agricultural production has occurred through the growth in the size of the land base. Between 1860 and 1920, 432 million additional hectares of land were brought under cultivation. An equivalent amount was added during the succeeding fifty years (Richards, 1984). The regions which registered the largest increase in production in the nineteenth and early twentieth centuries were the regions with the largest additions to their cropped area. Since the 1940s, however, yield growth has contributed a much larger share of the growth in total production than expansion in physical area. Worldwide between 1950 and 1980, area expanded by 26 per cent, average yield by 80 per cent and total production by 126 per cent. In an analysis of sources of growth in crop production in ninety developing countries for the fifteen-year period beginning in 1961, Scrimshaw and Taylor (1980) found that new cropped land contributed 16.9 per cent, irrigation 16.6 per cent, fertilizer use 40.2 per cent and other factors 26.3 per cent. More recently (1972–82) for developing countries as a whole, yield growth contributed 70 per cent to the growth in production (see Fig. 3.2). For their developed counterparts the emphasis on yield growth has been even greater. Since 1960 yield growth has been responsible for more than 90 per cent of the growth in production (Barr, 1981). Figure 3.7 summarizes annual rate of changes in output and inputs for developed and developing countries.

The overriding importance of yield growth as a contributor to food production growth, combined with the need in the immediate future to expand that production, has raised a number of questions regarding yield trends and their stability.

As we saw in Barr's (1981) study, average world cereal yields consistently increased during the 1960s and 1970s. A more recent study of the

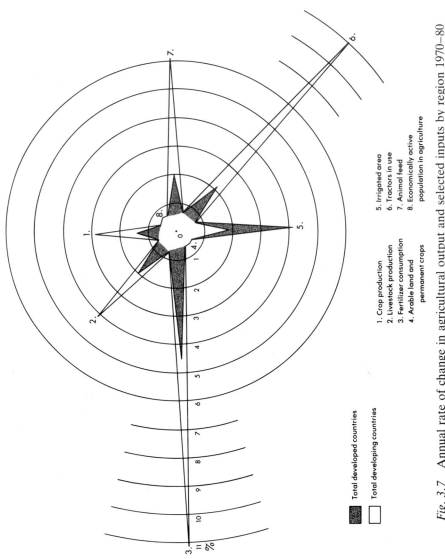

1. Crop production
2. Livestock production
3. Fertilizer consumption
4. Arable land and
   permanent crops

5. Irrigated area
6. Tractors in use
7. Animal feed
8. Economically active
   population in agriculture

Total developed countries

Total developing countries

Fig. 3.7 Annual rate of change in agricultural output and selected inputs by region 1970–80
Source FAO (1983a)

growth of yields for ninety-two countries over a twenty-three year period, beginning in 1960, found that yields increased at a constant annual rate of 41 kg per hectare per year (Tarrant, 1987). While there were no signs globally of significant change in growth rates (either upward or downward), a finer grained examination of the data does reveal significant variations in individual country's average rates of growth. Western Europe, the United States, Japan, South Korea and China showed average annual increases in yield in excess of 60 kg/ha. In contrast the Middle East, Australia and the Soviet Union showed only marginal gains (<20 kg/ha). Most of Africa and parts of South-East Asia showed absolute declines in yields from 1961 to 1983.

Just as there is variation among countries in the average growth in yields, so there is variation in the stability of growth. Whereas yields in North America and Western Europe display fairly constant growth trends, yield growth in Indonesia and Japan is increasing and decreasing respectively.

Other research into yield trends for wheat for the period 1945–81 revealed that although yield growth was increasing globally it was not uniform (Kogan, 1985). Not only were the 1960s the period with highest rate of change in yields, but countries varied significantly in their growth trends (see Fig. 3.8). Numerous important wheat-growing regions (including parts of Europe, the USSR, North America and Australia) representing 40 per cent of world wheat production experienced a decline in their growth rates. Only a relatively small area, mostly in the Third World, actually experienced increasing rates of growth in yield.

A variety of explanations account for the differences in yields and their growth. The slowing of yield growth and even the appearance of yield ceilings can be explained in terms of the optimization of the interaction of genotype and the environment (Jensen, 1978). The degree to which climatic resources meet the technology/genotype requirements determines the rate of growth (increasing or decreasing). As the compatibility between climate and technical resources declines, so will the rate of growth in yields (Kogan, 1985). Countries experiencing increasing rates of growth have adopted and/or developed technology which is highly compatible with the environment. Increasing marginal returns to factor inputs would be experienced.

The reversal of growth rates for many African countries attests to the significance and importance of drought, as it does to the technological and social/organizational capabilities needed to combat it. A more in-depth discussion of this problem follows in Chapters 7 and 8.

For many Third World nations, average yields and the growth in those yields remain below those in developed countries. Although the adoption of Green Revolution technology and new farm management practices boosted yields in numerous regions of Asia and Latin America during the 1950s and 1960s, growth subsided in subsequent decades. In part this

51

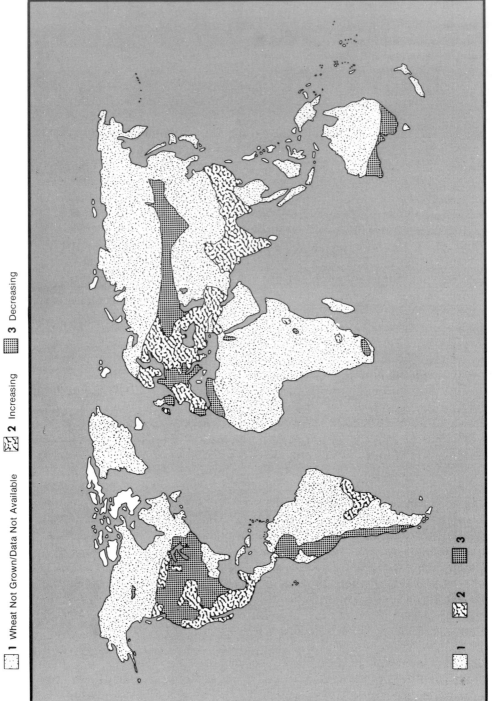

1 Wheat Not Grown/Data Not Available   2 Increasing   3 Decreasing

Fig. 3.8   Rate of growth in wheat yields c. 1948–1978

reflected a slowdown in the diffusion of technology as irrigation potential and land suited to production were exhausted. Equally important were changes in energy prices, poor price incentives, lack of investment in rural infrastructure and insistence by some governments on giving a higher priority to the export cash-crop sector than to the indigenous food sector.

The International Rice Research Institute (IRRI) has conducted research into the yield gap – the difference between actual yield and maximum potential yield. Herdt and Barker (1979) attributed the gap to a number of bio-physical and socio-economic constraints. Since maximum possible yield is normally achieved only under experimental conditions, a more realistic measure is potential farm yield. Research suggests that this yield gap exists primarily because of inadequate or unreliable rainfall, failure to match the right seed with right environment and a host of social, cultural and economic factors that affect the efficient allocation of knowledge and resources (Herdt and Barker, 1979). It is not always economically attractive to overcome all biological constraints to production. Also, technological knowledge or availability of technology may be limited. Without improved markets, greater incentives and more research, farmers rarely approach their economic ceiling, let alone their technical ceiling, in developing countries.

It is thus clear that large differences exist in yields and yield growth among countries. Research by Tarrant (1987) also suggests that the absolute and relative spatial variability of cereal yields is increasing. Countries are becoming less like each other in their yield trends. While some of the increased variability can be attributed to drought and other climate extremes in Africa, as well as the increased sensitivity of new high-yielding seed varieties to moisture stress and pest, the majority of it, in the view of Tarrant, is due to unequal access and use of agricultural technology. Certainly, in the case of North America and Western Europe the increased uniformity of agricultural practices and technology has decreased the relative spatial variablility of yields within these regions.

Perhaps more difficult to explain are the year-to-year differences in production. While no general trend exists towards an increase in the relative variability of inter-annual cereal yields, a significant group of countries, including Australia, China, most of Africa and central America, have increasing annual variability in yields (Tarrant, 1987). These observations can also be extended to increased variability in food production. Hazel (1984) has suggested that new seed/fertilizer-based technologies are characterized by high variability in semi-arid regions with limited irrigation. Moreover, the inability to apply new technology uniformly on a year-to-year basis because of price escalations in inputs or supply bottlenecks can also contribute to increased variability in yields and production.

The implications of these findings are that with increasing spatial variability in yield, the inequalities in food production will grow, as will the need for greater trade in cereal. And with increasing year-to-year variability for some regions, the need for additional food stocks and food aid will increase.

Land base

As agriculture has become increasingly science-based in North America, Western Europe, Japan and Australia, land has become relatively less important in the production process. The United States is a good example (see Fig. 3.9). There, non-land inputs contribute approximately three times as much to output as land. Much of the inducement behind the substitution of non-land for land inputs has been economic. Since the 1960s land values have risen at a faster rate than most other inputs. Farm real estate values increased by an average 200 per cent in real terms for the period 1960–80 (Huffman, 1981).

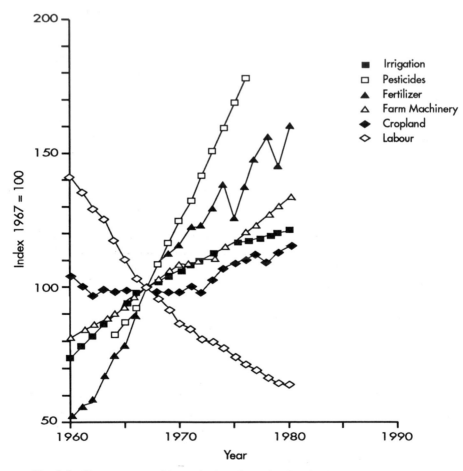

Fig. 3.9 Resources used in agricultural production in the United States 1960–80
Source Conservation Foundation (1982)

Although land values were rising during the 1960s, surplus grain conditions encouraged the large-scale retirement of land from production. Idle land reserves peaked in 1972, but with subsequent poor harvests, 24 million hectares were brought back into production by 1980. Idle land appeared once again as record harvest levels and poor markets created surplus conditions in the mid-1980s. Seen in this context, land and not yields was the chief means over the very short term by which output was deliberately checked or expanded. As will be discussed later, most of the developed nations of the world have used or are now using the majority of the potential arable land base. Land reserves are generally of lower quality than their cultivated counterparts, and would be relatively costly to convert. Long-term growth in production must therefore come, at least in developed countries, from yield growth.

Developing countries stand out from their developed counterparts in the growth and potential for growth of their arable land base. From 1960 to 1980 area under cultivation for grains grew by 15 per cent compared to 4 per cent for developed countries. It is estimated that developing countries have used only about 36 per cent of their potentially arable land (Buringh, 1977). The majority of unused reserves is to be found in Africa and South America. Like Western Europe, Asia has very little room for growth. True to its potential, Latin America experienced the greatest rates of growth in its arable land base of all major regions of the world. Brazil's cultivated area grew from 17.5 million hectares in 1950 to 44 million hectares in 1976. And by the next century it is expected to exceed 100 million hectares (FAO, 1978b).

Although Africa experienced the second highest rate of growth in its arable land base, the growth has been uneven, with expansion in the 1970s considerably behind that achieved in the 1960s. The drought in the Sahel has caused an actual retrenchment in the arable land base in some areas. Other factors responsible for the slowdown in growth include the increased cost of providing transportation and basic infrastructure, shortages of labour and the poor performance of the Sub-Saharan African economy (average annual growth in GDP in 1970s of 2.4 per cent, compared to 5.1 per cent for all developing countries).

Irrigation

The early civilizations of the Mesopotamians, Mayans and Chinese owed much of their prosperity to a cropland base sustained by irrigation. In the nineteenth century the development of agriculture in India and Egypt was largely the result of large-scale irrigation projects. Then, as today, irrigation was a key input in maintaining a population–food balance. Irrigation allows for effective control over two essential conditions for optimal plant growth–the timing and quantity of water supply. It relies upon surface and groundwater sources using diverse methods of storage (cisterns, reservoirs, tubwells) and distribution systems (pumped and gravity-fed channels).

Of the 1.4 billion hectares of arable land in use in the early 1980s, 270 million hectares or 19 per cent were irrigated, with the developing world accounting for over three-quarters of irrigated area. Approximately 30 per cent of the world's food production takes place on irrigated lands.

Developing countries possess not only the largest irrigated areas (China and India alone account for about half of these), but also the greatest potential for expansion and development. Irrigated area has grown in excess of 2 per cent per year since 1960, consuming 60 per cent of all fertilizers and accounting for 40 per cent of all crops grown in the developing world. Most significant, between 50 and 60 per cent of the increases in agricultural output from 1960 to 1980 was derived from the expansion in irrigated area (World Bank, 1982).

Irrigation is a key factor underlying increases in cropping intensity or multiple cropping. Multiple cropping refers to the number of harvested crops taken from a plot of land. If the entire arable land base is cropped and yields two crops per year, cropping intensity would equal 200. Areas with extensive irrigation have high cropping intensities: China (150), Taiwan (165), Bangladesh (155) and Egypt (190), (Hrabovszky, 1985). Africa, the region with the smallest irrigated area, experienced only small additions to that base (1.27 million hectares to 1.87) between 1965 and 1975. Consequently cropping intensity increased only from 106 to 109, with little growth in overall production. Much of the success of Mexican agriculture since 1940 is attributable to the growth and expansion of irrigated area (and an increase in cropping intensity), in combination with the use of fertilizers and high-yielding variety grains.

Given the arid nature of the Near East, water is the major limiting factor in agricultural development. Approximately 20 per cent of the cultivated area is irrigated, with proportions as high as 100 per cent in Egypt. Consequently, Egypt has one of the highest cropping intensities in the world. Other countries in the region, because of the scarcity of water and need for fallowing (to store moisture) have significantly lower cropping intensities (65).

The single most important factor affecting yield of rice in the Far East has been the growth and development of irrigation systems. India increased its irrigated area from 30 to 39 million hectares in the decade following 1970. Thailand, Nepal and Bangladesh had some of the highest annual growth rates in irrigated areas during the same period. Countries with the highest proportion of net cropped area irrigated are Pakistan (75 per cent), China (50 per cent), Sri Lanka (49 per cent), West Malaysia (48 per cent) and Republic of Korea (41 per cent). Like Mexico, the diffusion and adoption of high-yielding variety grains led to the growth in irrigated lands and the increase in yields. It is to these phenomena that we now turn.

56

New seed varieties and energy-intensive inputs

The use of fertilizers, pesticides and herbicides in combination with new seed varieties in both irrigated and rainfed areas has provided a major impetus to the growth in yields in the post-war period and has commonly been referred to as a Green Revolution in developing countries. Yields in cereals were roughly comparable in North America and in the developing world until the 1940s. Fertilizer application at this time was minimal (except for Japan and parts of Western Europe), as was the use of new cultivars which would make the most efficient use of nutrients. One of the common problems in applying chemical fertilizer to traditional varieties of grains is that most of the additional nutrients go to vegetative growth and not to the head of the plant. With an elongated stalk the plant tends to lodge (or flatten) before ripening. New cultivars solved these problems with their shorter stalks and larger heads. They also allowed for higher densities per unit area through smaller leaves and root systems (Jenning, 1976). As Norse (1979) observed, the technology itself was neither new nor revolutionary. The plant-breeding techniques had been developed in 1908 and applied in Taiwan and Korea during Japanese 'colonial rule' in the 1920s and 1930s. The revolutionary aspect 'was the extensive organizational effort which went into the production and dissemination of the seed of the new varieties' (Norse, 1979: 29).

Although irrigation was used in many developing countries in the 1940s and 1950s as a means of increasing yields, it was not until the 1960s that fertilizers and high-yielding variety grains, in combination with other energy intensive outputs, were actively applied. Mexico provided the first large-scale testing for the alteration of tropical and sub-tropical traditional agriculture into a higher yielding system. During the 1940s the Rockefeller Foundation and Mexican Ministry of Agriculture joined forces to improve crop yields. One of the major limiting factors in Mexican soils was the availability of nitrogen. It was found that a four-fold increase in yield (1 to 4 tonnes/ha) could be achieved by applying 100 kilograms of nitrogen/ha in combination with high-yielding varieties of corn (Wellhausen, 1976). For wheat it was found that the introduction of rust-resistant dwarf varieties of wheat, in combination with guaranteed water supply (through irrigation) and high inputs of fertilizer, would result in dramatic increases in yields. Hence in Mexico from 1950 to 1970 wheat output increased more than four times and corn 2.5 times.

In the 1960s the diffusion of these methods and techniques to other countries such as the Philippines, Pakistan, India, China, Indonesia and Thailand, resulted in similarly dramatic impacts on yields and outputs. High-yielding varieties were developed for rice, sorghum and other coarse grains. And new wheat and maize varieties were developed which were more site-specific. In the case of rice, the IRRI was instrumental in developing and diffusing new rice varieties. The first of these (IR-8)

57

quickly boosted yields in the Philippines and held the promise for a transformation of the agricultural landscape from one of low yielding to high yielding. It was not long after its introduction, however, that IR-8 like many other new varieties was decimated by pests and diseases. Despite the number of rice seed varieties (100,000-120,000), the difficulty and challenge has been to develop a genetic base which satisfies the need for higher yields and at the same time is resistant to pests and disease.

The initial growth in fertilizer consumption took place in developed countries. By the late 1960s, developed countries consumed over 80 per cent of global fertilizer consumption. The developed market economies were by far the most important consumers of fertilizers. During the next decade, the developed countries' share of total fertilized consumption decreased to 72 per cent. Throughout the developing world, annual rates of increase in fertilizer consumption of 10 per cent were common. The Far East and South America are the two leading consumers of fertilizer in the developing world. Africa registered the lowest share of fertilizer use.

The relationship between fertilizer use and yield levels is a close one (see Figs 3.10 and 3.11). Differences exist which are attributable to different environmental attributes as well as to labour and technological inputs. Countries with the highest yields such as Japan, the United Kingdom, the Netherlands and Germany also have the highest fertilizer applications. With wheat, the Netherlands and the United Kingdom had yields in 1945 as high as yields obtained in the United States in 1980. In the 1980s yields are almost three times US levels (6 tonnes/ha) and fertilizer use four times. Japan stands out as possessing the highest rice yields (3 tonnes/ha in 1930 and 6.5 tonnes/ha in 1970). In this context, Ruttan (1980) argued that crop variety improvement was directed toward the selection and breeding of more fertilizer-responsive varieties of rice.

Unravelling the exact contribution of new varieties and fertilizer to yield and production growth can be difficult because of the complex interactive effects between the two. Estimates of the impact on production of the introduction of new cereal varieties between 1939–64 range from a low of 0.7 (per cent/year) in the Netherlands to 1.4 (per cent/year) in the United Kingdom (Norse, 1979). In Manitoba, Canada, yield increases attributed to improved wheat varieties for the period 1962–78 averaged 0.7 per cent/year (Ridley and Hedlin, 1980). In the United States, Jensen (1978) has concluded that 49 per cent of productivity growth in wheat in New York State, from 1935 to 1975, was due to genetic factors and 51 per cent to technological (or energy-intensive factors). And lastly, new varieties of rice and chemical inputs accounted for a yield increase of 1.7 per cent per annum (compound) or 82 percent of the annual growth in yields in the Philippines (Herdt and Barker, 1979).

Other important energy-intensive inputs which have dramatically affected production have been various forms of mechanical technology (tractors, pumps, harvesters), insecticides and herbicides. The United

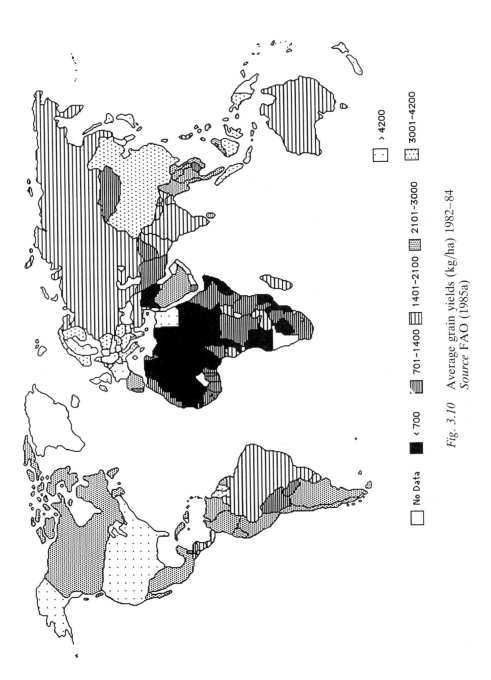

Fig. 3.10   Average grain yields (kg/ha) 1982–84
Source FAO (1985a)

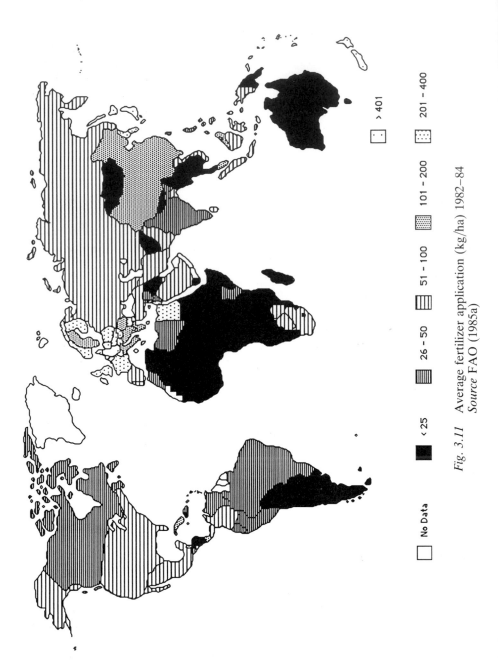

Fig. 3.11 Average fertilizer application (kg/ha) 1982–84
Source FAO (1985a)

States is the archetypal example of employing machinery to boost output (see Fig. 3.8). Of total energy inputs in 1970 into the production process for corn in the United States, fully half are accounted for by machinery and fuel, followed by fertilizers (30 per cent), electricity (6 per cent), drying (4 per cent) and a variety of irrigation, pesticide/herbicide applications (Pimentel, 1979). Since 1945 in the United States, the relative importance of machinery and fuel has decreased and that of the remaining inputs increased. Although total energy use has almost tripled during this period, yield growth/ha for corn has increased by 2.3 times. Decreasing marginal returns are therefore occurring.

Weaknesses of the green revolution

In concluding this section, some comments are required on the relative success of the Green Revolution. Developed countries have derived enormous net benefits from the use of more energy intensive and science-based forms of production. It was that very experience that inspired many Western countries, particularly the United States, to attempt to recreate the same success in Third World countries.

There is no question that the diffusion and adoption of this technology enhanced the productive capabilities of Third World countries' agricultural bases and was responsible for the large gains in food output. What is not clear about the Green Revolution is its impact on the average farmer and consumer. Since the technology required a minimum of energy-intensive resource inputs, it favoured land-owning classes, particularly larger and well-educated ones. This in turn further reinforced inequalities within many societies. Until there is more income and greater access by the poor to land and other resources, nutritional levels will not rise significantly. Hence in purely quantitative terms the Green Revolution was successful. But this statement ignores important distributional issues which are critical to the overall success of a programme. Attempts through purely technological means to combat inequality and poverty are bound to fail.

Summary

In the last three to four decades global food supply has expanded at an unprecedented rate. Growth rates for cereal production have been generally higher in less-developed countries than in their developed counterparts. Industrialized countries have seen food production per capita expand more rapidly than food consumption per capita. In developing countries food production per capita has expanded more slowly than food consumption per capita.

The growing gap between what a country could produce and what it required, defined in either nutritional or economic terms, was being bridged by increased food imports. For Eastern Europe, the Soviet Union and a number of middle-income developing countries the growth in effective demand accelerated the growth in food consumption and food imports. An increasing proportion of the annual cereal harvest was being diverted to livestock feed in these and other regions. Although lower-income developing countries expanded their consumption of grains, at a faster rate than production, the lack of income growth and effective demand in these countries still guaranteed that average annual food consumption would remain below minimum caloric and protein requirements.

Since the early 1970s the food trade balance of industrial countries has risen sharply while the opposite trend has occurred for developing and East-European non-market economies. Developing countries have relied upon export crops to earn foreign exchange. Unfortunately, these crops have displaced food crops and their economic value has declined relative to the value of major cereals.

The major source of growth in the food systems of both developed and developing countries comes from a variety of intensification strategies which have boosted yields and cropping intensities and in turn production. The adoption of Green Revolution technology, first by Mexico, followed by countries of the Indian subcontinent, China and other regions of South-East Asia, required dramatic increases in energy-intensive technology. With increased reliance upon fertilizers, irrigation, herbicides/pesticides and mechanization there was also a shift to a more science-based agricultural system involving new high-yielding variety grains principally for wheat, maize and corn.

While the success of the Green Revolution can be questioned on equity grounds, since it generally benefited a certain class of farmer capable of adopting the technology, it was successful in expanding yields and ensuring that food production kept pace with population growth.

Yet most developing countries are faced with a serious yield gap. The failure to approach expected yield levels arises from numerous socio-economic and bio-physical constraints. Moreover, the fact that yield growth is slower in a number of African, Asian and Latin American countries than in Western industrialized countries strongly suggests that the benefits of advances in agricultural technology are diffusing too slowly. This may be as much a political/cultural issue as an economic one. Regardless of the source, the need remains to provide the resources and technology which are adoptable and affordable to those regions which badly need to enhance their agricultural production and consumption possibilities.

CHAPTER 4

Prospective studies of food and agriculture

Setting the stage

If the last chapter was concerned with recent trends in the consumption and production of food, this chapter focuses on the prospects for food production over the intermediate to long term. The rear-view mirror approach is cast aside in favour of a forward-looking one. Future adequacy of food resources is assessed in relation to estimates of future food requirements and the productive possibilities of the food system regionally and globally. To address these issues, a number of studies and models will be examined to provide an assessment of food and agricultural prospectives.

Concern over the adequacy of the resource base generally and the food resource base specifically, during the last two or more decades, has spawned a diverse set of 'prospective' research on regional and global agricultural production potential and carrying capacities. From a conceptual perspective, agricultural development rests upon the interaction of three spheres – the biosphere (land, water, genetic resources); the technosphere (technological resources); and the sociosphere (social, economic and political systems), (Kassas, 1982). By varying assumptions about land and technical resources, allocative efficiency of the economic system, or acceptable costs of development, it is possible to expand or contract productive capacity (see Fig. 4.1). Whether or not that capacity is sufficient to meet the nutritional needs of the population depends on assumptions regarding growth in populations and income, acceptable calorie/protein levels in diet and the major food sources from which these are to be derived, as well as distribution and trade. Research into these areas is highly simplified, when compared to the real world, as well as highly speculative and subject to error. There is no single view or correct approach which provides definitive answers.

Prospective studies of food supply can be distinguished according to

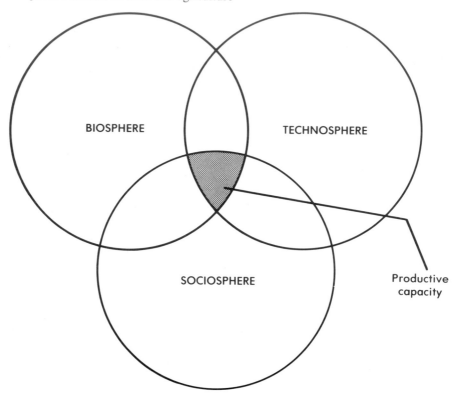

Fig. 4.1 Basic components underlying agricultural development

many different dimensions or criteria relating to complexity (scale, level of aggregation, sectors, time horizons), purpose (description, forecast or prescription), method/approach (optimization/equilibrium, input–output, systems-dynamic, econometric) and reliability. In what follows, an attempt is made to provide answers to basic questions on both the output and input side of the food equation from a resource/ecological, socio-economic and resource-economic perspective.

Resource/ecological studies

Clark, Revelle and Buringh

Initial studies of food production potential made assessments of land resources available for crop production, their capability to produce protein and calories and, if fully utilized, their carrying capacities. After examining climatic resources of the world, Clark (1967) concluded that the world possesses the equivalent of 7.7 billion hectares of standard land (land that is capable of producing a good crop per year or the equivalent in grazing) if tropical lands are equivalent to two units of standard land, and 10.7

billion hectares if tropical lands are equivalent to five units of standard land. Arguing that a subsistence diet requires approximately 680 grams per day or 250 kg of grain equivalent/yr (which at 3.2 calories/gram equals approximately 2200 calories per day) and that the North American diet is eleven times subsistence level, he concluded that approximately 2000 square metres (or 2250 square metres if requirements of forest land are included) would be needed for each person to sustain a high level (North American) of consumption. If world agricultural land resources are between 7.7 and 10.7 billion hectares of standard land equivalent, this land could feed between 34 and 49 billion people.

Revelle's (1976) study of land resources available for rainfed and irrigated cultivation under intense management produces similar results, but at different food energy requirements. He estimated that there are 4.2 billion gross cropped hectares (usable land times number of crops/yr) that are capable of producing high yields with present technology. Deducting 10 per cent of gross cropped area for non-food crops and assuming a yield of half of that attained in the US Mid-West (or 3000 kg/ha), 11.4 billion tonnes of food grains or their equivalent could be grown. Since the food energy in 700 grams of wheat, rice or corn equals human daily energy requirements of 2400 calories, this potential output is sufficient to feed a population of 40 billion. Moreover, 3.6 billion hectares of grazing land could produce between 25 to 50 million live-weight metric tonnes of animal products.

In an attempt to estimate absolute maximum food production of the world, Buringh et al. (1979) first divided the world into 222 broad soil regions. For each of these regions, data were collected on soil, climate, vegetation and water resources, as well as topographic conditions. From this information the potential size of the rainfed and irrigated agricultural land base was calculated, as previously discussed in Chapter 2. These figures in turn were adjusted for soil and water deficiencies. From a potential agricultural land base of 3.7 billion hectares, only 1.7 to 1.9 billion hectares are usable after adjustments for soil and moisture constraints are made. Following these calculations, estimates for each region's potential dry matter production were made from estimates of mean monthly gross photosynthesis per hectare for a standard crop. Final estimates of maximum production of dry matter were made by multiplying land area (rainfed and irrigated) times per hectare dry matter production adjusted for soil and moisture contraints.

Table 4.1 provides a continental breakdown of these calculations. To make these calculations comparable to standard food consumption units they were converted to grain equivalents (1 kg dry matter = 0.43 kg of grain). On this basis the authors estimated that maximum production of grain equivalents per year could be 50,000 tonnes or 40 times the cereal production prevailing in the mid 1970s or 32,390 tonnes if the present ratio of cultivated land to total arable land were used. On average, 26 tonnes of

Table 4.1 Potential arable land resources and productivity by region

Region	TA	PDM	PAL	IPAL	MPDM	PIAL	IPALI	MPDMI	MPGE
South America	1,780	75.5	616.5	333.6	25,224	17.9	340.7	25,710	11,106
Australia/									
New Zealand	680	70.5	225.7	74.2	5,297	5.3	76.1	5,462	2,358
Africa	3,030	79.5	761.2	306.5	24,162	19.7	317.5	25,115	10,845
Asia	4,390	55.0	1,083.4	433.5	24,966	314.1	581.6	33,058	14,281
North/Central									
America	2,420	47.5	628.1	320.0	15,443	37.1	337.5	16,374	7,072
Europe	1,050	37.0	398.7	233.1	8,289	75.9	247.1	9,653	4,168
Antarctica	1,310	–	–	–	–	–	–	–	–
Total	14,840	60.5	3,714.1	1,700.9	10,3381	470.0	1,900.5	11,5372	49,830

Key
TA – Area of a region (10^6 hectares)
PDM – Potential production of dry matter (10^3 kg/hectare/year)
PAL – Potential agricultural land (10^6 hectares)
IPAL – Imaginary area of PAL with potential production without irrigation (10^6 hectares)
MPDM – Maximum production of dry matter without irrigation (10^6 tonnes/year)
PIAL – Potentially irrigable agricultural land (10^6 hectares)
IPALI – Imaginary area of PAL with potential production including irrigation (10^6 hectares)
MPDMI – Maximum production of dry matter including irrigation (10^6 tonnes/year)
MPGE – Maximum production of grain equivalents including irrigation (10^6 tonnes/year)
Source adapted from Buringh et al. (1979)

grain per hectare per year are capable of being produced, compared to a global average of around 2 tonnes per hectare per year in the mid 1970's.

Since economic, social and political considerations are absent from the study, the estimates cannot be thought of as attainable globally and should not be used as a basis for estimates of ultimate carrying capacity of the land. Even though there are indications that some of the regional yield estimates are not far off those obtained in experimental conditions under very intensive management, many other factors must be taken into account before these figures can be used. This study also differs from the previous ones in terms of the estimate of the ultimate size of the arable land base.

Potential population-supporting capacities

The Food and Agricultural Organization in conjunction with the International Institute for Applied Systems Analysis (IIASA) have taken the work of Buringh et al. (1979) considerably further in their study, *Potential Population Supporting Capacities of Lands in the Developing World*

(FAO/UNFPA, 1979; FAO/IIASA, 1982; FAO 1984a). They too have used climate and soil information in combination with specific crop resource requirements to define agro-ecological zones. This information in conjunction with assumptions regarding technical inputs (low, intermediate and high) and the size of the arable land base provided the basis for making different assessments of rainfed production potential. When the estimates were compared with population projections, a rough measure of population-supporting capacity of the land and self-sufficiency levels was provided.

If the entire potential arable land base of the 117 countries studied is used for agriculture, approximately twice the 1975 populations (1.9 billion) could be supported (see Table 4.2). Values greater than one in Table 4.2 indicate self-sufficiency potential in food. At low levels of inputs, in 1975 all regions (except South-West Asia) could more than meet their food needs. The situation becomes much less positive (except at high-input levels) by the year 2000. The population of the study region by the end of the century is expected to be 3.6 billion. As many as 64 of the 117 countries at low-input levels would not be able to meet their food requirements. Even at high-input levels, nineteen countries would remain critical (FAO, 1984a). If the potential arable land base is adjusted for the use of land for non-food cash crops, forestry, urban and built-up uses as

Table 4.2 Regional potential/needs ratios (potential population supporting capacities divided by 1975 or 2000 populations)

Input level	Africa	South-West Asia	South America	Central America	South-East Asia	Average
Year 1975 ratios						
Low	3.0 (1.9)[a]	0.8 (0.5)	5.9 (3.9)	1.6 (1.09)	1.1 (0.7)	2.0
Intermediate	11.6 (7.7)	1.3 (0.8)	23.9 (15.9)	4.2 (2.1)	3.0 (2.0)	6.9
High	33.9 (22.9)	2.0 (1.31)	57.2 (38.1)	11.5 (7.6)	5.1 (3.4)	16.6
Year 2000 ratios						
Low	1.6 (1.1)	0.7 (0.5)	3.5 (2.3)	1.4 (0.9)	1.3 (0.8)	1.6
Intermediate	5.8 (3.1)	0.9 (0.6)	13.3 (8.9)	2.6 (1.7)	2.3 (1.5)	4.2
High	16.5 (10.9)	1.2 (0.8)	31.5 (20.9)	6.0 (4.0)	3.3 (2.2)	9.3

[a]Figures in brackets represent a one-third reduction in land area
Source after FAO (1984a)

well as a higher average calorie/protein intake to offset inequalities in distribution, then approximately one-third of the previously-used land is lost. Table 4.2 gives fractions of 1975 and future populations that regional lands can sustain. Under these diminished land-resource conditions the necessity to increase inputs increases further. The list of countries on the critical list with low inputs expands from sixty-four to seventy-five and with high from nineteen to twenty-nine (FAO, 1984a).

There is considerable spatial variation in population-supporting capacity and food self-sufficiency levels. While Africa has the potential at low-input

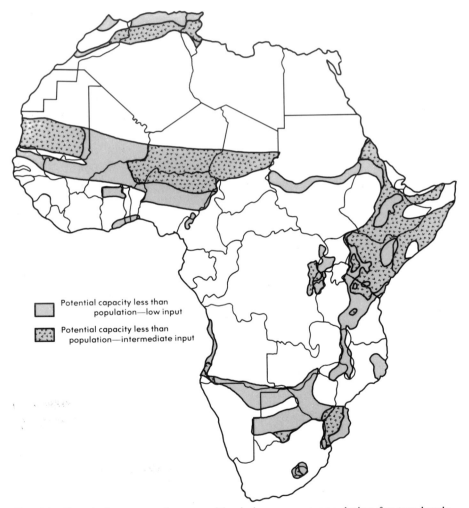

Fig. 4.2   Population-supporting capacities below current population for two levels
          of technological input
          Source FAO/IIASA (1982)

levels to feed three times its current population, this potential assumes that all arable land is cultivated and that food will move freely among countries. Figure 4.2 illustrates African population supporting capacities which are less than present populations with low and intermediate inputs. These critical areas whose lands cannot meet existing population densities cut across national boundaries,reflecting the importance of soil and climatic conditions.

> The critical zones extend across the Maghreb, in mountain and coastal areas. They stretch across the Sahel between latitudes 20 °N and 12 °N, taking in the northern savanna areas of Ghana, Togo and Nigeria. The most densely populated areas of Kenya are critical, along with a densely settled crescent along the great lakes from southeast Uganda through Rwanda and Burundi to parts of Malawi. In the south, critical zones straddle the continent, from the coast of Angola through Botswana and Lesotho to southern Mozambique. (FAO, 1984a: 22)

Much of the humid tropics stands out as having excess potential population-supporting capacity because of its large potential arable land base and its relatively small population size.

This FAO study has emphasized what could be achieved under different land, water and technological inputs. Whether the potential can or will be achieved is another question. Africa uses only 21 per cent of its arable area, South-East Asia 92 per cent, Central America 49 per cent and South America 15 per cent. The majority of the critical countries (sixty-four by the year 2000 under low-input conditions) were considered land-scarce by the FAO. Sixty-six per cent were cultivating more than 70 per cent of the potentially cultivable area (see Fig. 4.3). Other features or characteristics of these critical countries include high fertility rates and population growth, environmental deterioration, low fertilizer applications and low yields.

Socio-economic studies

While the previous studies and models provided a general assessment of regional and global food production potential, they were expressions of a limited number of factors (bio-physical and technological) which shape and determine the ultimate productive capacity of the food system. Useful as these studies are in providing a standard or benchmark against which existing and expected requirements can be compared, they are nevertheless relatively simple. From a very different perspective production potential can be evaluated using economic, social and institutional criteria. The attempt is not to define absolute production capacity, but a penultimate estimate such as feasible supply capacity, given knowledge and assumptions regarding economic, social and institutional environments. Hence Yeh et al. (1977: 37–38) define feasible supply where 'the supply curve becomes

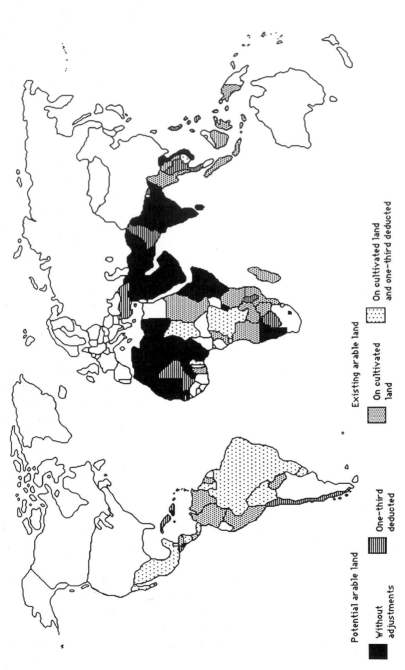

Fig. 4.3 Critical countries at low input level (supporting capacities below population) according to adjustments in the arable land base
Source after FAO (1984a)

very unresponsive to price because quality land, fertilizers, other conventional inputs and management are at such limits that additional output comes only at substantial costs . . .'. Although the potential for expanded production exists, it can only be realized at an uneconomic level.

In what follows we examine some of the better-known and important studies and models. Although using different methods and guided by different rationales, they provide general answers to questions about the future growth and availability of food, the sensitivity of the system to income, price and policy changes, the necessary inputs required to meet certain predetermined growth objectives and, to a very limited extent, the environmental implications of growth in the food system.

Future of the world economy

The 1970s represented the United Nations' second development decade during which a number of objectives and growth targets were set out for the year 2000 and beyond. To determine how realistic these objectives were and whether the growth targets could be achieved, a number of studies were undertaken by the Centre for Development Planning, Projections and Policies. One of the more ambitious was a study, *The Future of the World Economy*, which used a global input/output model of the world economy (Leontief, 1977). The purpose of the model was to show under different development scenarios the inter-relationships among the various production and consumption sectors by region (fifteen in all) and the environmental implications of four development scenarios for 1980, 1990 and 2000. Food and agriculture receive considerable attention in the model.

Under one scenario the most optimistic growth rules for population and the economy are externally specified in such a way as to halve the income gap between developed and developing countries by the year 2000. World agricultural production would have to increase three to fourfold compared to 1970 to meet this projected growth in demand. The model indicates the feasibility of this by projecting output and trade and estimating input and capital requirements. Table 4.3 profiles the ouput and input requirements by region for this scenario. Less optimistic scenarios show higher rates of population growth and/or lower rates of GDP per capita. The developing world shows a fourfold to ninefold increase in agricultural production. This contributes to a change (not shown) in the developing world's share of agricultural output from 36 per cent in 1970 to 62 per cent in 2000. However, this is not accompanied by a change in agricultural self-sufficiency for developing countries. Without the planned growth in output, existing self-sufficiency levels would decline drastically.

To achieve these higher levels of output, the land resource base will have to increase by 30 per cent or 229 million hectares above 1970. Latin America and Tropical Africa are targeted to have the greatest increase in the cultivated land base. The land resource base remains static in North America and Western Europe. The land/yield index indicates by how much the land resource base would have to expand to achieve the agricultural output levels in 2000 if yield remains unchanged from 1970 (see Table 4.3).

Yields are not expected to remain static. Yield growth in all regions is higher than arable land growth. Since the yield growth calculations are based upon assumed levels of agricultural land expansion, any shortfall in this expansion will require even greater growth in yields. Since the study itself points out that estimates of yield growth are too high for the Middle East and Japan (two land-scarce countries), food self-sufficiency levels will probably have to be sacrificed and food imports increased.

Irrigation is expected to play an important role in expanding yields – 80 million new hectares from 1970–2000 – as will the growth in other energy-intensive inputs such as fertilizers and machinery. In short, a new technological revolution is required. But to turn this 'physical possibility into a reality', many public policy measures in the area of irrigation, land reclamation, public and private investment, credit facilities, land reform and resettlement of labour will have to be designed. Capital requirements alone for opening up new land and expanding productivity are expected to

Table 4.3 Land requirements and land productivity in 2000 (scenario X)

Region	Agricultural output	Land/Yield index	Arable land	Land productivity
Developed market				
North America	196	215	111	194
Western Europe	130	162	100	162
Japan	176	269	100	269
Oceania	192	296	183	162
Centrally-planned				
Soviet Union	164	215	100	215
Eastern Europe	143	186	100	186
Asia (centrally-planned)	488	333	120	278
Developing market				
Latin America (medium-income)	495	517	166	311
Latin America (low-income)	532	460	140	328
Middle East	950	612	126	487
Asia (low-income)	506	376	113	331
Africa (arid)	409	371	131	282
Africa (tropical)	438	492	152	324

Index 1970 = 100 per cent

Source after Leontief (1977)

exceed 1970 levels by a factor of 3.3–6. Careful and sustained investment is therefore critical.

Although the original aim of the study was to 'study the environmental aspects of the future world economy', unfortunately there is little documentation of agricultural pollutants (except pesticides) and nothing on degradation problems and in turn the costs of abatement. Hence the actual environmental implications of the various scenarios are not at all clear. As a result the following conclusion of the study is premature.

> The principal limits to sustained economic growth and accelerated development are political, social and institutional in character rather than physical. No insurmountable physical barriers exist within the twentieth century to the accelerated development of the developing regions. (Leontief, 1977: 10–11)

Global 2000

Another major study (and global modelling effort) *The Global 2000 Report to the President* (Barney, 1980: 77) came to similar conclusions as the previous one: 'The world has the capacity, both physical and economic, to produce enough food to meet substantial increases in demand through 2000.'

There are, however, a number of significant qualifications which distinguish this study from *The Future of the World Economy*. The most noteworthy is that the food sector must grow at near record rates simply to sustain current consumption. Furthermore, this growth will place increasing pressure on the resource base, an indication of which will be an increase in the real cost of producing food, particularly if petroleum prices increase. Before pursuing these issues more critically, the structure of the model and its results are needed.

In the Food and Agriculture Model, a number of long-range food projections are made using different assumptions regarding population, income, weather and petroleum price increases. The model itself (multi-sector, multi-region and general equilibrium) reflects the functioning and interrelationship of three sectors (grain, oilseed and livestock) through a series of one thousand demand, supply and trade equations by region and sector. The parameters for the equations were calculated largely from conditions prevailing worldwide between 1950 and 1975.

Three alternative sets of projections were made. In Alternative I, the baseline projection, population and income grow at the median rate of 1.8 and 1.5 per cent respectively to the year 2000. Weather and trade policies were assumed to be the same as in the previous twenty-five years, and energy prices are either held constant or doubled. In Alternative II, the optimistic scenario, population growth is lower (1.5 per cent), but income growth is higher (2.4 per cent). Weather conditions are assumed to be more favourable to crop growth than during the previous twenty five years (yields rise by the equivalent of one standard error from 1950–75 regional yield trends) and petroleum prices are constant. Lastly, under Alternative III, the pessimistic scenario, population growth and per capita income growth are 2.1 and 0.7 per cent respectively. Less favourable weather conditions than those which prevailed during the previous twenty-five years are assessed. Yields are one standard error below Alternative I. The doubling of petroleum prices by 2000 is also assumed.

Table 4.4 provides a summarized cross-section of model projections for production, consumption and trade by region for the three previously discussed scenarios. The variation in outcomes emphasizes the importance of exogenous variables such as population, income, energy prices and climate in affecting demand for and supply of food. Although food output is expected to double worldwide (over 1969–71) by 2000, per capita consumption will only increase by 26 per cent under the most optimistic scenarios. Alternative I shows a range of values because of the impact of different climate conditions upon yields. Globally, in the year 2000 yields fluctuate by +7.2 per cent. These gains are also unevenly distributed, with less-developed countries experiencing considerably smaller increases both in consumption and production than industrialized or centrally-planned economies.

Self-sufficiency levels decline and trade in cereals increases as the baseline (I) scenario is approached for centrally-planned and less-developed countries in 2000. Traditional exporters are expected to continue to play an important role in balancing world supply and demand, although countries such as Canada and Australia are expected to become less important as domestic markets expand.

In many developing countries the food problem is seen as much as a difficulty of increasing effective demand as it is of increasing supply. Typical agricultural economies in South Asia and much of the Sahel and Central Africa are expected to experience effective demand lagging behind nutritional demand. Real price increases for grain (30 per cent under scenario II for 1969–71 to 2000) are expected to limit their ability to compete internationally for exported grain, while the increased costs of inputs such as energy will dampen any intensification strategies. Other important factors affecting the price and hence consumption of cereals by developing countries include the shift to more livestock products by centrally-planned and middle-income developing countries.

To meet the income and population-generated growth in demand, the projections suggest that a significant increase in the share of the world's resources devoted to the food sector will be required. The demand for additional land resources will vary significantly by region with absolute constraints effective by 2000 in Western and Eastern Europe, Japan, South and East Asia and parts of Central America. The study argues that 'Arable areas in many of these regions will quite likely begin to contract before

Table 4.4 Per capita grain and total food production, consumption, and trade (alternatives I, II, III)

	1985 Grain (kg)			1985 Food (1969–71 = 100)			2000 Grain (kg)			2000 Food (1969–71 = 100)		
	I[a]	II	III	I	II	III	I	II	III	I	II	III
Industrialized countries												
Production	18.9–663.8	719.2	669.7	112.9–104.5	115.2	105.0	838.5–769.8	847.5	716.9	128.8–118.4	131.8	108.8
Consumption	613.7–587.3	656.9	569.4	108.8–104.9	115.2	102.1	735.0–692.4	798.3	619.2	127.7–121.2	139.1	110.0
Trade	◆105.1–◆76.5	◆62.3	◆100.3				◆103.5–◆77.4	◆49.2	◆97.7			
Centrally-planned countries												
Production	415.5	452.5	369.6	116.7	127.6	107.2	451.1	489.2	375.3	129.6	135.6	112.8
Consumption	432.5	458.5	400.4	122.4	125.0	115.9	473.9	495.1	396.5	135.8	138.4	119.0
Trade	◇21.0	◇6.0	◇30.8				◇22.8	◇5.9	◇21.2			
Less-developed countries												
Production	182.0–189.4	190.4	178.3	101.7–106.5	106.7	99.1	195.1–197.1	210.2	176.6	109.5–110.8	119.5	99.1
Consumption	203.0–201.6	207.8	191.8	107.7–106.7	110.8	101.8	210.2–205.5	219.4	189.5	111.0–108.6	116.7	99.0
Trade	◆21.0–◇12.2	◇17.4	◇13.5				◇14.6–◇8.4	–9.2	–12.9			
World												
Production	337.7–332.6	354.4	315.4	109.5–108.5	114.0	103.0	352.2–343.2	373.0	302.0	117.0–114.5	126.0	104.0
Consumption	337.7–332.6	354.4	315.4	109.5–108.5	114.0	103.0	352.2–343.2	373.0	302.0	117.0–114.5	126.0	104.0
Trade												

Note ◆ indicates export; ◇ indicates import

[a] Scenario I ranges in value reflect yield variations

Source adapted from Barney (1980)

2000 as demand for land for non-agricultural uses increases and as the economic and environmental costs of maintaining cultivated areas near physical maxima become prohibitive' (Barney, 1980: 97). The lion's share of the growth in the arable land base is expected to take place in less-developed countries (particularly those in South America). Worldwide arable land per capita under Alternative I is expected to decrease from the present 0.39 hectares per capita to 0.25 with the greatest decrease taking place in lesser-developed countries (from 0.35 to 0.19).

Given the relatively small role land is expected to play in production growth, the role of land augmenting inputs such as fertilizers takes on added significance. First, to double food production by 2000 under Alternative I required a trebling in fertilizer application over 1971–75. Second, the diminishing marginal returns to increasing fertilizer use globally (7:1 in 1985 and 5.5:1 by 2000) will require disproportionate increases in energy-intensive inputs to sustain the growth rate in production. However, these values are heavily influenced by the high value of use in developing countries. In this regard developing countries which currently use relatively low amounts of fertilizer will undoubtedly show higher marginal returns than many of their developed counterparts.

Other resource-augmenting inputs, particularly irrigation systems, will require large increases in public and private investment, with the former by far the most critical factor in terms of meeting the expansion in productive capacity. Other costs, specifically environmental costs, are not directly incorporated in the model although they are discussed in some detail. For example:

> Problems have been most marked in countries where man–land pressures are greatest, where agricultural technologies are primitive, where soil conservation measures are limited and where climate factors do not favour intensive cultivation . . . 'Future problems are likely to continue to be associated with pressure to expand agriculture into marginal areas and to utilize marginal resources more intensively'. (Barney, 1980: 104)

Agriculture toward 2000

The findings of the *Global 2000* report do not stand in isolation. A concurrent study by the FAO (1982a) *Agriculture Toward 2000* (*AT 2000*) points to growing food deficits, and slow growth in per capita food production and consumption if present trends persist. *AT 2000* examined three scenarios: a continuation in existing relationships (trend), improvement in the economic performance of developing countries in line with the growth objectives of the UN's development scenarios (optimistic growth, A) and a more modest rate of growth (medium growth B). The emphasis of the study is on the performance of the food sector in ninety developing countries.

In the trend scenario, historical growth rates in production and demand for ninety developing countries (excluding China) were extrapolated to the year 2000. Where necessary, adjustments were made to the extrapolation to ensure that resource constraints were not exceeded. The results indicate that although some modest improvements can be expected among middle-income countries, the majority (two-thirds) of the countries would show no improvement in nutritional levels and would have to import substantial quantities of cereals simply to retain their nutritional position. Other disquieting tendencies are also expected to occur, such as decline in the average size of holdings, a worsening of the unequal distribution of production assets and incomes, over-exploitation of fragile soils and a decline in production potential in irrigated areas.

In contrast, Scenario A (the one we will devote most attention to since it demonstrates what is possible) indicates the scope for adjustment in the previous situation, with changes in economic performance and population growth of developing countries. Projections are made on both demand and supply sides of the food equation, in accordance with assumptions about 'desirable' levels of economic growth and feasible agricultural production. In demand projections, demand for food is estimated on the basis of exogenously-determined projected population (medium UN projections) and GDP (7 per cent per annum for the next twenty years) assuming constant relative prices for twenty-seven commodities. In supply projections, feasible supply is estimated by first identifying six land–water situations (based on FAO agro-ecological zones), twenty eight potential crops, six livestock commodities and four management levels. Yield for each crop and land-use class was identified by management level and, from this, resource requirements could be derived. From demand estimates it was then possible to determine production needs. These were compared with what is feasible in terms of resource requirements. If not feasible, production estimates were down-scaled to accommodate the feasible supply conditions. From these calculations it was possible to estimate import requirements over the next twenty years and general levels of self-sufficiency.

In terms of the cereal sector, demand outstrips production in both the trend and optimistic (A) scenarios. The deficits are largest in middle-income countries where the indirect consumption of cereals for livestock feed becomes increasingly important (see Table 4.5). As a result, only Latin America is expected to have a self-sufficiency ratio that exceeds one (under Scenario A). The cereal deficit for the ninety developing countries ranges from 63 to 132 million metric tonnes by 2000.

The calculations for growth in production were based upon three factors: arable land, cropping intensity and yields. The majority of growth in productive capacity will come from higher yields (60 per cent) followed by an expansion in cultivated area (26 per cent) and lastly by increasing cropping intensity through fallow reduction and double cropping (14 per

Table 4.5 Agriculture Toward 2000: cereals-sector results

| | 1966/68 | | | | 1979/81 | | | | Projected 2000 | | | | | | | |
| | | | | | | | | | Trend | | | | Scenario A | | | |
	pdn	dmd	bal	SSR	pdn	dmd	bal	SSR	pdn	dmd	bal	SSR	pdn	dmd	bal	SSR
World	1,040	1,039	1	100.0	1,461	1,460	1	100.0								
Developing countries	429	452	−23	94.9	652	720	−68	90.5								
Ninety study countries	282	299	−17	94.3	413	461	−48	89.5	636	768	−132	82.8	786	850	−63	92
Africa	37	40	−3	92.4	44	57	−14	76.0	61	110	−48	55.9	108	133	−25	81
Far East	148	161	−13	92.0	227	237	−9	96.1	358	384	−26	93.9	405	423	−18	95
Latin America	59	55	3	105.6	88	95	−8	91.9	146	168	−22	86.6	184	180	4	102
Near East	39	44	−4	90.2	54	78	−7	75.5	71	106	−35	67.1	89	114	−24	78
Low-income	156	172	−16	90.9	228	244	−16	93.9	349	404	−55	86.3	429	457	−28	93
Middle-income	126	127	−1	98.9	185	217	−32	85.5	287	363	−76	79.0	358	393	−35	91
Other developing countries (including China)	147	153	−6	96.0	239	258	−20	92.4								
Developed countries	610	586	25	104.2	809	740	69	109.3								
Market economies	396	369	27	107.3	556	443	113	125.5								
Centrally-planned	214	216	−2	98.9	253	297	−44	85.2								

Key
pdn = production; dmd = demand; bal = balance; SSR = self-sufficiency ratio
Demand equals production plus imports minus exports
SSR (per cent) equals production over demand
Cereals includes wheat, rice (milled) and all coarse grains
Source after FAO (1983a)

Table 4.6 Inputs to production, ninety developing countries

Inputs	Year 2000[a] Scenario		Growth rates 1980–2000 (per cent per year) Scenario	
	A	B	A	B
Current inputs (value equivalent)	307	252	5.78	4.73
Agricultural inputs	233	197	4.13	3.45
Inputs from outside agriculture	392	314	7.07	5.89
Arable land	120	115	0.90	0.71
Irrigated area (arable)	141	129	1.72	1.27
Irrigated area (harvested)	162	146	2.43	1.91
Tractors	553	417	8.92	7.40
Fertilizer	514	412	8.53	7.33
Pesticides	240	207	4.47	3.70
Commercial energy (in oil equivalent)	494	383	8.32	6.94
Improved seed	317	280	5.93	5.29
Cereal feed	304	258	5.71	4.85
Labour requirements (man-days)	146	137	1.91	1.60

[a]*Index* 1980 = 100

Source After FAO (1983a)

cent). Wheat yields are expected to increase from 1.42 to 2.29 tonnes per hectare and rice from 2.11 to 3.17 tonnes per hectare. Irrigation, fertilizer and improved seeds are seen as the basic means for increasing yields (see Table 4.6). Improved seeds account for 42 per cent of crops planted and this is to increase to 67 per cent by 2000. Fertilizer use is expected to increase by over 8 per cent per annum, and irrigation, the most costly of the capital intensive inputs, could expand from 103 million to 150 million ha by 2000.

Much of the existing irrigation system would have to be improved simply to sustain current production levels. Fully-equipped irrigated areas as a percentage of irrigated areas rise from 60 per cent to 77 per cent. New and improved irrigation schemes are expected to cost annually $13.4 billion (1975 US dollars) by 2000, and gross annual investment requirements in agriculture for irrigation, transport, storage and marketing is expected to be $52 billion in 1980 and $107 billion by 2000. Cumulative gross investment exceeds $1.5 trillion dollars by 2000, with per capita (1975 US dollars) investment ranging from $700 in Africa and $930 in Far East to $4200 in Latin America.

Scenarios A and B estimate the maximum sustainable growth rate in production, given the previously-discussed assumptions. Both soil- and water-conservation measures are expected to play an important role in ensuring and enhancing the productive potential of the land. This is all the more important when one considers the cost of bringing new land into production, plus the fact that an estimated 60 per cent of the population in developing countries will face critical shortages of land by 2000. Water resources will also be in tight supply as competition from non-agricultural sources increases and as the usable proportion becomes fully allocated. The greatest opportunities in improving output from irrigation agriculture come from improvements in existing systems, through drainage, better delivery ratios and more efficient application techniques.

Like the *Global 2000* study, *AT 2000* anticipates increasing pressure on land resources 'on the edge of deserts, in high rainfall tropical soils and steep mountain areas'. Lack of any systematic assessment of the magnitude of these pressures prevented adjustments being made to the production estimates. Unlike the *Global 2000* study, *AT 2000* does not anticipate a large increase in the proportion of the world's income that might be devoted to agriculture. It is this point, along with assumptions about increases in real food prices, that distinguishes the two studies and serves as a basis for criticism of the *Global 2000* report. Johnson (1984: 105) took issue with assumptions in the report regarding increases in the cost of energy and in turn its impact on real food prices. Among his concerns was that 'there is no simple relationship between energy prices, as represented by petroleum prices, and the costs of inputs that have a high energy content.' Not only have real energy prices decreased, but real food prices (1982) are below 1970 levels. Moreover, he argued that the assumption that agriculture will require an increasing as opposed to a decreasing proportion of the world's resources contradicts historical trends in which agriculture has tended to capture smaller and smaller shares of gross domestic product.

If these represent shortcomings in the *Global 2000* study there are equal difficulties with *AT 2000*. Since it is largely a normative study it has set out 'desirable' levels of economic growth and its consequences for the demand for and supply of agricultural goods. These desirable levels of economic growth of 7 per cent for twenty years are unlikely to materialize. With the exception of a few middle-income developing countries there is no indication for the bulk of the ninety developing countries that economic growth has come close to the desirable levels set down by the study.

International relations in agriculture

The last study to be examined in this section describes and explains the world food situation and how policy can change that situation. Model of International Relations in Agriculture (MOIRA), (Linnemann, 1979) is a general equilibrium agriculture sector model where production (one sector) and demand (two consumption sectors) for food, nationally and globally, are balanced at assumed price levels. A prime focus of the study is to evaluate the sensitivity of the outcomes of the model to alternative assumptions about the future development of exogenous variables (e.g., population and income growth and income distribution) and to determine the policies which hold the promise of reducing world hunger. No consideration is given to the role or impact of environmental or energy factors.

A number of simulation runs are made by varying important exogenous variables and then comparing these results with those of the standard run which represents a forecast of food conditions based upon past trends (see Table 4.7). Self-sufficiency ratios tend to improve for developed countries but decline for developing countries with significant regional variations. Although diets or amount of consumable protein improve, total food deficit increases, as does the number of individuals below the minimum food standard.

Variations in this standard run in terms of changes in economic growth outside of agriculture, population growth and income distribution outside agriculture reveal the sensitivity of the food system. A lower (by half) income growth rate of the non-agricultural sector reduces the prices for food in the agricultural sector, diminishes production and increases the food deficit. On the other hand, a reduction (by half) in population growth rates has a beneficial impact on income growth and food prices. Consequently, the world food deficit is 30 per cent lower than in the standard run. Thus population growth rate is seen as a primary factor affecting the availability of food. Lastly, as income equality is reduced by half of the level between 1975–2010 for the non-agricultural sector, world hunger is substantially decreased. Average food consumption per capita grows faster than in the standard run and self-sufficiency levels are higher than in the standard run. The authors argue that 'This simulation run illustrates the thesis that the hunger problem is to a large extent a problem of income distribution' (p.300). The role of income distribution was examined, however, only for the non-agricultural sector.

Resource – economic studies

Limits to growth

Conspicuous by its absence in the previously-discussed studies is an explicit account of the dynamic feedback process between agriculture and its host environment. Some of the studies acknowledge that environmental deterioration such as land degradation would ultimately lower productive potential, while others made reference to the fact that land and water supplies could act as constraints to further growth in production. The difficulty of incorporating these considerations into any modelling exercise are manifold, not just in terms of the availability and quality of the data,

Table 4.7 Results of MOIRA simulations (standard run)

	1966	1975	1980	1990	2000	2009
Total agricultural production (10^8 kg cons. prot.)						
World	1,943	2,495	2,970	4,094	5,340	6,530
Developed countries	743	910	1,067	1,517	1,896	2,194
North America	403	497	580	855	1,009	1,151
European Community	147	182	218	297	377	434
Developing countries	599	749	941	1,237	1,774	2,344
Latin America	181	241	297	434	631	905
Tropical Africa	66	82	96	145	208	297
Middle East	58	72	96	128	220	287
Southern Asia	265	321	409	467	624	736
Food production per capita (kg cons. prot.)						
World	46	50	53	61	68	73
Developed countries	86	102	110	130	147	160
North America	107	121	129	148	163	173
European Community	90	103	108	126	141	153
Developing countries	30	30	33	37	43	48
Latin America	43	48	52	63	76	89
Tropical Africa	25	25	27	34	40	47
Middle East	38	40	46	56	71	78
Southern Asia	26	25	26	27	29	29
Self-sufficiency ratio consumable protein						
Developed countries	96	92	97	107	110	109
North America	142	143	149	174	175	176
European Community	59	60	67	74	81	82

Developing countries	106	102	104	93	93	91
Latin America	123	113	110	103	100	101
Tropical Africa	111	104	102	98	93	92
Middle East	87	85	88	58	65	65
Southern Asia	100	101	108	95	97	95
Percentage of population in agriculture						
World	52	46	42	36	32	29
Developing countries	66	60	57	53	48	45
Latin America	45	38	36	32	28	25
Southern Asia	70	64	61	57	52	48
Price indicators of world food market (DFP: 1965 = 0)	−8	60	431	301	422	442
World hunger						
Total food deficit (WHUNG) (10^8 kg cons. prot.)	15	29	40	43	62	97
Million people below minimum food standard	180	350	480	520	740	1,160
Percentage of WHUNG located in agricultural sector	76	85	35	42	19	15

cons. prot. = consumable protein
Source after Linneman (1979)

but also in terms of accurate measurement of the important interrelationships.

To examine these and other complex interrelationships, a project was initiated by the Club of Rome 'to understand the options available to mankind as societies enter the transition from growth to equilibrium . . .' (Forrester, 1971: viii). A global simulation model (World 3) was developed using a systems-dynamics approach, the results of which were published under the title *Limits to Growth*. (Meadows et al., 1972). Other global systems-dynamic modelling efforts followed (Meadows et al., 1982).

Despite heavy criticism of assumptions, design and conclusions of these models, particularly *Limits to Growth*, they were a useful exercise in understanding some of the interrelationships among bio-sphere, technosphere and socio-sphere. In the interests of brevity and because of the importance of agriculture, only the technical report of the World 3 Model of the *Limits to Growth* study will be discussed (Forrester, 1971 and Meadows et al., 1974).

World 3 is a single region model containing five sectors, two of which grow exponentially – population and capital – and three whose capacity for growth is limited – agriculture (land and other inputs), non-renewable resources (fuel and mineral inputs) and pollution. In the agricultural sector of the model it is assumed that there is a limit to the productive potential of the earth's food resources. This arises from the assumption that agricultural land, fertilizer output, yield growth and the ability of the environmental system to absorb pollution are all limited.

Moreover, although technology has the ability to expand yields, it does so through diminishing or marginal returns to inputs. In turn, investment in expanding agricultural production through land and yield increases, also experiences decreasing marginal returns. Other important assumptions which underlie the model include: investment in yield and arable land increases are based upon whichever has the highest marginal productivity; capital-intensive use of land can lead to persistent pollution of the land; land fertility declines when the level of persistent pollution becomes high; and land fertility regenerates itself with proper land maintenance.

Figure 4.4 illustrates for the simulation model the interactions among the basic components that are assumed to determine global food production. The model examines the growth and availability of food in terms of six sets of relations or loops: (1) investment in expansion of arable land base; (2) investment in increasing agricultural inputs; (3) land erosion and urban industrial use; (4) land fertility by impairment; (5) land fertility regeneration; and (6) immediate food increase from discontinuing land maintenance.

Investment in agriculture is governed by demand for food which is estimated in per capita terms by growth in industrial output. Since capital is required for expansion in new land and intensification, the relative share of investment dollars depends upon the comparative productivities of each

84

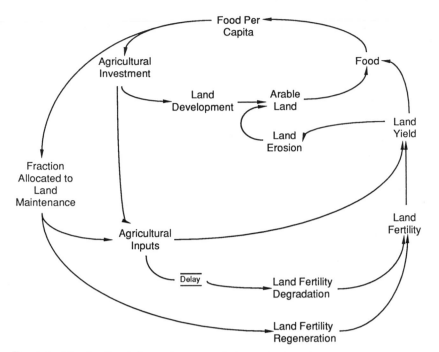

Fig. 4.4 The feedback loop structure of the agricultural sector
    Source after Meadows et al. (1974)

strategy. Affecting the relative marginal productivities are a number of cost considerations. For land development, costs are expected to rise exponentially with declines in the size of the potential arable land base (reserve).

Yield growth is a function of agricultural inputs. As input increases yields also increase as a multiple of the natural land fertility (set at 600 kg per hectare per year). In all cases the process of diminishing returns is present so that yields increase but at a decreasing rate. Both land supply and yields possess ceilings which ultimately check food production.

Other factors affecting the growth in yields and land availability are air pollution, land erosion, urban industrial use and land fertility degradation. Regeneration of fertility is considered possible with proper maintenance.

The standard run illustrates the impact of exponential growth in exogenous components (population and capital) upon food production and food availability (see Fig. 4.5). Yields and arable land reach their ceilings of 4000 tonnes/ha at 2050 and 2.5 billion ha at 2025 respectively. Food production per capita per annum reaches its height of 700 kg at the same time as the potential arable land base is fully exploited. The potential arable land base declines as land is required for urban and industrial uses. As development costs for new land rise exponentially, more investment switches to intensification to increase yields. Yield growth eventually

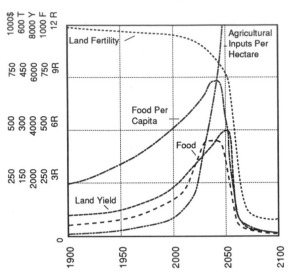

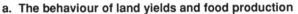

a. The behaviour of land yields and food production

KEY

**$** - Development Cost ($ per ha)
T - Land Fertility
Y - Land Yields
F - Food Per Capita
MUDE - Land Removed for Urban Industrial Purposes (mil. ha/yr.)
BPL - Billions

b. The behaviour of arable land

Fig. 4.5   Limits to growth study – standard run in which exogenous inputs continue to grow
   Source after Meadows et al. (1974)

declines as land fertility drops largely from high land erosion. As the pressure on the land-resource base intensifies from increasing population numbers, less money is spent on maintenance and conservation of the land-resource base, leading to even higher rates of erosion and to further declines in yields. Per capita food availability falls below minimum requirements in 2060.

To test the sensitivity of the model to possible errors in the two leading constraints to production (arable land base and yield ceilings), a number of different assumptions were used regarding endogenous relationships for the size of arable land base, yield ceilings, declines in land fertility and land-erosion programme. The outcome is to delay from ten to thirty-five years the decline in the peak levels of food production per capita. Where conservation is pursued, fertility held constant and no land erosion takes place, food production and yield plateau at approximately 10.5 billion tonnes/yr and 6000 tonnes/ha respectively. Because population continues to grow exponentially beyond 2050, per capita food production must decrease.

By modifying the growth rates in the exogenous inputs so that they level off in the year 2000 (see Fig. 4.6), it is possible to sustain high levels of food production and food production per capita (approximately 150 per cent higher than 1970 levels). This is contingent upon minimizing the land removed for urban-industrial uses (approaches zero in 2020), land erosion and declines in land fertility (no declines after 2000). The study concludes with the following statement: 'the stabilization of growth results in lower food production in the short term but avoids the negative side effects that decrease the capacity for food production thus ensuring higher and more stable levels of food in the long term' (p. 360).

The difficulty of balancing short- versus long-term interests (and costs) rests in part with the price of food. The *Global 2000* report observed in this regard that 'The real food price increases projected for the decades ahead could well make the short-term costs of environmentally positive agriculture seem high and the long run costs of an environmentally negative agriculture seem small' (Barney, 1980: 104). Producer and consumer costs must therefore, whenever possible, adequately reflect the total costs of production and consumption decisions in order to encourage environmentally-positive agriculture. This is a more difficult challenge in developing countries, but one which still should figure prominently on development agendas.

Criticisms of the *Limits to Growth* study are extensive and not unwarranted. To treat the world as a single unit using global averages masks large and important geographical variations in resource quality and response to excessive population pressure on the land-resource base. Another weakness is the lack of self-regulating mechanisms in the model, particularly with respect to the response of population and the economic system to declines in living standards. The model is also based upon

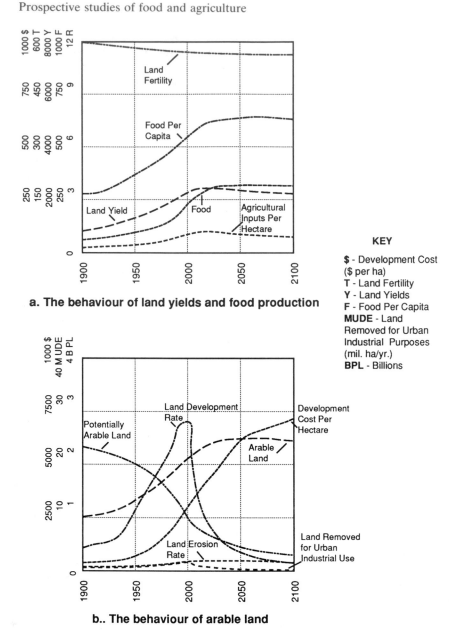

a. The behaviour of land yields and food production

b.. The behaviour of arable land

Fig. 4.6   Limits to growth study – equilibrium run in which exogenous inputs level off in the year 2000
Source after Meadows et al. (1974)

pessimistic assumptions regarding the ameliorating influence of technological innovations. Incorporating into the World 3 Model different assumptions about the positive and formative role technology would play, Boyd

88

(1972) demonstrates that after an initial decline in the quality of life through rapid population growth, investment in new technology lowers pollution, expands food output and uses resources more efficiently. Consequently, population growth rates slow and eventually stabilize with an increase in food and quality of life.

Summary

What insights have been gained by reviewing and evaluating these diverse prospective studies on food and agriculture? The first set indicates that the earth has the bio-physical potential to meet the nutritional needs of a vastly larger population, although the potential does not necessarily conform with the needs of the regional population base. While good progress has been made in expanding agricultural production, a number of trend scenarios in the socio-economic studies indicate that food self-sufficiency and nutritional levels will decline for a large segment of the global population, unless existing resource–production relationships change. Even with changes there are still a significant number of countries which will face higher food deficits which will be translated into increasing levels of undernutrition or food imports.

The forces and conditions underlying the great imbalance in the way in which people consume and produce food, and the prospects for change, have been highly simplified. In the socio-economic studies the food problem then was seen to be as much a demand as a supply problem. The emphasis was on lowering population growth rates while expanding growth in GDP and per capita income to lower-income disparities and to expand effective demand for food. Growth in supply would be dependent on expanding yield through a complex combination of land-augmenting factors, principally fertilizer, irrigation and new seed varieties, technological transfers and an improved economic and financial environment, including higher prices and more capital. Public investment is seen as performing a very important role in increasing resource inputs.

While implicit in these studies was the notion that limits to sustained economic and agricultural growth were political, social and institutional rather than natural, significant resource constraints were identified. Increases in both land and water supply would be accompanied by real increases in the costs of production. The need for better management and improvements in the efficiency of these resources is therefore of paramount importance.

The environmental implications of expanded production were for the most part ignored, as were the innumerable trade-offs that must be made between agricultural and other uses of important land and water resources in a growing society.

Although the *Limits to Growth* study tried to circumscribe the growth of a society by resource and environmental factors, there was insufficient attention paid to how the market and technology may respond to impending scarcity and indeed how some regions may out-perform others. More work must be done on these resource and environmental factors and the way in which they interact with the food system to either limit growth and/or prevent the system from reaching its potential.

CHAPTER 5

Population pressures and the demand for land resources

Issues in the demand for land resources

Land resources are characterized by a number of features. Spatially they are fixed, yet the flow of goods and services we derive from them is not. They are prized for different qualities – space/location, amenities, resources – and, in many cases, are able to fulfil many different functions. Hence the diverse potential uses for land resources, the competing demands for those resources and the numerous conflicts which arise from that competition are hallmark features of any land-use system. The intensity of these conflicts is due to a complex host of factors on both the demand and supply side of the land-use equation.

The continued growth in derived demand for land resources, driven by increases in population and income in the face of an inherently finite resource, has led many to question the long-term sustainability of continued growth in population. While there is a common-sense appeal to this view over the long term, the reality over the short to intermediate term is more complex, with the implications for agriculture and food production far from clear. For example, the growth in food production on a declining land base in industrialized countries attests to the importance of substitution and technological enhancement of factors of production. Although there is no consensus on how far substitution can be carried, it must be limited since the factors of production are interdependent. Land is of course required for the production of non-land factors of production.

Figure 5.1 conceptualizes some of the major land-use impacts and alternatives arising from growth in population and income. The derived demand for land to satisfy food, fuel, housing, industry, transportation, wood products and recreation needs can be met or accommodated in numerous ways. Existing space can be 'intensified', imports can be increased and migration can take place or, conversion of that space from one use to another can occur. Agriculture may expand its area at the

91

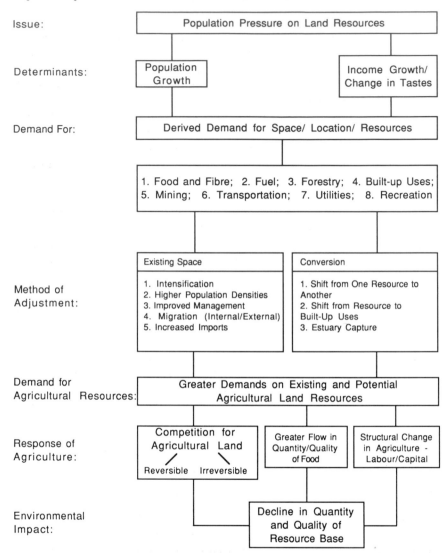

Issue:

Determinants:

Demand For:

Method of
Adjustment:

Demand for
Agricultural Resources:

Response of
Agriculture:

Environmental
Impact:

Fig. 5.1 Response of agriculture to population pressures

expense of another use, such as forestry or wilderness areas, or agricultural land itself may be consumed.

The method of trading-off one land use for another is not important here. What is important, though, is that while substitution and intensification are common occurrences in societies, so is land-use conversion. A growing society requires land not just for agriculture, but also for many other purposes. Also, a growing society requires more water and other resources essential to agriculture. How much will be demanded depends on growth in income, level of economic development, and the elasticities of demand and supply. Information on the elasticity of demand with respect to land resources is fragmentary. However, we know that for advanced industrialized countries income elasticities are low and approaching zero for food, whereas they are high and positive for goods and services derived from land such as recreation and housing.

Regardless of level of development, a growing society places additional demands upon the flow of goods and services from agriculture. The shift to higher protein diets with growth in income underlines this point. Moreover, many developing countries rely upon cash crops from the agricultural sector to earn foreign exchange.

Agriculture's response to these changing demands manifests itself in a variety of structural changes. In developed countries the typical model has been decline in farm workers and farm numbers but increase in farm size. In developing countries the growth of rural populations has encouraged farm fragmentation, a decline in farm size and an increase in the numbers of landless workers. Alongside this phenomenon there has been an increase in the commercialization of agriculture and an inequality in land-ownership patterns. The environmental impact of these increased demands is generally a decline in the quantity and/or quality of the resource base. To offset these declines additional lands must be brought into production and/or an increase in energy subsidies is required.

Although it is not possible to document precisely the responses of land uses to growing populations in such countries as diverse as Britain and Holland, Canada and the United States, and India and China, it is possible in this chapter to outline in general terms the growth in population and incomes, some of the expected land-use requirements for those populations, and to evaluate critically the implications for agriculture.

Background on population and income growth

Historical analyses of world population growth have portrayed it as an exponential function of time, particularly since the industrial revolution. Today the majority of this growth is taking place in developing countries where the gap between birth and death rates remains high as does total fertility rate. The demographic transition has been realized in some developing countries, such as China, but may not occur for sometime in numerous others such as Sri Lanka and Kenya. Practically all industrialized countries have reduced birth rates in line with death rates to create very modest rates of growth in total population. Figure 5.2 highlights the differences among groups of countries in birth/death rates and rates of natural increase.

Another historical analysis of population growth employing the same aggregate data uses a logarithmic scale over a longer time period (see Fig. 5.3). The first great advance in population occurred at the beginning

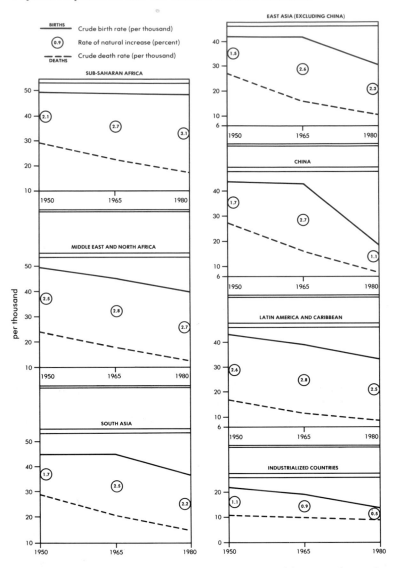

Fig. 5.2   Birth and death rates and rates of natural increase for region 1950, 1965
and 1980
Source after World Bank (1984)

of the Agricultural Revolution 10,000 years ago and the second about 300
years ago at the start of the industrial–scientific revolution. This second
approach emphasizes the role of new technology and the limits of that
technology, first in triggering growth and second, in dampening that
growth when an equilibrium is attained between population and resources
(Deevey, 1960). How large the world population will be at the next

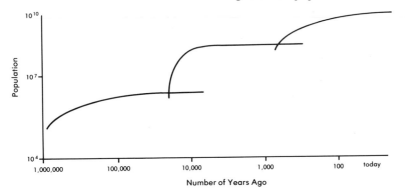

Fig. 5.3   The growth in world population from 1 million BP to the present, using a logarithmic scale
Source adapted from p. 198 The Human Population, E.S. Deevey.
(1960). © Scientific American Inc. *All rights reserved.*

equilibrium (if in fact one does take place) and exactly when it will occur is open to conjecture. Long-term UN projections of a stable global population range between 7 and 14 billion and occur between 2060 and 2110 (World Commission on Environment and Development, 1987). The difference between these estimates is a function of when replacement-level fertility is reached. The earlier fertility levels are brought down to replacement levels, the sooner an equilibrium is reached.

There is no question that technology and human ingenuity have expanded the carrying capacity of land and allowed for a truly remarkable expansion in individual and total resource consumption. As previously noted, Simon (1981) has argued that population growth is not a problem since there are no real natural resource limits. Population growth in his view creates opportunities which in turn expand the welfare of society. While price trends for major commodities have historically shown a downward trend indicating decreasing not increasing scarcity it can be argued that these are the product of unique or unusual circumstances which may not prevail in the future. Examples are large-scale emigration from Europe to the New World involving specific groups of countries, cheap energy supplies, an abundance of land resources in North and South America, and a rate of population growth that was less than growth in technological innovation. In the absence of these and other conditions the consequences of continued rapid population growth could be devastating for any real improvement in nutritional levels, standards of living and general material well-being for developing countries. Certainly the results from the socio-economic models discussed in Chapter 4 strongly support this interpretation. Although our specific concern is with the implications for agriculture, it is essential to preface these discussions with a brief comment on the economic, social and environmental consequences of population pressures.

The degree to which rapid population growth impedes economic growth and social welfare is unclear. Numerous examples exist where the benefits of economic growth are largely offset by rapid population growth. In West Germany, population is stable but economic growth is around 2 per cent per annum. If this continues to 2004, GDP per head will be 40 per cent higher than in 1987. For Kenya to realize a 40 per cent increase in GDP over the same period, economic growth will have to be in excess of 6 per cent per annum if population growth remains at its present rate of 4 per cent per annum (*The Economist*, 1987a).

A relatively small group of middle-income developing countries such as South Korea, Taiwan and Singapore have experienced high growth rates in population (over 2 per cent per annum from 1955–80), but double to triple growth rates in GDP. In contrast, since 1973 China has, with its low population growth of under 1 per cent, realized an average annual growth in per capita GDP of 9.7 per cent. A much larger group of low-income countries has experienced high rates of growth in population but not in GDP per person. Among these are Mexico, Brazil, Nigeria, Mozambique, Turkey, Ethiopia and Kenya. While patterns are difficult to decipher, since low rates of economic growth are also associated with low levels of population growth, it would appear that population growth in excess of 2 to 2.5 per cent per annum greatly decreases the prospects for improvements in living standards.

Some economies have the capacity and ability to absorb population growth while others do not. It has been argued that population growth can affect economic growth in three principal ways – private savings, availability of capital per person, and economic efficiency (World Bank, 1984). Private savings may be considerably reduced or non-existent when there are high fertility rates and large numbers of dependents. Rapid population growth requires capital resources to be spread over more and more individuals. This process of capital widening (as opposed to capital deepening) is often counterproductive in provision of education and medical services. And in rural areas where fertility rates are high, the availability of capital per worker is low, preventing the growth in the productivity of the workforce. Lastly, improvements in the efficiency of allocation of human, capital and national resources are often sacrificed with rapid population growth because of a variety of social and political pressures which threaten national and regional unity.

The environmental implications of rapid population growth and increasing pressure on the land-resource base are manifested in many forms. Large-scale deforestation, abandonment of farmland, soil erosion, desertification, increased sedimentation of rivers, water pollution and a reduction in genetic diversity are some of the commonest and most significant expressions of these pressures as well as of poor management practices. Some of the worst examples of environmental degradation (e.g., Brazil, Nepal, Haiti, Madagascar and the Sahel) have taken place in traditional cultures where high population pressures on the land-resource base were combined with scarce capital, technology and resource management skills.

The *Global 2000* report (Barney, 1980) forecast large increases in the populations of traditional cultures. Given their reliance on agriculture, based on either herding or shifting cultivation, future environmental repercussions are expected to be significant. For herding the major problem will be the overuse and in turn degradation of a common property resource – grazing lands. The 'tragedy of the commons', as Hardin (1968) has so graphically described it, is destined to repeat itself over and over again unless there is some form of institutional control of use of land. Equally important is shifting cultivation (Barney, 1980). It is estimated that 25 per cent of the world's land surface is occupied by people practising shifting cultivation. If adequate fallow periods are used, soil fertility can be restored and therefore shifting cultivation can be a sustainable practice. However, with increased population pressures the fallow period will diminish as will the soil fertility. This in turn is expected to place increasing pressure on marginal lands.

Some implications for agriculture

Increasing densities

Agriculture is still an overwhelmingly resource-based system. Losses of existing or potential arable land through conversion (which we will examine in detail in the next section) can affect current and future food production prospects. In an earlier discussion (Chapter 4), we examined the various estimates for future availability of land. While globally these appeared to be abundant, there appeared to be particular pressure points such as China, India and other parts of Asia, the Middle East and Europe. More specifically, Hrabovszky (1985) has observed that countries with high pressure on arable land resources can be classed into three groups: the alluvial high-rainfall monsoon areas of Asia such as the Ganges–Brahmaputra Basin and South-East Asian rice-growing areas; the low rainfall savannahs of North Africa, Asia and Latin America; and the young volcanic highlands of the tropics and sub-tropics such as Java, the Philippines, Himalayas, East African Highlands and Andean and Central American highlands where there are few land reserves left to develop.

Future growth in food production in these areas would have to come from intensification and not from expansion in the cultivated land base. And even in those regions such as Africa and South America with a seeming abundance of land, numerous constraints in the form of technology, water, pests and diseases seriously limit the potential of the land ever being achieved. We saw in Chapter 4 that with available technology and inputs numerous countries of Africa (Ethiopia, Kenya, Niger, Nigeria and Namibia) are unable to support existing populations. In short there is considerable spatial variation in the 'criticality' of land resources and in turn the 'flexibility' for food production and other uses of the land in the future (Smit and Flaherty, 1984).

A traditional approach to measuring the existing population pressure on land resources is the man–land ratio. There are major problems in the use of this ratio since the quality/productivity of the arable land base (measured in terms of climatic resources, intensity, fertility, etc.) varies considerably among countries, as does carrying capacity. Moreover, the ratio provides no measure of qualitative demands on the resource base from variations in income. Nevertheless, the ratio allows for a broad-brush assessment of land-use pressures and, when combined with measures of available land, of the significance of land lost from agriculture. Figures 5.4 and 5.5 highlight by country the ratio of population to constant arable land for 1984 and 2000, based upon UN population (medium) projections.

While North America, Australia, Argentina and the Soviet Union (the major grain producers today) do not change their low man–land ratio status, numerous other countries show significant increases in the average numbers to be supported on the arable land base. In Bangladesh the man–land ratio is expected to increase by approximately 30 per cent over a twenty-year period beginning in 1980. Even higher population densities are found on the island of Java in Indonesia where irrigated agriculture supports populations averaging twenty persons per hectare. This is not apparent in Fig. 5.4 because Java is averaged with the rest of the islands of Indonesia. Since about 75 per cent of the island is cultivated, with little or no prospects for expansion of arable land – largely due to the steeply-sloped and rough terrain – a large scale 'Transmigration' programme has been implemented to resettle the population to other sparsely-populated islands, such as Sumatra and Irian Jaya. The government has succeeded since 1964 in resettling one-quarter of Java's natural population increase (World Bank, 1984). Brazil has also attempted to ease population pressure on its agricultural land base in the north-east through its Trans-Amazon Programme. And in Ethiopia, forced emigration from the drought-stricken northern half of the country to the south-west, financed by international agencies, is meant to relieve the pressure on the land. These examples show that unless intensification and/or outmigration takes place it will be difficult to sustain per capita food consumption without large-scale importation of food. Since many countries are unable to afford this they must resort to various forms of food aid and relief. In the early 1980s Egypt was the largest single recipient of food aid, followed by Bangladesh, India and the Sahelian area of Africa.

Changing demands

Aside from the problem of losing much, if not all, of a country's additional annual production to a rapidly expanding population, there is the related

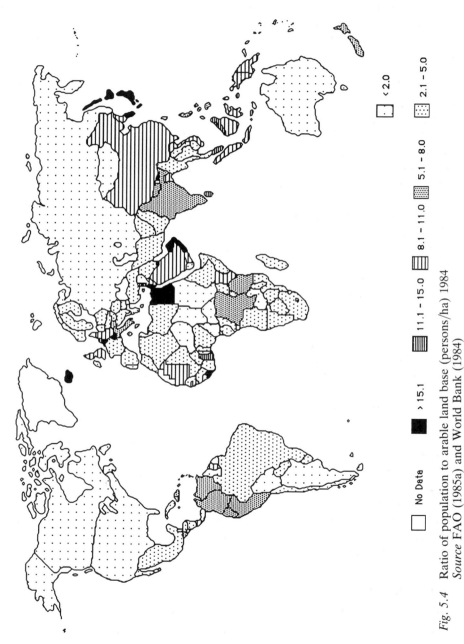

Fig. 5.4 Ratio of population to arable land base (persons/ha) 1984
Source FAO (1985a) and World Bank (1984)

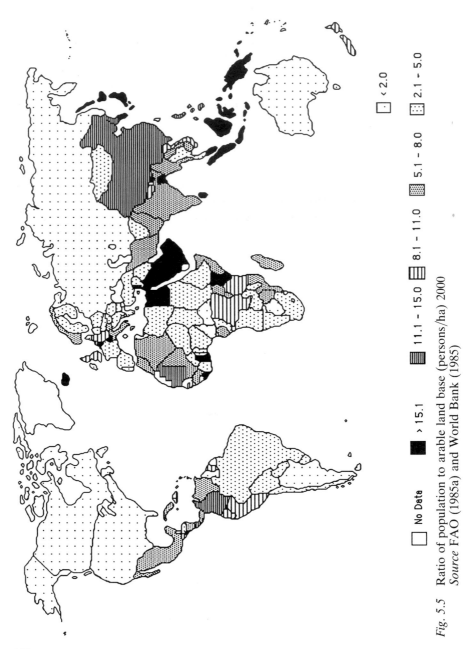

Fig. 5.5 Ratio of population to arable land base (persons/ha) 2000
Source FAO (1985a) and World Bank (1985)

Legend:
No Data · < 2.0 · 2.1 – 5.0 · 5.1 – 8.0 · 8.1 – 11.0 · 11.1 – 15.0 · > 15.1

problem of the growth in effective demand as income expands. Societies with high and/or rapidly expanding incomes place different demands upon the agricultural resource base, relative to their economically-backward counterparts. The emphasis on high-protein diets shifts agricultural resources to the livestock sector and increases the overall importance of grains as an animal feed source and not a direct food source.

As Borgstrom (1980) notes, the cereal and pastureland base of the world is called upon to meet the nutritional needs not of 4.6 billion persons (the earth's population in 1981), but the equivalent of 21 billion persons – the present population plus domestic livestock of 16.8 billion measured in population equivalents. Carrying capacity burden of the earth's green plant cover in protein terms is already much higher than is recognized by conventional measures. And this burden promises to become much larger. One study of world ruminant populations estimated that by the year 2000, cattle, buffalo and sheep/goat populations will be 27, 29 and 40 per cent higher than in 1972 (Fitzhugh et al., 1978).

At the heart of this different notion of carrying capacity is that growth in income, particularly among the populations in developing countries, will produce a major shift in the indirect consumption of grains. Table 5.1

Table 5.1 Annual grain consumption per capita in the twenty most populous countries, 1975

	Kilograms (per capita)[a]
United States	708
USSR	645
Spain	508
France	446
Federal Republic of Germany	441
Turkey	415
Italy	413
United Kingdom	394
Mexico	304
Egypt	286
Japan	274
Brazil	239
Thailand	225
People's Republic of China	218
Bangladesh	203
Pakistan	171
Philippines	157
Indonesia	152
India	150
Nigeria	92

[a]Represents direct and indirect consumption

Source after Brown (1978)

indicates average per capita grain consumption (direct and indirect) for a cross-section of countries. Individuals in the USA and USSR, with their heavy consumption of animal protein, consume on average four to six times as much grain as individuals in Nigeria and India. If the developing world is to increase its average per capita consumption of plant energy in the way that South Korea and Taiwan are now doing, yields, land area and/or imports will have to expand. For a static population with a rising income the growth is sizeable; for an expanding population with a rising income the demands on the agricultural system are nothing short of monumental.

Many countries will be unable to achieve higher nutritional levels through their own agricultural production systems. Large regional transfers in grain and oilseeds will therefore figure prominently in a more affluent and nutritionally richer world. (See Chapter 3 for a discussion of the present dimension of grain exports.) Short-term dislocations and bottlenecks are to be expected. Mellor and Johnston (1984) have documented and analysed the dramatic increases in food imports by emerging middle-income developing countries, such as South Korea and Taiwan, as consumption has outstripped production. The inability of these countries to meet their food needs arises from rapid income growth and a high effective demand for livestock, combined with an inability of the agricultural sector to adjust, at least over the short term, to these demands. Many other countries, both those with planned and market economies, such as the USSR, Cuba, Iran, Saudi Arabia and Japan, have shown dramatic increases in cereal imports because of similar divergences.

While a relatively small number of industrialized countries are actively involved in the export of grains, oilseeds and livestock, a much larger number of developing countries are involved in the export of non-cereal cash crops, such as tea, coffee, sugar, soya beans, cocoa, cotton, palm oil and bananas. These products are grown to serve the higher-income demands of industrialized countries and to provide the major source of export earnings for non-oil-producing developing countries.

Because of the need to boost export earnings, largely to service foreign debt in places such as Brazil and Mexico, increased importance has been attached to the development of this commercial cash-crop sector – often to the detriment of traditional agriculture. Not only has this intensified the competition for agricultural land with the need to develop more marginal lands, but it has contributed to the creation of a class of seasonal workers who have few alternative sources of income and access to the land.

In Sudan, for example, approximately half of the cultivated land is devoted to the cash-crop sector (mostly cotton in the Gezira irrigation scheme) with the remaining land devoted to traditional farming and grazing. The competition for land intensified in the 1970s as World Bank loans financed the expansion of mechanized commercial rainfed farming. In part this was made possible by granting of leases on lands which formerly were part of the public domain and used by nomads and small farmers (Bennett, 1987). The displacement of the peasant population from their traditional land holdings and their increasing integration into a wage economy that was based upon a few internationally-traded commodities made the indigenous population particularly vulnerable to the vagaries of climate and international prices. When drought struck in the 1980s the population at large had neither the income to purchase nor the means to produce food.

Similar examples of the conflict between commercial export agriculture and traditional self-sufficient agriculture can be found in Brazil and the Philippines. North-east Brazil has become a major exporter of sugar and soya, at the expense of land available for local food production. And in Negros Occidental Province of the Philippines, known as 'Sugarland', large tracts of land have been removed from food production and sugar production by the large land-owners because of depressed world prices.

The environmental implications of food for export policies are as alarming as the social implications. Large areas of rainforest in Latin America have been destroyed to make way for a rapidly expanding cattle industry created for the consumption of pet food and hamburgers in North America. And in West Africa, during colonial rule, French taxation policy encouraged farmers to grow peanuts for the export of vegetable oil at the expense of subsistence food sector. As peanut production expanded northward to offset declining soil fertility and to sustain foreign exchange earnings, nomads were forced further into the drier margins of the Sahel providing the original preconditions for the famine (Kumar, 1988).

Rural workforce and farm fragmentation

The ability of countries to realize higher incomes and to transfer them to the population at large will depend at least in part on solving the formidable problem of accommodating the rapidly-growing rural work-force. Developing countries stand in sharp contrast to developed countries in this regard. In Western industrialized countries during the nineteenth and the early twentieth centuries, the increasing mechanization and pro-ductivity of farms, coupled with the demand for a large industrial work-force, allowed the growth in rural population to be absorbed into urban industrial areas and the modern wage economy. In contrast, the majority of low-income developing countries still have over 60 per cent of their work-force engaged in agriculture. As that rural work-force continues to expand, with few prospects for absorption into the urban-based work-force, the problems of underemployment and diminishing returns to labour loom large.

In India between 1953–54 and 1971–72 there was a 66 per cent increase in rural households but only a 2 per cent increase in cultivated area. The number of marginal holdings of less than 0.5 hectares increased by over

100 per cent, while their average size decreased from 0.11 to 0.05 hectares (World Bank, 1984). Thus wage rates have declined in those areas unable to expand output commensurate with the growth in labour supply. In Kenya non-wage employment in agriculture absorbed more than 80 per cent of the increase in the labour force during the 1970s (World Bank, 1984). At the same time a number of middle-income countries have managed to transfer labour out of agriculture for many of the same reasons that Western industrialized countries were able to do some fifty to a hundred years ago.

A country with even greater population pressures on the arable land base is China. Only about 4 per cent or 100 million hectares are available for cultivation, given moisture, relief and soil constraints. During the 1970s there were approximately 50,000 communes averaging 635 hectares with a working population of 13,000 persons. Between 1977–84 the communal system was abandoned and replaced by a highly egalitarian land redistribution system. *The Economist* (1987a: 6) observed that 'when the distribution was over, the 180 million Chinese households found themseves with farms of roughly equal size and value. China as a whole found itself with 180 million farms that were too small.' Average farm size is now less than half a hectare. In the dominant rice-producing province of Sichuan, efficient use of fertilizer and machinery does not occur until parcel size is three to four times larger than existing parcel size (*The Economist*, 1987a).

If parcel size is too small in India and China, growing evidence suggests that it is too large in Latin America (Todero, 1985). Large land-holdings or *latifundios* in Brazil are on average thirty times larger than the family farm or *minifundios*. Yet they invest only eleven times as much. Average productivity per hectare is also lower.

The structural transformations of the labour force for many developing countries will be slow even if growth rates can be reduced and surplus labour absorbed into a modern wage economy. In the meantime, improved management, redistribution of land, an increased emphasis on multiple cropping and the transfer to these economies of technology of a labour-using form, as opposed to labour-saving form, will be an essential feature in warding off diminishing returns to labour and sustaining per capita consumption levels.

Competition for agricultural land

Some recent changes in cropland base

The world's ice-free land surface is estimated to be approximately 13.4 billion hectares. In 1975, 11 per cent of that total was devoted to cropland, 22 per cent to grassland, 31 per cent to forests, 3 per cent to non-agricultural uses and the remaining (33 per cent) to other uses (Buringh, 1981). Table 5.2 highlights these uses according to the land's potential

Table 5.2 Global land-use by land class x10⁶ ha) 1975

Land use	High	Med.	Low	Zero	Total
			Land class		
Cropland	400	500	600	0	1,500
Grassland	200	300	500	2,000	3,000
Forest-land	100	300	400	3,300	4,100
Non-agricultural land	0	0	0	400	400
Other land	0	0	0	4,400	4,400
Total All Land	700	1,100	1,500	10,100	13,400

Source after Buringh (1981)

productive capacity for agriculture. The overwhelming percentage of the total land mass (75 per cent) has little or no potential for agricultural production because of moisture, soil, temperature and relief constraints. This assumes no dramatic change in technology and/or market conditions that would alter the marginal nature of these lands.

Given the extent of these constraints, the major land uses, principally cropland, grazing and forestry, must rely for their combined operation and growth upon a common but limited set of flow resources. Moreover, these same uses must compete with more intensive uses of the land from urban/industrial sources. As an example of the joint suitability of land, Figure 5.6 traces shifts in major land uses during the 1970s within four industrial countries. Whereas agricultural land augmented the forest base in all four countries, it is only in the USA and Japan that forests were used for extension of the agricultural land base. Although both forestry and agricultural land serve most of the space needs of a growing urban/industrial society, agricultural land represents the largest share of that supply.

Agricultural land also represents the major source of land for urban development in China. Although we shall examine the process of land conversion in developed countries in more detail later in this chapter, it is useful at this stage to highlight the experience of a developing country. Smil (1984) provides information on the statistical dimensions of the losses and gains of agricultural land in China from 1957 to 1977. One estimate places the loss of agricultural land to urban and rural construction at 33 million hectares or 30 per cent of the 1957 total arable land base. Reclamation of land of 21 million hectares created a net loss of 12 million hectares of prime agricultural land. As a result of these losses combined with the addition of 300 million people, per capita land availability fell from 0.172 ha in 1957 to 0.104 ha in 1977.

The loss of agricultural land to suburban development in China has often meant the decline in local vegetable production. In Beijing the growth of housing and industrial uses of land claimed 30 per cent of the land within

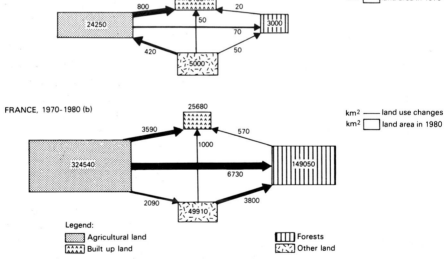

Legend:
- [dotted] Agricultural land
- [AAAA] Built up land
- [IIII] Forests
- [dashed] Other land

Notes: a) Selected major land use conversion
       b) Estimated net land use changes

Fig. 5.6   Land use in selected OECD countries
             Source OECD (1985)

the municipality and two-thirds of all vegetable areas in close proximity to the city (Smil, 1984). Similar problems of lost vegetable production have occurred within the vicinity of Shanghai.

Shifts in global agricultural land

Some lands with little productive potential can be improved and intensities on existing land can be increased. Given the joint suitability of the productive land base for developed uses, grazing, forestry and agriculture, however, the competitive outcome among these uses results in the growth in one sector being at the expense of another. What types of shifts are expected to take place over the near future among these and other land uses and what will be the prime agents underlying these shifts?

Buringh (1981) attempted to answer these questions to the year 2000 with special emphasis on changes in potential productive capacity of the arable land base as a result of losses to other uses and degradation. A number of assumptions were made concerning the expected growth in population and density of that growth, gains in agricultural land through intensification and changes in each land use's share of productivity classes. Because of these assumptions and the incomplete data base the results must be interpreted with caution. Table 5.3 summarizes the major findings of this study.

The growth of population and the needs of the existing population are responsible for the non-agricultural use of approximately 200 million additional hectares between 1975–2000. Of that total, 120 million, 62 per cent of which is highly productive, is expected to be transferred directly from the cropland base. The remaining 80 million hectares will be supplied from forest-land and grassland. Other sources of loss of cropland are erosion, desertification and toxification. Some of this degraded land shifts to a less intensive use, either in the form of grassland or forest-land. However, all the other losses (built-up, desertified, toxified) are considered irreversible, at least under present economic and technological conditions. These irreversible losses of cropland and all productive land (including grassland and forest-land) are equal to 220 and 300 million hectares of land respectively, between 1975 and 2000.

To compensate for the losses in productive capacity and meet the nutritional needs of a growing population, additional lands must be brought into production. In addition to the equivalent area required to replace that lost to urbanization, another 375 million hectares are needed for the growing population. The equivalent of 75 million hectares will come from intensification and 300 million from other uses. It is assumed that all of these additional lands including grasslands are taken from forest-land. In fact total forested area is expected to decrease by 600 million hectares, whereas grassland area remains constant.

Hence by the year 2000 the cropland base is expected to be 1800 million hectares, an increase of 300 million hectares over 1975 but a much higher proportion of medium- to lower-grade land contributes to the output of food than in 1975. Non-agricultural uses of the land are expected to be 50

107

Table 5.3 Estimated change in the global land budget by land class, 1975–2000

	Cropland			Grassland				Forest-land				Non-agri-cultural land	Other land	Totals
	H	M	L	H	M	L	Z	H	M	L	Z			
LAND USE IN 1975	400ª	500	600	200	300	500	2,000	100	300	400	3,300	400	4,400	13,400
Debits (deterioration)														
Loss by erosion		40				15			10	10				75
land converted into lower class			10		5	30				30				
Loss by toxification	25	15												50
land converted into lower class					5	5							50	
Loss by desertification						30				10				50
land converted into lower class			10										50	
Loss by non-agricultural use	75	25		30	10	10			20	10				200
land converted into lower class			20									200		
Loss by shifting cultivation								25	25					50
land converted into lower class									25	25			50	
Net change	100	80	50	30	10	40		25	20	35*		0	200*	100*

Table 5.3 (cont.)

Credits (reclamation)													
For Increasing Population reclaimed from lower class	25	175	100					30	100	100	70		300
For Replacing Lost Cropland reclaimed from lower class	20	150	50					10	60	80	70		220
For Replacing Lost Grassland reclaimed from lower class					30	40		5	20	25	20		70
Net change	45	325	150	0	30	40	0	45*	180*	205*	160*	600	4,500
LAND USE IN 2000	345	745	710	170	320	510	2,000	30	100	230	3,140	600	13,400
Net change (2000–1975)	−55	245	110	−30	20	10	0	−70	−200	−170	−160	200	100	0

[a] All values are in millions of hectares

*Denotes net gain (deterioration) or net loss (reclamation)

H = High yields. Two or more crops per annum. >60% of potential maximum yield

M = Good yields. 40 to 60% of potential maximum yields

L = Low yields. 20 to 40% of potential maximum yields

Z = Very low yields. <20% of potential maximum yields

Source adapted from Buringh (1981)

109

per cent larger than in 1975, a growth proportional to the same increase in population.

National estimates of future losses of agricultural land

The actual growth in population during the next twenty years is expected to differ dramatically in rate, quantity and distribution between developed and developing countries. Table 5.4 illustrates the striking difference in share of total population living in urban areas by region as well as the growth rates, actual and anticipated, for urban and rural regions. The rapid growth rates of urban population in developing countries can be traced to high rates of natural increase in these regions, but also to large-scale emigration from rural regions. Unlike the growth in urban areas in developed countries, the move to the city is as important as population decentralization in affecting urban growth patterns in developing countries. By the year 2000, if current growth rates continue, there will be twenty cities in the developing world with populations over 10 million (there were only three in 1978) and only four cities of that size or larger in the developed world (the same as in 1975). However, in proportional terms, this process of urbanization is not as dramatic as the absolute growth in individual urban agglomerations would imply since rural areas will also continue to capture a significant share of the growth of population. Industrialized countries are unique in their negative or very low growth rates in rural regions.

Table 5.4 Rural and urban population growth, 1950–2000

| Country group | Percentage urban population | | | Average annual percentage growth | | | |
| | | | | 1950–80 | | 1980–2000 | |
	1950	1980	2000	Urban	Rural	Urban	Rural
All developing countries	18.9	28.8	43.4	3.4	1.7	3.4	1.1
Excluding China	22.2	35.4	43.3	3.8	1.7	3.5	1.1
Low-income							
Asia	10.7	19.5	31.3	4.4	2.0	4.2	0.9
China	11.2	13.2	38.6	2.5	1.8	3.3	0.2
India	16.8	23.3	35.5	3.2	1.8	4.2	1.1
Africa	5.7	19.2	34.9	7.0	2.5	5.8	1.5
Middle-income							
East Asia and Pacific	19.6	31.9	41.9	4.1	1.8	3.1	0.9
Middle East and North Africa	27.7	46.8	59.9	4.4	1.6	4.3	1.6
Sub-Saharan Africa	33.7	49.4	55.2	3.1	1.0	2.9	1.7
Latin America and Caribbean	41.4	65.3	75.4	4.1	0.8	2.9	0.4
Southern Europe	24.7	47.1	62.3	3.8	0.5	2.9	0.2
Industrial countries	61.3	77.0	83.7	1.8	−0.7	1.0	−1.1

Source after World Bank (1984)

How will these expected growth rates in population affect the demand for land resources, particularly agricultural land? Not all of the land converted for non-agricultural purposes will have agricultural potential and not all consequences will be irreversible for the agricultural sector. The majority of the land consumed, however, will have potential for agriculture and will be irreversibly affected by hydro-electric projects, transportation systems and the growth of settlements. Numerous factors contribute to differential rates of land consumption among countries: the initial size/density of the population, stage of development, population and income growth, rate of urbanization and type of settlement, transportation system, government policy and a variety of historical circumstances.

Buringh provides no regional breakdown of his estimates, nor is it clear what share of this non-agricultural use is comprised of urban versus rural settlement. This is an important issue in any attempt to understand the land-resource implications of a growing population. Cities or urban forms of settlement are far more parsimonious in their use of land than rural forms of settlement which tend to rely upon single-storey technology.

To examine this question and expand upon Buringh's study, UN information on average population densities for urban and rural areas, and the projected growth in urban and rural populations for a twenty-year period (1980–2000) were collected (UN, 1980). Since little information existed on rural population densities for most countries, it was assumed that future growth would take place at twelve persons per hectare, or 0.08 hectares per person. Weighting the urban and rural population projections by their respective current densities provided a measure of the demand for rural land. These figures were then adjusted downward by 25 per cent to indicate only agricultural land (cropland and grassland). This value was then expressed as a percentage of total arable land base.

Table 5.5 provides a regional breakdown of projected losses of agricultural land from built-up activities in both urban and rural areas. Asia is expected to consume the greatest quantity of agricultural land both in absolute terms and relative to its cropland base. It is followed by Africa and Latin America. Given the large expected increases in rural populations and their relatively low population densities, the demand for land resources in these regions is particularly high. From 1980 to 2000 this translates into a global loss of 37.9 million hectares of land consumed for rural development and 14.9 million hectares for urban development, for a total of roughly 53 million hectares or 3.7 per cent of the existing arable land base. This is approximately twice the amount estimated by Brown (1978) who considered only the loss of land to urban populations, but is only a little more than one-half the amount estimated by the FAO (1982a) for the loss of land to non-agricultural activities in developing countries between 1975–2000.

On an annual basis this loss of land to development is equal to 2.6 million hectares per year, compared to Buringh's estimate for non-

Table 5.5 Land consumption by region, 1980–2000 (000s of ha/percentage of arable land)

Region	Urban[a]	Rural[b]	Total
Canada and USA (15)	1,888.00/0.8%	815.06/0.3%	1.1%
Africa (179)	825.10/0.5%	8,552.60/5.2%	5.7%
Latin America (102)	2,047.70/1.4%	1,479.10/1.0%	2.4%
Asia (65)	8,811.50/2.0%	25,267.70/5.9%	7.9%
Europe (30)	465.20/0.3%	669.90/0.5%	0.8%
USSR (37)	775.00/0.3%	1,187.50/0.5%	0.8%
Australia and New Zealand (15)	126.50/0.2%	26.25/0.06%	0.26%
World	14,939.00/1.09%	37,988.11/2.78%	3.7%

[a]Urban density is in brackets for each region (persons per ha)
[b]Rural density = twelve persons per ha
Data sources World Bank (1984); UN (1980 and 1985); FAO (1985a)

agricultural use of 6 million hectares per year. This discrepancy could be due to the differences in estimated densities of population and share of rural population growth of the total, as well as an allowance in Buringh's study for other forms of development. In terms of lost production potential, the historical siting of cities on excellent agricultural land, and evidence by Buringh, would suggest that because of the quality of land lost, the impact on output will be greater than the percentage decrease in arable land lost.

While a 3.7–6 per cent loss in the global cropland base does not appear to be excessive and could be accommodated through intensification and new lands, an analysis of the regional picture reveals more significant impacts. Figure 5.7 provides the estimated loss of a country's arable land base from urban and rural development between 1980–2000. Europe and North America indicate modest declines in overall cropland base of less than 1 per cent, whereas a number of Asian and African nations indicate precipitous losses. The *Global 2000* report (Barney, 1980) projected, for a cross-section of industrialized countries, cumulative losses of agricultural lands of 2.5 per cent from 1978 to 2000. China is expected to lose 4 per cent of its base to various forms of settlement. This may be a serious underestimate since much of the demand for rural housing originates from the need to replace ageing facilities with new ones. Smil (1984) argued that if present trends continue, per capita availability of farmland will decline to 0.068 ha by 2000. Estimates of rate of land loss for the USSR may also underestimate the challenge to the cropland base. For example, major reservoir flooding in the 1960s and 1970s claimed 2.3 million hectares of which one-fifth was prime land (Gustavson, 1979). Bangladesh is expected to lose 29, Malaysia 24, Indonesia 20 and South Korea 17 per cent. Similarly high rates are expected in Africa, where Kenya leads the list at 33, Rwanda 29, Ghana 20 and Egypt 14 per cent.

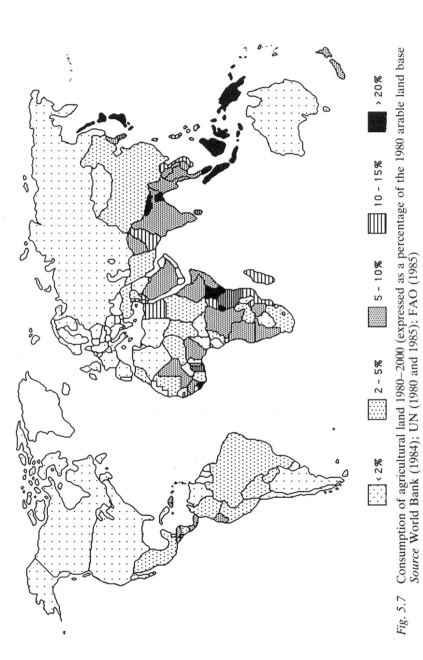

Fig. 5.7 Consumption of agricultural land 1980–2000 (expressed as a percentage of the 1980 arable land base *Source* World Bank (1984); UN (1980 and 1985); FAO (1985)

113

It should be emphasized that these values are only indicative of outcomes if current trends continue. The picture in Latin America is far more promising, with the exception of Central America and parts of the Caribbean, where El Salvador, Guatemala and Haiti will need 18, 10 and 8 per cent of their cropland bases respectively for other types of development. Critical factors affecting these proportions include not only the growth and density of population, but also the size of the existing arable land base. A number of the countries discussed above will have to change one or more of these variables if per capita land availability of the food system is not to be seriously constrained.

Process of agricultural land conversion

We have examined generally and, at large scale, some of the major land-use requirements of an expanding population and the land-use implications for agriculture. The process of agricultural land conversion has been studied in great detail in most Western industrialized countries. The results from these studies, although far from being definitive, reveal a number of common dimensions relating to the overall context of development and to the response of the agricultural sector to development pressures in a far more informed and systematic way than for developing countries. It is a discussion of these dimensions that concludes this chapter.

Context of development

The growth and spread of cities, including their closely associated support structures of transportation, communications, water supply and energy networks, impact on agriculture directly and indirectly (Furuseth and Pierce, 1982). The direct effects, the most visible and damaging to the flow characteristics of the resource, represent the actual conversion of land from agriculture to a more 'intensive' use. The indirect effects, which are far more complex and difficult to measure precisely, relate to a real or perceived change in the environment for farming, and, in turn, alterations in a whole host of factors which relate directly to the short- and long-term viability of the farm unit. Unlike direct effects, the indirect effects may be either positive or negative, conferring benefits or costs for agriculture. It should be emphasized before examining these effects that not all the losses in agricultural land or changes in the structure of farming in the urban fringe are due to urban-based forces. Farmland abandonment, and changes in product mix and the structure of farming in general within the vicinity of urban areas may also be due to non-metropolitan forces such as uncompetitive agriculture and changes in agricultural technology (Bryant, 1976).

One of the major reasons for conflict between agriculture and the growth of settlement arises from the joint suitability of the land for both uses, and the fact that historically the initial location and subsequent

114

growth of many cities was tied to good agricultural land and the development of agricultural surpluses. A number of researchers have examined the degree to which urban regions contain a disproportionate share of high-quality agricultural land. In a review of these studies in Canada, the United States and Britain, Hansen (1982) found that indeed a bias existed in the location of high-capability land within urban regions of North America – particularly Canada but not in England and Wales. For example in the United States a selection of urban regions comprising 17 per cent of the national area contained 28.4 per cent of class 1 and 2 land; and in the case of Canada, urban regions comprising 3 per cent of the total land area of the country contained 34.4 per cent of class 1 and 2 land.

The concern over the loss or threat of loss of this land arises not simply from the quality of the land base itself (e.g. class 1 or 2), but also from the climatic resources associated with it which together define the potential capability of the land. Lands of high capability have fewer risks of crop failure, offer higher yields and have a much larger range of production possibilities or crop options.

In many countries in northern or high latitudes such as Canada, Sweden and the USSR, the relatively large land bases are at odds with their production possibilities because of limitations in soil and climatic resources. Although Canada is the second largest country in the world it is only able to use about 5 per cent of its surface area for crop production and only 0.5 of 1 per cent of the area is free of significant limitations (soil and climate) for crop production. Considering that over 50 per cent of the population coincides with the best 5 per cent of the farmland (Williams et al., 1978), the loss of prime agricultural land has more significance in terms of future production potential than for a country such as the United States. This situation must be understood within the context of the demand for agricultural land for non-agricultural purposes, the replacement value of these converted lands and the size and quality of the agricultural land reserves available for future agricultural purposes.

The United States

To understand this context it is necessary to estimate the quantity and quality of lands lost, intensity of use and reserve potential. During the 1960s the conversion of agricultural land (cropland, pasture-land and range-land) to non-agricultural uses was somewhere between 0.370 million hectares and 0.448 million hectares annually. The National Resources Inventory (NRI) of 1977 estimated that during the preceding ten years the rate of conversion of agricultural land climbed dramatically to between 0.734 and 0.855 million hectares. Some of this land was not developed but merely incorporated into urban boundaries. Plaut (1980) estimated that of the one million hectares of rural land converted or annexed, 29 per cent was cropland but 36 per cent prime land since some of the range- and

115

pasture-land had high capability. In the 1982 NRI, only direct conversion of agricultural land to built-up uses was measured. For the 1977–82 period, average annual rate of conversion to urban uses was almost identical to the 1960s level (USDA, 1987). Between 1959 and 1982 built-up and rural transportation uses increased from 20 to 30 million hectares.

Although the proportion of cropland to agricultural land converted is not known, the previous 1982 NRI study and a study by Zeimetz et al. (1976) would place the figure between 30 and 40 per cent. Hence cropland conversion to built up use ranges realistically between 0.122 and 0.179 million hectares annually. If Zeimetz's study of fifty-three fast-growth countries is an accurate indication of the efficiency or intensity of land use, then approximately 69 hectares of land are required for each 1000 increase in population.

Evidence suggests that the density of new development is lowering. According to the 1980 US census, which includes annexed as well as built-up land as part of the growth of urban areas, there has been an increase in the amount of converted land per person from 0.1 hectares/person (1960–70) to 0.18 in (1970–80). Other studies (Heimlich and Anderson, 1987) indicate that this trend is apparent in both Standard Metropolitan Statistical Areas (SMSA) and non-SMSA, with the latter displaying the lowest density development.

Calculations of future land-use needs and their cropland equivalents are at best guesstimates. Hart (1976) suggests that for the US between 13 to 15.5 million hectares of rural land will be converted to urban use by 2000. Assuming that 30 per cent of this will be cropland, then between 2.32 and 2.7 per cent of the current cropland base will be consumed or, more importantly, the equivalent of between 7 and 8.4 per cent of the total cropland reserve (estimated to be as high as 55 million hectares). Using higher annual rates of land conversion, based on the 1977 NRI, Plaut (1980) argued that an equivalent of 12.4 per cent of the cropland base and 44.5 per cent of the prime agricultural land reserve will be consumed by 2000. Even when Plaut's rates of prime land conversion are reduced by half, the loss of an equivalent of 22 per cent of the prime land reserve is still a significant amount.

Raup (1980) has argued that the scale of the non-agricultural demands for cropland during the 1960s and 1970s may prove in the long term to be episodic. There are a number of important factors to consider. The development from 1956–75 of a major state and interstate highway system demanded enormous quantities of land. The interstate system alone consumed 700,000 hectares directly and many times that amount for access and rights of way. Interstate highways require about 4 hectares per km and interchanges 20 to 40 hectares. This same highway system provided improved access to the surrounding countryside encouraging suburban, exurban and in many cases sprawling development. Housing starts between 1968 and 1977 were consistently higher than either the 1960s or 1980s. And a restructuring of the population proceeded further, despite falling birth rates through a process of counter-urbanization or rural renaissance. Many non-metropolitan areas during the 1970s were growing at nearly double the rate of their metropolitan counterparts (Berry, 1980). This accounts in part for the lowering of densities of new development, as discussed earlier. Hence, while the US can expect a decline in the absolute amounts converted, because of a slower growing population and a completed transportation infrastructure, the consumption of land per capita may continue to rise.

A further factor intensifying the competition for agricultural land is the importance of grain exports to the rural economy. These exports documented in Chapter 3 will continue to form an important source in the demand for agricultural land. One could argue that without this external demand and farm support subsidies, not only would farmland prices be lower but rates of land conversion would be much higher.

Canada

In Canada there are no comparable estimates of rural land converted to urban and built-up purposes. Estimates for cities over 25,000 persons (about 65 per cent of total population) place the annual average loss of rural land to urban centres at approximately 16,500 hectares. Extrapolating that to the whole population would yield an annual loss of 23,500 hectares. In addition to the absolute quantities of land consumed, the rural to urban land conversion process differs from the American process in two other important respects. First, the per capita consumption of land converted tends to be higher. Despite this difference there has been a progressive increase in land consumption rates (or increase in per capita consumption) from 60 ha per 1000 in the period 1966–71 to 72 ha per 1000 in 1971–76, and to 119 ha per 1000 for the subsequent five years, much like the increase in the United States. For the Windsor–Quebec Axis in Central Canada, the most heavily populated region of the country, Yeates (1985) argued that the increase of land consumption rates reflects increasing wealth and/or decreasing family size. The lowering of densities of development is analogous to the process occurring in the United States. Canada, like the United States, has also undergone a decline in population growth from the 1970s onwards, as well as a restructuring of the geographic concentration of growth to smaller centres (Preston and Russwurm, 1977; Joseph et al., 1988).

The second difference relates to the proportion of high capability land converted to urban purposes and the size of the reserve cropland base. During the five-year period beginning in 1976, about 50 per cent of the land urbanized was of high capability. This compares with cropland proportion of 63 per cent during 1966–76. These high proportions relative to the United States reinforce earlier findings on the bias of settlement for

117

good agricultural land. Within a 160 km radius of Census Metropolitan Areas in Canada lies 55 per cent of the class 1–3 land in Canada.

Almost half of the high capability land converted to urban purposes during the late 1970s had a high agro-climatic rating. Agro-climatic ratings indicate the agricultural value of land from a climatic perspective by taking into consideration duration of frost-free period, significant moisture shortages and summer heat. Typical values for the best agricultural land in Canada located in south-western Ontario range from 2.5 to 3, whereas in extremely dry areas of the Canadian Prairies or very short growing season regions in the Peace River district of Alberta and British Columbia, values range from 1 (the lowest) to 1.5. If these ratings are used to scale or weight land-capability classes, then to replace the 45,000 hectares of converted class 1–3 land throughout Canada between 1976–81 would require the equivalent of over 100,000 ha of land in the Peace River region of Northern Alberta and British Columbia. The prime source of land with some agricultural potential in Canada lies in the north, particularly the Peace, where there are some 13 million ha of class 3 but mostly class 4 land. In terms of class 1 equivalents this land would be equal to no more than five million hectares. This comparison ignores, as did the earlier one, that these northern lands regardless of their abundance cannot be used to grow the same range of crops.

Canada like the United States has additional land resources that can be used to help offset the loss of land to urban expansion. However, the quality of these lands and the restrictions they place on the types of crop that can be produced preclude any sort of direct transfer of production. Moreover, it is unclear at this stage what economic conditions are required. In other words, how responsive or elastic are land supplies to changes in price? While considerable quantities of land in the United States have historically been retired from production because of low prices and returned under high prices (or subsidies), there is little evidence to suggest what prices would be required for marginal lands to be brought into production in northern Canada. Greater emphasis will have to be placed on intensification strategies in the south if the lost land resources are not to interfere with long-term growth in production.

Britain

The question of the need for intensification as the land-resource base diminishes under different demand conditions has been examined for land-scarce Britain (Edwards and Wibberley, 1971). By cross-correlating different 'demand for output' scenarios to the year 2000 with annual growth in output per hectare, it was possible to define land-use requirements. These requirements were measured in terms of percentage of land area or production capacity necessary to meet demand in 2000. Table 5.6 reveals that if demand increases by 50 per cent over 1965 levels (150) and production per hectare expands by 2.75 per annum, to boost overall output per hectare by 96.4 per cent over 1965 levels (196.4), then demand can be met by 76.4 per cent of the land-resource base in the year 2000. An 8–20 per cent decline in land area and in turn production capacity are indicated as contours in Table 5.6. Combinations above the 20 per cent contour indicate situations where the growth in demand can be met by growth in output per hectare, even if 20 per cent of the land-resource base is lost. Combinations below that contour represent the opposite. For example the value 87.8 can be achieved with a 15 per cent loss of agricultural land, but not a 20 per cent loss. The worst situations occur when growth in demand, because of income and population growth, is high, but where gains in productivity are modest. Only small percentages of agricultural land can afford to be lost.

The actual loss of agricultural land in Britain to built-up uses has declined steadily from a peak of about 25,000 ha per year in the 1930s to less than 10,000 ha per year in the late 1970s (Ilbery, 1985). Like Canada the distribution of urban development is highly uneven across the country, with percentages as high as 18 per cent for the South-East, an area with the best agro-climatic resources. Best (1981) has argued that with the

Table 5.6 The balance between the demand and supply of agricultural output in 2000. Non-agricultural demands have been met (using a linear output trend)

Demand for output produced on farms in the United Kingdom in 2000 (1965 = 100)	Annual increase in output per hectare (% linear trend)			
	2.5	2.75	3.0	3.25
	Output per Hectare in 2000 (1965 = 100)			
	187.5	196.4	205.0	213.8
130	69.3	66.2	63.4	60.8
135	72.0	68.7	65.9	63.1
140	74.7	71.3	68.3	65.5
145	77.3	73.8	70.7	67.8
150	80.0	76.4*	73.2	70.2
155	82.7	78.9	75.6	72.5
160	85.3	81.5	78.0	74.8
165	88.0	84.0	80.5	77.2
170	90.7	86.6	82.9	79.5	20% loss
175	93.3	89.1	85.4	81.8
180	96.0	91.7	87.8*	84.2	15% loss
185	98.7	94.2	90.2	86.5
190	100.7	96.7	92.7	88.9*

8% loss   10% loss   *% of land required to meet demand

Source after Edwards and Wibberley (1971)

119

slowdown in the rate of agricultural land conversion, the high proportion of land already devoted to agriculture and the shift in the highest rates of urban development to the north and west of the country, the loss of agricultural land will have relatively little effect upon the productive capacity of British agriculture.

Indirect effects of urbanization on agricultural lands

Prior to and preparatory for the direct consumption of agricultural land by urban and built-up uses are a number of changes in the size and structure of farms, proportion of idle land, the value of land and capital investment, number of non-farm residences, amount of off-farm work and, perhaps most importantly, changes in the farmer's attitude regarding the environment for farming. These changes are commonly referred to as indirect effects of urbanization which may be beneficial for farmers and farming because of changing market opportunities and other factors, but which more often than not are harmful to the farm environment. Although difficult to document, these negative indirect effects may influence production potential far more than the direct effects discussed above.

In his classic study of the urbanization of the Niagara Fruit Belt in Ontario, Krueger (1959) suggested that these indirect effects may alienate twice as much land from productive use as direct effects. In another study of land conversion in the Windsor–Quebec Axis of central Canada, Yeates (1985) found that for every hectare consumed directly, five more were affected indirectly. Although theoretically most of this land is not irrevocably lost during this process, from a practical perspective the loss of agricultural services, the price of the land and hence its opportunity cost, and proximity to development, effectively preclude most future agricultural options. Regardless of whether these ratios are 2:1 or 5:1, the important point is that use of direct conversion figures may seriously underestimate the quantity of land whose production potential is irretrievably lost or functionally removed from production.

There are beneficial relationships between agriculture and nearby urban centres. Research in North America and France has illustrated numerous ways in which agriculture has adapted to the changing environment for farming. Because of the high opportunity cost of owning farmland in the urban fringe, many farmers have resorted to renting farmland with considerable success. Although this may dictate the type of agriculture, for example, crop production as opposed to livestock/milk production which tends to be more capital intensive, important products are produced.

Proximity to markets affords additional opportunities for marketing specialty products. Bryant (1981) found this to be the case in the Île de France region. As well, improvements in services resulting from higher population densities and greater part-time job opportunities, with greater proximity to urban centres, may be a sufficiently large incentive to offset the real and perceived costs of farming in the urban fringe. According to Bryant and colleagues (1982), the resilience of the agricultural sector to the pressures of urban growth depends on the size and growth rates of cities. Case studies of farm activity in the urban fringes of large and medium-size Canadian cities suggest size of centre appears to be the most damaging condition for agriculture and not rate of growth, since many fast-growing medium-sized cities exhibited healthy agricultural sectors within their urban fringes. At the level of the farm community and individual farm, the concept of thresholds has been used to explain the minimum requirements to sustain viable farm enterprises. Land prices, sizes of farms and non-farm population densities are all subject to threshold values which when exceeded seriously hamper agricultural production.

The most conventional explanation underlying the decline in the farm sector in peri-urban areas or in the rural–urban fringe relates to the disinvestment on the part of farmers because of high levels of urban anticipation and hence uncertainty regarding the future for long-term production. Urban anticipation is expressed in many forms to include rising land values, increasing densities of population and, related to that, complaints and externalities originating from non-farm residents, a rise in taxes and a decline in the overall 'rural' character of an area. The unwillingness to invest further in production, at least capital-intensive production, leads to a decline in output and eventually to the cessation of active farming (Sinclair, 1967). Modifications to this approach recognize that some labour-intensive activities can prosper under intensive urban pressures, as well as some capital-intensive enterprises, so long as that capital is mobile as in the case of farm machinery (Bryant et al., 1982).

Summary

The growth of societies demographically and economically places a wide variety of demands and pressures upon their land-resource bases. For agricultural lands these demands and pressures manifest themselves in the intensification of production to produce more and better-quality food, in the shift to cash crops for export markets, in structural change in the use of labour, capital and technology, and in the conversion of land to non-agricultural uses. The response of agriculture and the sustainability of the above practices vary, reflecting the large differences by country in the combinations of population, resources, technology, income and political/institutional structures.

In numerous developing countries continued high growth rates in population within the context of limited access to additional land resources and alternative forms of employment have increased land fragmentation, the size and density of the rural work-force, and have led to a decline in the quality of the environment for agricultural production. While there is no definitive answer to the question, 'Is rapid population growth the cause or the effect of poverty?' the development experience of most countries would suggest that a dampening of population growth, changes in population distribution through migration and improved access to agricultural resources is imperative before income and welfare can be improved.

Pressures on the agricultural base in developing countries also come from non-agricultural uses of the land. To accommodate a rapidly urbanizing society, the conversion of a relatively high proportion of agricultural land will be necessary. Whereas African and South American countries may have additional land resources to offset these losses, a number of Middle-Eastern and Asian countries do not. For these regions loss of agricultural land will diminish the productive capacity inherent in the system and will necessitate increased dependence on external food sources and the need to expand productivity further.

A number of middle-income countries which are relatively land-scarce, such as South Korea and Taiwan, are already in this situation. Rapid growth in population and income has placed heavy and insupportable demands on the land-resource base. While these countries have the flexibility to trade manufactured goods for food and thereby relieve the potential land constraint, this is only possible over the long term if Western countries continue to have the additional land resources and production capabilities to offset these food deficits.

For the foreseeable future, North America and Western Europe have adequate agricultural land resources to meet the food demands of middle-income developing countries, as well as the food demands of a relatively stable but affluent domestic population devoted to the consumption of high protein and caloric diets. Demands for goods and services from the land other than agricultural have precipitated large-scale conversion of farmland. In the United States the loss of farmland, although large, will not greatly affect production potential because it represents a small proportion of the arable land base; there is still scope for expansion in that base and there has been a decline in the importance of land as a result of tremendous yield/productivity growth. In contrast, the threat to production potential as a result of farmland conversion is much larger in Canada, given the quality (agro-climatically) and proportion of land lost as well as the limited scope for expansion of cultivated area. There is even more force to this argument if the indirect effects of land conversion are included.

Europe too has limited scope for expansion so that declines in area must be offset by increases in yield/productivity. The high level of agricultural subsidy in the European Common Market has ensured productivity growth throughout the 1970s and 1980s. Unlike most developing countries, the structural changes in developed countries have favoured an increase in farm size and a decline in the rural/agricultural work-force. In the absence of subsidies within the EEC this would have occurred to an even greater extent.

The inability of Eastern Europe and the Soviet Union to meet their rising food demands, which are largely income-induced, suggests that the pressure on land resources, given current technology, is indeed high and will continue to worsen.

CHAPTER 6

Water resources and agriculture

Context of water use

Water, like arable land resources, is highly variable in its spatial distribution. Chapter 2 highlighted this variability in terms of the balance among precipitation, evapotranspiration and run-off. Unlike land, however, water resources are variable over time, displaying seasonal as well as year-to-year differences. The end result of this variability is that only a fraction of the total run-off is usable for humans, plants and animals, and that the usable proportion often fails to coincide with the requirements of humans and other life forms. Human intervention into the environment has aimed at redressing the balance by transferring water resources from surplus to shortage regions and by constructing storage facilities. Within an agricultural context, water and not land, in many regions of the world, is the chief limiting factor to growth and development.

This view of the critical importance of water is not only shared widely today by scientists and development specialists, but was recognized in most of the earliest civilizations whose growth and power were intricately tied to the adoption of irrigation systems. By controlling and manipulating the use of water for agricultural purposes, the early hydraulic societies in the Nile and Tigris–Euphrates valleys, and in India, China and Peru were able to concentrate production to enhance yields, reduce the relative size of the agricultural work-force and support a large population. In Iran (some 5000 BP), rainfed agriculture supported 1.2 persons per sq. km compared with six persons per sq. km for irrigated systems. Cities in the Tigris–Euphrates region approached 100,000 inhabitants, and total population reached 17 million (Heathcote, 1983).

Irrigation systems, however, cannot be appreciated or understood outside the context of the social organizations which manage them. Wittfogel (1970) has argued that there has been a complementary relationship between the basic means of production, in this case irrigation, and certain

124

social organizations. In those regions with the water potential for large-scale irrigation development, the specialization and division of labour was required, as was a highly-centralized and hierarchical form of administration. At the apex of the system was a king or emperor, supported by priests who managed the bureaucracy and the division of labour, all of which existed by and for the irrigation system (Heathcote, 1983).

The reasons underlying the demise or downfall of these hydraulic societies are far from clear. Toynbee (Tomlin, 1978) has argued that it was the failure of the civilizations themselves which led to the loss of command over the physical environment. The technological failures, in the form of waterlogging of the soils and siltation of canals, were the effects rather than the cause of social breakdown. Wittfogel (1970) saw the social organization, although dedicated to the protection of the irrigation system, as being non-innovative and hence unable to handle many of the technical problems which inevitably arise in any irrigation system through prolonged use. As productivity declined from land degradation, neither the division of labour nor the large concentrations of population could be sustained.

Regardless of the veracity of these interpretations, irrigation systems today, as then, are valued for their land-saving and yield-augmenting roles. Other benefits associated with the spread of irrigation include the potential for expanding area cultivated and a larger range of crops. Perhaps most importantly, irrigation provides a more secure environment for crop production by reducing the risks associated with periodic and unstable rainfall, and in the process, improves the economic and income performance of agriculture.

As previously argued, a significant if not a dominant share of the growth of future food production is expected to come from the improvement and extension of irrigated area. Irrigation systems today, like those in hydraulic societies, are faced with a fixed supply of water resources, but unlike the past, there are many more competing demands for that water from non-agricultural sources. Moreover, the growth in demand for food products and the impact on the quality of the resource are certainly higher than in the early pre-industrial civilizations. In appraising the world water situation, Biswas (1978: 64) has noted that 'the essential water problem is how best to reconcile increasing use of a fixed supply with the needs and constraints of human society, in a way that will maintain a stable environment.'

Seen within this context, the pressure to develop and regulate water resources for consumptive and non-consumptive uses will increase, as will the need to manage the resource more effectively. If societies are to achieve the numerous benefits associated with irrigation, then policies dealing with water and food inter-relations must consider the economic, social, geographic and environmental context within which development is occurring (Rogers, 1985). Water development occurs within and between river basins, with a whole host of on-site and off-site environmental effects.

The economic and social context of this development is framed as much by international economic conditions and terms of trade as it is by the availability of capital, labour and expertise within the country itself. The development issue, however, cannot be separated from the management issue. Mismanagement has only recently been identified as one of the key problems affecting supply in both new and existing systems.

In this chapter we examine some of the major issues relating to the use of water resources for food production, with special emphasis on irrigation systems.

Irrigated lands – physical and economic realities

Growth in irrigated area

From 40 million hectares of land in 1900, irrigated area increased almost seven-fold during the intervening eighty-five years to occupy about 18 per cent of arable and permanent cropland, and to contribute roughly a third of global food production (Rangeley, 1987). Table 6.1 profiles the change in gross irrigated area from 1950 to the present. The 1960s saw the greatest gross addition to the irrigated land base, averaging some six million hectares annually, but this declined to around four million hectares annually during the 1970s. The exact amount of irrigated land that is currently in active use is unknown. Aside from the definitional problem of what is irrigated land, there is the equally complex problem of what is actually being used, since poor maintenance, periodic use and land degradation have reduced the usable proportion of the irrigated land base. It is common in South East Asian countries, such as the Philippines, during the dry season that at least 25 per cent of the wet season irrigated area receives no water at all (Norse, 1979).

Irrigated land's share of cultivated land, illustrated in Figure 6.1, probably exaggerates its areal importance, particularly in developing countries. Regardless of the measurement problems, irrigation agriculture figures prominently in the composition of agricultural land-use systems throughout Asia and the Middle East. In fact, these regions today possess approximately three-quarters of the world's irrigated area. Table 6.2 indicates for

Table 6.1 Gross irrigated area by continent (million ha)

	1950	*1960*	*1970*	*1985*
Europe (Including part of Soviet Union)	8	12	20	29
Asia (Including part of Soviet Union	66	100	132	184
Africa	4	5	9	13
North America	12	17	29	34
South America	3	5	6	9
Australia and Pacific	1	1	2	2

Source after Rangeley (1987)

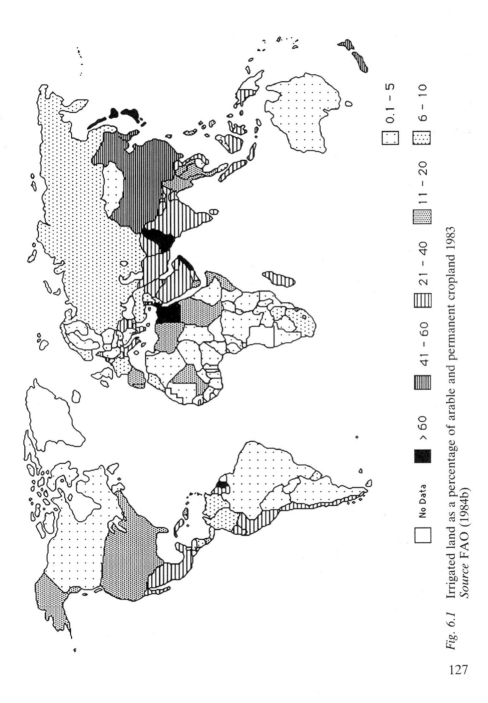

Fig. 6.1 Irrigated land as a percentage of arable and permanent cropland 1983
Source FAO (1984b)

Table 6.2 The contribution of irrigation to food production c.1985

Country	Irrigated area/ cultivated area (%)	Irrigated food production/total food production (%)
India	30	55
Pakistan	65	80
China	50	70
Indonesia	40	50
Chile	35	55
Peru	35	55
Mexico	30	N/A

Source after Rangeley (1987)

a number of countries the contribution these irrigated lands make to national food output.

The variation in the importance of irrigated land among countries as indicated in Figure 6.1 can be explained in part at least by the persistent variation in the population–land balance. Populations in these regions can only be supported by relatively intensive horticultural systems of production, since land is the scarcest factor of production. Irrigation affords the opportunity for high productivity through yield and cropping intensity enhancement, particularly for rice. A precondition for this support and productivity is a favourable balance between availability of water in the form of stable run-off and water requirements as dictated by gross water demand. Furthermore, labour is abundant, which facilitates the development and maintenance of these systems. The scarcity of labour and the relative abundance of land in North America encourages less intensive forms of agriculture and less reliance on irrigation.

Techniques of irrigation

The impressive growth in irrigation systems during the last thirty years can be traced to a number of interdependent factors. Perhaps the most important was the shift in technology from diversion techniques to reticulation. Diversion techniques rely upon naturally-occurring peak water supplies with minimal storage or impounding to irrigate crops (see Fig. 6.2). In contrast, reticulation techniques are more thorough and complex in their distribution and control of water supplies. Numerous large-scale damming projects and pumping installations provide the means and wherewithal to distribute scarce water resources over time and space. Agriculture is often only one of a number of uses of the water, with hydro-electricity also figuring prominently.

The existence of cheap energy during the third quarter of the twentieth century encouraged energy-intensive pumping systems with concomitant increases in withdrawals from groundwater sources. Technology, in other words, favoured the use of certain systems such as the sprinkler and centre pivot system in the United States. As Holdgate et al. (1982: 134) observed: 'The development of deep wells and application systems that did not require extensive distribution channel networks reduced costs, and in many cases also became more efficient in the sense of requiring less water for a given crop output.'

Water requirements and supply constraints

The future growth of irrigation systems and ultimately their contribution to growth in food production depends upon the growth in demand for water resources for agricultural and non-agricultural uses, the potential for growth in water supply (from surface-water and groundwater sources), and the scope for change in the efficiency with which water is used by all

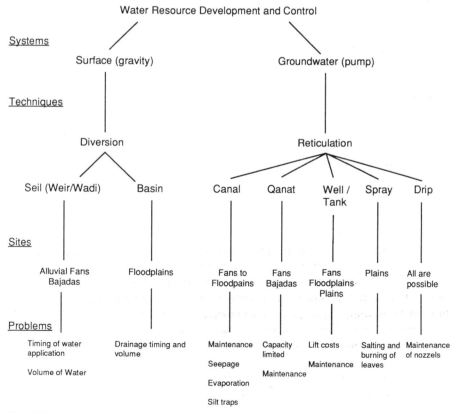

Fig. 6.2a Irrigation systems

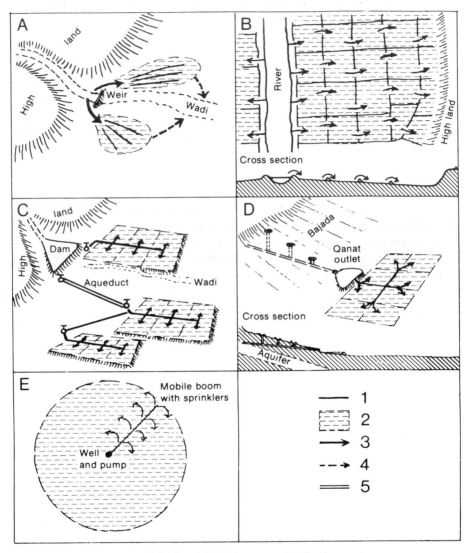

Fig. 6.2b A schemata of distinguishing features of irrigation systems
Key: (A) Seil (flood) system: (B) Basin system; (C) Reticulation system
(dam and canals); (D) Reticulation system (qanat or foggara); (E)
Centre pivot sprinkler system. 1 – dykes or walls; 2 – irrigated areas; 3
– water movement; 4 – drainage of excess water; 5 – canals
Source from Heathcote (1983)

sectors. Given the low-value use of water in agriculture and the trend towards increasing industrialization and population growth in developing countries, agriculture's share of total water withdrawals is expected to decline over the next two decades.

Holy (1971) projected slower rates of growth in agricultural withdrawals of water resources than in urban and domestic uses with, in turn, a decline in agriculture's share of water use from 70 to 51 per cent between 1967 and 2000 (see Table 6.3). The *Agriculture Toward 2000* study, discussed in Chapter 4, envisaged a 40 per cent increase (in scenario A) in irrigated area, (for ninety developing countries, excluding China) from 105 million hectares to 148 million hectares, most of which was to take place in India and Far Eastern countries. This reflects a relatively modest annual growth rate of 1.7 per cent to the year 2000, in part due to the increasing scarcity of cheap sites, and hence the increasing marginal costs of development as well as reliance on repairing and improving existing irrigation systems. Similarly, Norse (1979) argued that while many developing countries in the wet and dry tropics have great potential for expanding irrigated area, the greatest potential lies in improving the existing irrigation system.

The majority of the irrigation development in Asia is for the expansion of rice cultivation, which already accounts for three-quarters of food grain consumption there. A report to the Trilateral Commission on food production in Asia noted that rice is the most suitable and highest-yielding crop for the monsoon climate of Asia. Proper water control was seen as the key factor to increasing paddy yields in Asia (Gasser, 1981).

Some appreciation for the potential for growth in water consumption/withdrawal and the exigencies of water supply now and in the future was gained in a very general discussion of water resources in

Table 6.3 Estimates of world water use, 1967, and projections to 2000

	Total use		Projected rate of growth, 1967–2000	Proportion of total use	
	1967	2000		1967	2000
	(million m³)		(% per year)		(%)
Agriculture					
Irrigation	1,400,000	2,800,000	2.1	70	51
Livestock	58,800	102,200	1.7	3	2
Rural domestic	19,800	38,300	2.0	1	1
Other					
Urban domestic	73,000	278,900	4.1	4	5
Industry and mining	437,700	2,231,000	5.0	22	41
Total	1,989,300	5,450,400	3.1	100	100

Source after Holy (1971)

131

Chapter 2. In regional terms there were three classes or groups of water-users that possessed different development/management options. Likewise, Biswas (1978) has characterized the different water supply/demand relations of countries as follows:

(1) At one extreme are regions or countries which have abundant natural supplies of fresh water and relatively low demand, most of which can be satisfied by minimal regulation of water resources (e.g., major areas of tropical Africa and South America). This is equivalent to Stage I of David's (1978) conceptualization of water basin development (see Fig. 6.3). Irrigated area in these regions has the potential to expand from 49 million hectares to 185 million hectares (Norse, 1979).

(2) At the other extreme are regions with scarce supply and high levels of demand, which can only be met by complete regulation of the drainage system. Unlike the former group, there is little scope for increasing supply, only a decrease in net demand by making more efficient use of existing supplies of water. Seen within the context of David's scheme, water basin development has evolved to its most complex stage, where water flow is fully committed and regulated both within and between basins (Stage III). Large and complex infrastructures are required for this stage, as is a high level of management and technical expertise (Widstrand, 1980). Egypt would be an archetypal example of this situation.

(3) Between these two extremes lies another group, where demands can be met by partial regulation of flow and quality (e.g., India and the United States). In these situations, various options exist for augmenting supply or decreasing net demand. This is a typical (and intermediate) stage in river basin development, in which not only a growing number of uses besides agriculture must be accommodated, but the problem of deteriorating water quality must be addressed for the first time. It has been argued, however, that despite the scope for further regulation the potential for expanding irrigated area in such places as the Soviet Union and the United States is low. This assessment is based not so much on physical constraints but economic ones, since large-scale inter-basin transfers would be required (Norse, 1979).

Implicit in the above discussion on the potential for augmenting supplies is the notion that withdrawals of water cannot exceed usable supply. While this is true over the long term, over the short term there are numerous regions, particularly in the United States, where groundwater resources are withdrawn at rates in excess of recharge. The mining of groundwater and hence the physical reduction in the size of the aquifer are short-term solutions to the problem of scarce and limited water resources. Desalinization is also a means for augmenting supply (as currently practised in the

Middle East), but is generally economical only in application to high-value uses.

Economic considerations

Before examining water supply and demand situations for a select number of regions, the issue of the cost of irrigation needs to be addressed. Globally, the majority of agricultural investment, if not water-resource development, is dominated by expenditure for the extension, upgrading and maintenance of irrigation systems. Much of the capital assistance for the Green Revolution in Mexico, India, Pakistan and the Philippines was targeted on irrigation extension and drainage systems. During the 1970s, the majority of Middle Eastern countries allocated from 60 to 81 per cent

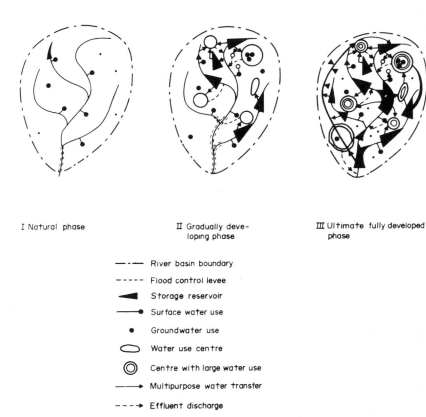

I Natural phase   II Gradually deve-   III Ultimate fully developed
                       loping phase   phase

—·— River basin boundary

- - - - Flood control levee

◀ Storage reservoir

———• Surface water use

• Groundwater use

⬭ Water use centre

◎ Centre with large water use

———→ Multipurpose water transfer

- - -→ Effluent discharge

———➤ Large-scale water transfer

o Private water use

Fig. 6.3 David's three states of water-basin development
Source from Widstrand (1980); after David (1978)

of their agricultural investment to irrigation. China, in 1982, spent more than 50 per cent of agricultural investment on irrigation and drainage (Rogers, 1985).

Total and per-hectare costs (fixed and variable) vary according to the scale of the project (gravity diversion versus tube wells or lowlift pump), type (new land or renovation/improvement), quality of water and the need for drainage. *Agriculture Toward 2000* estimated that the cost of constructing new irrigation systems (in 1975 dollars) ranged from $300 per hectare, for controlled flooding and improved impounding facilities, to $7000 per hectare, for full sprinkler systems. In addition to this, in regions where there is little tradition of irrigation, such as Africa (exclusive of Egypt and Sudan), Rangeley (1987) noted the costs are often $10,000 per hectare or more. Drainage costs are estimated as between $1000–2000 per hectare, so that the global average cost per hectare is between $5000–6000. Rehabilitation or upgrading costs are considerably lower – in the neighbourhood of $200–300 per hectare.

In examining the representativeness of these costs and their stability over time, two observations need to be made. First, there is little evidence of the existence of economies of scale in irrigation development. Costs tend to increase proportionately with the size of the project (measured in area). There is, in fact, evidence of diseconomies of scale in some very large projects.

Second, if per hectare costs for irrigation development are adjusted for inflation and plotted against time, they display a positive relationship (Norse, 1979). This should not be surprising, since in numerous countries such as China and India, low-cost sites have already been developed. In this regard, Rogers (1985: 275–6) noted that 'China is now on an increasing-cost part of the supply curve for irrigation, and is already suffering from problems related to over-exploitation of groundwater.' Hence, the previous cost estimates for enlarging and maintaining irrigation systems have tended to be optimistic, undervaluing the financial burden many of these projects will exact in the future.

Table 6.4 illustrates UN targets for growth in irrigation and drainage to 1990, and Table 6.5 indicates the cost associated with financing new and improved irrigation systems for 1974–85. Fifty-nine billion dollars (in 1974 dollars) are required for improving and expanding irrigation systems exclusive of capital outlay for drainage. In the previously-discussed report to the Trilateral Commission it was estimated that in order to meet Asia's rice requirements from 1978 to 1993, roughly $50 billion would have to be invested in irrigation and other production-augmenting factors (Gasser, 1981).

Exactly how these and other proposed enhancements of irrigation systems are to take place, and the ratio of benefits to costs of different strategies, is unclear. The high opportunity cost of capital has influenced the scale of projects and, in turn, the source of water (Rangeley, 1987). To

Table 6.4 Irrigation and drainage in developing market economies (1975) and targets (1990)

	Africa	Latin America	Near East	Asia	Total
Irrigation		*(Thousands of ha)*			
Equipped irrigation area, 1975	2,610	11,749	17,105	60,522	91,986
TARGETS					
New irrigation	960	3,101	4,295	13,848	22,204
Improvements to existing irrigation	783	4,698	9,789	29,718	44,988
of which minor	522	2,349	6,368	17,614	26,843
major	261	2,349	3,421	12,104	18,135
		(Km^3)			
Increased water demand	20	33	44	341	438
Drainage		*(Thousands of ha)*			
Equipped drainage area, 1975	7,044	46,585	18,212	62,501	134,342
Improved targets, 1990	5,900	19,245	9,643	43,396	78,184
in irrigated land	1,177	2,018	7,076	42,152	52,423
on non-irrigated land	4,723	17,227	2,567	1,244	25,761

Source after UN Water Conference (1977)

obtain a cubic kilometre of water through damming costs an estimated $120 million. This is two and a half to four times the capital cost of obtaining an equivalent amount of water from underground reservoirs (Ambroggi, 1980). A high discount rate tends to favour those projects with high operating costs but low capital costs. Hence, pump schemes, with their relatively small capital requirements and moderately high operating costs, have been economically superior to gravity diversion dam schemes. In India, private sector groundwater systems have proliferated in number (power pumps have grown from 85,000 in 1951 to 2.7 million in the 1980s) and shown a much higher rate of return than larger surface projects.

Despite this fact, and the estimated annual deficit arising from irrigation projections of $330 million, the most recent five-year plan in India allocates 69 per cent of its funds to major and medium projects, but only 14 per cent to small-scale irrigation, which is normally served by ground-water (Rogers, 1985). However, it is still argued that despite the economic disadvantages of large projects, they have proved to be more resilient with changing economic fortunes than those with high operating costs, and are less vulnerable to declines in management standards evidenced recently in a number of developing countries (Rangeley, 1987).

Regional examples of supply/demand relations

Egypt

Egypt is unique in the world in its dependence upon and control of a single river – the Nile (see Fig. 6.4). The opening of the Aswan High Dam in

Table 6.5 Estimated cost of water and land development, 1974–85 in millions of dollars (1974 prices)

	Renovation and improvement of existing irrigated area			Equipping new land for irrigation			Development of new arable land		
	Millions of ha	Total estimated cost	Foreign exchange component	Millions of ha	Total estimated cost	Foreign exchange component	Millions of ha	Total estimated cost	Foreign exchange component
Far East	28	11,700	3,500	15	22,000	11,000	24	9,500	500
Near East	12	6,700	2,700	3	7,400	5,000	10	2,500	250
Africa	1	500	200	1	2,400	2,400	34	1,500	570
Latin America	5	2,100	100	4	6,200	2,500	85	12,800	2,500
Total	46	21,000	6,500	23	38,000	20,000	153	30,000	3,820

Source adapted from Lindh (1979)

1969 afforded complete control of Nile Waters (Phase III of David's scheme of river basin development), allowing all of its arable land base to be irrigated (except for a small rainfed coastal band). In the agricultural sector, the control over surface waters has permitted the extension of new

AREAS OF RECLAIMED LAND

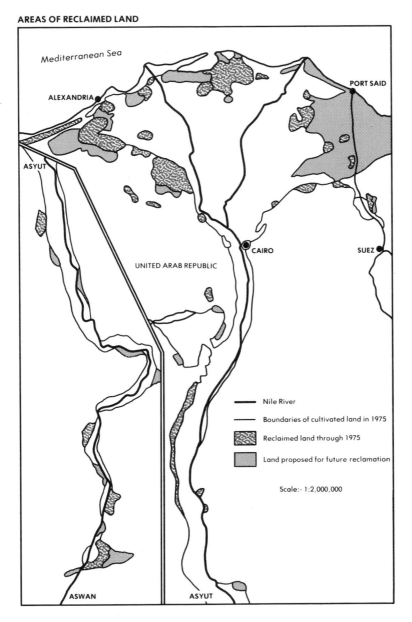

Fig. 6.4 Land reclamation in Egypt 1975
Source USDA (1976)

lands, improved security of supply of water resources, rural electrification and expanded employment opportunities. Given the rapid and expected continued growth in population (2.8 per cent per annum), will these highly regulated and fixed water resources be sufficient to meet the needs of the agricultural sector and domestic and industrial uses?

The average annual flow of the Nile is 84 billion m^3, of which, according to international agreement, 55 billion m^3 are allocated to Egypt, 18.5 to Sudan and 10 billion m^3 for evaporation and seepage. The actual storage capacity of Lake Nasser is 164 billion m^3. Apart from the relatively small quantities of water required for navigation, domestic/industrial and hydroelectric uses (four billion m^3 annually), the total flow is allocated to the agricultural sector (see Table 6.6). In the mid-1970s, agriculture consumed approximately 26 billion m^3, the remainder went directly to return flow, raising water tables and/or increasing groundwater supplies. In a study of the shares of water used for irrigation and drainage in the delta, fully half went toward drainage. Since only about one-half of this drainage is

Table 6.6 Estimated water use from Aswan High Dam, 1974

Item		Amount (billion m^3)
Crop-consumptive use for 6.2 million feddans[a]		26
Losses in the system:		
On-farm	14	
Conveyance	11.2	
Total	———	25.2
Required diversion and direct use from the Nile		51.2
Supplemental water:		
Return flow	2.3	
Reuse of drainage	2.5	
Groundwater	0.4	
Total	———	5.2
Total required release from Aswan Dam for irrigation		46.0
Required released for other uses:		
Industrial, domestic, etc.	1.0	
Navigation and power (January)	3.0	
Total	———	4.0
Pumped into the sea		6.0
1974 release from Aswan High Dam (actual)		56.0

[a] 1 feddan = 0.43 hectares

Source after USDA (1976)

required for leaching purposes, the remainder (7.75 billion m^3) is considered excessive.

The issue of irrigation efficiency thus becomes an important one. Efficiency in the use of water is estimated at between 44 to 58 per cent which, according to a USDA (1976) report, is a very low proportion for a river like the Nile, which lends itself well to the recovery of losses. Part of the problem can be traced to the use of and dependence on age-old irrigation practices. Also, water is treated as a free good with minimum controls. The environmental implications of the inefficient water use (which is examined in detail in the next section and in Chapter 7, which deals with land degradation) are significant. Because of canal seepage and excess applications in the absence of proper drainage systems, water tables have been raised, contributing directly to the waterlogging of the soil and to an increase in salinity levels, mainly in the northern part of the delta (Fig. 6.4). An estimated 840,000 ha are affected by high soil salinity levels in this area.

The water problem in Egypt is not so much a supply problem as a management one. Irrigation efficiencies have considerable scope for improvement. Projects designed to increase the flow of Lake Nasser (the reservoir of the Aswan Dam) are expected to add almost ten billion m^3/year, and groundwater resources, which are now under-utilized, are predicted to add up to five billion m^3/year (Barrada, 1987). The New Valley running along the western side of the Nile from Cairo to Lake Nasser is thought to have good groundwater potential (see Fig. 6.4). By the turn of the century, domestic and industrial demands for water are expected to increase to four billion m^3. At the same time, to meet the food and fibre needs of the burgeoning population (75 million by 2000), cropping intensities and irrigated area must increase. Expansion of irrigated area could prove to be the most intractable problem. In 1897 Egypt possessed 2,076 million irrigated hectares. By 1985, this had increased in net terms to 2,394 – about 2.5 per cent of the total area. Expansion of urban areas on to irrigated land has been an important factor underlying the slow growth in irrigated land. Cultivated area per person is 0.05 today, compared to 0.214 in 1897. In the mid 1980s, the number of land-holdings stands in excess of 2.9 million – the average size of which is 0.84 ha (Barrada, 1987).

The problem with respect to increasing land supply is two-fold. First, the old lands found primarily in the delta and the Nile Valley (representing over 80 per cent of cultivated area) are, as already observed, undergoing various forms of degradation, most of which can be alleviated through better drainage. An exception is the loss of delta lands to the sea. Where the high flow of the Nile once counteracted the erosive effects of the sea, the reduced flow of the Nile as a result of the Aswan Dam leaves an exposed and vulnerable land mass. Second, lack of good arable land with relatively few limitations is 'the primary constraint for horizontal expansion around the Nile and near the delta' (USDA, 1976: 81). For example, lands in the West Coast zone and New Valley depression are generally of Classes III and IV and are unlikely to contribute greatly to enhancement of production. New or reclaimed lands (brought into production since 1952) comprise 16 per cent of land currently cultivated, but contribute only 3 per cent of total national production.

Seen in this context, adequate land resources and not water resources represent the prime constraining input in the expansion of agricultural production. Growth in the future will depend upon intensification strategies that expand productivity without diminishing the productive potential of the land.

United States

In contrast to the situation in Egypt, there has been a dramatic growth in irrigated lands since the turn of the century in the United States. The majority of this growth has taken place in the semi-arid and arid western states, that are west of the 100th meridian. Unlike the eastern half of the United States, this region is unable to sustain high productivity dryland agriculture. Having said this, the eastern half (particularly the states in the south-east and around the Great Lakes) has increased its share of irrigated area from 11 per cent in 1964 to 16 per cent in 1982.

The development of irrigated agriculture throughout the United States is closely tied to the increasing regulation and control of river basin flow through a proliferation of water projects for dams, reservoirs, canals and drainage systems. The institutional framework for much of this development took place through the Bureau of Reclamation which, after its establishment in 1902, was charged with reclaiming arid western lands through irrigation. This it did, with the expansion from 162,000 hectares in 1910 to 4.45 million hectares by 1980. The Bureau also became increasingly involved in supplying water for industrial, municipal, energy and recreational uses, and in major flood-control schemes.

The growth in the water withdrawal and consumption by all of the above uses has placed increasing pressure on a limited resource base. Figure 6.5 illustrates water withdrawals and consumption by functional use. Agriculture accounts for over 40 per cent of all freshwater withdrawals and over 75 per cent of total consumption (USDA, 1987). Because agriculture is a low-value use for water, and given the increased demands by urban and industrial uses for water, it is expected that agriculture's share of total water consumption will decline. Although the consensus is that the United States is not faced with a water-supply crisis, the adequacy of regional supplies is questioned, particularly when adequacy for agriculture is defined in economic as opposed to physical terms.

In 1982 irrigation systems were in place in 20 million hectares, of which 85 per cent were to be found in the seventeen Western states (USDA,

1987). These same states account for approximately 84 per cent of all freshwater consumption in the nation. Surface water use for the western states has changed little since 1955, reflecting the increased cost of new supplies, competition from other sources and the fact that 'relatively little surface water remained to be developed within the areas with the most favourable growing conditions' (Frederick and Hanson, 1982: 71). Under these conditions supply shortfalls were inevitable, particularly when below-average rainfall occurred.

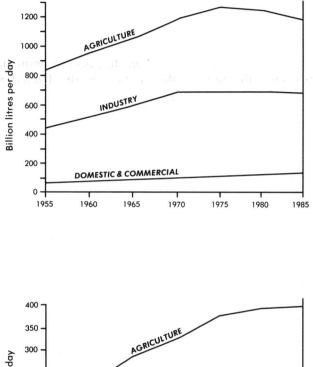

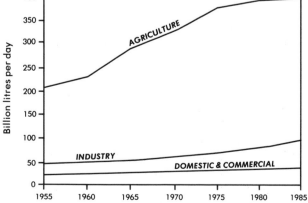

Fig. 6.5 Water withdrawals (top) and water consumption (bottom) by functional use for the United States 1955–85
Source USDA (1987)

Under average rainfall conditions, total water use (which includes instream uses) exceeds streamflow in approximately 66 per cent of the region's irrigated land. Consequently, the growth in irrigated area since the mid-1950s has been fed by groundwater supplies. In 1955 these supplies represented 26 per cent of water withdrawn, and by 1975 their share of withdrawals had reached 39 per cent or 69 million cubic decametres. For both the Northern and Southern Great Plains, the dependency on ground-water sources is close to 80 per cent of total withdrawals (see Table 6.7). The major source of this groundwater is from the Ogallala Aquifer. A variety of technological breakthroughs, such as high-speed engines, turbine

Table 6.7 Ground and surface water withdrawn for Western irrigation, 1950–75 (per 1000 acre-feet)[a]

Region and Source	1950	1955	1960	1965	1970	1975
Northern Plains						
Groundwater	786	1,636	2,839	4,068	6,165	11,209
Surface	2,220	2,292	3,702	2,910	2,950	3,120
Total	3,006	3,929	6,540	6,978	9,115	14,329
Groundwater as percentage of total	26	42	43	58	68	78
Southern Plains						
Groundwater	1,850	7,470	9,252	13,300	9,610	11,100
Surface	3,130	4,173	3,570	2,910	2,910	2,780
Total	4,980	11,643	12,822	16,210	12,520	13,880
Groundwater as percentage of total	37	64	72	82	77	80
Mountain						
Groundwater	5,285	9,906	12,226	11,400	11,311	14,450
Surface	42,300	53,860	45,411	47,200	52,200	50,900
Total	47,585	63,766	57,637	58,600	63,511	65,350
Groundwater as percentage of total	11	16	21	20	18	22
Pacific						
Groundwater	10,270	12,002	11,575	12,830	19,100	19,260
Surface	18,900	27,700	25,365	26,500	29,600	31,600
Total	29,170	39,702	36,940	39,330	48,700	50,860
Groundwater as percentage of total	35	30	31	33	39	38
Seventeen Western states						
Groundwater	18,191	31,014	35,892	41,598	46,186	56,019
Surface	66,550	88,025	78,047	79,520	87,600	88,400
Total	84,741	119,039	113,939	121,118	133,846	144,419
Groundwater as percentage of total	21	26	32	34	35	39

[a] 1 acre-foot = 1.233 cubic decametres
Source after Frederick and Hanson (1982)

centrifugal pumps, centre-pivot sprinkler systems and low-cost fossil fuel, stimulated the growth in use of groundwater supplies. Inasmuch as these groundwater resources are still considered vast, numerous areas are undergoing overdrafts or mining. Figure 6.6 highlights surface and ground-water depletions now or in the near future in excess of 70 per cent. It has been found that 'flows diverted for offstream uses deplete streamflow by more than 70 per cent in 16 of 79 subregions in the contiguous U.S.' (USDA, 1987: 7–3). If groundwater mining is defined as use of groundwa-ter equivalent to 10 per cent or more of annual off-stream consumption, the affected areas roughly correspond to those in Figure 6.6 in which an average year's water use exceeds streamflow (Frederick and Hanson, 1982).

Not only do these overdrafts threaten surface-water flows, but they also contribute to subsidence and salt-water intrusion. They ultimately threaten the viability of many agricultural communities. Perhaps the best example of this problem is in the Texas High Plains. Texas (unlike most Western states) has no formal licensing or prior appropriation of groundwater, so that a doctrine of absolute ownership entitles property owners to pump water at whatever rate they deem necessary. Given the crucial importance

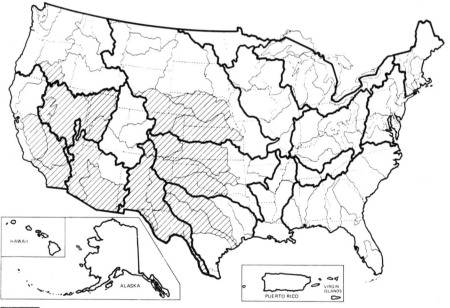

 Indicates subregions where total water use exceeds total streamflow in an average year.

Fig. 6.6 Regions of the United States where total water use exceeds total streamflow in an average year
Source Frederick and Hanson (1982)

of water to the agricultural economy, water has been pumped at rates in excess of replacement, leading to a decline in the volume of groundwater storage, and in some cases to the abandonment of irrigated land. Walker (1980) estimated that annual overdraft of water in the Texas–Oklahoma High Plains area is equivalent to the natural flow of the Colorado River (47,300 million litres/day). Walker expects water pumping to decline by approximately 50 per cent over the next half century.

The limits imposed by supply are economic in nature. A recent study of irrigation costs in the High Plains found that pumping cost increases (from increased fuel and equipment cost) were directly attributable to declining groundwater levels (Sloggett and Mapp, 1984). The rise in cost, and more precisely, the impact upon agriculture, is tied to a variety of factors, including groundwater depth, rates of decline, subsurface features, energy cost, prices of crops, conservation measures and alternative uses for the water.

Since agriculture is a low-value use of water, the growth of more intensive uses is often at the expense of agriculture. In California the value added in agriculture in the use of a cubic kilometre of water is $75 million, compared to $5 billion for industrial use (Ambroggi, 1980). In Arizona, existing and anticipated population pressures on the state water resources during the 1970s led to the passage in 1980 of a comprehensive water-planning law. Agriculture's share of total water consumption is to be reduced to accommodate municipal and industrial needs. Through the introduction of withdrawal fees, metering, specific allocations of water for agriculture and the sale of water rights, the state expects to reduce irrigated area from 0.526 million hectares to 0.324 million hectares by 2020, which should balance water accounts (*The Economist*, 1983).

The common property characteristics of the resource and/or overly generous licensing within the context of historically cheap energy prices are the main source of supply problems and inefficiency, not only for ground-water but also for surface water. The development and control of surface water by the Bureau of Reclamation has rarely required the farmer to pay operating, let alone fixed, costs. In one analysis of federal subsidies for eighteen irrigation districts, subsidies as a percentage of full cost ranged from a low of 57 per cent to a high of 97 per cent (Frederick and Hanson, 1982). Another study by the San Francisco Federal Reserve Bank in 1981 reports that the average price paid by farmers in California's Central Valley for federal water was $4 per cubic decametre, whereas the marginal cost, replacement average cost and historical average cost were $264, $39 and $19 per cubic decametre respectively. The federal subsidy in the Central Valley alone amounted to $1 billion between 1948 and 1981 (*The Economist*, 1983).

When water prices are so low, consumption tends to be pushed to that point where utility approaches zero. Thus, inefficiencies in the use of water are at the heart of the supply problem. Given agriculture's overwhelming share of the western United States' consumption of water, small changes in efficiencies through improved pricing and allocation will allow for significant increases in consumption of other uses. Irrigated area itself, through better conservation of water resources, has the potential for modest increases in size.

India*

India has been remarkably successful since 1970 in expanding food output at a faster rate than population, due in no small part to the growth and improvement in irrigation systems. The control of water resources in river basins, where approximately 80 per cent of the population resides, is essential. With relatively abundant rainfall (averaging 1100 mm/yr), but of a highly seasonal nature (four to five months of monsoonal rain), storage and containment facilities are vital to this control.

Table 6.8 provides estimated water use for 1973/74, and the ultimate potential of water use. As in Egypt, agriculture is the dominant user of water resources, but unlike Egypt, the groundwater share of total use is considerably larger. The ultimate potential of surface water (700 billion m^3) is based upon estimates of future storage capacity, as well as a recognition of hydrologic, geologic and topographical constraints restricting the use of river water. Storage capacity, which stands at about 150 billion m^3, can be enlarged to no more than 350 billion m^3 (but with 100 billion m^3 lost to evaporation). The remaining 450 billion m^3 of the 700 billion m^3 potential will come directly from streamflow. Given current rates of growth in use, it is estimated that the surface potential will be totally committed by 2025.

Table 6.8 Indian water resource use

Water source/use	Ultimate potential	1973/74
	(Billion m^3)	
Surface-water	700	250
Irrigation	510	240
Other uses	190	10
Groundwater	350	130
Irrigation	260	110
Other uses	90	20
Total water use	1,050	380
Irrigation	770	350
Other uses	280	30

Source after Gasser (1981)

*Based upon Gasser, (1981)

Of the fourteen major rivers that account for approximately 85 per cent of total average surface water flow, few if any can be totally controlled as with the Nile. The Brahmaputra River Valley is too narrow to permit the development of adequate storage facilities, with 80–90 per cent of its water escaping to the sea. The Ganges, with its extremely broad, fertile and heavily populated floodplain, makes control of more than 50 per cent of the monsoon flood extremely difficult. Proposals have been made to develop an enlarged ground and surface-water balance for the Indus and Ganges basins. This involves a heavy reliance on groundwater pumping during the dry season, when surface water is scarce, and a dependence on canal deliveries during the flood season. Just as surface-water storage would play an integral role in storing surplus supplies, so would underground storage systems which could be artificially enhanced during the flood season.

While approximately 80 per cent of the average annual flow of the twelve other major rivers can be controlled, only about one-half of the medium and minor river flow can be stored because of the periodic nature of the rainfall combined with poor sites for storage. If the full potential outlined above is to be achieved, significant inter-basin transfers will have to occur from the Brahmaputra to the Ganges, from the Himalayas to Rajasthan, and from the rivers of the Western Ghats, to the eastern-flowing rivers of the Deccan and Southern Plains region.

Groundwater resources are physically vast, perhaps three times the usable potential, but economically inaccessible in many regions of the country. Most of the development of groundwater resources is expected to take place in the heavily-populated large river valleys and in the alluvial plains of the Punjab, Uttar Pradesh, Bihar and West Bengal.

Management problems abound in the use and development of water resources for irrigation purposes in India. Waterlogging is a common problem in the Indus and Ganges basins, as are alkalinity and salinity in the South. Poor water quality, the result of salt/fertilizer-laden return-flow irrigation waters and domestic pollution, has seriously contaminated an estimated 70 per cent of the usable water. The efficiency of surface-water use in irrigation is about 43 per cent, compared to 70 per cent for groundwater use. Like Egypt and the United States water rates do not accurately reflect the fixed and operating costs of irrigation systems, although the methods of determining cost to the farmer appear to vary – from systems based on crop area and volume of water used, to increments based on the benefit to the farmer and to the state.

As noted previously, despite the superior economic performance of groundwater systems, the state has allocated the bulk of its water investment to large-scale diversion and storage schemes, which serve multiple uses such as flood control and increasing security of water supply for domestic/industrial purposes.

146

Ecological aspects of irrigation

Ecologically, irrigation systems can be viewed from two contrasting perspectives. Without doubt, the adoption of irrigation systems has permitted the growth in cultivated area for a variety of cultivars (particularly rice), expanded yields and increased overall cropping intensities. The net effect of these changes has been an overall growth in food production and a tremendous increase in the carrying capacity of the land. Irrigation systems may also have a beneficial effect upon the landscape by improving ground cover and reducing the effects of wind and water erosion. From a very different perspective, through modification of the groundwater and water–salt balance, irrigation has contributed over the long term to the destruction of a significant amount of high-quality arable land. It has also contributed to a number of off-site environmental problems, such as contamination of water quality and the transmission of water-borne diseases. While the benefits still far exceed the costs, the trade-offs in the future may not favour the growth in irrigated systems as they did in the past.

In this section, we examine selectively some crop–water relationships concerning potential yield and production benefits of irrigation, and follow with a brief evaluation of some of the main on-site and off-site environmental costs or externalities created by irrigation systems.

Crop–water relationships

In Chapter 2, examples were given for various cereals of potential versus actual or average yields. The gap between the two was explained in terms of the existence of pests, weeds, diseases and unfavourable physico-chemical environments. This last factor, which reflects a variety of growth-limiting factors (principally nutrients, heat and water), accounted for over two-thirds of the shortfall in yield. Lieth (1987) has observed that temperature is the chief limiting factor affecting net primary production poleward of 40° latitude, whereas precipitation exercises the greatest control equatorward.

The main purpose of irrigation is to regulate the moisture content of the unsaturated root zone according to crop requirements. Water requirements among crops vary considerably in terms of *quantity* (rice requiring twice the amount of water on average than wheat, and high-yield variety (HYV) almost twice traditional varieties of grain), *quality* (e.g., salt-sensitivity), and *timing* (with consistency in application far more significant for rice than for wheat or millet). Boyer (1987) has argued, however, that even with successful control and application of water, where there is a basic equality between actual crop evapotranspiration (ETa) and maximum crop evapotranspiration (ETm) crops can undergo daily water deficiencies and hence are considered water-stressed. 'The effect occurs because the rate of water loss by the crop exceeds the rate of water gain sufficiently to cause dehydration that inhibits metabolic processes' (Boyer, 1987: 233). He goes on to add that the deficiency cannot be alleviated by additional rainfall or catchment control. Instead, plants need to be modified genetically so that physiological and metabolic features of the plant will be more moisture-stress tolerant.

Leaving aside the fact that irrigation does not meet the total water needs of crops, it nevertheless meets the majority of those needs, allowing for higher yields and multiple cropping. The intensification of crop production through various levels of fertilizer application and water control has boosted productivity significantly in Asian countries (see Fig. 6.7). Not only have these strategies allowed for almost a trebling in individual crop yields, but they have nearly doubled harvested area, contributing to a four-fold increase in productivity (Ambroggi, 1980). Consequently, Japan requires only about one-sixth of the land that India does to meet the average person's dietary requirements.

Irrigation waters should not be seen only as a means of alleviating water stress. Where HYV crop hybrids require more water than traditional

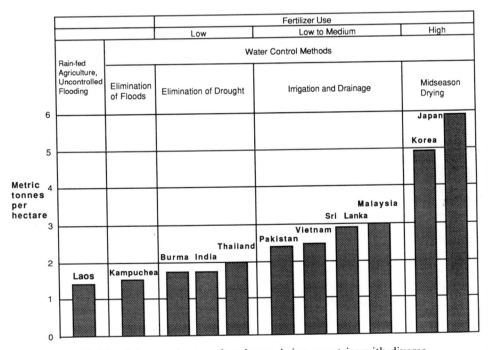

Fig. 6.7 Yields of rice per hectare for eleven Asian countries with diverse agricultural technologies
Source adapted from Water, R.P. Ambroggi (1980) © Scientific American Inc. All rights reserved.

148

varieties, they also require nutrients. It is estimated that irrigation increases the plant's response to fertilizers from 25 to 100 per cent. In Figure 6.8, we are able to examine the individual and combined effects upon yields of grains in Pakistan of changes in these two basic inputs – fertilizer and water. Successively greater applications of water cause significant upward shifts (although at a decreasing rate) in the fertilizer–yield response curve. The individual curves reveal diminishing marginal returns to fertilizer inputs, regardless of the water inputs.

Environmental effects

Although irrigation systems share the same basic purpose – the provision of water for agricultural production – they vary enormously in their scale

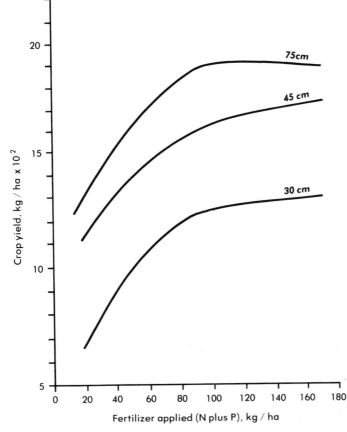

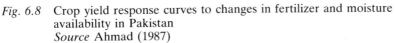

Fig. 6.8 Crop yield response curves to changes in fertilizer and moisture availability in Pakistan
Source Ahmad (1987)

and type (gravity versus pressure), reliance on surface and groundwater sources, methods of distribution and conveyance, water quality and efficiency. The real complexity, however, of irrigation systems arises not so much from technical considerations, which are indeed demanding, but from the fact that they create changes in all major ecosystem regimes, leading to significant and often adverse changes in soil, water, vegetative and animal systems.

Changes to aquatic environment

The perennial water bodies, created through the development of drainage ditches, canals and reservoirs, all of which are rich in nutrients and organic matter, are an excellent host environment for weeds and algae. Numerous examples exist (Mussayes Project in Iraq and Aswan Dam in Egypt) where the growth of hydrophilous plants has seriously reduced the efficiency of storage and distribution systems. There is a close association between organic growth in the aquatic environment and the spread of insects and pathogens for both plants and animals. Irrigation affords an opportunity for the establishment and migration of locusts and other insects in environments which normally would be inhospitable. Weeds provide a protective and nutritional environment for the Bulinus snail, which is an intermediate host for the debilitating urinary and intestinal disease schistosomiasis. The disease can spread rapidly, afflicting as much as 80–90 per cent of the resident population (Worthington, 1977).

Irrigation water also provides an environment for mosquito larvae, which are responsible for the transmission of malaria and yellow fever, common in such highly-irrigated areas as Egypt, Syria, Iraq and Iran. The growth and spread of the tsetse-fly, the vector for the transmission of sleeping sickness, is intricately tied to modifications of the water balance in regions such as in the Sudan, from Lake Nasser, and in Zambia from the Kariba Reservoir. Other diseases associated with the spread of irrigation canals include cholera, dysentery, hepatitis and typhoid.

Modification of soil and water regimes

The storage, conveyance and field application of irrigation waters alters local and regional water balances in the hydrological cycle. A critical interface for the exchange of moisture between surface and groundwater zones is the unsaturated root zone or soil moisture zone, the intended destination of irrigated water. This zone has been described as the 'heart of the continental branch of the hydrological cycle' (Worthington, 1977: 19). Alterations in the moisture content of this area lead to the following changes in salt and water regimes: modification of the atmospheric branch of the cycle; modification of surface run-off; modification of the groundwater regime; and modification of water quality beyond the soil moisture zone.

While irrigation leads to higher levels of evapotranspiration and possibly higher precipitation levels, locally and regionally, the deleterious effects of irrigation on the productive potential of the food system originate from modifications to run-off and groundwater (Worthington, 1977). Changes to the hydrologic cycle take many forms. In the Kabini project of India, the construction of a dam required a submersion area of 2430 hectares. By the time lands were cleared to relocate displaced villagers, a total of 12,150 hectares of primeval forest had been cut in the catchment area. Local rainfall in the area declined from 152 cm to 114 cm. Increased rates of siltation seriously reduced the life of the project (Jayal, 1985). Before the construction of the Aswan Dam in Egypt, the annual flood of the Nile Valley brought with it important nutrients (minerals and trace elements) for the adjoining fields and important sediments for the continued stability and growth of the delta (approximately 100 million tonnes/yr). With the construction of the dam, the majority of the sediment remained in the reservoir – reducing its capacity – and nutrients, although still available through irrigation water, showed a marked decline. The decline in streamflow in the Nile was such that alluvium deposition was not sufficient to counteract the effects of coastal erosion.

Other effects of decreased streamflow include the raising of water temperatures, decline in oxygen content of water and a general diminishment in the number and quality of animal and plant habitats, particularly in estuarine environments. Irrigation waters themselves, through gravity and flood systems, often increase sediment loads in streams and reservoirs through sheet and rill erosion. As we shall see in Chapter 7, in the United States the inefficient or excessive use of irrigated water and its application in particularly erosion-prone areas that are hilly and sandy (in the Northern Great Plains) has added significantly to off-site costs in the form of siltation of streams and rivers, and on-site costs in terms of lost nutrients and deterioration in the physical structure of the land.

The process of secondary salinization, alkalization and waterlogging of soils in irrigated lands (to be discussed in detail in Chapter 7) affects an estimated 50 per cent of all lands currently under irrigation, and is responsible for the abandonment of 20–25 million hectares (Kovda, 1979). Irrigation systems alter the water balance and water–salt balance in the soil moisture zone through changes in groundwater levels by two principal means, the impact of which will depend upon climate, soil characteristics, surface cover, terrain, mineral content of subsurface materials, and existing groundwater levels. One means is where seepage from reservoirs and distribution systems (because of uninsulated surfaces) recharges groundwater and leads to increases in horizontal groundwater flow, directly increasing water tables and waterlogging in discharge areas. Since much of the substratum is rich in soda, sodium and other salts, the water is easily mineralized. The evaporation of groundwater brought to the surface by capillary action concentrates the salts in the soil moisture zone.

The other means of affecting water and salt balances is where excess surface irrigation water percolates through the soil moisture zone to the groundwater level. This process of negative accretion (as opposed to positive accretion with upward movement of water) leaches out salts in the root zone through a continuous downward movement of water so long as drainage is adequate. If inadequate, water tables will rise, leading to waterlogging and excess concentrating of salt near the surface.

Kovda (1977) has argued that it is groundwater levels and the mineralization of groundwater that are the chief sources of secondary salinization and not saline irrigation water. This is not to say that salinity of irrigated waters is unimportant. Research in the Soviet Union has shown during the 1970s that mineralization of water grew from 0.2–0.3 g/l to 0.6–1.0 g/l, largely as a result of the increasing role of evaporation, reduced stream flow, return flow from irrigated areas and wastes from urban centres. Under favourable drainage, water with a salt concentration of 2–7 g/l can be used for irrigation. The higher the concentrations, of course, the greater the necessity for leaching and proper drainage (Kovda, 1977).

In both of the above examples of alterations to the water balance (seepage and excess water), proper drainage systems are required to lower the water table in low-lying discharge areas below the equilibrium level. This is also required in the irrigation areas themselves, to prevent waterlogging and the movement of salts to the active root zone or soil surface. Reducing excess applications of water, but at the same time meeting leaching requirements, would also reduce waterlogging problems.

Given the presence of salts in the soils and substrata of many irrigated regions of the world, both streamflow and the return flow of irrigated water tend to have high salt concentrations. For the Colorado River, an international agreement between Mexico and the United States has required the latter to desalinate downstream waters entering Mexico. Similar transboundary problems exist along the Euphrates River.

The excess water from irrigation systems also becomes contaminated by fertilizers, such as nitrates and phosphates, and pesticides, affecting groundwater and/or run-off to streams, rivers and lakes. Most of this non-point pollution can be traced to agricultural origins. Another aspect regarding water quality deserves mentioning. Excessive pumping or mining of groundwater supplies, particularly in coastal areas, can contribute to salt-water intrusion into aquifers, seriously limiting their usefulness for irrigation or urban/industrial purposes.

Human dimensions of irrigation

Just as irrigation development creates significant changes in the natural ecology of a region, it also creates changes in the human ecology and social structure of a region. Agricultural development, through expansion and improvements in irrigation systems, has numerous economic, social, political and psychological objectives. Balancing these numerous objectives is an age-old problem with different emphases reflecting different conditions, requirements and exigencies of the host country or region. Although highly simplified, projects in developed countries tend to be oriented towards production enhancement, with little emphasis (Japan is an exception) on the issues of rural employment and poverty, self-sufficiency and the overall improvement in social welfare. It is exactly these considerations that feature prominently in the justification for improvements to or extensions of the irrigation systems in developing countries. Enhancement of food production is also a primary concern, particularly as a national goal, but it is in concert with these other objectives.

As previously discussed, the choice of type and scale of project depends on the relative economic advantages of large-scale surface-fed systems versus small-scale groundwater-fed systems, in conjunction with the potential for exploitation of either of these sources of water. The human/social impact of these schemes will depend on the type of project. Large-scale capital-intensive systems are the most disruptive in terms of people and resources, whereas small-scale groundwater projects normally build upon the existing social structure (Yotopoulos, 1980). It follows that the context or milieu within which development occurs is also important. Those regions which already have high-density populations will have to make more adjustments than their lower-density counterparts, regardless of the scale/type of system used.

Exactly how various objectives will be achieved and, in turn, how successful they will be at meeting social objectives in the long term will depend on choice of development strategies. Development strategies may favour traditional holdings and tenure systems. Alternatively, they may expand the opportunities for participation in agriculture through land extension. Or, they may favour certain agro-industries and agro-businesses. The implications of each strategy for farm size, labour productivity, distribution of gains, crops grown (cash or food) and general agricultural efficiency will be different. A number of examples from developing countries illustrate interrelationships discussed above, and how they benefit and improve the welfare of the rural population.

In Asia, the problem of the land-poor is particularly acute. The land-poor are those with no land who work as labourers on a seasonal basis, or those whose holdings are too small to sustain them (Silliman and Lenton, 1987). Women represent a significant and growing proportion of this group. Since the land-poor depend upon land-owners for employment, the nature of the relationship will determine future employment opportunities and the trend toward mechanization.

One of the fundamental dilemmas in irrigation development is that the social structure may not exist to provide for the diffusion of benefits to the land-poor. The established social order in Southern India, for example, with its caste hierarchy, is prejudicial to certain landless groups. Similarly, in pre-revolution Iran, agricultural employment or sharecropping was based largely on the largesse of relatively few landlords. Silliman and Lenton (1987), in a review of the literature on the direct and indirect benefits of irrigation to the land-poor (mostly in Asia), have suggested on the other hand that there is a positive relationship between irrigation and employment. In their view, there are both short-term employment opportunities derived from the construction of the irrigation system itself, and long-term employment from increases in cropping intensities. This is despite the fact that much of the potential, particularly with HYVs, has not been realized.

In another study of the equity effects of irrigation in South-East Asia, it was found that irrigation increased the income of all factors of production (Rosegrant, 1986). Large farms in Indonesia, the Philippines and Thailand have not benefited more than small farmers and landless labourers. The increase in labour income is closely tied to the change in cropping intensity induced by irrigation. In Thailand, income to hired labour is 30 per cent higher with irrigation.

Table 6.9 categorizes some of the major indirect gains and losses to the land-poor through irrigation development. Mechanization plays an important role in affecting the land-poor. The land-intensifying mechanization tends to improve employment by expanding cropping intensities, whereas the labour-displacing reflects a shift to equipment which decreases the total demand for labour.

The relationship between land-poor and land-owner, as well as the development strategy chosen, influences the benefits to the farmer. In China, until the late 1970's communes served as basic administrative and organizational units for major irrigation projects, involving the integration of large and small dams, reservoirs and canals. These systems, although uneconomic in the strict sense, afforded major opportunities for achieving self-sufficiency in agriculture – including fish and fowl production – and meeting other needs such as drinking water, as well as a variety of industrial and power uses (Yotopoulos, 1980). Despite a push towards mechanization, a growing labour force has been absorbed into the agricultural sector without sacrificing productivity per unit of labour. As Silliman and Lenton (1987: 166) argued: 'China has also shifted the demand for labour upward, from less to more productive and renumerative tasks.'

In Iran, the Dez Irrigation Project (DIP) in Khuzestan attempted to address both social and economic goals with a variety of programmes favouring traditional small-scale agriculture and modern large-scale cash-crop agri-business (Ehlers, 1977). The programme highlighted some basic incompatibilities in terms of meeting these objectives (see Table 6.10). Except for a relatively few villages and a small percentage of the total area, the region was transformed from 'backward and small-scale peasant farming to spectacular large-scale and market-oriented agri-business'

(Ehlers, 1977: 90).

While the small-scale traditional farming sector, previously dominated by sharecroppers, was able to expand its labour force with irrigation, its productivity per unit of land and labour remained low. The modern agricultural enterprises were comprised of three systems: agro-industries – state-run sugar plantations; agri-business – large-scale, foreign-owned, highly-mechanized, cash-crop enterprises; and farm corporations – or large-scale, highly-mechanized, collective farm enterprise controlled by an agricultural shareholder's company. It was concluded that although the last two enterprises were able to meet the demand for agricultural products, this could only be accomplished with a diminished work-force. Only in the case of agro-industries was it possible to realize and combine the advantages of large-scale market-oriented farming and the employment of a large rural labour force (Ehlers, 1977). In this context, type of ownership system and approach to mechanization were key factors in affecting the social benefits of irrigation development in Iran.

Employment opportunities for the landless or land-poor in many Asian countries can also be directly enhanced by irrigation through: (1) construction, operation and maintenance of irrigation systems; (2) approaches that permit the landless to own irrigation projects and sell water; (3) the allocation of water rights to the landless; and (4) allocation of land to the landless in new irrigation projects (Silliman and Lenton, 1987).

In countries where labour is in shorter supply than land, as in the Sudan, the last of the above four means of improving employment and social welfare of people has particular relevance. In Africa, Sudan ranks second only to Egypt in terms of the size of its irrigated area (1.9 million hectares). The largest of the irrigation projects is the Gezira scheme which covers nearly 800,000 hectares. Begun originally as an experimental pump scheme for growing cotton in 1911, the project allowed for the settlement and cultivation of new lands with the establishment of a systematic gravity irrigation system. Agreements with Egypt over water allocation allowed for large capital investments in storage, distribution systems and infrastructure. The scheme initially benefited a large number of Bedouin settlers by formalizing access to the land to grow food crops in return for their labour and a cotton crop. During the 1960s and 1970s an attempt was made to diversify the crop base of the scheme through the production of wheat, rice and sorghum. The push towards import-substitution stalled in 1978 when the World Bank recommended an increase in cotton production to offset balance of payments problems (Bennet, 1987).

A large seasonal work-force of three-quarters of a million for the Gezira and nearby Rahad cotton scheme became increasingly dependent upon a highly volatile commodity. With the decline in cotton prices and the lack of access to other land because of the rise in importance of mechanized agri-business farming in rain-fed areas, these seasonal workers are becoming increasingly marginalized. The highly-centralized and authoritarian

Table 6.9 Indirect gains and losses to the land poor

Type of gain	Who gains	Under what conditions
(1) Increase in employment in construction of irrigation projects	Male and female agricultural labourers	Labour-intensive construction methods
(2) Increase in number of days of employment, and levelling off of peaks in agricultural employment	Male and female agricultural labourers	Irrigation-induced agricultural intensification
(3) Increase in wage rates for agricultural labour	Male and female agricultural labourers	Irrigation-induced agricultural intensification; no surplus labour to keep wages from rising
(4) Growth in nonfarm employment	Male and female agricultural labourers	Irrigation-induced agricultural intensification
(5) Return migration	Male and female agricultural labourers	Irrigation-induced agricultural intensification
(6) Lower food prices	All sections of rural society but particularly the poor (who spend a disproportionate amount of their income on food).	Payment in cash rather than kind
(7) Non-agricultural use of water, including uses that improve health	Those living close to major canals and distributaries	Year-round irrigation, with access by villagers to canals or groundwater

Table 6.9 (cont.)

Type of loss	Who loses	Under what conditions
(1) Increase in land prices	Marginal farmers pushed off land; landless tenants	Actual or anticipated irrigation-induced agricultural intensification
(2) Market competition between irrigated and rainfed farmers	Marginal rainfed farmers	Irrigation-induced agricultural intensification
(3) Displacement because of irrigation construction	Those located in areas marked for reservoir sites, etc.	Inadequate compensation structures
(4) Increase unpaid workloads for women	Women	
(5) Increase in water-borne diseases	Particularly agricultural workers	Presence of endemic waterborne diseases; lack of preventive health measures
(6) Labour displacement	Agricultural workers displaced by mechanical threshing, herbicides, etc.	Effect of irrigation-induced mechanization greater than that of increased productivity
(7) Waterlogging and salinity	Small farmers, sharecroppers displaced by induced waterlogging and salinity	Irrigation-induced waterlogging and salinity

Note Certain groups of people may be doubly or triply disadvantaged
Source after Silliman and Lenton (1987)

Table 6.10 Economic and social effects of different types of agriculture

	Agricultural productivity	Effects of industrialization	Development of human labour-force
Agro-industries	+	+	+
Agribusiness	+	+	−
Farm corporations	+	○	−
Traditional farming	○	○	+

Key
+ Positive development
− Negative development
○ No changes
Source after Ehlers (1977)

Gezira irrigation scheme may be run in an efficient fashion as Yotopoulos (1980) suggests. Nevertheless, it has failed to provide the basic means either through direct food crops or higher incomes to improve the welfare of the indigenous population.

Management issues

In this section we examine some of the basic issues relating to the improved management of water resources. To ensure adequate supplies of water to meet present and future demands will require a mixture of demand and supply management. Increased efforts will be required to alter society's water requirements, particularly through efficiency gains and to increase the usable supply of water.

Irrigation performance

Despite the impressive production achievements of irrigated agriculture during the last quarter century, the vast majority of irrigated systems have not performed according to expectations or potential. Performance can be evaluated in many different ways, but generally it refers to yield and cropping intensity enhancement, as well as to extension of irrigation systems to new lands. The failure to achieve expected growth in productivity and extension of irrigated area generally is seen as a water allocation problem in which management, and not ultimate physical supply, is the key issue. In most regions, neither physical nor economic limits have been approached, even though a number of regions are on the increasing cost section of the water-supply curve. Hence, the supply of water has not been the chief constraint affecting the performance of irrigation systems. At least three dominant recurring aspects arise in discussions of water allocation problems: (1) the efficiency and effectiveness of water use; (2)

environmental aspects of irrigation development and operation; and (3) the
reliability and predictability of irrigation waters.

Efficiency and effectiveness

The efficiency and effectiveness of water use, particularly as they are
affected by the operation and maintenance of a system, are by far the most
critical concerns in water management. Efficiency has a direct bearing on
the other basic issues. Effectiveness generally refers to the degree to which
irrigation systems have fulfilled various social, economic or political goals,
while efficiency – a narrower concept – normally refers to the productivity
or balance between output and inputs of a system. Systems may be
efficient without being effective (Widstrand, 1980).

Irrigation water-use efficiency can be defined in a number of ways. Most
commonly, it refers to the percentage of the quantity of water diverted
from the original source which actually reaches the root zone. Against this
'project' or overall definition of efficiency are distribution efficiency and
farm efficiency. The former represents the percentage of diverted water
from the original source which reaches the irrigated area, while the latter
refers to the percentage of water under a farmer's control which is
effectively used by crops (Worthington, 1977). In the United States, for
example, project efficiencies average 41 per cent, distribution or conveyance systems average 78 per cent, and on-farm efficiencies average 53
per cent.

In most developing countries, because of higher rates of evaporation and
poorly-designed and insulated reservoirs, efficiency levels tend to be much
lower. In the Indus Valley 106 out of 175 million cubic decametres are
diverted into a distribution and storage system. Approximately 3.2 million
farms on 13 million hectares received 79 million cubic decametres from the
diversions and another 32 million cubic decametres from groundwater
supplies, for a total of 111 million cubic decametres. Of this total, 43
million are lost from poorly-maintained earth channels from the public
canal system to the farmers' fields and 68 million decametres are left to the
farmer, of which 30 million are lost in field applications. Hence, only 38
million cubic decametres ever reach the crops (Widstrand, 1980).

Efficiency of water use must also be considered at the level of the actual
plant. As we have seen, quantity and timing are critical to achieve high
yields and cropping intensities. All too often water is applied excessively
and/or at the wrong time. The choice of the most efficient-water use
strategy is not a simple one, since it depends upon and is conditioned by
irrigation technology, energy costs, cropping patterns, soil characteristics
and rainfall patterns, to name just a few. Where water is a limiting factor,
the choice often becomes one of maximizing returns per unit of irrigated
water. In Iraq water has been applied over a large surface to allow more
farmers to benefit from irrigation. However, in numerous other areas, such

as South-East Asia and Egypt, the strategy is to maximize returns per unit land.

The Environment

Efficiency problems resulting from the operation and maintenance of irrigation systems manifest themselves environmentally in a number of ways, such as excessive pumping and diversions leading to waterlogging, and salinization and alkalization of the soil. But the environmental aspects of irrigation are compounded by poor initial planning and design of these systems. The most obvious and recurrent of the design problems is lack of adequate drainage and return-flow networks. In developing and developed countries alike, drainage has been of secondary importance – to be accommodated once the irrigation system becomes operational. Even in the Central Valley of California, the most intensively irrigated area of the United States, areas such as the Tulare Sub-basin have no natural outlet or drainage, leading to an alarming increase in salinity and high concentrations of selenium. Numerous examples exist in India and Pakistan, where the bulk of development funds for irrigation went to storage and distribution systems, but not to drainage, seriously weakening the long-term viability of the projects.

Reliability

The third theme frequently discussed in water allocation problems is the reliability of water supply. Although irrigation systems are designed to improve water availability, many are plagued in total or in part by unpredictable flows, making optimal use of water for plant growth a rarity. While some reliability problems can be traced to the design of systems with inadequate storage facilities, and competition from alternative uses such as power development, there are enormous bottlenecks and shortfalls in supply created by poor management and administration of the ongoing operation of the system. The most typical source of unreliability in South Asia is over-watering at the head of the source (much of which is consumptive use of water), with a commensurate decline in water availability in the lower reaches of the system. Other factors contributing to unreliability relate to under-utilization of groundwater supplies, which seriously limits cropping intensities, and progressive land fragmentation, which requires expansion in the number of distribution systems and contributes to further losses of water (Widstrand, 1980).

System design and operation

Hardware bias

All three aspects of water-allocation problems are intricately linked to problems in the design, operation and maintenance of systems. There is a

160

growing consensus that most of these problems derive from the failure of both market and non-market institutions to design and administer irrigation systems with efficiency and equity goals in mind. Bhuiyan (1987) argued that there is an inherent 'hardware bias' in the development of irrigation systems such that the means or technique for the capture and distribution of water becomes the overwhelming emphasis, with little regard given to the need for irrigation institutions and their role in development of software (see Fig. 6.9). Such mechanistic approaches, which assume that irrigation systems are almost self-regulating and that the farmer's behaviour is rational, tend to repeat the same mistakes over and over again, in part because of poor ex-ante and almost non-existent ex-post evaluations. Ecological and social ramifications of irrigation projects are

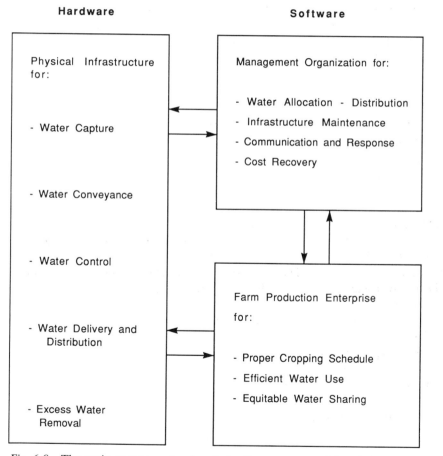

Fig. 6.9 The main components of an irrigation system model and their major functions in relation to system performance
Source after Bhuiyan (1987)

161

given little attention. Given these shortcomings in institutional arrangements, it is useful to examine some of the more salient market and non-market features and lessons which can be learned from these experiences to improve the system.

The role of the market

In most countries, water is treated as an open-access resource and as a social good with only nominal charges attached to its use. All open-access or common-property resources have traditionally been subject to varying degrees of misuse, over-exploitation and third-party effects. With water, these problems take the form of excessive consumption or mining of groundwater, waterlogging of fields, excessive return flows, lowering of water quality and siltation of dams and canals. While water may have many of the characteristics associated with open-access resources, it is very much a commodity the supply of which is often contingent on large and sustained levels of investment. As a commodity it has economic value, and that (scarcity) value should be reflected in the costs associated with its production and use.

The existence of large-scale subsidies, as we saw in the case of irrigation development in the American West and the use of average cost calculations, have meant that the cost to the user is far below its replacement. In the construction of the Auburn Dam in the Siena foothills of California, supplies of irrigation water are expected to cost $51/cubic decametre. Yet, the US Bureau of Reclamation is proposing to average this cost into total regional supply, which will increase average cost from $4 to $15/cubic decametre – still only a third of the cost to provide the water (Rogers, 1985). Generally, the costs recovered from irrigation schemes barely cover operation and maintenance, let alone fixed capital costs. Hence, users of water tend to undervalue the resource, leading to excessive use and its mis-allocation.

By introducing a levy or charge on the use of irrigation water so that it reflects its marginal cost (the actual cost of producing it without averaging), a number of important goals would be achieved: (1) it would provide a basis for the recovery of financial cost and the maximization of benefits for society; (2) it would encourage water conservation; and (3) it would provide a tax on those who benefit most from the use of irrigation (Widstrand, 1980). There is no doubt that higher pricing would affect the demand for the commodity. Research into water use in agriculture in the United States shows that there is a definite decrease in demand as the price of water increases, with demand elasticities ranging from −0.3 to −2. Direct evidence of the relationship between price and water conservation is to be found in the higher levels of water-use efficiency (and higher marginal value products) in the use of groundwater, where pumping charges are borne by the farmer, as compared to surface-water systems, where generally they are not. Moreover, not only do higher prices lead to greater efficiencies in the use of water, but they also lead to production of higher-value crops and a greater emphasis on multiple cropping patterns (Rogers, 1985).

Reliance on a market price for water to encourage conservation, promote efficiency and reflect the cost of production is plagued by a complex of problems including: variations in the quality of water, third-party effects, lack of control over access (free-rider problem), cost of meters and inexact nature of distribution systems. Not surprisingly, flat rates have been popular, but these do little to diminish the demand for water.

Of equal significance, however, is the fact that reliance on pricing to achieve conservation and higher efficiency could be regressive in socio-economic terms (Rogers, 1985). Irrigation development fulfils many objectives, one of which is to reduce rural poverty. By increasing efficiency, one does not necessarily increase effectiveness of irrigation programmes. A number of highly undesirable consequences could follow from the implementation of market-value systems for pricing. In strict agricultural terms, it is unclear what would be the impact on the viability of the agricultural sector of additional costs of production. If markets are available it may encourage a shift to intensive or higher-value crops. More importantly, very poor farmers may not be able to afford higher costs for water, and so lose their land to wealthier farmers.

Institutional control and decision-making

Problems associated with reliance on the market underline the need in all countries for an *ad hoc* approach to the institutional regulation of water supply. Approaches will vary according to the level of economic development, type of economic system, relative scarcity of water, the availability of recurrent financing, labour supply and concentration of decision-making and control. In developing countries, farmers' groups, associations and co-operatives play different roles in water management because of different levels of responsibility *vis-à-vis* the central water authority. In China, a high level of autonomy and independence has been achieved by the peasant in irrigation development. The emphasis is on co-operation and on the use of irrigation to further the process of rural development and social transformation. But the applicability/transferability of this and other approaches (e.g., the Taiwanese water users' associations) to other countries such as India or Bangladesh, is in doubt, if for no other reason than the large number of small land-holdings that are currently organized under farmers' associations. The transfer to modern co-operatives and associations has been successful in large centralized irrigation systems such as those in the Sudan and Egypt. Widstrand (1980) observed, however, that in other African countries, the traditional social groupings along class or tribal lines often reject the adoption of modern co-operatives.

The performance and success of irrigation projects is also influenced by the place of the farmer in the overall decision-making and chain of command. Bhuiyan (1987) has noted that one of the reasons for the poor performance of irrigation systems is the lack of direct input by farmers in decision-making, and of communication between the farmer and the water agency. A different model has been tried for small irrigation projects in the Philippines. Although the project may be agency-developed, it is community-owned and managed, with farmers participating not only in the direct operation and management of the system, but also in initial design.

The management of water supply in such a way as to achieve a high level of efficiency and to meet many of the diverse goals expected of irrigation development requires thorough planning, including knowledge of various consequences of, and an administrative framework for, decision-making, establishment of standards and rules, financing and general allocation of water. Even having established this set of institutions, irrigation is still subject to the vagaries of climate (short- and long-term), the price of agricultural commodities, and general economic conditions. Despite the long history of irrigated agriculture, important questions remain unanswered regarding such things as the appropriate scale of development, large or small; the desirable form of decision-making, centralized or decentralized; the emphasis to be placed on new or old irrigation systems, and the importance attached to other uses of water.

Summary

Water is an important limiting factor in food production in many regions of the world. The growth and spread of irrigation systems has been aimed at easing those limits by redressing the balance of water supply over space and time. Irrigated agriculture's ability to enhance yield and increase cropping intensities has consistently increased its share (a disproportionate share based on land area) of overall food production. This share is expected to increase further as numerous development strategies in Third World countries are aimed at improving and/or extending irrigated agriculture. Whether these development strategies will be successful at creating sustainable systems depends among other things upon reconciling an inherently fixed supply of water with a growing demand, from a variety of sectors, while maintaining the environment. This is the major challenge facing these systems requiring a healthy balance between development and management.

Important development issues relate to the scale of projects and the method of water supply. Whereas small-scale lift-pump schemes are flexible, accessible and normally have a more favourable benefit-cost ratio *vis-à-vis* other types of projects, they are contingent upon the availability of groundwater. In contrast, large-scale gravity-fed or diversion schemes have high initial capital outlays and are capable of supplying not only irrigation water but hydro-electricity which can serve as the basis for rural industrialization. A formidable barrier to expansion of irrigation systems in China and the United States is the cost or economic supply of controlling additional water resources. Most low-cost sites have been developed, declines in groundwater levels have increased pumping charges and alternative users are able and willing to pay more for the water. Combine these conditions with the already large foreign debt situation of many Third World countries and the development prospects for new irrigation systems diminish.

Just as water supply in itself may not be the chief factor impeding irrigation development, similarly supply is not the main factor affecting the performance of irrigation systems. Here management is seen as the critical factor underlying numerous water-allocation problems. These problems were examined in terms of: (1) efficiency and effectiveness; (2) environmental aspects; and (3) reliability and predictability of water flow. Improvements in efficiency were seen as a form of demand management and one of the most important changes to be made if agriculture is to have sufficient water supplies for the future. While irrigation normally increases the carrying capacity of the land, it is also responsible for large-scale degradation of fertile land through waterlogging, salinization and alkalization. Inefficient design and applications of water, seepage and poor drainage limit the effectiveness of the system, while contributing to environmental deterioration, decreased life of the project through sedimentation and the transmission of water-borne diseases. Reliability problems are also linked to inefficient and excessive use of water near the source of the system.

The human dimensions of irrigation development and management are equally complex. Irrigation has the potential to increase returns to land, labour and other inputs across a large range of farm sizes and conditions. The landless poor in South-East Asia have benefited from increased employment opportunities in irrigated regions. Other regions, such as the Sudan, have been less successful largely because of the choice of crops grown and the export-based agricultural policies.

As a rural development strategy, irrigation can serve both efficiency/productivity goals and equity or income-distribution goals. To achieve these goals in developed and developing countries, institutional methods of water control and allocation must be devised according to the specific social, cultural and economic requirements of an area. While reliance on pricing mechanisms may be effective in Canada and the United States to counter the problem of the excessive use of a free good, this would impose unfair burdens on water-users in many Third World countries.

The effectiveness of irrigation projects in expanding the food, employment and income prospects for a region ultimately depends upon managing

165

them as social and physical systems. The design, operation and maintenance of these complex systems require as much attention to the decision-making, and social/organizational context as to engineering parameters.

CHAPTER 7

Land degradation

Defining the process

No other human-induced process affecting agriculture, with the possible exception of climatic change, holds the potential for such far-reaching and long-lasting impact as soil degradation. The FAO (1977a: 3) has defined soil (land) degradation as 'a process which lowers the current and/or the potential capability of soil to produce (quantitatively and/or qualitatively) goods or services'. Soil or land degradation then affects the 'flow' or renewable characteristics of soils by reducing the (potential) biotic productivity of the resource. Closely-related issues are environmental effects in the form of excessive siltation of streams, rivers, lakes and reservoirs, and numerous socio-economic effects that stem directly from the problems of productivity declines and environmental deterioration.

Change in soils over geologic time is a natural process. The interaction of climate, vegetation and parent material may produce either aggradation or degradation. The critical factors affecting 'normal' or geologic degradation are the climate and a host of bio-physical factors peculiar to the land – soil, topographic conditions, and vegetation. The critical factors affecting non-geologic or accelerated degradation are the above two sets of factors and human intervention in the form of cropping, grazing, rotation systems and management. This intervention in the environment alters the relationship between climate and land by altering the 'natural resistance' of land to what Riquier (1982 and FAO, 1979b) has termed the 'aggressivity of climate'.

Figure 7.1 illustrates the relationship between soil productivity and the degradation/aggradation process. As land-use and management practices change, so does the process of aggradation and accelerated degradation. Soil productivity may decline rapidly, reflecting a high and accelerating rate of soil degradation to produce a totally exhausted land-resource base (1). Or, productivity and hence degradation, may decline at a decreasing rate ultimately to achieve some equilibrium state either naturally (2) or through some improved management strategy (3). Alternatively, the productivity of the land may be enhanced (land aggradation) through a definite land-improvement programme (4). Thus, changes in soil productivity reflect the dynamic process of degradation/aggradation. Measurement

167

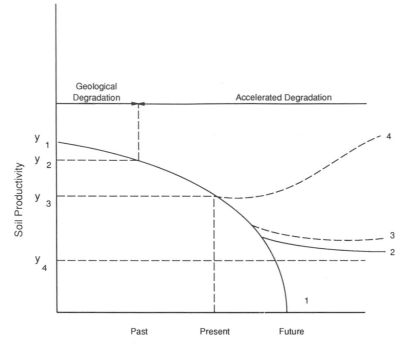

Fig. 7.1 Soil productivity as influenced by the degradation ↔ aggradation process
Source adapted from Riquier (1977)

of the process is based upon changes in soil productivity over two time periods or the differential change in productivity with respect to time (Riquier, 1977). Other measures of degradation include the potential – extrapolation of present trends into the future – and the risk – the analysis of the hazard to current and/or potential productivity resulting from an alteration of the biotic status quo (FAO, 1979b).

Land degradation and its associated processes can be categorized in many different ways (Coote, 1983; FAO, 1979b). In the discussion that follows, land degradation is divided into three major groups by selectively combining previous typologies based upon the most significant process (see Table 7.1). The choice is not without its weaknesses, since there is considerable overlap among the categories. Nevertheless, it affords an opportunity to preview and summarize much of the technical material to be discussed in this chapter before proceeding with a more in-depth look at degradation.

Physical/biological loss to soils occurs through wind/water erosion and oxidation of organic matter. It leaves a variety of visible (desertification/gulleying) and invisible (nutrient/humus loss) imprints on the landscape. This form of land degradation is by far the most extensive, threatening present and future environments for food production and, at

168

the same time, generating considerable off-site costs. Whether the degradation arises from erosion or oxidation, the ability of the soil to retain moisture and nutrients and to provide a foothold for plants is weakened. Actual impact upon yield potential depends on such factors as the erosivity of rainfall, the erodibility of the soil, depth of topsoil and plant cover and, on the manner in which agricultural practices interact with the environment to affect the natural resistance of the land.

The second major category, chemical change, deals with a host of conditions such as salinization, acidification and soil contamination which alter or perpetuate soil chemistry harmful to food production and in some cases human/animal life. The growth of irrigated cropland has been accompanied by the growth of salt content in soils. The risk of soil salinization is highest in these environments with high rates of evapotranspiration. In tropical climates, the low-base status (low cation exchange capacity) of a high percentage of the soils, in combination with high rainfall, leads to leaching of nutrients and ensures an acid soil chemistry. High soil acidity is also a problem in temperate climates because of artificial fertilization, lack of natural soil buffers and atmospheric sources of sulphur and nitrogen. And soil contamination from heavy metals in sludge, pesticides, fertilizers and atmospheric pollution (PCB/radioactive fallout), although not extensive, is of particular concern adjacent to urban/industrial areas.

Structural change, the third category, involving the compaction of soil, and its associated increase in bulk density, waterlogging and profile disturbance, is confined mainly to regions where irrigation is practised without proper drainage, where heavy machinery is used and where mining/energy development is occurring. Most compaction problems are due to poor farm management, such as excessive tillage and use of land during wet periods. Profile disturbance highlights the problem of the joint but incompatible uses of land for agriculture and energy projects such as pipelines and open pit-coal and other mineral developments.

Despite the importance of all three categories, the following analysis will concentrate on the agricultural effects of the first two categories, with particular emphasis on the problems of wind/water erosion and secondary salinization. These latter problems represent the greatest threats to a continuation of a renewable agricultural base.

The general impact of all of these forms of degradation is to reduce actual or potential productivity of the soil and/or to increase the cost of producing food in the absence of mitigating technology. Both issues raise serious questions regarding the sustainability of our present agricultural practices. The need for the conservation of the flow characteristics of soil resources has been emphasized by a wide variety of national and international organizations. In 1980, the UN sponsored World Conservation Strategy (International Union for Conservation of Nature and Natural Resources, 1980) indicated that sustainable development is premised upon

Table 7.1 A typology of land degradation/desertification

Type	Physical/biological loss	Chemical change	Structural change
Form	W–Wind erosion E–Water erosion OM–Oxidization of organic matter	S + A–Alkalization and salinization SC–Soil contamination A–Acidification L–Leaching	C–Compaction PD–Profile disturbance WL–Water logging
Source/process	E–Sheet and rill erosion; gully erosion; mass movement; flooding inundation OM–Microbiological; artificial fertilizer use	A–Atmospheric and terrestrial sources of sulphur and nitrogen S + A–Changes in water salt balance SC–Heavy metals and organic compounds L–Percolation	C–Heavy machinery PD–Anthropogenic excavation WL–Raised water tables
Critical factors	W–Windspeed and soil moisture; vegetation cover E–Rainfall erosivity and soil erodability; slope; ground cover and crop management; animals; erosion control OM–Temperature; soil moisture; carbon/nitrogen ratio; crop residues; topography; vegetation cover; PH; manuring; artificial nitrogen use	A–Efficiency of ammonium-based fertilizers; presence of sulphates in fertilizers; soil buffering capability (dependent on calcium and magnesium availability); acid rain; low-based low cation exchange capacity S + A–Excessive application of irrigation water; high PET; poor drainage; fallowing; vegetation cover; salt in geologic sub-stratum	C–Excessive tillage; humus content; moisture content of soils; soil texture PD–Surface mining and pipelines WL–Excessive application of irrigation water; poor drainage; subsidence

Table 7.1 A typology of land degradation/desertification (*cont.*)

Type	Physical/biological loss	Chemical change	Structural change
		L–High permeability; fallowing; lack of vegetative cover	
		SC–Type of pesticide; organochloride vs. organophosphates; climatic conditions; proximity to airborne contaminants such as PCBs	
Impact	W + E–*Offsite*: siltation and increased turbidity; water pollution; clogged ditches and reduced life of hydroelectric projects; decline in soil production of sites receiving deposits. *Onsite*: decline in nutrients and water retention abilities; reduced yields; increased costs of farm production	A–Increase in toxic levels of manganese and aluminium; reduction in nitrification and nitrogen uptake adversely affects aeration from earthworms and other soil fauna	C–Reduction in soil aeration; subsurface water movement and rooting zone depth creates surface ponding and plow pan; requires increased energy expenditure
		S + A Production loss through impediments to water nutrient uptake; moisture stress; reverse osmosis	WL–Reduction in soil aeration; declines in productivity
	OM–Irreversible decline in organic matter; loss of water-retention abilities; greater risk of erosion; decline in yields; higher levels of CO_2	L–Loss of organic matter; mineralized nitrogen; declines in productivity	PD–Removal of topsoil; declines in organic content and mineral nutrients; loss of productivity
		SC–Toxic to livestock, humans and microflora	

171

Table 7.1 A typology of land degradation/desertification (cont.)

Type	Physical/biological loss	Chemical change	Structural change
Measurement	W–Wind erosion equation (in tonnes per hectare per year) E–Universal soil loss equation (in tonnes per hectare per year); sediment delivery ratios (in tonnes per hectare per year) OM–Change in humus/carbon content within 30 cm of surface	A–Changes in pH; decrease in base saturation (in percent per year) S + A–Increase of electrical conductivity (in mmhos per cm) of saturated paste; and increase in exchangeable sodium (in percent per year) L–Percentage declines in carbon SC–Percentage increase in toxic elements (in ppm per year)	C + WL–Increase in bulk density (in grams per cm^3 per year) or decrease in permeability (in cm per hour) PD–Change in soil profile/horizons
Area/extent	W + E + OM–Wind erosion particularly acute in arid regions; water erosion in regions of high intensity rainfall with minimal natural vegetation; organic matter loss in most regions using modern/industrial agricultural methods	S + A–Most arid regions with high evapotranspiration SC–Urban/industrial regions; localized L + A–Tropical regions those with low-based soils	C–North America WL–Numerous irrigated regions, particularly the Middle East PD–Areas of strip mining in North America and the Soviet Union

Table 7.1 A typology of land degradation/desertification (cont.)

Type	Physical/biological loss	Chemical change	Structural change
Indicators	W–Dust storms, dust clouds, desert pavement, ripple marks, formation of hummocks or dunes, accumulation of sand against grass stems, tree boles, hedges, fences, road embankments, roots exposed	A–Advent of plants resistent to acidification; to low pH, in fallow or following crop or between rows of crop (plants vary according to ecological region)	C–Platy or laminary structure of soil surface, or massive structure more or less compacted and indurated in dry seasons, plough pan increase in run-off and decrease of water available in soil, roots limited in depth stopped short at compact horizon
	E–Rills (small water channels), muddy water, mudflows, gullies, erosion pedestals, exposed roots of trees and shrubs, changes in colour of bark on trunks and stems, soil deposits on gentle slopes, exposed parent material, uneven topsoil, gravel, sand and silt deposits in stream channels, trampling displacements by grazing animals, changes in vegetation species, sediment deposition in reservoirs	S + A–Efflorescence or salt crust on soil surface, edges of irrigation furrows, river banks, barren spots or unhealthy plant growth	PD–Degradation of seed bed and poor gemination of seed
		L–Lack of response to fertilizers	WL–Sealing and crusting of soil surface after storms, mud and water stagnation after storms
		SC–Dispersed clay in puddles after rainfall, sticky soil, increase of plant disease, appearance of toxicity symptoms on leaves: iron, copper, manganese, boron, zinc, deficiency symptoms of potassium, sulphur and phosphorous	C + PD + WL–Decrease of yields
	OM–Decrease of organic matter, lighter soil colour, increased sealing, crusting, run-off, decrease of earthworms and rodents, decrease of response to fertilisers	A + S + AL + SC–Decrease of yields	
	W + E + OM–Decrease of yields		

the conservation of living resources. Similarly, in 1981, the FAO adopted a World Soil Charter which set out a variety of themes and resource conservation principles and safeguards (Dudal, 1982). Emphasis was placed on the need for resource inventories, encouragement of those uses of land which preserve the greatest range of future options, consideration of the long-term gains from conservation, the importance of proper incentives and technology, the removal of land tenure arrangements which impede sound soil conservation, and education and information on the most appropriate approaches to manage the land. The UN sponsored Brundt-land Commission (World Commission on Environment and Development, 1987) argued that conservation of land resources would form an integral component of strategies for sustainable long-term development.

Few would question the value and validity of these principles, but achieving conservation has been, and will continue to be, a difficult task because of the differing perceptions of farmers and politicians of the seriousness of the problem, how it can best be tackled technically and administratively, who pays (regardless of responsibility), the financial resources available for amelioration and, perhaps most importantly, the high rate of discount most decision-makers apply to future income/rewards from land resources. The costs of conservation are often far more apparent and real than the benefits over the short term. There is often, therefore, little incentive to undertake small-scale schemes, much less major con-servation schemes. Combine this situation with the poor income perform-ance of much of the earth's agricultural system, and it becomes painfully clear why relatively little has been done to check land degradation worldwide.

Physical/biological loss

Measures of soil erosion

Humans have become important agents affecting global rates of erosion. Where human 'occupation is intense and is directed toward the use of land for cultivated crops, the difference is one or more orders of magnitude greater than when the land is under complete natural vegetative cover such as grass or forest' (Judson, 1968: 366). By comparing sediment yields of 'undisturbed' watersheds against their 'disturbed' counterparts, it is possi-ble to make inferences regarding the degree to which humans accelerate erosion. If we were to correlate land-use change with sedimentation and erosion rates, we would find that, at either end of the ecological con-tinuum, urban land and permanent forest and grassland produce minimal rates of erosion. In contrast, on a point-specific basis, construction and deforestation create some of the highest rates of erosion and sedimenta-tion, followed by general cropping and grazing activities. Because cropping and grazing are by far the most extensive of these activities, they tend to

174

be the main source of sedimentation. It remains difficult, however, to separate the numerous influences on erosion rates between land uses and between purely geological and accelerated erosion, and to determine the specific locations of the loss. Despite these problems, sediment yields are used to estimate erosion due to human intervention in an environment of mixed land activities. Caution should therefore be exercised in the interpretation of these estimates.

Sediment delivery

Attempts to estimate pre-occupation rates of erosion in the United States suggest that average rates of erosion were $3\,cm/1000$ years or 78 tonnes/km^2/yr (0.78 tonnes/ha/yr). Present rates of erosion in the United States including dissolved and solid sediments have doubled, with annual sediment loads estimated at 3.6 billion tonnes. The major source of the sediment (between 40–50 per cent) comes from the agricultural land which occupies one-quarter of the land base (Crosson, 1983 and Golubev, 1980). Globally, it is argued that the transport of sediment by rivers to the ocean has increased from 9.3 billion tonnes annually in pre-agricultural times to 24 billion tonnes (Judson, 1968). Others have argued that soil erosion in the world is five times higher than that which occurred during pre-agricultural periods (Golubev, 1980). Agriculture's exact share of this increased sedimentation is not known, but as in the United States it would represent a major proportion of the total.

Estimates of erosion using suspended sediment loads for major rivers reveal significant variations among drainage basins and among continents. Table 7.2 ranks some of the major rivers of the world according to the size of their drainage basins and indicates estimated soil erosion. It has been observed that in the United States there is an inverse relationship between the sediment delivery ratio and the drainage basin area. Sediment delivery ratio refers to the proportion of delivered sediment to gross soil loss at watershed outlet. Hence, as drainage basins increase in size, there is a log-linear decrease in the associated sediment delivered, with the ratio decreasing from close to 100 per cent for very small drainage basins (< 2.6 square km) to under 10 per cent for large drainage basins (> 260 square km) (Crosson, 1983).

While the universality of this relationship has been questioned because of differences in catchment relief characteristics, soils and vegetation, there are no alternative approaches to measuring erosion on a large scale (El Swaify et al., 1982a). Table 7.2 provides estimates of water-based soil erosion calculated with a sediment delivery ratio of 0.05, since all the drainage basins represented are in excess of 260 square km.

Immediately apparent from Table 7.2 is that areas with high population density and intensive agricultural systems are correlated with high rates of soil erosion (Yellow, Ganges, Irrawaddy and Red), whereas those with low

Table 7.2 Soil erosion estimates from annual suspended sediments

River (country)	Drainage basin $(10^3 km^2)$	Discharge (m^3/sec)	Average annual suspended load		Estimated soil erosion	
			$(10^6 tons)$	$(tons/km^2)$	$(tons/km^2/yr)$	$(tons/ha)$
Amazon (Brazil)	5,776	182,000	363	63	1,260	12.6
Congo (Angola)	4,014	39,000	65	16	320	3.2
Mississippi (United States)	3,230	17,900	312	97	1,940	19.4
Nile (Egypt)	2,978	2,600	111	37	740	7.4
Yangtze (China)	1,950	21,900	499	256	5,118	51.1
Missouri (United States)	1,380	1,960	218	160	3,200	32.0
Niger (Nigeria)	1,114	7,086	5	4	80	0.8
Ganges (India)	1,076	15,500	1,455	1,352	27,040	270.4
Orinoco (Venezuela)	950	29,000	87	91	1,820	18.2
Danube (USSR)	820	6,190	19	24	480	4.8
Mekong (Thailand)	795	11,100	170	213	4,260	42.6
Yellow (China)	680	1,500	1,819	2,800	56,000	560.0
Irrawaddy (Burma)	430	14,000	299	695	13,900	139.0
Red (China)	120	3,900	130	1,083	21,660	217.0
Po (Italy)	55	1,450	15	280	5,600	56.0
Kosi (India)	62	1,770	172	2,774	55,486	555.0

Data sources Baumgartner and Reichel (1975); Crosson (1983); El-Swaify and Dangler (1982a); Robinson (1981); UN (1966)

population densities and undeveloped agriculture have relatively low rates of soil erosion (Amazon and Congo). To infer a simple causal relationship would be misleading, however, since there are other critical factors such as soil and slope characteristics, and rainfall intensity. Two examples illustrate this. The Yellow River, in its journey from Tibet to the Pohai Sea, cuts through the wind-deposited loess soils of Shansi and Shensi Provinces, picking up the majority of its sediment load. The steep slopes, high-intensity rainfall and very low organic matter content make the soils extremely susceptible to erosion. Robinson (1981) reports that average annual rates of erosion in this area are 100 tonnes/hectare. Similarly, the Kosi River in India has unusually high rates of sedimentation, in part because of topographical and soil conditions.

Universal soil loss equation

As a first approximation in estimating water-driven soil erosion, a sediment-delivery approach allows some useful comparisons. More reliable approaches, on a smaller scale, estimate the loss of topsoil through samples and the Universal Soil Loss Equation (USLE) and Wind Erosion Equation (WEQ). The USLE calculates rates of soil loss as a function of rainfall characteristics, soil erodibility, slope length and degree, cropping practices and erosion control. The WEQ estimates rate of soil loss as a function of soil erodibility, surface roughness, wind speed and duration, field length and vegetative cover (Larson et al., 1983).

Regional estimates of soil erosion

North America

The 1982 US National Resource Inventory data base of soil erosion was derived from the application of USLE and WEQ equations to one million sample sites. An estimated 3.1 billion tonnes of soil are eroded annually from the cropland base and an additional 1.1 billion from rangeland (USDA, 1987). Sheet and rill erosion were estimated to be 11 tonnes/ha, and wind erosion 7.6 tonnes/ha, for a combined average erosion loss of 18.6 tonnes/ha in the United States as a whole. The Northern and Southern Plains and Corn Belt are the dominant regions where cropland is eroding in excess of T or tolerable levels.

Excessive rates of erosion are normally defined as a loss of topsoil greater than the natural rate of soil formation or what is termed the tolerance ('T') value. T values vary according to topsoil depth and other factors affecting the resilience of the land. Excessive rates of erosion are not to be confused with accelerated rates of erosion. Erosion above the geological rate is accelerated, but it may not be excessive. T values vary from 2.5 to 12 tonnes, depending upon the depth of topsoil and use of land (e.g., cropland or grazing). Generally, 11 tonnes/ha/yr is used in the United States as the standard limit of annual erosion consistent with maintaining the long-term productivity of the land in deep soils. If one accepts this level of erosion as not impairing the productivity of the soil, then the figure of 18.6 tonnes from the US National Resource Inventory translates into an excessive loss of topsoil of 1300 million tonnes.

In Canada there are no national estimates of rates of soil loss from wind and water erosion. Regional analyses of the problem indicate trends similar to the United States. In Eastern Canada, slopes in excess of 5 per cent have recorded soil erosion by water as high as 26 to 56 tonnes per hectare. In Ontario, level cropland devoted to corn is losing on average 12 tonnes per hectare. And in Western Canada wind erosion claims an equal if not greater quantity of soil (Coote, 1983).

There are numerous weaknesses in the use of T values. These values represent a gross and not a net measure of loss of soil, in that not all of the soil is washed into the river system and no account is taken of soil formation which is around one tonne per hectare per year. Also, these values do not take into account topsoil depth (Crosson, 1983). Apart from these difficulties, it is still fair to say that a significant portion of the US and Canadian cropland bases are eroding at *potentially* excessive rates. Brown (1981) argued that the topsoil loss from the United States on an annual basis is equivalent to the loss of 307,000 hectares of cropland. Figure 7.2 indicates areas of most serious erosion.

Approximately 58 per cent of the cropland base in 1977 required conservation treatment. In 1985 the US Congress passed the Food Security Act. Recognizing that over-production was creating economic and environmental stresses, Congress allowed for the retirement of 18 million hectares of highly erodible cropland in a conservation reserve. The Act also discourages the conversion of highly erodible land and wetlands to cropland (USDA, 1987).

Asia

Like the United States, India has made a major effort at keeping an account of the changing quality of its land-resource base. Although no complete or unified inventory exists, sufficient information from direct and indirect measurements indicates a truly alarming situation. India cultivates a much higher percentage of its total land base (44 per cent) than the United States (15 per cent) but a smaller total area. Actual per unit rates of erosion and total loss of topsoil are among the highest in the world. Conservative estimates of net soil loss place it around 5 billion tonnes, or two to three times the level estimated for the United States. This translates into annual (gross) per unit rates of loss of 34 tonnes/ha/yr. When estimates of erosion are made on the basis of sediment delivered, the average rate of loss becomes a staggering 250 tonnes/ha/yr (El Swaify et al., 1982a). This figure reflects all land uses and includes sediments from areas outside of India, such as Nepal and China, since the estimates are based on drainage basins. Figure 7.3 highlights major areas and types of erosion in India. Approximately 86 per cent of the entire sub-continent has serious wind and water erosion problems. Much of the water erosion is from flooding. Between 1953 and 1981, 100 million hectares of fertile valley bottom land were seriously inundated by floodwaters. One of the most serious occurrences was in 1978, when 10 million hectares were flooded in the Punjab, displacing 65,000 persons. Of the cultivated land

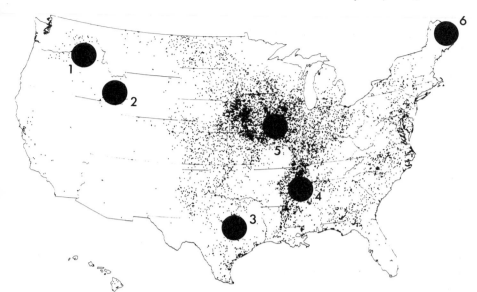

Cropland Sheet and
Rill Erosion: 1977
Total for United States
is 2,000,000,000
Data for Alaska not available

1 dot = 250,000 tons

1 *The Palouse,* covering parts of Washington, Oregon, and Idaho, is dryfarmed to wheat, barley, peas, and lentils. Most of the cropland is hilly, with slopes of from 15-25 percent. Runoff from melting snow and heavy rains cause erosion of 50 to 100 tons per acre.

2 *Southeastern Idaho* cropland is planted in hard red wheat one year and left fallow the next to conserve moisture. Erosion occurs during intense summer rainstorms and even more destructive rains in late winter, when a thawed layer of soil moves downhill over frozen subsoil. Annual erosion may reach 16 tons per acre per year on 35 percent slopes.

3 *Texas Blackland Prairie* is an important farming area, with two-thirds of the land in crops, mainly cotton and grain sorghum. Rainfall averages 30 to 50 inches a year on the gently rolling land. Many soils in the area are highly erodible, and erosion is appreciably higher than the national average.

4 *Southern Mississippi Valley,* including parts of five states, is about one-third cropland, much of it sloping to steep. The soils are deep, fertile, productive, and erodible. Many row crops are grown without adequate conservation practices, and annual soil losses on much of the land reach 20 tons per acre or more.

5 *The Corn Belt States* experience some of the highest erosion rates in the country: in 1977, Iowa cropland lost an average of 9.9 tons of soil per acre; Illinois, 6.7 tons per acre, and Missouri, 10.9 tons per acre.

6 *Aroostook County, Maine,* is famous for its potatoes. They are grown on slopes ranging from nearly level to 25 percent. The upper 2 feet of soil have been lost since cultivation began, lowering crop yields. Some sloping fields are losing as much as an inch of soil a year.

Fig. 7.2   Some serious erosion areas in the United States
Source adapted from USDA (1980)

179

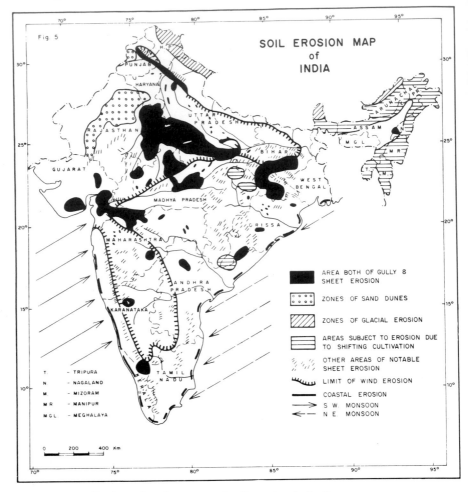

Fig. 7.3   Distribution of major types of soil erosion in India
          Source FAO (1977)

base, an estimated 60 per cent requires soil-conservation measures. The most severe form of erosion is gully and ravine erosion, affecting an estimated 8000 ha/yr.

Other regions of tropical monsoon Asia have very high rates and risk of soil erosion from wind and water. Nepal, Indonesia, the Philippines, Sri Lanka, Nepal and Thailand – with their high rainfall, steep slopes, and cropping and deforestation patterns – have all experienced greatly accelerated rates of water-related soil loss. This loss is manifested in the form of sheet and rill erosion, but, equally seriously, in gullying, landslides, underground tunnelling and flooding. It has been estimated (El Swaify et al., 1982b), for example, that three-quarters of the arable land in the Philippines is seriously eroded. Also, although poorly documented as to quantities removed, wind erosion is responsible during ploughing in early spring for the movement of large quantities of very fine soil particles eastward from North Asia over the Pacific (Brown, 1984). A similar phenomenon occurs over North Africa, transporting large quantities of soil westward over the Atlantic.

In the Loess Plateau of Northwest China, mentioned earlier, some of the highest rates of soil erosion in the world are to be found. Smil (1984) noted that the potential for erosion in the region is exceedingly high, given the light and easily erodible character of the soils, the high-intensity rainfall in the summer and the strong seasonal winds. While these factors set the precondition for erosion, Smil (1984) argued that the actual agent for change was the Maoist 'grain-first' policy which during the 1950s led to deforestation and cultivation of grassland. Nearly four-fifths of the region is seriously eroded. In Huang He basin not only have grain yields declined in step with the erosion, but large-scale silting of water-control projects has occurred.

In other regions of China, rice multi-cropping policies of the government have ignored traditional wet- and dry-crop rotation schemes, contributing to waterlogging of the soil. And with the decline in the use of green manures and legume crops, organic matter of the soil has declined (Smil, 1981 and 1984).

Africa

In tropical Africa, the documentation on erosion is unsystematic. An exception to this is the recently-completed maps of present and potential land degradation for North Africa and the Middle East (FAO, 1979). Earlier assessments of the risk of erosion were done by Fournier (1962). He found a close correlation between suspended sediment loads of rivers and measures of rainfall intensity and topography for large drainage basins. This information provided the basis for estimating the risk of erosion in Figure 7.4. No attempt was made, however, to hold constant human intervention or the role of vegetation or soil type in contributing to that erosion.

Significant proportions of Africa and practically all of Madagascar have high (10–20 tonnes/ha/yr) to very high (>20 tonnes/ha/yr) erosion risk. East Africa, including Tanzania, Kenya, Ethiopia and Somalia, are noteworthy. All four countries have experienced extensive sheet and gully erosion in semi-arid and upland areas. Sediment yields in the semi-arid regions of Kenya for forested, agricultural and grazing land use increase by a factor of ten for each land use. Erosion rates are as high as 200 tonnes/ha/yr in overgrazed areas (Dunne, 1977). These values contrast sharply with geologic erosion rates of 0.79 tonnes/ha/yr during the late Tertiary and late Quaternary in Kenya (Dunne et al. 1978, quoted in El Swaify et al., 1982a). Both Ethiopia and Somalia have some of the most

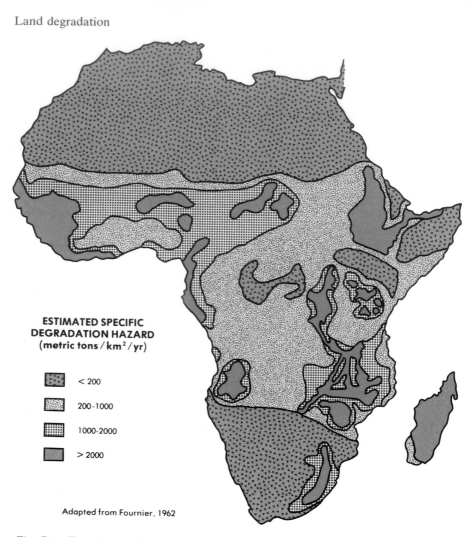

ESTIMATED SPECIFIC
DEGRADATION HAZARD
(metric tons / km² / yr)

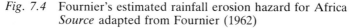

< 200

200-1000

1000-2000

> 2000

Adapted from Fournier, 1962

Fig. 7.4   Fournier's estimated rainfall erosion hazard for Africa
Source adapted from Fournier (1962)

wind and water erosion-prone areas of the world. In the case of the East
African highlands, occupying much of Ethiopia, where the Nile derived
much of its silt naturally, the process of deforestation and the grazing and
cultivation of mountainous areas has accelerated sheet and gully erosion at
an unprecedented scale. Virgo and Munro (1978) have suggested that
erosion rates of the Central Plateau region of the North exceed 180
tonnes/ha/yr.

Tropical America

Although lowland areas of Tropical America have a high potential for
erosion, if only because of the erosivity of the rainfall, this is doubly the

182

case in upland regions with their high rainfall and steep slopes. In Chapter 5, reference was made to the increasing pressure placed on marginal lands by shifting cultivation. A recent study of current and future importance of agriculture in steep slopes of tropical America supports this interpretation (Posner and McPherson, 1982).

In high-altitude areas of Central America, Caribbean and South America live 10–50 per cent of the national population and 30–60 per cent of the agricultural population. Posner and McPherson (1982) argued that situations of the recent past, such as importance of steep slopes to agricultural production, increase in number of small farms in these regions, but a decline in the size, the extreme poverty in these regions, and the growth in rural population will continue well into the future. In their view this will place increasing pressure on the existing base and on newly-cultivated lands as fallow periods shorten, farm size declines and the absolute number of farmers increases.

Although no precise evidence exists as to rates of erosion large-scale deforestation in Haiti (only 7 per cent of original forested area remains) and highlands of Central America would suggest that in the absence of alternative approaches the cultivation of these lands is not sustainable over the long term.

The Soviet Union

One of the major food-producing regions of the world, with heavy emphasis upon cereal production and mechanized farming, is the Soviet Union. Approximately 120 million hectares of arable land, or about 50 per cent of the arable land base, are subject to erosion. Some five million hectares have experienced a 60 per cent decrease in yields from normal levels (Golubev, 1980). Major sources of wind and water erosion are in Kazakh SSR and in the Volga, North Caucasus, Urals and Siberia (Kogan, 1983).

Brown (1984) argued that the Soviet Union is losing topsoil as rapidly, if not more rapidly, than the United States. He cited Soviet research in the Baltic and Rostov regions that shows a mean annual soil loss on bare fallow of 59 tonnes/ha and 46 tonnes/ha respectively. A critical time of year for erosion is during snowmelt, when the unprotected ground becomes a plastic medium with negligible infiltration. On the assumption that erosion in the USSR occurs at the same rate as in the United States, excessive soil loss is estimated to be 2500 million tonnes or 9.8 tonnes/ha in excess of tolerable levels of soil loss.

Causes of erosion

While the exact dimensions of the risk and extent of soil erosion remain unclear and poorly documented, the causes and a number of the consequences are well understood. Reference has already been made to a variety of these factors, their relative importance being as much a function of the great variety in the cultural practices in food production as of the heterogeneity of the resource base available for and affecting agriculture. Although it is not possible to undertake an exhaustive survey of these factors, we can highlight some of the more salient and generalizable features.

The point was made earlier that accelerated land degradation was the product of the interplay of three factors: climate, natural resistance of the land and human intervention. Human intervention is expressed in many ways, but generally, within the context of soil erosion, it is a process in which, as populations expand, the demand for food, fibre, space and energy expands, placing increased pressure on a finite land-resource base. Demand growth may be indigenous as in China and India, or largely exogenous as in Canada, the United States and Australia. Nevertheless, the theory, expressed perhaps most forcefully by Brown (1984), Eckholm (1976) and Borgstrom (1980), is that increasing population pressure (income and population growth and increase in livestock numbers) forces increasing intensification of the existing system and extensification onto marginal and hazard-prone lands. Often associated with these strategies are poor land-management practices, varying from abandonment of crop rotation to overgrazing and deforestation.

The context of these growth pressures is equally important in affecting rates of erosion. Norse (1979) has argued that in Africa pressures on the land-resource base are particularly severe when high population growth rates and technological developments are combined with a static social and economic situation. Related to this problem is the inability of the growing rural population to gain access to suitable land resources for cultivation purposes. Although lack of access to the land may be related to physical limits in the supply of arable land, more commonly it is due to land tenure and cash crop systems which ultimately make hazard-prone lands the main alternative outlets for expansion in cultivated area for the peasant population. Poverty can be both a cause and an effect of poor land-management practices. There are numerous examples (one of which will be discussed in Chapter 8) of international aid contributing to the increase in population pressures on hazard-prone lands. And finally, in developed countries the economic and policy context is important in affecting erosion. Agricultural policy through subsidies has encouraged the cultivation of erosion-prone lands. Moreover, the cost-price squeeze affecting many North American farmers during the 1980s has been detrimental to any individual long-term conservation schemes. Let us examine in more detail some of the direct natural and human-based factors responsible for accelerated erosion.

In both Canada and the United States, severity of water erosion is due to the interactive effects of the intensity of rainfall, slope of land, type and rotation of crop (row or close-grown), extension of irrigation onto sloping land, soil conditions, and tillage practice. Wind erosion is due to soil conditions (particularly soil moisture), wind velocity, size of fields and the tillage system. Throughout the eastern half of North America, where rainfall intensity is high and combined with row crops such as corn, potatoes and cotton, erosion rates tend to be very high. Table 7.3 illustrates erosion rates by cropping system for different cultural practices or contour cropping approaches.

In western portions of the United States, where 18.5 million hectares of land are irrigated, approximately 35 per cent is located on erodible and 21 per cent on highly-erodible cropland. The northern and southern plains have the highest percentage of their cropland base on erodible lands. Although centre pivot irrigation has contributed to gully erosion by permitting the cropping of hilly, sandy soils, the most extensive erosion stems from flood and furrow systems on lands that have not been properly levelled (Frederick and Hanson, 1982).

Wind erosion in both Canada and the United States is usually highest in areas with bare summer fallow and excess fall tillage. Quantity of surface mulch is a critical factor, affecting the impact of wind velocity. Conservation tillage experiments have demonstrated that soil loss due to wind erosion in Nebraska for a wheat–fallow rotation was reduced from 6.5 to 24 tonnes/ha/yr on bare fallow, to 1.8–1.9 tonnes/ha/yr on stubble mulch fallow (Fenster, 1977). The decline in winter irrigation in the southern High Plains because of the high cost of water has reduced cover crops and accelerated erosion rates (Frederick and Hanson, 1982).

The emphasis in North America on achieving higher grain yields through increased artificial fertilizer application, largely for the international grain market, has reduced the need for traditional crop rotations (legumes), reduced the amount of fallow, increased continuous cultivation of corn and wheat, and pushed production onto lands that were either semi-arid or had high slopes. The value of fallowing is controversial. On the one hand, it contributes to increased soil moisture (and nitrogen mineralization in semi-arid areas). On the other hand, it can expose the soil to the increased risk of wind and water erosion because of lack of vegetation cover. In the Canadian prairies, there is consensus that erosion can be reduced by a reduction in summer fallow in all but the driest areas (Rennie et al. 1980).

If accelerated erosion in North America is due in part to increased international demand on land resources for food and fibre, it is even more the case for most of Asia and Africa. Not only is the agricultural system called upon to meet the needs of growing and more affluent populations, but extensive amounts of land are given over to the production of cash crops for the export market. India cultivates a significantly higher percentage of its total land base than either Canada or the United States, much of which is characterized by natural constraints such as flood hazard, low vegetative cover, slopes in excess of 15 per cent, aridity and high rainfall erosivity.

Most of India and other areas of Asia and Africa are subject to high

185

Table 7.3 The relation of run-off and erosion to contour farming and strip cropping

Location	Cropping system	Rows up and down slope		Cultural practice Rows on contour		Land strip cropped	
		Run-off (%)	Erosion (tons/ha)	Run-off (%)	Erosion (tons/ha)	Run-off (%)	Erosion (tons/ha)
Bethany, Missouri	Corn–wheat–clover			7.7	4.4	7.6	1.9
Southern New York	Potatoes–oats–clover	15.7	34.7	5.2	2.8	1.9	0.3
Temple, Texas	Cotton	13.6	35.2	4.6	13.2		
Southern Illinois	Corn–oats	11.7	10.8	8.3	6.3		
	Corn–soybeans	12.1	13.7	5.5	5.6		
Western Iowa	Corn–oats	11.5	56.4	7.4	22.6		

Source after *Prarie Farm Rehabilitation Administration* (1983); Baver et al. (1972)

seasonal (monsoonal) rainfall. In Bombay, 94 per cent of total rainfall (1800 mm) falls between June and September. Cropland is subject to severe water-erosion pressure during this time, particularly during planting, when ground cover is minimal. As previously mentioned, excessive run-off creates frequent flooding and torrents (or chos) and periodic destruction of cropland. Historically, terracing in its myriad forms (e.g., bench and narrow base or bunding) has been used to reduce erosion by reducing slope and to conserve water for both paddy and non-paddy agriculture. Expansion of agriculture into areas without proper terracing has accelerated gully and ravine damage in the north of India. During the eight-month dry season in India, the risk of wind erosion is high. Here vegetation cover, soil moisture and grazing practices have become critical factors, particularly in Gajarat and Rajasthan in the north-west.

In other areas of South and South-East Asia, a litany of factors can be identified to explain accelerated soil erosion. Since the Second World War, the increase in the demand for lumber and land for cultivation has accelerated deforestation. The most notable example of this is the Diptercarp forest in South East Asia, valued for its hardwoods. Sri Lanka (since the nineteenth century) and (Peninsular) Malaysia (since the 1940s) have undergone extensive clearing and development – for tea and coffee in the former and rubber, palm oil, bananas, tea and pineapples in the latter. Since much of this development occurs in steeply-sloping terrain, mass movement and very high sedimentation are common.

El Swaify et al. (1982a) argued that erosion on tea and rubber plantations can be checked by good management and the use of soils with low susceptibility to erosion such as ultisols. Severe erosion on alfisols 'is due to high soil erodibility, low infiltration rates, uncontrolled population settlement patterns and lack of adequate (protective) cropping sequences' (El Swaify et al., 1982a: 32). A similar explanation of high erosion rates can be applied to Thailand, the Philippines and Indonesia. Lack of terracing in upland areas, deforestation because of the practice of swidden, or slash and burn, agriculture and lumbering, in combination with high monsoonal rainfall, are the commonest and most important contributors to excessive erosion and sedimentation of rivers and streams.

The destruction of vegetative cover in regions of high-erosion risk in Africa is likely the most important factor contributing to erosion (both wind and water) and sedimentation. Overgrazing pressures, the use of forests for fuel and the expansion of cultivated areas in upland regions all contribute to the denuding of the landscape. East Africa (Kenya, Tanzania, Ethiopia) provides classic examples of the damage arising from the operation of all of these factors. Increased grazing pressures, trampling, deforestation, lack of crop cover during the beginning of rains and cultivation of steep slopes without terracing – combined with periodic drought conditions – have set the stage for an ecological disaster resulting in greatly reduced carrying capacity of the land.

Erosion effects

Offsite

Both wind and water erosion exact a heavy toll on the biophysical, economic and social environment. Although our primary concern is with the (on-farm) productivity effects of erosion, the (off-farm) environmental and social impacts require examination.

The human disturbance of natural drainage basins through deforestation and agricultural operations has accelerated the rate of erosion and increased run-off and the sediment loads of rivers and streams. The downstream or offsite effects of erosion are numerous, but they are expressed in three principal forms. First, increased sedimentation has raised stream beds and reduced their capacity. In a variety of environments with intense (periodic) rainfall patterns, particularly monsoonal, the risk of flash flooding and damage to property and person is very high. In the North China alluvial plain, the Yellow River is suspended above the surrounding countryside by three–ten metres because of the deposition of sediment from the loess plateau (Robinson, 1981). This requires constant expansion of dyking. The threat of flooding in the densely-populated area of China is as real as the size of the river's load. In Bangladesh, flooding in coastal regions has exacted a very heavy toll. Apart from the loss of life, the economic consequences of flooding can place serious strain on local and regional economies from lost crops and damaged production potential because of sediment deposition to damaged roads, bridges and infrastructure. Similar problems of increased flooding because of changes in hydrology and increased sedimentation can be found in East Africa, South-East Asia and in Columbia, Peru and Bolivia.

The second major consequence of off-site sedimentation is increased siltation and reduction in life-expectancy of dams and reservoirs. Numerous examples exist world-wide, again primarily in tropical areas, where observed rates of siltation of reservoirs/dams are significantly higher than assumed, so that the life-expectancy of these projects is reduced. Pimentel et al. (1976) estimated that in the United States agriculture contributes approximately 3 billion tonnes of water-born sediment. The cost of correction in terms of dredging and reduced life in reservoirs was in the order of $500 million annually in the 1960s. In India, observed rates of siltation for reservoirs are often three to six times what is predicted (Centre for Science and the Environment, 1982).

The Kisongo Reservoir in Tanzania, built in 1960 to enhance the quality of the range for cattle, has in approximately twenty-five years lost most of its capacity. The life expectancies of the Aswan High Dam (Egypt), Amblukao Dam (Philippines) and the Mangla Dam (Pakistan) are longer than the Kisongo, but nonetheless relatively short at a hundred, thirty-two and seventy-five years respectively from date of construction (El Swaify et al., 1982b). As the capacity of the systems is reduced, their value for flood control is reduced, as is their usefulness as a source of irrigation water and hydro-electric power generation. This is nowhere more apparent than in the Sanmenxia Dam at the gorge of the Three Gates in Henan, China. Approximately 60 per cent of the storage capacity was lost between 1958 and 1973. Subsequent attempts to reduce siltation by increasing discharge during flood seasons have limited its usefulness for irrigation, power production and flood control (Smil, 1984).

The third major effect of off-site sedimentation is increased nutrient loading in rivers, lakes and streams, with a variety of impacts ranging from eutrophication of lakes to contamination of surface-water and groundwater. In regions with fertilizer-intensive farming systems, such as California and the US Mid-West, run-off is enriched with nitrogen and phosphorus.

These offsite impacts or effects are responsible for real environmental or social costs. Since the farmer and other groups have passed along these costs to the rest of society in the form of the loss of reservoir capacity, flood damage and water pollution, the environmental cost to the farmer is minimal or non-existent. This raises not only social efficiency questions regarding the wise use of resources, but also equity questions as one group (farmers) affects the income/well-being of another group (consumers of water). Similar questions of efficiency and equity arise in considering the on-farm or productivity effects of erosion. It is to these effects and the potential for amelioration which we now turn.

Onsite

Productivity effects of wind and water erosion are in many instances less visible than off-site effects, but they are every bit as pernicious to the environment and to society. In fact, in Latin America, land degradation generally has been referred to as 'terremoto silencioso' (Dudal, 1982). The loss of productivity through decline in soil productivity (existing or potential) originates from the loss of nutrients (chemical effect) such as nitrogen, phosphorus, potassium, calcium, magnesium and sulphur, and micronutrients such as manganese, iron, copper, zinc, iron and molybdenum. It also originates from the loss of humus and organic matter and a physical decline in rooting zone depth (physical effect). Whereas these are critical factors underlying declines in yield, there are a host of other factors which intervene to affect the loss of nutrient and topsoil depth. Important among these are soil type and structure, topography and cropping systems. It has been difficult to isolate the effects of these factors on yield and provide a macro measure of yield changes even in the United States, the scene of the most detailed and intensive research to date.

The loss of soil nutrients and organic matter varies by region, but in those areas with high rainfall, steep slopes and loss of vegetation cover, the losses are high. In one study of the nutrient losses in run-off and sediment from alfisols under the above erosive conditions (with 10 per cent slope),

189

bare fallow lost approximately 600 kg/ha/yr of nutrients, and maize and cowpea approximately 40/kg/ha/yr (Lal, 1976). The intricate relationship between loss of topsoil, slope and nutrients is indicated in Fig. 7.5 for Hawaii. On a national scale in the United States, wind and water erosion

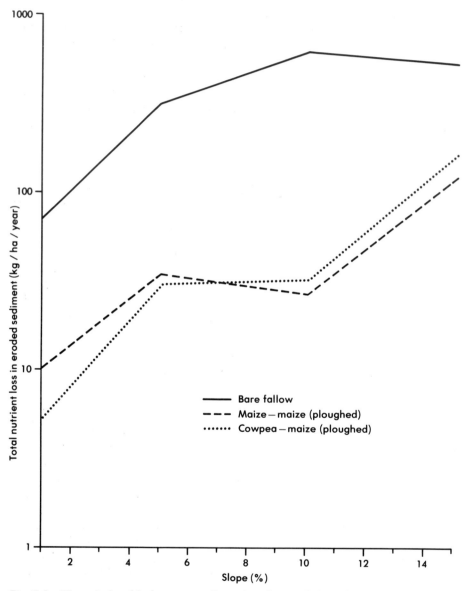

Fig. 7.5 The relationship between soil nutrient loss and slope for three cropping cultures
Source Lal (1976)

are responsible for the annual loss of an average of 3.7 kg/ha of nitrogen, 2.9 kg/ha of phosporus and 54 kg/ha of lime worth over one billion dollars annually. In India, it is estimated that 8.4 million tonnes of nitrogen, phosphorus, and potassium are lost annually through water erosion (Centre for Science and Environment, 1982).

The impact that these nutrient losses have on yield and productive potential depends upon the efficiency of nutrient uptake and the use of artificial fertilizers. The heavy use of artificial fertilizers in developed countries has in many instances offset nutrient loss and prevented yield declines. In 1982 the United States consumed 8.3 million tonnes of nitrogen fertilizer for agriculture and produced 333 million tonnes of grain. Canada has a similar output-to-nitrogen ratio (40: 1). Since the efficiency of fertilizer uptake is rarely 100 per cent (more normally 40 to 60 per cent), and since nitrogen uptake for plant growth comes from other sources, it is not entirely valid to use the above ratio to indicate lost potential. Nonetheless, these figures give some idea of the potential for lost productivity over the long term if artificial fertilizers are not used. This is particularly the case for numerous developing countries, which have neither the energy nor capital resources to sustain productivity through fertilizer use.

Crosson and Stout (1983) found in reviewing a number of studies that nutrient loss in deep- and medium-textured soils can be remedied by the addition of artificial fertilizers. However, where erosion reduces tilth, water retention abilities of the soil and rooting depth, yield losses will often persist even with the addition of fertilizer. Similarly, a Canadian study (Prairie Farm Rehabilitation Administration (PFRA), 1983) found that in many regions of the Prairies, despite the use of fertilizers to offset nutrient loss, yields cannot be restored beyond 85 per cent of their potential. Even without erosion, cultivation of virgin soil accelerates organic matter decomposition. And even with additional applications of nitrogen to offset this loss and to rebuild humus, soil organic matter declines to an equilibrium level between 40 to 60 per cent (Barney, 1980).

Physical loss or change in the structure of soils has been examined extensively by region, crop and soil type in the United States. A number of studies has shown that as topsoil is removed, yields diminish, but with considerable variability. Lyles (1975) found for a number of regions of the United States that for every cm decrease in topsoil (which is roughly equivalent to 100 to 130 metric tonnes/ha), wheat yields decreased an average of 40 kg/ha. Other studies emphasize the importance of topsoil depth as opposed to topsoil loss (e.g., cm/yr.) on soil productivity. Huat (1974), quoted in El Swaify et al. (1982a), shows corn yields in Iowa of 3200 kg/ha with 5 cm of topsoil and 6988 kg/ha with 30 cm of topsoil. Larson et al. (1983) examined two Major Land Resource Areas (MLRA) of the US corn belt with serious erosion problems. Assuming the 1977 rate of erosion would continue in the areas (31 and 38 tonnes/ha/yr) during the next 50 to 100 years, they calculated the impact on soil productivity. In the area with deep loess (three to twelve metres) in which root growth and water storage vary little with depth, productivity was affected by no more than 5 per cent over 100 years on slopes of 6–12 per cent. In the second area, productivity effects were much more substantial (23 per cent over 100 years on slopes between 6 to 12°). Topsoil depth was less than in the previous case and the loess was overlayed by unconsolidated sands, silts and clays and, in some cases, fragipans.

Figure 7.6 illustrates how important topsoil depth and subsurface material are in affecting productivity. As erosion proceeds, productivity effects are greatest in example C (Rockton), in which topsoil is thin and subsurface material is unconsolidated. In essence, 'the soil is viewed as an environment for root growth and water depletion' (Larson et al., 1983: 219). So long as that soil has a favourable profile with good surface and

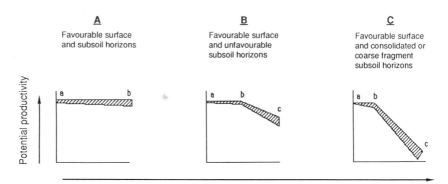

Concept of eroding productivity

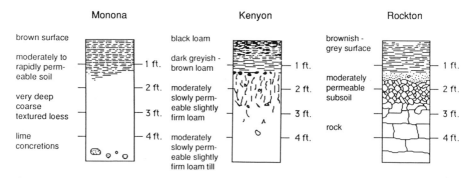

Characteristics of three soils from the Corn Belt.

Fig. 7.6 Illustration of eroding productivity concept and three select soil profiles
Source after Pierce et al. (1983)

sub-surface conditions, erosion will have little impact on productive potential over the medium term. In the absence of these conditions, fertilizer applications will be unable to restore the soil's full potential once the rooting depth and water retention capabilities have been damaged.

Larson et al. (1983) used these results to indicate the productivity effects of soil erosion nationwide. The authors argued that if 1977 rates of erosion continued, the productivity of US cropland would be reduced by 5–10 per cent during the next 100 years. This is equivalent to the loss of 8.4 (over 50 years) or 16.8 million (over 100 years) hectares of productive cropland. More recent estimates of productivity losses during the next 100 years based upon 1982 erosion rates (which are lower than 1977) indicate national productivity would decline by only 2 per cent (USDA, 1987). Nevertheless, areas with shallow soils and steep slopes such as the Central California Coast Range and Great Valley of Virginia are expected to lose over half of their productivity.

Since erosion is a cumulative process, to what degree have previous rates affected production potential? Past erosion in the United States is estimated to have reduced yields by 10–15 per cent (Pimentel et al., 1976). And estimates of loss in production annually from both wind and water erosion are one billion bushels or 6.2 million metric tonnes (Dregne, 1978). Similar estimates have been made for Canada. It has been suggested, for example, that during the last sixty-five years, the loss of potential production has been 4.65 million tonnes of grain annually. Given the cumulative nature of erosion, this represents roughly 14 per cent of total crop production averaged between 1969–78 (PFRA, 1983).

By combining past and expected productivity effects from erosion, we create a more complete picture of the magnitude of decline in the potential productivity of the food system. Much of this decline has and will continue to be offset by shifts in (through technological change) and movements along (through increased inputs) the production function.

Soil conservation

Inasmuch as new technology and increased energy inputs represent solutions, albeit indirect, to the problems of erosion, they fail to deal with the problem of irreversible losses in soil productivity. The size and gravity of these losses is not known beyond the figures quoted above for Canada and the United States but it has prompted numerous suggestions for soil conservation. We have already discussed a number of practices which reduce accelerated erosion. The use of terracing, double cropping, contour ploughing, strip cropping, mulching, wind breaks, crop rotation and conservation tillage are some of the more important means for conserving food land resources. Conservation tillage is perhaps the most recent of these (1960s in the United States), and is one which holds considerable promise in developed countries and in those countries of the developing world with the potential for mechanization. Conservation tillage practices differ from conventional tillage in three ways: '(1) they rely on some instrument other than the moldboard plough to prepare the land for planting; (2) they leave enough residue from the previous crop on the soil surface to significantly reduce erosion; and (3) they rely more on herbicides and less on mechanical cultivation to control weeds' (Crosson and Brubaker, 1982: 95). In 1981 approximately 27 per cent of US harvested cropland was under either minimum till or no-till operations. Yields are comparable with those under conventional tillage, particularly in drier environments and where the growing season is not too short. Moreover, Crosson (1981) argued that costs are between 5 and 50 per cent less, because the savings from reduced tillage more than offset increased herbicide costs. It is because of this economic advantage that conservation tillage has become important.

The above suggests that farmers will adopt erosion control measures when it is economic to do so. The corollary to this is that failure to adopt conservation measures is due to their high short-term costs in relation to their benefits. In other words, so long as the cost of conservation measures exceeds the benefits in the form of higher yields, there is little inducement to undertake conservation. Of course, conservation may not take place because of other obstacles such as ignorance, lack of information and capital, and government policies such as price ceilings on agricultural products. Putting these aside for the moment, how should society assess the need for conservation?

We have seen how 'T' values are used to determine if erosion rates are excessive. They act as a guide or standard against which society can judge the need for conservation. But we have also seen that 'T' values are very gross measures and, in many instances, tell us little about productivity effects. Are we adversely affecting future generations by allowing erosion to continue in excess of 'T' values? Some argue that technological change has offset the productivity effects of erosion and kept the cost of production down (Crosson and Stout, 1983). Moreover, 'T' values say nothing about the most appropriate time of the application of conservation measures. It is within the context of these weaknesses that Crosson and Stout (1983: 81) proposed an alternative standard – 'that avoidance of higher production costs be substituted for 'T' values as the criterion for judging when erosion is excessive.' As soon as the present value of the productivity losses exceeds the present value of the cost of conservation measures, action is justified and socially efficient.

This is a much more sophisticated and complex approach to conservation. Its success would depend on assumptions about the rationality of farmers, the free flow of information and the perfection of the market. Even under these ideal conditions it would deal, however, only with on-site or productivity effects and not off-site effects. In other words, all the costs of the farmer's decisions would not be internalized. To do this, farmers would have to bargain with affected parties to reduce sedimentation. Agreement would only be 'efficient' when the cost of removing the sediment is less than the cost to society of the sedimentation (Crosson and Frederick, 1977).

Regardless of the approach or combination of approaches (physical/economic), there are numerous obstacles to ensuring that public interests in the productivity of the land are being protected. Crosson and Brubaker (1982) argued that the public interests may not be protected because: (1) the market may underestimate the social value of and future demand for agricultural land, and (2) farmers may not recognize and respond to its true social value. The first error can arise from an exaggerated importance attached to the role of technology in increasing yields in the future. As well, given uncertainty about the future, society may want to give more weight than the market to protecting the productivity of agricultural land. If indeed this is the case, the cost of conservation would have to be more broadly borne than on the shoulders of farmers alone. Concerning the latter problem, the fact that farmers may be unaware of social value and therefore under-invest in erosion-mitigating programmes may be partially a reflection of ignorance, lack of capital and access to information, and insecure tenure. Crosson and Brubaker argued, however, that generally farmers in the United States are rational, and the access to capital and information can be improved.

In numerous developing economies, an additional set of factors operate which make it difficult to protect society's long-term interests in the land. The absence in many cases of secure tenure and/or rights to the land, lack of income/capital, inadequate resource information and pricing of agricultural products, and severe population pressures are likely to prevent many countries from properly valuing the land resource base. The existence of a large and uncontrolled common property land resource base used for livestock and crop production is in itself one of the greatest 'soft spots' in attempts to widen compliance with respect to conservation measures.

Chemical change

Dynamics of salinization

Unlike soil erosion, the process and occurrence of salinization of soils is located primarily, although not exclusively, in arid and semi-arid regions of the world. The soils and substrata of these regions are rich in water-soluble salts, particularly sodium salts. These salts and/or their ions restrict the growth of most domesticated plants for food production.

Salt-affected soils, as previously noted, are commonly divided into two main groups: (1) the saline group, which refers to soils affected by sodium salts such as sodium chloride and sodium sulphate; and (2) an alkali group (soda salinization), which indicates soils affected by sodium salts capable of

195

alkaline-hydrolysis such as sodium bicarbonate and sodium carbonate (Szabolcs, 1979). This latter group may also be found in more humid climates. Soils may be both saline and alkaline at the same time, depending on the proportion of sodium to calcium and magnesium in the salts.

The natural water–salt balance or budget of a region is governed by complex interacting factors including climate, geological, hydro-morphic and chemical conditions, and vegetation. To reiterate and expand upon the earlier discussion, the concentration of salts or efflorescences in the upper soil horizons reflects a salt regime in which leaching actions from run-off are very slight in relation to the upward movement of mineralized groundwater from capillary action. The process of evaporation and transpiration are critical determinants in affecting the sub-surface movement of water. The presence of soluble salts in groundwater can be traced to the composition of the parent material, to weathering and to sea-spray. In many arid regions, the accumulation of salts in sub-surface sediments represents an interrupted hydrologic cycle (Pels, 1978). Intervention by humans, however, completes this cycle by the transfer of historically-deposited salts into the groundwater system and unsaturated root-zone area.

Generally, human intervention responsible for completing this cycle is in two forms: (1) irrigation; and (2) the replacement of perennial plants with annual (commercially-grown) crops. As we saw in Chapter 6, the introduction of irrigation radically changes the natural water–salt balance increasing the extent and risk of saline and alkaline soils. Secondary salinization and alkalization occur when the natural drainage system is unable to accommodate the additional water input, causing a rise in groundwater levels. As the water table comes closer to the surface, capillary action transports dissolved salts to the active root-zone and surface areas. Waterlogging is often associated with this. The critical depth of the groundwater varies from one to four metres, according to a variety of climatic and hydro-morphic conditions, but generally the higher the salt content of the groundwater, the greater the depth through which this saline solution can damage crops.

There are examples, particularly in irrigated projects of ancient origin, where there was sufficient drainage capacity to handle additional water supply without greatly altering the water–salt balance. However, the overwhelming majority of irrigation projects do not have this capacity. Drainage to the sea or to some other outlet is insufficient, and secondary salinization occurs. Failure to properly level fields, excessive seepage from irrigation canals and tubwells (as high as 40–50 per cent) and inefficient application of water all add to the subsoil water supply.

Problems of salinity and alkalinity also occur because of the application of brackish, saline and alkaline waters. Increasing mineral content of irrigation water can be traced to a variety of conditions. The most

196

significant factors contributing to higher soluble concentrations are an increasing percentage of surface and groundwater used for urban and industrial purposes, which leads to higher salt concentrations; surface run-off from irrigated cropland which is often contaminated with salts; and the growth in reservoirs and canals for irrigation purposes, which exposes the water to evaporation and therefore increasing salt concentrations.

Problems of salinity occur as well in non-irrigated environments. Dry-land salinity, which occurs through the process of saline seep, also reflects a change in the quantity and movement of groundwater. This change is brought about by modifications to the vegetative cover (perennials to annuals), to certain cultivation practices such as summer fallow, and to the management of surface water, including snowmelt. The net effect of these practices is to increase subsurface water-flow with a high saline content from recharge to discharge areas, leading to salt accumulations.

Distribution of salt-affected soils

The generalized distribution of salt-affected and potentially salt-affected soils (saline and alkaline) is illustrated in Figure 7.7 and Table 7.4. Throughout Eastern Europe, the Middle East and Asia, large tracts of land have been affected by increasing salinity, mainly as a result of poor drainage from irrigation systems. Close to 70 per cent of the 30 million hectares of irrigated land in the Middle East (Egypt, Iran, Iraq and Pakistan) suffer from moderate to severe salinity problems (Schaffer, 1980). In Iran, some 7.3 million hectares of the 16.8 million hectare arable land base are saline. In neighbouring Iraq, approximately half of the 3.6 million hectares of irrigated land suffers from secondary salinization and waterlogging – largely in the middle and lower Rafidian Plain (El Gabaly, 1977). Similar risks of secondary salinization and alkalization exist in India, where expansion of food production through poorly-designed irrigation schemes was achieved at a very high environmental cost. Approximately seven million hectares of land suffer from salinization and alkalization effects, the majority of them occurring in the central and western portion of the Indo-Ganges plain, Gujarat and irrigated areas of Rajasthan. Excessive application of water, canal seepage and poor drainage are common problems throughout much of India. These practices are particularly critical in soils with high water-retention abilities, such as the deep and medium black cotton soils found throughout India. China has had a similar spread of saline soils with the growth of irrigation and the potential for increasing the salt-affected soils is as great again if irrigation is expanded.

Similarly, in Australia, as irrigated areas have expanded, so have saline- and alkaline-affected soils (Pels, 1978). But these problems also afflict rainfed agriculture through saline seep in much of the interior of the continent. Some 120 million years ago a rise in sea level flooded the

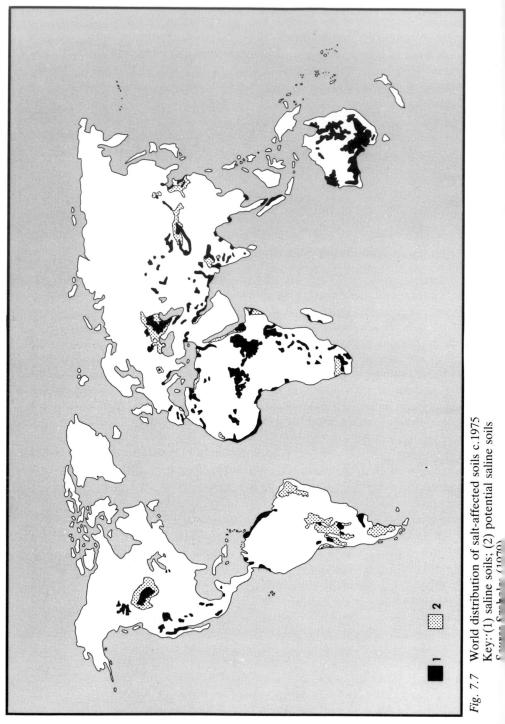

Fig. 7.7   World distribution of salt-affected soils c.1975
Key: (1) saline soils; (2) potential saline soils
Source Szabolcs (1979)

Table 7.4 World distribution of salt-affected soils

Region	Area Thousands of ha	Percentage of total land area
North America	15,755	0.9
Central America	1,965	0.7
South America	129,163	7.6
Europe	50,804	4.6
Africa	98,521	3.5
South Asia	85,108	7.9
North and Central Asia	211,686	7.2
Southeast Asia	19,983	5.9
Australasia	357,330	42.3

Source after FAO (1978b)

interior lowlands. As sea levels declined 50 million years later, an inland sea remained centred on the Lake Eyre Basin in South Australia. Table 7.5 highlights the distribution of human-induced salt-affected soils (for rainfed and irrigated lands). Perhaps the worst area is the Murray–Darling river system in South-East Australia (New South Wales, Victoria and South Australia), where chronic salinity problems have been described as the 'greatest environmental disaster of the century' (McWilliam, 1981).

The Soviet Union is also plagued by existing saline and alkaline soils and a high risk of further damage if the growth of irrigation continues. The problem is most acute in the South-East, Transcaucasia and Central Asia,

Table 7.5 The areas of man-induced salt-affected agricultural land in Australia (1980–81)

	Non-irrigated Land area (1980–81) (× 10 ha)	Salt-affected area (× 10 ha)	(%)	Irrigated Land area (1980–81) (× 10 ha)	Salt-affected area (× 10 ha)	(%)
Queensland	157,244	590	0.38	255.7	0.6	0.2
New South Wales	64,485	924	1.43	714.6	8.4	1.2
Victoria	14,154	150	1.06	546.5	92.0	16.8
Tasmania	2,167	5	0.23	32.7	0	0
South Australia	62,321	1,255	2.01	79.5	21.5	27.0
Western Australia	115,775	607	0.52	24.7	0.5	2.0
Northern Territory	77,600	682	0.88	n.a.	n.a.	n.a.
Total	493,746	4,213	0.85	1,653.7	123.0	7.4

Source after Aston (1987)

where intensive secondary salinization took place between 1920–40 (Kovda, 1979). Considerable progress has been made in the Syr Darya Basin by means of lining canals with impermeable material, constructing vertical mechanized drainage (tube wells) to inhibit the rise of groundwater, and creating deep horizontal drainage systems (Kovda, 1977).

To gain a better understanding of the effects of irrigation on the delicate water–salt balance in arid regions, we should turn to Figure 7.8. In the

Solutions

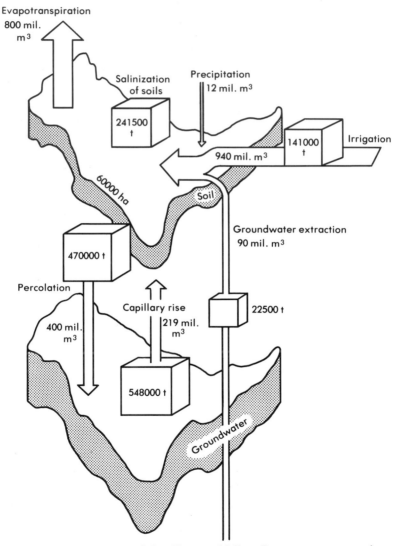

Fig. 7.8 Irrigation area of the Chancay Valley, Peru: average annual water and salt balance
Source after Schaffer (1980)

Chancay Valley of Peru, the Tinajones Irrigation area (100,000 ha) was created by diverting water from the Rio Chancay and creating a reservoir in this rainless coastal zone. Inefficient applications of already mineralized water and poor drainage have systematically raised the water-table and increased the salinity of soils. Of the 60,000 hectares of land represented in Figure 7.8, 241,500 tonnes of salt are deposited annually, for an average deposit of 4 tonnes/ha (Schaffer, 1980). Other areas of Latin America such as Mexico are plagued by soil salinity problems, usually from poor drainage. There are 5 million hectares of irrigated land in Mexico, of which 10 per cent have soil saturation extract levels from 4 to 20 mmho/cm (the reciprocal of resistance measured in ohms). The north-western region of Mexico has approximately half of all the salt-affected soils. An esti-mated 55,000 hectares of irrigated land have been abandoned in Mexico.

More extensive in area than irrigation-induced salt-affected soils, dryland salinity-affected soils are common throughout the arid and semi-arid regions of the world. Some of the best documentation exists for Australia and North America. Australia is one of the most seriously affected regions of the world, with some 357 million hectares of soils affected by problems of alkalinity and salinity – almost half of its total area. The Great Plains of North America (North and South Dakota, Wyoming, Montana, and the three prairie provinces of Manitoba, Saskatchewan and Alberta) possess about 590,000 km^2 with hydrological conditions conducive to saline seep (PFRA, 1983). Rates of area increase in salt-affected regions have been reported as high as 10 per cent per annum, with the fastest rates occurring during wet cycles. A four-fold increase in salt-affected soils occurred in Saskatchewan from 1960 to 1977. The practice of summer fallow (crop–fallow system) has been identified as one of the principal mechanisms by which increased percolation of water increases groundwater supply which, in the course of its movement over impermeable bedrock and glacial till, becomes mineralized. In low-lying areas, these waters are brought to or close to the surface, resulting in salt accumulations (see Fig. 7.9).

Ameliorative measures

Although the solution to a number of irrigation-induced salinity and alkalinity problems is reasonably clear, the economic benefit/cost ratio to society of amelioration is not, nor is the question of who should pay and how benefits are to be distributed. In the Colorado River Basin, increasing salt concentrations of the river were threatening the viability of nearly 400,000 irrigated hectares in a number of south-western US states, as well as in Mexico. Salt concentrations at the Imperial Dam (the lower basin) were as high as 879 mg/litre in 1972, but have since decreased to 722 mg/litre. In 1974 the Salinity Control Act was passed, authorizing construction of major desalinization plants at a cost of $280 million. In 1985 estimates of total costs (since construction is still ongoing) are around

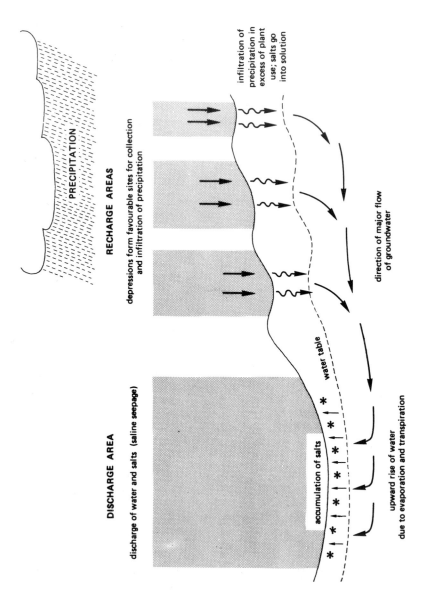

Fig. 7.9 The process of dryland salinity
Source after Lilley (1982)

$500,000,000. The benefits to the agricultural sector have been calculated at $39,100 per mg/litre decrease in the salt content of water. A 50 per cent decrease in salt content from 722 mg/litre to 361 would increase total benefits to $14 million annually, and would reduce potential gross salt-load of 9.3 tonnes/ha. Despite these perceived benefits, and the fact that substantial salt-load reductions could be achieved through inexpensive changes in irrigation management techniques, Gardner and Young (1985) have observed that only a few of the Bureau of Reclamation projects are economically feasible in cost–benefit terms, largely because they are capital-intensive solutions.

The question of who should pay is complex. A US Environmental Protection Agency report (1971) suggested that 37 per cent of the salt content of the river is due to irrigation. Should farmers therefore pay in relation to their contribution to total costs (benefit principle)? Should downstream users who suffer damages also share in the costs?

To the west of the Colorado Basin is the San Joaquin Valley, arguably the most economically profitable irrigated area in the world ($4.76 billion in farm products in 1977). Of the 1.8 million hectares of irrigated land, close to 155,000 hectares are affected by high brackish water-tables creating an annual loss of $31 million (Sheridan, 1981). This could rise to 272,000 ha by the year 2000 with an annual crop-yield loss of $321 million, unless improved subsurface drainage systems are installed. The problem is to extend on-farm drainage to most farms (only 40 per cent now have it), and to develop a system for disposing of this drainage water. Estimates of disposal cost for large-scale water diversion projects are in excess of $258 million, and are in themselves not without environmental impacts, since they would affect delta wetlands in the San Francisco Bay area. Cost to the farmers is estimated at between $112 to $190 per hectare per year, while benefits to farms in drainage problem areas are estimated at $335 per hectare per year (Sheridan, 1981). A number of farmers on the eastern side of the valley are not seriously affected to date, but fear that they too will have to share in the costs of improving drainage systems. Alternatives to these master drain projects include improved water conservation, disposal of water into a salt lake in the Carrizo Plain, and a desalinization plant (Gardner and Young, 1985).

Solutions to the problems of dryland salinity are much less capital-intensive than for soils salt-affected from irrigation. Continuous cropping systems, the return of land to permanent pasture and/or more natural vegetation, improved drainage, and the use of deep-rooted crops such as alfalfa to restrict the movement of saline waters are some of the least expensive, but most successful, conservation approaches.

Productivity effects

Both saline and saline-sodic (alkaline) soils limit plant growth by affecting water uptake and nutrient-exchange processes. They may also have toxic effects through the presence of certain trace elements such as boron, selenium, manganese, cadmium and vanadium. Also associated with saline and alkaline soils are changes to the physical properties of soils, including surface crusting which retards root and water penetration, reduced aeration capacity, cracking and filtration losses in heavy-textured alkaline soils, decreased permeability and overall reduction in water-storage capacity.

In identifying saline and alkaline soils, two measures are used: one measures the electrical conductivity (EC) of a saturated soil sample in mmho/cm, and the other measures the relative importance of sodium as exchangeable sodium-to-total-cation exchange capacity (ESP). Saline soils have an EC in excess of 4 mmho/cm and and an ESP of less than 15 per cent. Alkaline soils have an EC greater than 4 mmho/cm and an ESP greater than 15 per cent (Cox and Atkins, 1979). Figure 7.10 shows the relationship between yield and soil conductivity for different species of plants. Most vegetable crops are highly sensitive to salt, as are corn and

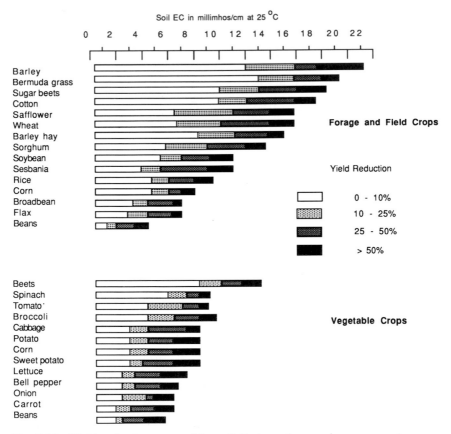

Fig. 7.10   Yield reductions caused by salinity in various major crop species
Source adapted from Cox and Atkins (1979)

soybean. Wheat, sorghum and safflower are moderately sensitive. Barley, sugarbeets, cotton and bermuda grass are very tolerant.

The actual impact of salt-affected soils on national crop production is difficult to calculate, given the quality of information available. General estimates of yield decrements for major crops from salt-affected soils in Mexico have been made. A knowledge of the extent of soils at different salinity levels, information on the tolerance of crops to different salt levels, and a model of the general yield response of crops as a function of soil electrical conductivity (illustrated in Table 7.6) provided a basis for the calculations. An estimated one million tonnes of food a year are lost because of high soil salinity levels. Wheat and sorghum show the largest average and total declines of the five crops grown (Aceves-Navarro, 1987).

Although no dollar value was attached to these losses, it would be significant, particularly since the losses are cumulative. In the Canadian Prairies, economic analyses of lost crop production from saline seep place it at roughly $25 million per year, beginning in 1983. The cumulative value (expressed as a benefit to the area if it were alleviated) of conservation

Table 7.6 Total yield decrement for some given crops in areas affected by different salinity levels in the Mexican irrigation districts

Crop	Affected surface (ha)	Y_{100} (t/ha)	EC_{Y_x} (dS·m^{-1})	$EC_{Y_{100}}$ (dS·m^{-1})	EC_{Y_0} (dS·m^{-1})	$Y_{100}-Y_x$ (t/ha)	Total yield decrement (t)
Corn	90,000	3.5	6.0	2.0	10	1.75	157,000
Soybean	90,000	2.3	6.0	5.0	10	0.46	41,400
Sorghum	135,000	5.0	10.0	5.0	14	2.78	375,300
Wheat	85,000	4.4	14.0	6.0	20	2.51	213,350
Barley	45,000	3.5	18.0	8.0	28	1.75	78,750
Wheat	55,000[a]	4.4	20.0	6.0	20	4.40	242,000

[a] Assumed mean yield in the abandoned areas

Note Equation for the calculation of the mean yield decrease per hectare for a given crop and a given soil salinity level is:

$$Y_{100}-Y_x = \frac{EC_{Y_x} - EC_{Y_{100}}}{EC_{Y_0} - EC_{Y_x 100}}$$

Where:

Y_{100} = Optimum yield per hectare for a given crop without salinity problems in the root zone

Y_x = Expected yield per hectare for a given crop with mean soil electrical conductivity in the active root zone equal to EC_{Yx}

$EC_{Y_{100}}$ = Threshold soil electrical conductivity after which yields per hectare decrease approximately linearly as salinity increases

EC_{Y_x} = Given mean soil electrical conductivity in the crop active zone

EC_{Y_0} = Given mean electrical soil conductivity in the active root zone at which the yield per hectare for a given crop is zero

Source after Aceves-Navarro (1987)

was estimated to be $465 million by 2000 – the present value of which is approximately $2.2 billion (PFRA, 1983).

The productivity effects of saline and alkaline soils can be severe. Alleviation requires either a reduction in the salt content of soils or the selection of salt-tolerant plants. Since these plants (particularly forage crops) tend to be of a lower economic value and to supply less of the conventional sources of nutrition, the overwhelming challenge will be to reduce salinity through a variety of preventive and ameliorative measures.

As with soil erosion, there are both on-farm and off-farm effects from increases in sodium in soil and water. We have seen how irrigation raises the water table and leads to increasing salt accumulation in the upper soil horizons. This may be the result of individual actions on the farm and/or neighbourhood effects from canal and reservoir seepage. With dryland salinity, the problem of off-farm external effects is particularly critical, since those in water discharge areas (leading to salt accumulations) suffer from the practices of those in water recharge areas. These external effects in both cases produce environmental costs which are difficult to internalize, requiring fairly broad-based solutions and compliance.

Desertification

The collective expression of numerous forms of land degradation is desertification. It has no precise meaning, but generally refers to a land degradation process in which human actions (normally in semi-arid and arid environments) weaken the resilience of the agro-ecological system and reduce the biological potential of that system, which ultimately leads to desert-like conditions. As Dregne (1985) has noted, the hazards and risk for human occupancy increase – in some cases dramatically – with desertification. Hence, the analysis of desertification is not concerned with existing deserts, but with the changes which take place in agro-ecological systems as a result of improper/inefficient management of grazing land, woodland area, and irrigated and rainfed cropland.

Within this context, Rapp (1974) argued that desertification commonly occurs when grazing, wood collection and cultivation of marginal lands expand during wet years, but cannot be sustained during very dry or wet conditions because of wind and water erosion. Moreover, in a UN publication on desertification (Secretariat of the UN, 1977: 16) it is argued:

> To the extent that desertification contains self-reinforcing elements, its effects may extend outward through a whole system of climatic and land-use belts. As arid pastureland turns into complete desert, neighbouring semi-arid land, once suitable for rainfed cropping, may deteriorate into arid pasture. But since the process does not spring from the desert cores, it need not always work outwards, and the

semi-arid or sub-humid cropland may be the first to deteriorate to desert status.

Desertification is not a new phenomenon. It has led to and/or been associated with the decline of hydraulic civilizations in the Mesopotamian Plain, and other areas of the Fertile Crescent, in the Indus Plain and in the Loessial Hills of China. But today, unlike the past, the pressure on the earth's arable land base has increased by a factor of forty or more. Much of the desertification is taking place in areas with already high and/or rapidly growing populations. These areas can ill afford to weaken the production potential of their food systems.

The 1977 UN Conference on Desertification, which was responsible for providing general estimates of the extent of the problem and the formulation of a plan to combat desertification, and a recent assessment of the progress of the UN plan (Mabbutt, 1984), have greatly enhanced our knowledge and understanding of the dimensions of desertification. There are still serious discrepancies in the spatial and quantitative assessment of the process, in part because of debate over the inclusion or exclusion of sub-humid land. And both the original and recent assessments are overwhelmingly physically-based, with little information on the socio-economic dimensions of the process other than populations affected. Notwithstanding these shortcomings, the second assessment confirmed the 1977 global estimates of desertification and populations affected, and identified the prospects for changes in the situation.

Figure 7.11 provides an original definition of the degree of desertification (exclusive of sub-humid lands). Existing deserts are portrayed as undergoing only slight desertification, whereas bordering and more humid regions are experiencing higher rates. This presumably reflects the notion that desert regions have reached an ecological climax or equilibrium with little or no change taking place in their ecological status. Similarly, the UN map of desertification has portrayed regions of the world according to the risk or hazard of desertification, with desert environments possessing the lowest risk.

The current estimates of desertification, including sub-humid lands, indicate that about 30 per cent of irrigated agriculture, 60 per cent of rainfed cropland, and 80 per cent of rangeland are at least moderately desertified. As much as 30 per cent of the rainfed cropland in dryland regions is severely or very severely desertified. Very severe desertification refers to an almost total collapse of the agro-ecosystem reflecting, in most cases, economic irreversibility of the land, whereas the remaining classes, although not economically irreversible, are responsible for significant (15–50 per cent) yield decrements.

At least 280 million humans living in rural areas – or 470 million if urban areas are included – are affected by at least moderate desertification. The majority of this total (60 per cent) live in rainfed croplands.

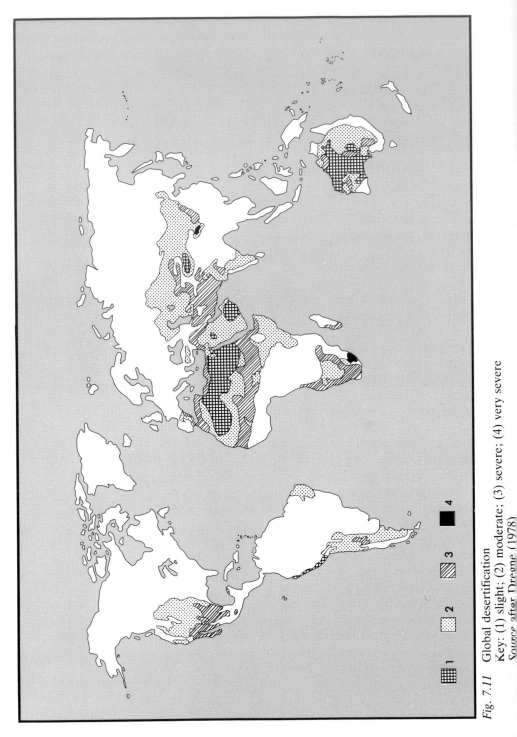

Fig. 7.11 Global desertification
Key: (1) slight; (2) moderate; (3) severe; (4) very severe
Source after Dregne (1978)

A regional breakdown of desertified areas and populations affected, cross-classified by production system, is provided in Tables 7.7 and 7.8. Mabbutt (1984: 12) has argued that 'Man's role as an agent of desertification is revealed by the way in which land use forms the main avenues of advance.' Accordingly, land-use categories provide a useful basis for

Table 7.7 Regional extent of lands at least moderately desertified (in millions of ha)

Region	Rangelands	(%)	Rainfed croplands	(%)	Irrigated lands	(%)	Total drylands	(%)
Sudano-Sahelian	342	90	72	80	0.8	30	415	88
Africa south of the Sudano-Sahelian region	200	80	42	80	0.6	30	243	80
Mediterranean Africa	68	85	15	75	0.5	40	84	83
Western Asia	98	85	15	85	3.0	40	116	82
South Asia	127	85	105	70	20.0	35	252	70
USSR in Asia	150	60	12	30	2.0	25	164	55
China and Mongolia	210	70	3	60	3.0	30	216	69
Australia	100	22	12	30	0.3	19	112	23
Mediterranean Europe	15	30	13	32	1.6	25	30	39
South America and Mexico	180	72	24	77	4.0	33	208	71
North America	125	42	33	39	4.0	20	102	40

Source after Mabbutt (1984)

Table 7.8 Rural populations affected by at least moderate or severe desertification, respectively, by regions (in millions of ha)

Region	Rangelands M[a]	S[b]	Rainfed croplands M	S	Irrigated lands M	S	Total rural population M	S
Sudano-Sahelian	13.5	7.0	36.0	20.0	1.5	0.5	41.0	25.0
Africa south of the Sudano-Sahelian region	8.0	4.5	32.0	20.0	1.0	0.5	51.0	27.5
Mediterranean Africa	4.0	2.0	11.0	6.0	1.0	0.5	16.0	8.5
Western Asia	4.0	2.0	16.0	9.5	12.0	4.5	32.0	16.0
South Asia	9.0	4.5	34.5	18.0	23.0	6.5	66.5	29.0
USSR in Asia	1.0	0.5	1.5	0.5	4.5	1.0	7.0	2.0
China and Mongolia	3.0	1.0	4.0	2.0	10.5	3.5	17.5	6.5
Australia	0.03	–	0.1	0.3	0.1	–	0.2	0.03
Mediterranean Europe	2.0	1.0	13.0	4.5	1.5	0.5	16.5	6.0
South America and Mexico	4.0	2.0	22.5	11.5	2.5	1.0	29.0	13.5
North America	1.5	0.5	2.0	0.5	1.0	0.2	4.5	1.2

[a]M = moderate
[b]S = severe
Source after Mabbutt (1984)

structuring generalizations about present and future impacts. All land-use classes in arid and semi-arid regions possess lands which are at least moderately desertified. In all categories, the developed world has a lower percentage of its dryland area moderately desertified than the underdeveloped world. Populations most affected by desertification are to be found in Third World countries of South Asia, the Sudano-Sahelian region and areas to the south, Western Asia, and South America; and the majority of this population is concentrated on the cropland base. Populations living on irrigated lands are the second most important group to be affected by desertification, followed by humans occupying rangeland areas. In terms of maximum loss of production, desertification is the greatest threat to irrigated regions in developed and developing countries.

While much of the preceding discussion concentrated on the present status of desertified environments, what about the process of desertification? First Mabutt argues that desertification is accelerating in rangelands that are already the 'most extensive manifestation of the problem' – in the Sudana-Sahelian region, Andean South America and South Asia – with most other regions showing little change. In terms of rainfed cropland, desertification is accelerating in tropical areas of Africa, South Asia and South America, including Mexico. One of the great pressure points is the cropland–rangeland interface in semi-arid regions (particularly Africa), where livestock numbers are increasing, as are human demands on the rainfed cropland base. In most other areas, desertification remains unchanged, with the exception of areas of Europe and North America, which have shown actual signs of decline in the process. For irrigated lands, most regions will still undergo the same rate of salinization and waterlogging, with some notable improvements in the Soviet Union.

Given the enormous variation of population densities in these arid and desert-like regions which range from less than 0.005 persons per km^2 in the Gascoyne Basin of Western Australia to over 50 persons per km^2 in the Luni Basin in the Rajasthan Desert of India, the human implications of these conditions and their correction are highly variable.

In Australia, which has a commercially-based agricultural system, it has been possible to combat desertification with a variety of programmes such as improved rangeland management, abandonment of marginal lands and amalgamation of holdings such as in the Murray Mallee of South Australia, without significant human cost. However, in the case of the subsistence economy of the Rajasthan Desert, in which population increases have averaged 3 per cent per annum, the pressure on the land resource base and the resistance to change are great. The conversion of rangeland to cropland during wetter years increases the threat of famine and endangers the stability in the system. Mabbutt (1978: 254) argued that 'The promise of a greater food return is at the cost of stability, for whereas in years of drought animal-based systems can continue to provide some subsistence, crop failure can be complete; and a cover of natural pasture provides a check against accelerated soil erosion where cultivated lands are left vulnerable.'

The control and amelioration of desertification is still in its infancy. While forestry projects have had some success, the long-term nature of many of these problems, the lack of capital, the emphasis on technical as opposed to socio-economic solutions, and the fact that most of the desertification occurs in poor, developing countries are serious and major impediments to redressing the balance. A more in-depth discussion of the causes and consequences of desertification is to follow in Chapter 8.

Summary

The dynamics of land degradation are best understood within the context of climate, the natural resistance of the land and human intervention into the environment. By affecting the balance between climate and land-base forces, human intervention has accelerated the natural process of degradation. The direct effects of degradation manifest themselves in the form of reduced crop yields, siltation of rivers and reservoirs, decline in water quality and a host of socio-economic impacts relating to cost of production, total viability of the local economy and to the risk of human habitation. While technology has the capacity to offset some of these effects, land degradation and sustainable agricultural development are incompatible over the long term.

Of the three major forms of land degradation, physical/biological loss stemming from wind and water erosion was considered the most extensive and problematic. Despite the use of different approaches to the measurement of the problem and the lack of systematic soil surveys, it was possible to identify areas according to erosion risk and/or rates of erosion. Without doubt, regions with high-intensity rainfall, steep slopes and lack of natural vegetation, have high risks and rates of soil displacement. Even though these conditions are found in numerous developing countries of the tropics and sub-tropics, such as China and India and Central America, leading to some of the worst examples of degradation, developed countries, such as Canada, the United States and the Soviet Union, are not immune to the problem. In these cases the environmental costs lead to significant economic costs in the form of lower yields, abandoned land, reduced life of water-diversion projects and the additional inputs to redress the balance.

The underlying causes of soil erosion, from both wind and water, vary enormously by agro-ecological region and development status. For many developing countries increasing population pressures within a relatively static social and economic environment have provided the preconditions for misuse of the land. Poverty, inequitable access to high-quality land resources and technology by the peasant population, government policy relating to export crops, land-tenure systems and the common property characteristics of land in many regions combine to produce non-sustainable development patterns. The situation is equally complex in developed countries, both planned and market-oriented. The misuse of the land can be traced to a rapidly expanding livestock sector, the intensification (or industrialization) of agriculture, increase in the food grown for export, and agricultural subsidies and policies. In North America the poor income performance of farmers and possible imperfections in the land market have discouraged land-resource conservation. Despite *billions* of dollars spent on soil conservation in the United States, the problem persists.

Various regional estimates of lost production potential from soil erosion indicate the need for and benefits of increased inputs and technological change to offset the effects of lost nutrients and declines in the physical properties of the soil. In numerous developing countries without access to technology and with limited resources, soil erosion has either decreased yield or imposed higher costs of production. Although support for the long-term benefits of conservation exist amongst governments and international agencies alike, disagreements exist over acceptable levels of erosion, over the use of physical or economic criteria as a basis for action and over responsibility for control and funding. While trade-offs inevitably must be made among present versus future interests and public versus private interests these trade-offs will vary among countries reflecting different economic, social and political milieux.

Chemical change to the soil in the form of an increase in salinity/alkalinity levels is generally human-induced, through the spread of irrigation and the replacement of perennial plants with commercially-grown crops. Most arid and semi-arid regions of the world are afflicted to varying degrees by this chemical change in the soil.

Whereas the spread of dryland salinity in North America and Australia can be traced to spread in the cultivation of cereals and the mismanagement of groundwater flow, the growth of salt-affected soils in irrigated areas world-wide is directly attributable to poor drainage, raised groundwater levels and the use of mineralized irrigation water.

The lost production from increased salt content of soils runs into billions of dollars annually because of reduced yields and/or abandoned land. Although well understood, preventive and ameliorative measures are costly and potentially environmentally disruptive to regions receiving the drainage water. Many of the issues relating to the reduction of soil erosion also apply to the reduction of soil salinity. Points of contention involve sharing of cost and establishment of standards and responsibility for use.

The collective expressions of soil erosion, loss of organic matter and chemical contamination of the soil in arid and semi-arid regions of the world have been described as desertification. Although associated with the famine in the Sahel, desertification is a far more extensive phenomenon, representing varying degrees of decline in the biological potential of large cropland and grassland regions of the world. Grasslands are particularly vulnerable to desertification, as is the interface between rangeland and crop production. Populations most affected by desertification are to be found in rainfed cropland areas of Third World countries.

Many causes of desertification can be traced to those factors identified earlier for soil erosion and salinization. Although this subject is to be examined in more detail in Chapter 8, the increasingly intensive use of dryland regions which are marginal at best for crop and livestock production is an important issue, as is poor management of water resources. Where migration was once the response to dry spells, limitations on movements and expansion of sedentary agriculture prevent this. Certainly, in some cases the demands made on these fragile lands could have been abetted by the use of better and higher-quality foodland resources, now committed to production of export crops.

CHAPTER 8

Climatic variations and food production

Weather and climate

If weather is defined in terms of short-term or day-to-day behaviour of the atmosphere, then climate represents some generalization of that behaviour over an arbitrary time period longer than a few weeks (Hare, 1979). Weather is often associated with annual yield conditions whereas climate is associated with the type and geographical extent of crops that can be grown. This distinction between weather and climate is, however, not altogether accurate, since climate is also associated with variations in yield over the long term.

Implicit in climatic variations are spatial and temporal changes in the thermal, light and moisture conditions necessary for plant growth. The availability of these atmospheric resources has a great impact on the productivities and extent of agro-ecological zones. Unravelling the relationships between weather, climate and food production is extremely difficult. The dynamic and often interactive character of the factors precludes most conventional forms of analysis. And as the geographic scale of the problem increases so does the number of relevant factors (Chisholm, 1980).

Historically, biological and mechanical technologies have extended the range over which crops can be grown and have boosted yields substantially. Increases in food production also owe much to favourable weather conditions. Unfavourable weather conditions or climatic variability may just as easily depress yields and affect area cultivated. The size of the increase or decrease depends on the length and magnitude of the change in climatic variations, on the physiological response characteristics of plants to changes in thermal and moisture conditions, to the changes in the environment for pests, weeds and diseases, and to the impact on soil organisms. In contrast to these first-order effects, which are biophysical in nature, are a number of higher-order effects which are social and economic in nature and which are expressed regionally and nationally (Parry and Carter, 1987). For example, climatic variations may affect yields which in turn may affect production costs, the choice of what to produce in the face of increasing uncertainty and ultimately the viability of the farm community. These are but a few of the effects and complex interactions which occur when the climatic environment for food production changes.

In this chapter we examine the relationship between, on the one hand, climatic change and variability and, on the other, changes in food production. Particular emphasis is placed on understanding first-order effects and interactions. Climate is treated as one of two major environmental driving forces, the other being crop/soil environment. As such, climatic change and variability, representing climatic variations, act as limiting factors or constraints to food production, with short- and long-term impacts for society.

Instability and change in climate

Climate can be defined and measured in many ways. Although there is no such thing as a 'normal' climate, by measuring average values for important climatic elements such as temperature and precipitation it is possible to define climatic states for monthly, yearly or decadal periods. Climatic change reflects a significant difference between two or more climatic states.

During the last two million years the world has undergone a series of glacial epochs separated by warmer and shorter interglacial periods. The last inter-glacial period, the Holocene epoch, began about 10,000 years ago. It was ushered in by a rapid rise in temperatures and with that, an increase in precipitation in many sub-tropical deserts of the world such as the now dry belt extending from the Sahara eastward to the Indus Valley and Rajasthan in North-Western India. It was these more humid conditions that provided the basis for the hydraulic civilizations at Harappa and Mohenjo Daro in the Indus Valley. As drier conditions returned, beginning approximately 4000 BP, desiccation prevailed with declines in the productive agro-ecosystems of these and civilizations in the Mediterranean basin.

More recent examples of climatic change can be found in the mediaeval warm phase (AD 800–1200) affecting Northern Europe, Iceland, Greenland and Canada, followed by the so-called 'Little Ice Age' (from 1550 to 1850) with very cold winters and short summers in temperate climates of Europe and North America (Hare, 1979). The warming–cooling trends of the present century reaffirm the instability of climate, but as yet do not indicate that significant climatic change is on its way, at least comparable to that during the Pleistocene. The rise in the concentration of carbon dioxide in the atmosphere and its possible green-house effect, which we shall discuss in detail later, is yet another scenario that may await humankind during the next 50–100 years.

215

Of more immediate concern is climatic variability. Climatic variability can be expressed in a variety of technical ways (see for example Hare, 1979 and Chapter 3), but for our purposes it can be simplified to reflect: climatic anomalies and sudden disasters; within and between year differences in climatic elements; and cyclical or quasi-periodic effects of several years (Oram, 1982). Although less extensive spatially and of shorter duration, climatic variability's agro-ecological impact is sufficiently large to induce extensive famine, to undermine development efforts to improve the viability of agriculture, to increase the cost of food production, to create social/political upheaval and to create general uncertainty regarding food security. Although there is no fixed interval to the droughts that have plagued the Sahel this century (at least five) they are sufficiently regular to be classed as quasi-periodic. As an area that is already on the dry margin of crop and livestock production, successive droughts have seriously weakened the ability of the Sahel to sustain even current population, much less the growth that is expected to take place over the next twenty years.

Against these periodic events stand the inter- and intra-annual variabilities which plague most production systems and account for the sizeable variation in yield from year to year. The crop failures of 1972–1973 lowered global per capita food production to its lowest point in twenty years. Reserves of grain worldwide were reduced from 20 per cent of world consumption to 10 per cent. Again, drought had struck, but this time in the more traditional grain-producing regions of the world. The return to more normal moisture conditions brought record harvests in 1977–1978 and again in 1985–86. The unpredictability of the required climatic resources for food production makes year-to-year planning difficult, but all the more important for its potential for smoothing out shortfalls and surpluses (Oram, 1982).

The last variety of climatic variability is the anomaly or natural disaster in the form of floods, typhoons, hurricanes and hailstorms. While their impact may not be extensive in large agricultural countries, such as the United States, their effect can be devastating on smaller countries, such as Bangladesh or Sri Lanka. This form of variability is notoriously difficult to predict, largely because of its random character.

Climate variability

The sensitivity of the global food production system to inter- and intra-annual variability and changes in the variability have become focal points for research. Questions are being asked about the correlation of drought and poor yields in one part of the world with that in another; about the tolerance levels of crops to variability, particularly traditional versus high-yielding varieties of grain; about the role of technology in offsetting variability; about the regions most susceptible to perturbations in the weather; and about the ways and means of reducing risk and uncertainty facing the individual farmer and countries as a whole. Although we cannot provide complete answers to these questions, it is possible to evaluate some of the major issues involved and highlight the production effects of climatic variability according to some major climatic regions of the world.

Measurement issues

Plant species currently grown for food and fibre are either relatively new varieties bred specifically for particular environmental conditions as with many high-yielding grains, such as maize, wheat and rice, or old varieties such as millet or sorghum which have adapted well over time to these conditions. Regardless of the type of plant, each will possess built-in tolerance levels to variations in moisture, photoperiod, heat, and growing season length. So long as these levels are not exceeded, impact upon yields will be small. Since each of these environmental parameters possesses a probability distribution, then the odds are that they will be exceeded once every three, five or ten years, etc., depending upon the region. Hence, every so many years drought, or frost or unusual wetness or some combination will create conditions that exceed the plant's natural tolerance and reduce yields. Conversely, yields may be particularly high with optimum combinations of thermal and moisture resources. Yields may also be reduced by changes (increasing variability) in the probability distribution of occurrences of anomalies (Fukui, 1979).

Droughts may now occur every four as opposed to six years on average. This may or may not entail a change in normals or average values. To illustrate these and related concepts, Figure 8.1 provides climatic states for thermal and moisture conditions. Each distribution shows the expected variability in thermal and moisture conditions with respect to normals, while changes in the positions of the distributions reflect either climate change (a shift in normals) or the weather conditions prevailing at different locations. Hence 'B' represents a shift to wetter and cooler conditions, with its own patterns of variability, whereas 'C' represents a shift to warmer drier conditions, with its own probability distribution of occurrence. Against this information stand hypothetical crop-yield tolerances according to moisture and thermal conditions. For each condition there are two distributions – a and b – the former representing more sensitive (hybrids) and the latter less sensitive (traditional) varieties. The degree to which changes in the normals and frequency of occurrence of moisture and temperature conditions coincide with a crop's moisture and temperature requirements (as indicated by tolerance distributions) will determine the success of crops grown.

Evidence of variability

Associated with the growth of world food production is a natural increase

217

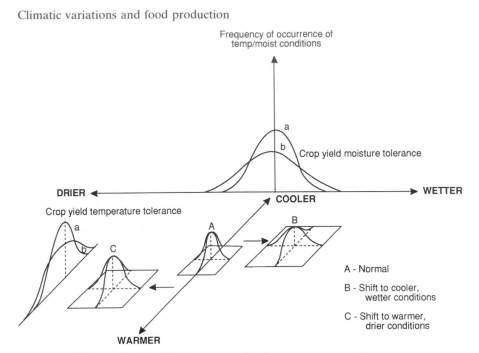

Fig. 8.1   Changes in the risk for crop production over space or time

in the variability of that production. As Tarrant (1987: 317) has argued: 'This is simply a result of stochastic variation about a mean.' Climate variability plays an important role in affecting that variability. In a study of yield variation over a twenty-three-year period (1950–73) for twenty-five major grain-producing regions of the world, it was found that one out of every three years would produce a total deviation in excess of 21 million tonnes from trend production. The author of the report noted that 'If the influence of weather were entirely random, the expected deviation would be 14.7 million tonnes' (Willet, 1976: 85). Moreover, there was evidence of spatial correlation between regions of the world in terms of their yield changes because of either favourable or adverse weather conditions.

Table 8.1 highlights by country examples of the absolute (standard deviation) and relative (coefficient of variation) variability of production. India possesses very high absolute variation in cereal production, but this is a relatively small percentage of average production. All North African and Middle-Eastern countries, with exception of Egypt, have high coefficients of variation. Cereal production in arid and semi-arid regions without the benefit of irrigation is particularly vulnerable to small changes in precipitation.

The variability of yields of specific crops underlines the critical import-ance of irrigation systems in stabilizing production. In Figures 8.2 and 8.3, for example, rice yields generally have a much lower coefficient of

Table 8.1 Variability in staple food production, 1961–76

	Staple food production instability		Probability of actual production falling below 95% of trend (%)	Correlation coefficient between total staple food production and consumption	Correlation coefficient between cereal production and total staple food production
	Standard deviations (thousand tonnes)	Coefficient of variation (%)			
Asia					
Bangladesh	765	6.4	22	0.90	0.99
India	6,653	6.4	22	0.89	0.99
Indonesia	1,040	5.4	18	0.92	0.94
Korea, Republic of	445	7.1	24	0.20	0.96
Philippines	346	5.7	19	0.03	0.99
Sri Lanka	107	9.3	29	0.56	0.91
North Africa/Middle East					
Algeria	531	28.9	43	0.78	1.00
Egypt	282	4.5	13	0.29	0.96
Jordan	119	65.6	47	0.63	1.00
Libya	56	28.0	43	0.62	1.00
Morocco	1,156	27.2	43	0.98	0.96
Syria	702	38.8	45	0.92	1.00
Sub-Saharan Africa					
Ghana	121	5.8	20	0.98	0.93
Nigeria	958	5.7	19	0.99	0.92
Senegal	335	18.6	39	0.99	0.81
Tanzania	430	12.7	35	0.98	0.09
Upper Volta	128	9.8	30	0.95	0.99
Zaïre	190	4.9	15	0.96	0.21
Latin America					
Brazil	1,631	5.2	17	0.92	0.60
Chile	215	11.1	33	0.54	0.99
Colombia	126	4.4	13	0.51	0.85
Guatemala	56	6.5	22	0.51	0.99
Mexico	1,060	7.7	26	0.53	1.00
Peru	197	9.8	30	0.37	0.97

Source after Oram (1982)

variation than wheat, although it must be emphasized that for some regions, such as China, the small relative variability would translate into large overall swings in food production.

Wheat production is plagued not only by moisture stress, as in Australia and Argentina, but also by variations in length of growing season and frost risk in Canada, the United States and the Soviet Union (see Fig. 8.3). More will be said on these regional variations later, but before doing that

219

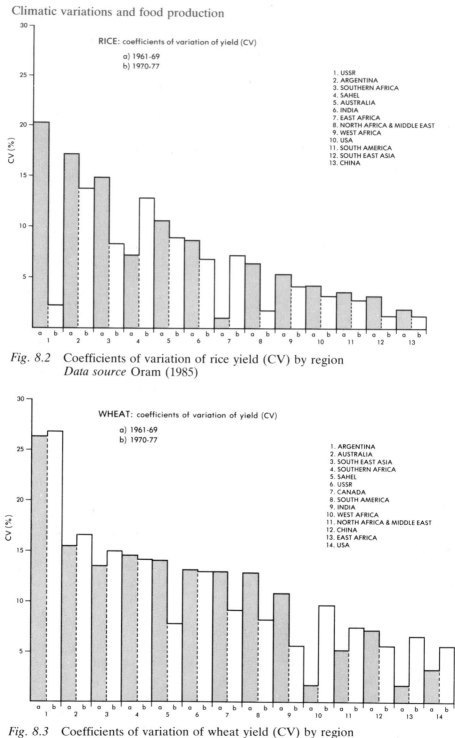

Fig. 8.2 Coefficients of variation of rice yield (CV) by region
Data source Oram (1985)

Fig. 8.3 Coefficients of variation of wheat yield (CV) by region
Data source Oram (1985)

two important questions must be considered. The first relates to a change in climatic variability while the second relates to the role of technology in affecting yield and production variability.

There is little unambiguous evidence to suggest that climatic variability is increasing. The 1970s were marked by greater extremes in temperature or precipitation than the previous three decades. The monsoons over India are becoming less predictable and average rainfall in the Sahel has declined since the 1960s. Hare (1979) suggested that the spatial and temporal variability of temperature has increased recently along with the poleward temperature gradient. This evidence would support a hypothesis that a cooling trend is occurring, increasing pole-to-tropics temperature gradients and intensifying disturbances through more vigorous atmospheric and oceanic circulations. An alternative hypothesis would be that a warming trend is occurring, reducing pole-to-tropics temperature gradients and hence weakening disturbances and instability in the climate system. There is other evidence, however, which suggests that at least for north and south non-tropical areas there is no increase in variability. Hare concluded that with the exception of the tropics there is no firm evidence of increasing variability in temperature.

This interpretation is supported by Tarrant's (1987) research, discussed in Chapter 3, in which globally there was no increase in year-to-year variability in yields. Having said this it should be stressed that inter-annual variability is increasing for some regions, particularly semi-arid regions. While climate accounts for some of the change in variability a more thorough explanation must address the interaction of climate and technology.

Technology is by far the most important factor affecting yield variability over the long term (between decades). Yields for corn and wheat in the United States have increased two and three times respectively since 1950. Irrigation, artificial fertilizers, pesticides and new hybrids have all contributed to the growth in output per unit area and expansion in cultivated area. These innovations have led to production/yield-stabilizing and destabilizing trends (Schneider, 1976). Irrigation is yield-stabilizing, so long as water is available at the right times and in sufficient quantities. Innovations that have the potential at least for destabilizing yields are the development of new seed varieties with a lower tolerance for changes in heat and moisture, increased reliance on energy-intensive inputs to sustain these new varieties (whose supply is uncertain because of price changes and distributional problems) and the spread of production into marginal areas. Recent research (Hazel, 1984: 1) 'supports the view that new technologies have contributed to increased yield variability, particularly in semi-arid regions with limited irrigation'.

Considerable controversy exists over the net effect of these trends. In other words, has technological change had an overall stabilizing effect upon yields? We saw earlier that year-to-year variability in yields in relative terms is not increasing. On a regional basis cereal yield variability showed a tendency to increase after 1971 in most of Africa, Australia, Soviet Union and the Middle East. Regions which show a decrease in year-to-year variability are Western Europe and Japan (Tarrant, 1987). Despite the adoption of Green Revolution technology in India, variability in grain production increased from the decade beginning 1967/68 relative to the previous decade (Hazell, 1982). This change had to do less with yield variability in traditionally-cropped areas and more with yield variability in more recently-cropped marginal areas. In Russia in two very different periods and management levels (1883–1915 and 1945–78) the climatic variability of cereal yield was essentially the same (Kogan, 1981).

During the 1960s in the United States it was widely believed that yield variability in good and bad weather had been reduced through technological enhancement of factors of production and that the prospects looked good for a continuation of this trend. To what degree had favourable weather conditions contributed to this situation? In a study of weather–yield interactions in the United States, Thompson (1975) used a statistical model to explain the variation in yield for corn, wheat and soybeans, based upon climatic data and technological trend variables. When technology was held constant at 1973 levels, so that the influence of weather on yields could be isolated, it was found that the low-yield variability from the mid-1950s to the early 1970s was due to abnormally good weather conditions. The model also demonstrated that even assuming the use of 1973 technology during the drought of the 1930s yield variability remained high. But even favourable weather conditions do not guarantee low-yield variability. In 1970 a mutant form of southern corn leaf blight spread throughout much of the US corn belt, devastating the corn crop based upon a relatively few hybrids.

The evidence suggests that by breeding crops with a narrower genetic base the new agricultural technologies have allowed for the expansion of yields and production. This strategy is successful, however, only under relatively controlled conditions. Deviations from these conditions because of climate variability, spread of pests, interruption in the supply of inputs, uneven application of technology and the spread of production into marginal areas have the potential to produce greater absolute if not relative deviations about a trend.

The main implication of these findings is that agricultural research needs to be devoted to the development of seed varieties capable of producing more stable yields under less than optimal growing conditions. Moreover, agricultural policy should not be based on the notion that technology leads to consistently high yields (Schneider, 1976). Policies, particularly those related to food reserves, must account for the risk of crop failure because of climatic anomalies and year-to-year variability in the system. This is all the more important when it is realized that poor harvests in one area are often correlated with poor harvests in another.

Production effects of climatic variability

Temperate regions (Humid and Dry)

Temperate regions (north and south) produce over 75 per cent of the wheat and coarse grain grown globally and supply approximately the same percentage to the world export market for grains. Although well suited to the production of grains, temperate regions are far from homogeneous in soils or climatic resources (see Fig. 8.4). The considerable variability in temperature and precipitation among the regions accounts for much of the spatial and temporal variation in yields over the short term. The temporal variation or year-to-year variability in yields due to natural factors such as weather, pests and diseases and human-induced factors such as markets and the price of grain, which affects the geographical extent of planted (and harvested) area, can be as low as 1 per cent and as high as 10 per cent of production (McQuigg, 1979). With this type of variation the relationship of production to consumption can quickly become imbalanced. In 1960 production of wheat and coarse grains exceeded consumption by 26 million metric tonnes, whereas in the following two years consumption exceeded production by 16 and 40 million metric tonnes respectively. Two or more years of consecutively poor weather conditions can easily reduce carry over stocks and hence remove surplus conditions.

Although it is difficult to generalize, moisture stress followed by temperature extremes would represent the two key limiting effects on yields. The physiological response of plants to these conditions varies according to species and the timing of the constraint. Wheat and soybean are more drought-resistant than corn. To highlight the production response of temperate regions to climatic variability we examine recent empirical evidence for three major grain-producing regions – the United States, Canada and the Soviet Union. (See Chapter 2 for a comparison of the climatic resources among these countries.)

The Soviet Union possesses the lowest average yields for wheat and coarse grain among these three countries and it possesses the highest relative variation. Some of this difference is due to relatively low proportions of area seeded to winter wheat, which is typically higher yielding, but precipitation is the major factor limiting both average yields and yield variations. Kogan (1981) has demonstrated an inverse relationship between variability of cereal yield and precipitation norm for the pre-growth and growing seasons (see Fig. 8.5). The lower the climatic norm of precipitation, the higher the climatic variability of yield (25–35 per cent). There appeared to be no difference in variability between state and collective farms and state strain-testing stations. Although the application of technology has considerably boosted yields in some areas of the Soviet Union since the Second World War, particularly in the Ukraine, Volga, North Caucasus and Chernozem districts, the level of variability has not been reduced.

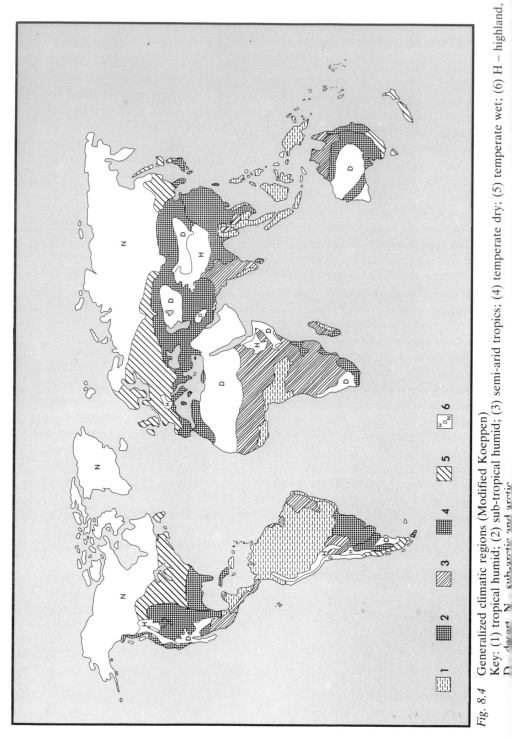

Fig. 8.4 Generalized climatic regions (Modified Koeppen)
Key: (1) tropical humid; (2) sub-tropical humid; (3) semi-arid tropics; (4) temperate dry; (5) temperate wet; (6) H – highland, D – desert, N – sub-arctic and arctic

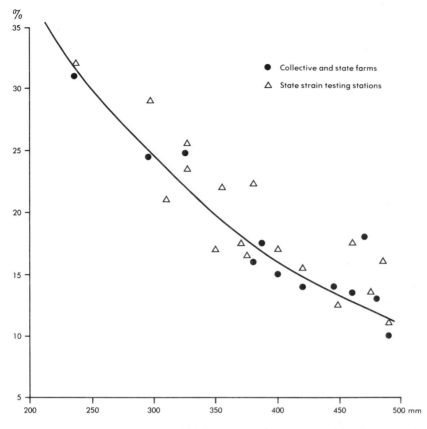

Fig. 8.5 Variability of cereal yield (percentage) versus precipitation norm for
January-September in the USSR.
Source Kogan (1981)

Not unlike the Soviet Union, grain production in Canada is subject to
many of the same vagaries in thermal and moisture conditions. There is no
doubt that climatic resources and their variability create substantial limits
for grain production compared to the United States. Figure 8.6 highlights
grain yields for the two countries over a sixty-year period. Whereas the
upward trend in yields in both cases is due to the application of similar
forms of technology (particularly increased application of fertilizers to new
seed varieties), the size of the variability with respect to the average trend
says much about the quality and consistency of the climatic resources of
the two regions. The growth of grain yields in the United States is heavily
weighted by the performance of the chief crop corn and the ideal climatic
resources available for its growth in the Mid-West. In Canada, wheat is the
chief crop grown in many areas at the climatic margin of production. The
risk of growing grain therefore is generally much higher in the Canadian

225

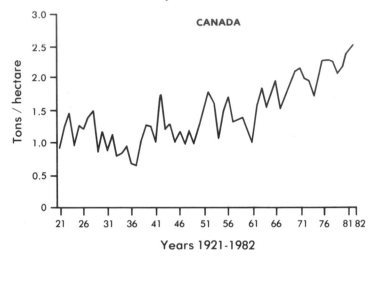

Fig. 8.6 Time series profile of grain yields in Canada and the United States 1920–82
Source USDA (1957) and (1983); Statistics Canada (1979) and Agricultural Canada (1983)

prairies than in the south. And while variation in length of growing season and average temperatures explains some of the difference, it also depends on the the amount of precipitation in June and August, the preceding winter's snowfall, and on the spread of grasshopper infestations during 'normal' conditions. Although fertilizer use has greatly expanded since the

226

Second World War, the efficiency of uptake of that fertilizer varies (directly) in relation to moisture availability.

The United States has not escaped the ravages of drought or temperature extremes despite the superior climatic resources available for grain production, particularly corn. Drought in 1974 and 1980 seriously reduced yields. McQuigg (1981) cited the case of extreme temperatures in 1980 in excess of 37.7° C. during the month of July. This prolonged heat-wave affected the flowering pollination process. The net effect was an 18 per cent decrease in yields from the preceding years.

The impact that year-to-year variations in weather and climatic anomalies have upon the supply of grains worldwide depends very much upon the correlation of crop failures and successes in different temperate regions of the world. It has been observed that the probability of a sharing of good or bad conditions worldwide was better than 50–50 during the third quarter of the twentieth century (Willet, 1976).

Humid tropics and sub-tropics

The tropics represent an incredible diversity of climatic and biotic resources. Of the hundred different bio-climates defined by Holdridge's World Life Zone System, thirty-nine are found in the tropics, compared to twenty-three in the warm temperate and sixteen in the cool temperate zones (Cooper, 1981). The tropics contain considerable climatic variability not only over space but also over time. The major expression of this variability is the year-to-year variation in precipitation which ultimately governs the region's surface and groundwater hydrology. Since the agricultural systems of the region are diverse, ranging from lowland intensive rice cultivation and flood-retreat agriculture to upland intensive rice and maize to slash and burn, the consequences of rainfall variability for food production differ considerably.

The high intensity and, in many cases, unpredictability of the rainfall, particularly during the monsoons, the greatly diminished rainfall for two to three months in many regions, the poor water-holding capacity of the coarse-grained soils and the high rate of evapotranspiration contribute in no small way to unstable water availability for agriculture. Fukui (1979) has observed that the core region of the Asian rice zone (Pakistan, India, Thailand and Kampuchea) is either marginal or prohibitive for rice production, unless irrigated systems are used.

Upland areas of the tropics are inherently risky places to grow crops. Upland rice and maize often suffer from inadequate rainfall and large scale land degradation, whereas sorghum and cassava are less prone to moisture stress and can prosper on relatively infertile soil. Many perennial crops such as coffee, tea, jute, rubber, palm oil and bananas have adapted well to the soil and climatic vagaries of upland tropical areas, although periodic low temperatures and frost have damaged coffee production in countries such as Brazil.

Lowland areas which produce the bulk of cereals and other directly-consumed food are affected by climatic variability in two principal ways. First, torrential rainfall of short duration commonly floods river valleys and coastal lowland areas, inundating that season's planted crop. Bangladesh suffers from extensive flooding throughout its deltaic environments. Second, and more importantly, rainfall variability in areas that are hydrologically marginal for rice production can, in the absence of other sources of water, create large variations in yield. The growth of rice depends upon the impounding of water in bunds from two sources – direct rainfall and some artificial supply of water. This artificial supply can take many forms ranging from complete control, as in sophisticated irrigation systems (phase II and III of David's water-basin control scheme), to redirecting stream/river run-off from catchment areas to simple holding ponds and reservoirs. Although these latter systems are a form of irrigation, only the first offers real security of supply.

The amount of water available for impounding depends upon many other factors in addition to rainfall, but the most important are the levels of technology available and natural or physical conditions of the land – such as the ratio of catchment area to rice land. A study of rice-yield variation in Thailand revealed that rainfall or seasonal water balance alone did not explain a large part of the variation in yield (Takaya, 1971). However, when the same variable was combined with the ratio of alluvial soil to catchment area, the degree of explanation increased considerably.

The control of water supply is the key factor in stabilizing the growth of rice yields in the tropics. The United States, USSR and Japan have some of the lowest coefficients of variation in rice yield, largely because of their highly-advanced irrigation systems. Since the variability of rice production in the tropics is less than for wheat and coarse grains in temperate and tropical areas, the region's food security is greatly enhanced.

Semi-arid tropics

Semi-arid tropical regions of the world (see Fig. 8.4), containing approximately 15 per cent of the world's population in some fifty countries and 13 per cent of the world's land mass, are most susceptible to climatic variability in the form of uneven rainfall (Swindale et al., 1981). The major regions with a long history of periodic crop failure and famine, which also contain the bulk of total arid population, are the Sahel and India. The problems of aridity and their consequences for crop growth are not unique to the tropical regions of the world since numerous temperate regions in the Great Plains and the Steppes of Russia are also plagued by insufficient moisture. There are, however, important and significant differences in water balance.

The majority of the rainfall in the semi-arid tropics falls during a two- to five-month period between April and October in the northern hemisphere, and October to April in the southern. This is at the same time when temperatures and transpiration are at their highest. Thus, the availability of moisture becomes the critical factor affecting growing season length which is often shorter than in more moderate temperate regions. Since evapotranspiration is so high, particularly at sowing time when ground cover is minimal or non-existent, minimum rainfall must be 400 mm, compared to 250 mm in temperate climates. Accordingly, given the same rainfall, average yields will be lower in tropical semi-arid regions than in temperate areas. Mattei (1979) estimated that with between 400–600 mm of rainfall, average yields of grains in temperate regions are 800–1000 kg/ha against 400–700 kg/ha in tropical areas. This underlines the significance of the variation in potential evapotranspiration between the two regions.

Since potential evapotranspiration is relatively constant, the main source of risk in agriculture derives from high intra- and inter-annual variation in precipitation (coefficient of variation of 20 to 30 per cent) (Swindale et al., 1981). The beginning and ending of the monsoons are critical factors affecting the availability of water and in turn the sequence of farm operations and crop development. Figure 8.7 indicates this sequence and its relationships to water availability. Growing seasons range from a minimum of 60–100 days to a maximum of 160–200 days, with rainfall exceeding PET from less than 60–100 days. Soil type plays a key role in growing season length, with shallow alfisols having the smallest water storage capacity and deep vertisols the highest.

Variability of the beginning and end of rains can have a great impact on sowing and ripenihg processes. Millet and sorghum, the two principal

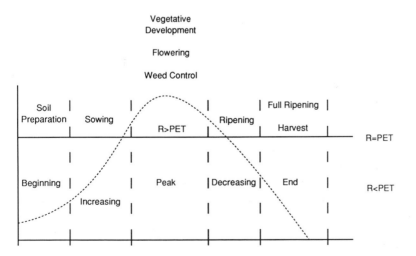

Fig. 8.7   The pattern of water availability in semi-arid tropics
Source adapted from Mattei (1979)

rainfed crops in non-irrigated semi-arid regions, show substantial yield decreases with late sowing. Mattei (1979) observed that in central Niger farmers have adapted to variability in the growing season with different varieties of millet. There are numerous other responses to the uncertainties of rainfall variability. Most of the crop varieties are traditional and well adapted to moisture stress, but not highly responsive to good conditions. Intercropping, as in the case of sorghum/pigeonpea in India, is a successful risk-averse strategy with a failure rate of one year in thirty-six, compared to the sole cultivation of pigeonpea or sorghum with failure rates of one in five and one in eight years respectively (Swindale et al., 1981). Fallowing is a common practice to restore soil moisture, but it is the adoption of irrigated systems which affords the greatest security against the vagaries of rainfall. The importance of conserving and improving soil moisture cannot be overstated. Since soils in most of the semi-arid tropics are low in nitrogen and phosphorous, fertilizer application is critical for growth in yields; but yield response to these fertilizers is poor unless there is sufficient soil moisture.

The single largest continuous extension of the semi-arid tropics lies south of the Sahara extending on the west from Senegal and Mali through Niger and Nigeria in West Africa to Chad, Sudan and the Ethiopian highlands to the East (see Fig. 8.8). The Sahel represents a transition zone between non-agricultural desert lands to the north in the Sahara and permanently settled and intensively-cropped areas to the south. Similar semi-arid conditions exist in most of the Indian subcontinent. Both of these areas have been subject to periodic drought and famine. Large soil moisture deficits are due to a variety of natural and human-induced circumstances – first we shall look at the natural factors.

Natural factors
Both the Sahel and India are dependent for their water supply on the annual northward extension of the tropical rains or monsoon. In the Sahel, summer monsoons originate in the South Atlantic and move northward with the advance of the zenith. The northern penetration of the monsoons is the critical factor affecting the adequacy of rainfall in the region. The deeper and longer the penetration of the monsoons, the greater the availability of rainfall (Bryson and Murray, 1977). The northern terminus of the monsoon is determined by the position of the inter-tropical convergence zone (ITCZ) which is the convergence of the tradewinds from northern and southern hemispheres. The currents from the south represent rising air, whereas those to the north represent subsiding air with very little moisture content. Closely related to the latitude of the ITCZ is the position of the sub-tropical anticyclone. This high-pressure system bordering the southern boundary of the westerlies moves poleward in the summer and equatorward in the winter. The positions of the ITCZ and the sub-tropical anticyclone display considerable annual variability.

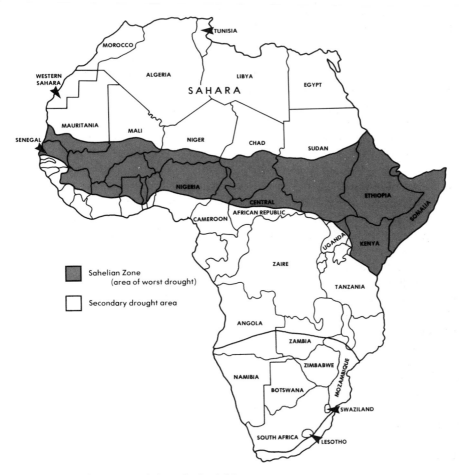

Fig. 8.8   Major areas of drought in Africa
Source adapted from Keating (1985)

The lower seasonal rainfalls from 1968 to the present are due to the failure of the monsoon to penetrate as far north as in the preceding twenty years (see Fig. 8.9). Research has shown that a displacement of one degree latitude of the ITCZ results in a shift of 17 cm of rainfall in Northern Nigeria (Bryson and Murray, 1977). Not surprisingly, the shifts in ITCZ, and hence in the northern positions of the monsoons, can then have a dramatic effect upon water balance. In 1972 a wide band throughout the traditional northern Sahel experienced conditions in which rainfall never exceeded potential evapotranspiration.

The variability in the position of the monsoons has been the subject of intense scholarly activity (with no conclusive findings) regarding the

231

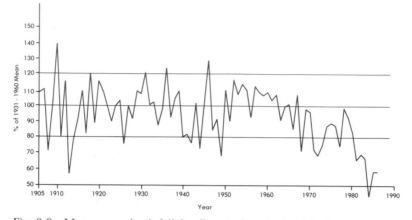

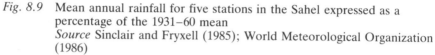

Fig. 8.9   Mean annual rainfall for five stations in the Sahel expressed as a
percentage of the 1931–60 mean
Source Sinclair and Fryxell (1985); World Meteorological Organization
(1986)

prediction of future changes in the extent of the monsoons on a year-to-
year basis. On the other hand, it has been determined that changes in the
equator to pole and surface to upper air temperature gradients have an
effect upon the position of the westerlies and the sub-tropical anticyclone.
Increasing carbon dioxide content and particulate matter suspended in the
atmosphere can affect solar radiation and in turn temperature gradients
(Bryson and Murray, 1977).

   In India, the northern penetration of the monsoons into the subcontinent
is also dependent upon the position of the westerlies and the sub-tropical
anticyclones to the south. If the westerlies shift to the north of the
Himalayas during the summer, the monsoons will penetrate well to the
north from the Indian Ocean. If the westerlies remain to the south, a
strong high pressure system limits the northern extent of the monsoons.
But the success or failure of the monsoons in Asia may also be linked to
the relative strength of the El Nino in the eastern Pacific. Evidence of
teleconnections can be found in the fact that the past twenty El Ninos have
been followed by fourteen poor or failed monsoons (*The Economist*,
1987b). As pressure falls over the Pacific, producing rain, it tends to be
associated with a rise in air pressure over Asia, providing an effective
block to the inward movement of warm moist air. The frequency of failure
of the monsoons has increased. During the last fifteen years the monsoons
failed five times in India compared to two times during the previous fifteen
years.

Human-induced factors
Such life-giving rains and their interruption in supply have had a critical
effect on the sustainability of agriculture in many semi-arid regions. But to

232

suggest that the failure of monsoon rains is the only agent underlying the increasing aridity of many of these environments is to ignore the real and on-going interactive effects of cultivation and pastoralism with the atmospheric/biotic system. Perhaps the Sahel offers the best example of this.

Two competing arguments have been forwarded to explain the increasing aridity and failure of this region to sustain its animal and human populations. One approach argues that the collapse of the biotic potential of the Sahel is due to extended periods of drought. Sandford (1983), a recent proponent of this drought hypothesis, has argued that water availability is the ultimate control or check. Indications are that the sub-Saharan drought between 1972 and 1987 has been the worst in 150 years, with the driest years of the present century occurring in the 1984–85 period (Kerr, 1985). He also sees the quantity of forage within reach of a dry-season water point as important. In cases of severe drought there is a tendency for overgrazing within the immediate vicinity of these natural or artificially created (bore-hole) water areas, producing what is termed 'sacrifice areas'. But in his view this is not human-induced and therefore cannot be considered desertification.

The second argument regarding desertification can be termed the 'settlement-overgrazing hypothesis'. In the view of Sinclair and Fryxell (1985: 990): 'The lower rainfall might have been the proximate trigger for the famine, but it was the prior overgrazing that was the ultimate cause.' The famine in the Sahel is human-induced through overgrazing, resulting in the spread of desertified environments. The authors cite evidence from numerous studies during the last ten years to support this alternative hypothesis. The major source of the problem derives from the concentration of forage and reduced migration patterns. They emphasize that the growth of cultivated areas to the south restricted access to traditional rangelands and, in combination with this, international development aid financed the creation of drill boreholes to improve access to groundwater reserves which concentrated grazing pressures. Reinforcing the effects of the previous conditions were improvements in medical and veterinary services which encouraged the growth in human and livestock populations. These factors led to significant overgrazing and, when combined with successive periods of drought, as between 1968–73 and 1980–84, the process of wind erosion and desertification took hold. It is from these nuclei that desertification spreads and interlocks with other nuclei – and not the spread of the edge of the desert that represents the process of desertification.

Sinclair and Fryxell have cited two studies which tend further to refute the drought hypothesis. Satellite imagery of a government ranch practising a rotational grazing system in the middle of the farm area of the Sahel revealed a green polygon (representing the ranch) surrounded by denuded vegetation. Both areas had received the same rainfall. Because the grasslands were not overgrazed they were able to withstand the sustained drought condition which according to meteorological records (See Fig. 8.9) are not unusual for the Sahel (at least prior to 1984–85).

Finally, the authors note that overgrazing may affect weather patterns themselves. An analysis of the radiation balance in the Sinai–Negev boundary between Egypt and Israel indicates that the Sinai with its overgrazed surfaces had higher reflectivity and cooler surface temperatures than the Negev which has little grazing, high plant cover and a lower albedo. This plant cover contributes to higher surface temperatures, leading to convective currents which at higher elevations condense to produce rainfall. Others (Hare, 1977) have also argued that alterations in surface vegetation may tend to have a positive feedback effect and actually prolong drought. And Norse (1979) has suggested that in the Sahel–Sudan zone the tendency during recent time has been for herd size to expand with favourable climate conditions on commonly-owned land which is decimated when drought conditions return. This cycle occurs over a ten- to fifteen-year period.

On the basis of these and other studies Sinclair and Fryxell propose a conceptual model of the interactive character of the biotic and atmospheric systems (see Fig. 8.10). This suggests that unless ameliorative measures are taken to reduce overgrazing, the ecological consequences will be severe. In terms of a continuation of food aid the authors (p. 991) noted that '[it] will both maintain the current imbalance between human populations and the land on which they depend, and encourage humans and livestock to emigrate south and start the overgrazing cycle again on new land while incorporating those additional peoples into the problem.'

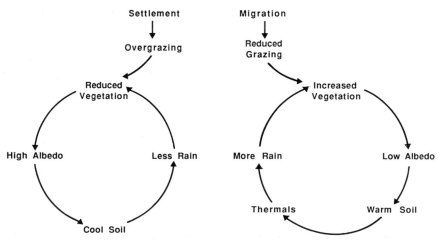

Fig. 8.10 Suggested sequence of the two climate-vegetation feedback systems in the semi-arid regions
Source Sinclair and Fryxell (1985)

Desertification is therefore not some isolated climate-induced phenomenon, but a failure, on a truly massive scale, to recognize and understand the interrelationships of people to the land. While applications of science to these environments will undoubtedly improve the prospects for change, we must also recognize other significant underlying factors which gave rise to these human pressures in the first place.

The civil war in Ethiopia has limited access by pastoralists to grazing lands. Cash-crop policies in Sudan for cotton and in West African countries for peanuts has led to the agricultural use of highly marginal lands with limited capability of sustaining long-term use. Many of these policies are directly linked to the internationalization of agriculture through agro-industries and the policies of the World Bank and the vital need for foreign exchange. Equally important in understanding the deterioration of these systems is the imbalance between population growth rates and technological developments (which influence herd sizes) and the ability of the social and economic environment to accommodate these changes (Norse, 1979).

Climatic change

Part of the concern over climatic variability is that it may be linked to climatic change in the earth's equilibrium climate. Increased variability and changes in the risk of crop failure may signal a significant change in normal conditions, indicating a long-term trend towards warming/cooling and drier/wetter conditions (as we saw in Fig. 8.1). Whereas the numerous Ice Ages accompanied by milder inter-glacial periods offer convincing evidence of climatic change, no comparable change has occurred during human occupation of the earth. Nevertheless, within the Holocene, the present inter- (or post) glacial period, significant shifts have occurred in average temperatures and precipitation. Compare the relatively moist conditions experienced throughout the Middle East (including North Africa and India) during the Altithermal Period (4500–8000 BP) with the drier conditions in these regions today and, the general cooling of Europe and North America from the sixteenth to the nineteenth century with the warmer conditions which exist today. While the consequences of these changes proved fatal for some hydraulic civilizations (Middle-Eastern), Europe survived in part because of superior technology and trade and because of a less marginal environment for food production.

The fact remains in these and other numerous cases of recent climatic change that relatively small changes in temperature can precipitate large changes in growing season length, soil moisture and general environment for crop production. The agricultural and human implications of this fact have not gone unnoticed. The search for indications of a changing climate and the factors underlying that change have attracted increasing attention in the scientific establishment. What then are the potential causes of climate change and what are the implications regionally and globally for agricultural production?

Sources of change

Tracing the origins and causes of climatic change requires temporal and geographic matching of changes in one or more external factors such as solar energy output, the earth's orbit, volcanic dust, CO_2 and other infra-red absorbing gases and continental drift with short- and long-term trends in the climate system itself. There is no single or unified theory explaining the long-term changes in the earth's climate. Whereas changes in solar energy output, continental drift and variations in the earth's orbit offer tentative but incomplete explanations of long-term climatic shifts, they offer little insight into more short-term fluctuations, such as the Little Ice Age, or even shorter-term cooling trends. Other natural factors, such as increasing atmospheric particulate debris through volcanic activity and internal variations in the climate system itself among the atmosphere, oceans, land and glaciers, particularly in the way energy is redistributed among these components of the system, may explain short term climate change (Schneider, 1976).

In contrast with natural external factors are numerous potential human sources of 'short-term' climatic change. Extensive land-clearing, overgrazing and the burning of fossil fuels have altered the earth's albedo or reflectivity, increased particulate matter in the atmosphere, changed a number of critical biogeochemical cycles and modified the atmospheric concentration of infra-red absorbing gases. Although not the only infra-red absorbing gas, carbon dioxide (CO_2) holds the potential for some dramatic changes in the earth/atmosphere radiation balance and in turn significant climatic change. Given the importance of CO_2, it is worth examining both its climatic and agricultural impacts.

Climatic impacts of increases in CO_2

Since the early nineteenth century, CO_2 concentrations in the atmosphere increased from approximately 265 to 316 ppm in 1958 to 345 ppm in 1985 – almost a 19 per cent increase. If current trends continue, the atmospheric concentration of CO_2 could double ($2 \times CO_2$) by the middle of the next century.

The dynamics of changes in atmospheric CO_2 are highly complex. Before the dawn of the industrial revolution a balance existed between the natural sources of CO_2 and the sinks or reservoirs of CO_2, principally the oceans and vegetative mass of the planet (Revelle, 1982). These sinks both absorb and release CO_2. With large-scale deforestation and the ten-fold increase in energy consumption from 770 million metric tonnes of coal equivalent (mmtce) in 1900 to 9000 mmtce in 1984, this balance was destroyed. The burning of wood and its oxidation after forest-clearing not only contributed to this increased output but limited through deforestation the capacity to absorb increases in CO_2. An even larger source of carbon than in forested areas is thought to exist in soil organic matter. As noted in Chapter 7, modern industrial agricultural methods are responsible for the breakdown of the matter and the release of CO_2 into the atmosphere. The net result is a dramatic rise in airborne CO_2 which over the last two decades represents approximately half of the cumulative total produced. Revelle (1982) has observed that since the rate at which the oceans can absorb the gas is lower than originally thought, because of the slow rate of mixing of ocean layers, this airborne fraction could increase. On the other hand a diminution in the rate of consumption of fossil fuels, particularly coal, and an increase in biomass would hold constant or reduce the fraction.

Carbon dioxide is considered the main gas which alters the heat balance of the earth by allowing short-wave solar radiation through but absorbing and re-radiating longer-wave radiation. This energy feedback mechanism has been termed the 'greenhouse effect'. A comparison of the earth's radiative equilibrium temperature ($-18\,°C$) with the earth's surface temperature ($+15\,°C$) reveals a shortfall of $33\,°C$. This difference is due to the presence of CO_2, and other gases in the atmosphere which increase the atmosphere's opacity, leading to a warming of the earth's surface. By extension, by altering the quantity of CO_2 in the atmosphere, humans are inadvertently altering the earth's thermostat.

Other important gases affecting atmospheric opacity include ozone (O_2) and water vapour (which is expected to increase with increased CO_2 levels and heat), as well as a number of trace gases such as methane (CH_4), nitrous oxide (N_2O) and chloroflurocarbons (CFCs). It is estimated that the combined climatic effects of these trace gases could be as large as from an increase in CO_2 concentrations (Wang et al., 1985). Some of these trace gases (N_2O and CFCs) are also thought to be responsible for a reduction in the ozone layer in the stratosphere which filters out incoming ultra-violet radiation.

Given these changes in the carbon cycle and receptivity of the atmosphere to long-wave radiation absorption, the obvious question is, how will the climate of the earth respond? It was hypothesized, almost a century ago, that increases in the atmospheric concentration of CO_2 would increase the surface temperature of the earth. Since that time a number of researchers have argued along similar lines, but it was not until the 1970s that concerted efforts were made to simulate comprehensively the likely impact on the earth's climate of changes in CO_2 emissions. Recent research on mean temperature variation (see Fig. 8.11) indicates that there was a gradual warming trend from the mid-nineteenth century to about 1940, a cooling trend for about twenty years and, since the late 1960s, a rise in surface temperature. But this most recent change is of too short duration to make any conclusive assessment of trends between CO_2 and

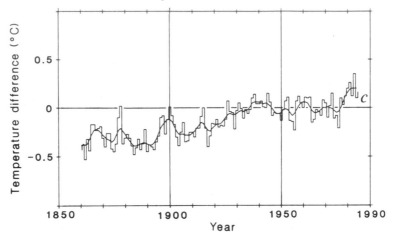

Global annual mean temperature variations since 1861, based on land and marine data
Source Jones et al. (1986)

radiation balance. Complicating that assessment are enormous interactive complexities of the components of the climate system, unknowns regarding surface-air temperature response to a rise in CO_2 and the role of the ocean in heat transport.

Recent research efforts

Generally, research into changes into the earth's equilibrium climate as a result of increasing CO_2 has pursued two separate but complementary approaches: mathematical or numerical modelling using general circulation models (GCMs), and the analysis of historical data from warm periods as analogues for the future (Wigley et al., 1980).

Analogue models

Analogue models offer a convenient snapshot of the future, based upon either regional reconstructions of paleoclimatic data or analyses of regional climates during warm years from recent instrumental records. The major difficulty with both approaches is that their value and accuracy as snapshots of the future depend on the similarities of boundary conditions of the past (e.g., between hydrosphere and cryosphere) with those of the future (Flohn, 1979). Wigley et al. (1980) observed that in all the major warm periods examined, boundary conditions differed.

Perhaps the best-known studies of past climates are by Kellogg (1977, 1978) and Butzer (1980). Both examined the distribution of moisture conditions from paleoclimatic data of the mid-Holocene (4500–8000 BP). The mid-Holocene or Altithermal was chosen because temperatures were

238

between 2 °C to 4 °C warmer than the present. Estimates of future warming of the earth's atmosphere through doubling of CO_2 suggest temperature increases between 1.5 °C and 4.5 °C (or average 3 °C ± 1.5 °C). Kellogg used pollen data from the Altithermal to construct a picture of changes in precipitation patterns relative to present patterns. That study and a similar one by Butzer (1980) showed a measure of agreement over drier conditions than now in central North America and wetter conditions than now throughout the Middle East and central India. The incomplete nature of the data and differences in outcomes with Butzer's study and two other studies analysing the temperature and precipitation differences between the recent past and today (Williams, 1979 and Wigley et al., 1980) prompted Kellogg and Schware (1981) to draft a composite view of moisture differences according to the previous studies. Reproduced in Figure 8.12, it reveals soil-moisture patterns appreciably different from today's patterns (see soil-moisture deficit map in Chapter 2). While there is general agreement over drier conditions in North America and wetter conditions in Africa, the Middle East and India, there are substantial regions where disagreement persists.

Given the dramatic differences in boundary conditions between the mid-Holocene and today, it is not surprising that there are differences between the two sets of studies used by Kellogg and Schware. Since the study by Wigley et al. (1980) offers a more detailed (temperature and precipitation) and arguably a more methodologically sound approach (since boundary conditions differ less), it is useful to examine these results. Wigley and colleagues selected the five warmest and coldest years between 1925–74 for northern latitudes (65 °N to 80 °N) and calculated the average temperature and precipitation differences for a composite of warm and cold years. Northern latitudes were chosen in part because of the belief that CO_2-induced changes will have their greatest impact in these northern latitudes. In the case of change in average surface temperature, the size of the gain increases poleward (see Fig. 8.13a) with the greatest changes taking place in winter compared to summer. While the trend is toward an increase in temperature, some regions to the south show negative differences.

In the case of changes in the pattern of precipitation, the warm-year group had annual precipitation of between 1 and 2 per cent above cold-year group. Numerical modelling results of changes in precipitation with $2 \times CO_2$ are in the order of 5 per cent. Figure 8.13b illustrates the spatial extent of these changes in precipitation. Large regions of central North America, Europe and Asia experience decreases in precipitation. If these changes are examined seasonally, Europe and Russia experience most of these reductions during the winter and autumn, whereas in the United States the reductions in precipitation occur during the summer and autumn. Further north, Canada experiences an increase in precipitation during the summer. The authors argue that these patterns of temperature

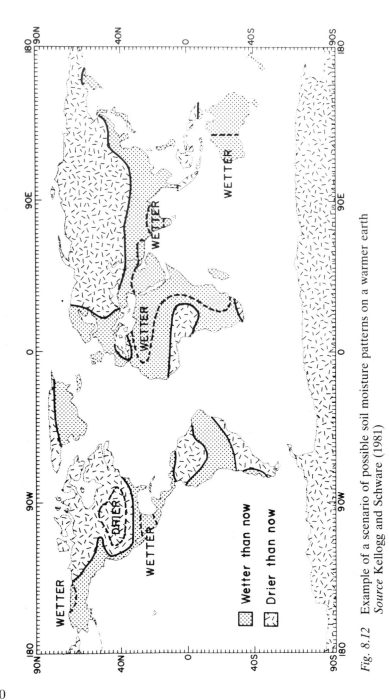

Fig. 8.12 Example of a scenario of possible soil moisture patterns on a warmer earth
Source Kellogg and Schware (1981)

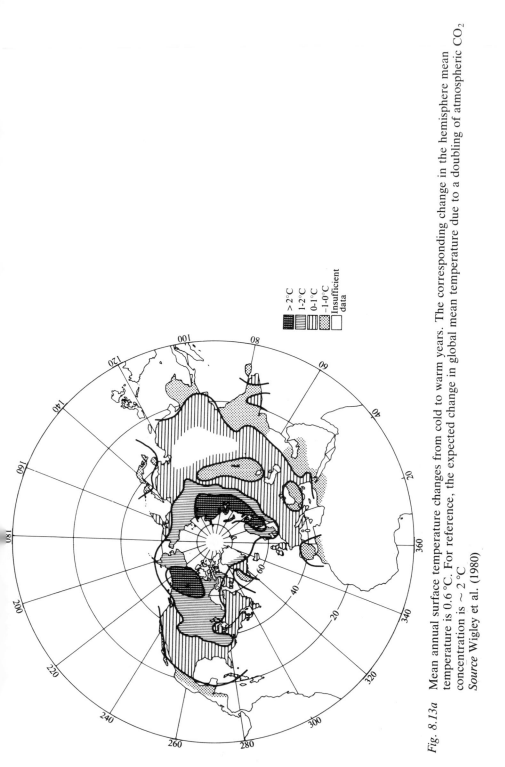

Fig. 8.13a Mean annual surface temperature changes from cold to warm years. The corresponding change in the hemisphere mean temperature is 0.6 °C. For reference, the expected change in global mean temperature due to a doubling of atmospheric CO_2 concentration is ~ 2 °C
Source Wigley et al. (1980)

> 2 °C
1-2 °C
0-1 °C
-1-0 °C
Insufficient data

241

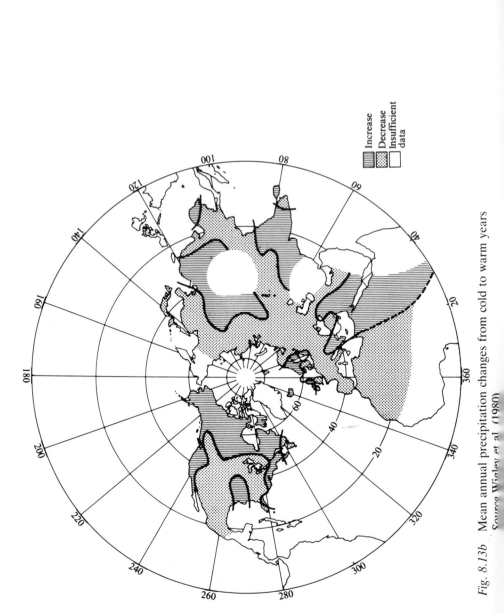

Fig. 8.13b Mean annual precipitation changes from cold to warm years
Source Wigley et al (1980)

and precipitation are scenarios as opposed to predictions of the impacts of future warming. They also point out that these scenarios are likely to take place only up until the turn of the century.

General circulation models

The second approach at simulating change in the earth's equilibrium climate from changes or perturbations in the atmospheric concentration of CO_2 is through numerical modelling using general circulation models. A number of these models, including those from the National Oceanic Atmospheric Administration (NOAA), Geophysical Fluid Dynamics Laboratory (GFDL) and Goddard Institute for Space Studies (GISS) have estimated latitudinal variations in temperature and precipitation assuming $2 \times$ and $4 \times CO_2$ under different boundary conditions. Although some integrating of atmosphere–ocean conditions occurs, these models are still very much atmospheric models with externally-prescribed boundaries. For example, most ignore horizontal and vertical heat transport of the oceans. Despite the weaknesses, the models have proven successful at simulating present large-scale climate conditions, including temperature, distribution of pressure and wind speed (Gates, 1985). Measures of present climate, including consideration of variability, act as control runs.

To test the impact of changing CO_2 levels, the models are run based upon higher levels of CO_2, holding constant all of the other factors and boundary conditions specified earlier in the control run. This 'perturbed' run may be time dependent, indicating the evolution of the climate to some equilibrium or, sudden, reflecting immediate increase in CO_2 levels (Kellogg and Schware, 1981). Given the complexity of the climatic system and the need to simplify it with a number of assumptions relating to such factors as sea ice, albedo, insulation cloud cover, the annual capacity of oceans, humidity and radiation, outcomes among models differ, as does their accuracy. What follows is a general summary of the more salient findings of these models, along with an example of one simulated run for temperature and precipitation.

Most of the GCMs show average surface-temperature increases of between 1.5 to 4.5 °C for $2 \times CO_2$. Although warming increased poleward in both hemispheres (but less in the Southern), there are large differences in the degree of warming among studies, with winter temperatures increases ranging from 2° to 8 °C for central North America. Maximum warming occurs during winter months in middle and high latitudes (Luther, 1985). The oceans are the least responsive of the earth's surface area to changes in CO_2 concentrations. In the GFDL GCM by Wetherald and Mange (Schlesinger and Mitchell, 1985), the positive summer temperature differences are greatest from approximately 30° N to 70° N. The high deviations for the Southern hemisphere, which are highly unlikely, are in part due to the inability of the original control run to simulate current conditions accurately.

Greater differences exist among the GCMs in their estimates of changes to precipitation and soil moisture. With increasing average temperatures, atmospheric humidity increases as does overall precipitation, but with important regional differences. North America, Europe and Central Asia show small declines in precipitation, whereas South and South-East Asia show considerable gains. When the temperature and precipitation data are combined to produce soil water differences, large deficiencies occur worldwide, with some of the largest in North America and Central Asia.

The considerable differences regionally among the models and the 'exaggerated' temperature changes require cautious use of the results. The need for caution is underlined by other factors, such as the large-scale spatial averaging approach used in GCMs, the sensitivity of the results to the heat capacity of oceans and other complex feedback processes (e.g., introduction of cloud cover) and the differing assumptions about future boundary conditions. Moreover, empirical evidence indicates the response characteristics of the atmosphere to changes from CO_2 may be much less dramatic than originally thought. Kimball and Idso (1983) argued that mean surface air temperatures are likely to rise no more than 0.25 °C with $2 \times CO_2$. Notwithstanding this point, Idso (1985) argued that while CO_2 concentrations may double, the benefits of these concentrations in the form of enhancing photosynthesis and water use efficiency are likely to be greater than the costs.

Impacts on agriculture

Changes in the earth's equilibrium climate affect the agricultural sector in terms of yields, qualitatively and quantitatively, crop inputs, cropping intensities and/or the area over which specific crops can be grown. Perturbations to the climatic system as a result of increasing levels of CO_2 and the likely changes to agriculture both at the macro (regional) level and at the micro (individual farming) level are far from clear. In a study of world grain production under different climatic scenarios (both warming and cooling), Johnson (1983) argued that the expected changes to production from different climatic scenarios would be less than historic inter-annual variation in yields. Moreover, until the year 2000, 'A 10 per cent change in either per capita income or population growth rates would generate roughly four times as large a change in world grain production as would be generated by either the Large Cooling or Large Warming scenarios' (Johnson, 1983: 26). This is not to deny the importance of climate but to place it, over the short term, within a broader perspective.

Change to climate at a magnitude to exceed the effects of inter-annual variability and perturbations caused by other factors such as technology and demand are unlikely to occur until well into the next century (Parry and Carter, 1984). Despite this long-time horizon, the possible significance of the impacts of gradual warming of the atmosphere on world food production is worth investigating.

The agricultural effects of changes in climate from increasing atmospheric concentrations of CO_2 have two dimensions. One expresses the direct climatological effects in terms of changes in temperature, growing season length, precipitation and soil moisture. The other expresses the biological effects from alterations to the efficiency of photosynthesis and to respiration.

Climatological effects

In evaluating the effect of climate change on food production, a number of contextual features need to be identified: (1) the crop's bio-physical requirements; (2) how closely matched these bio-physical requirements are within a given agro-ecological zone; (3) the yield response to changes in these requirements; and (4) the sensitivity of the environment in terms of growing season length and soil moisture to changes in temperature and precipitation.

The fact that global temperature may rise, with the greatest increases occurring in high latitudes accompanied by significant shifts in soil moisture, is a recipe for large-scale changes in productivity and range of crop production. Our present agro-ecological zones are expected to change and, with that change, suitability of these regions for crop production. Regions which are already on the margin of agricultural production, such as the arid and semi-arid regions of the world, will be particularly sensitive to changes in rainfall distribution (both in totals and in seasonality), whereas high latitude and altitude regions will be particularly sensitive to changes in temperature and growing season length.

Recent research on the sensitivity of agricultural production in a variety of northern regions to a warming trend has indicated favourable and unfavourable outcomes (Parry and Carter, 1987). Examples from Saskatchewan and North Japan (Hokkaido) will illustrate these outcomes. In the case of Southern Saskatchewan, Figure 8.14 profiles estimated effects of changes in thermal and moisture conditions upon such things as yield (first-order effects) and the economic environment for farming (higher-order effects). Under the GISS $2 \times CO_2$ scenario, where only temperature is adjusted (growing season temperatures are 3.5 °C to 3.6 °C above baseline for 1951–80), wheat production falls by 28 per cent with spring wheat yields diminishing by 15 to 37 per cent. Both drought frequency and wind erosion potential rise dramatically. Changes in the productivity of the economy translate into lower income and higher unemployment. Where precipitation is increased (9 to 14 per cent over baseline), along with temperature, total provincial wheat production falls by only 18 per cent with spring wheat yields decreasing from 4 to 29 per cent. The increased precipitation has clearly offset the effects of higher evapotranspiration.

The results from the first scenario, where only temperature is adjusted,

245

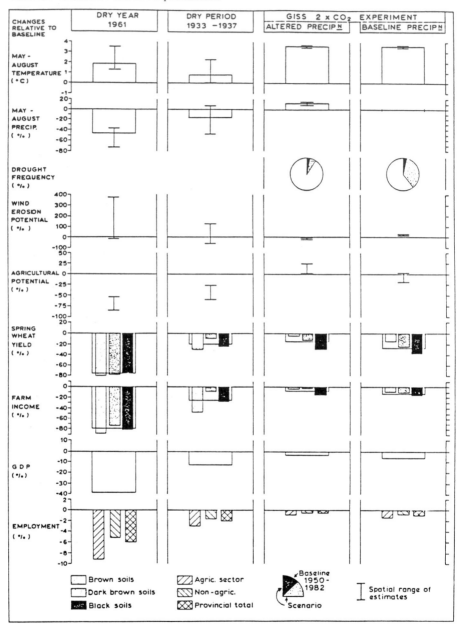

Fig. 8.14 Estimated effects of climatic variations on agricultural production in Saskatchewan. Baseline climate is 1951–80, unless otherwise indicated. Broad bars represent provincial mean values
Source from Parry and Carter (1987)

broadly conform with the estimated impact on agriculture of the 1930s extreme dry period. Compared, however, to the extreme drought of 1961 the first scenario is much less severe. It must be emphasized that these impacts reflect no adjustment in technology or farm-management strategies. Changes in either of these would, all other things equal, have a mitigating effect.

By comparison, rice production in Hokkaido, Northern Japan, is enhanced by a general warming trend under the GISS $2 \times CO_2$ scenario. With an increase in average growing season temperature, comparable to that of Saskatchewan, but a decline in precipitation of about 10 per cent, crop yields increase by 5 per cent, the upper limit of cultivation rises to 580 metres and overall rice production for the district increases by 11 per cent. The higher levels of production reflect, among other things, a reduced risk of cool summer damage and a significant reduction (27 per cent) in the coefficient of variation of yields.

More broadly based research, at least geographically, incorporating the heartlands and margins of grain production, point to a patchwork of gains and losses for agriculture from both GCM scenarios and analogue scenarios of CO_2 induced warming effects. Using different GCM scenarios, Santer (1985) found for Europe as a whole that biomass potential increased from 9 to 20 per cent with $2 \times CO_2$. The smaller estimate of biomass potential reflects a decrease in precipitation for southern Europe. In North America, Rosenzweig (1985) found that doubling of CO_2 would expand the winter wheat region northward and would push the fall-sown spring wheat region northward and eastward. Moisture was generally not a limiting factor, since adjustments were made to crop selection. Unfortunately, neither of these studies took evaporation into account, nor did they assess the role of CO_2 in affecting photosynthetic efficiency and respiration.

In Kellogg and Schware's (1981) composite diagram of changes in soil moisture (Fig. 8.12), some of the most important food-producing regions such as the United States, Canada, and the Soviet Union experienced drier conditions, while more moist conditions prevailed in others, such as China, India and South-East Asia. In terms of three principal grains (wheat, maize and rice), the anticipated decrease in moisture for some regions will limit production, whereas the increase in moisture for other regions will increase production.

Figure 8.15 provides by region for each crop the expected change in moisture conditions. The United States, the largest producer of maize, is expected to experience drier conditions in practically 85 per cent of its corn-growing area, while all of the wheat-growing regions of the Soviet Union, Canada and the United States are expected to be drier. Since a large percentage of the wheat grown in these regions is already close to the soil moisture margin of production, this trend could in combination with higher temperatures create moisture stress and declines in yields. In this regard, Thompson (1975) estimated that 2 °C increase in temperature and a decrease in precipitation (from 10 to 30 per cent of normal) would

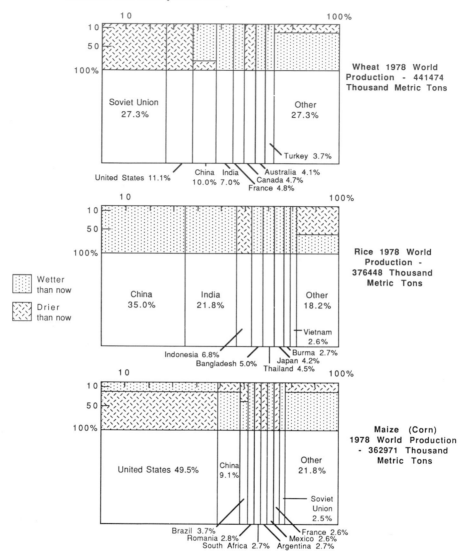

Fig. 8.15 World food production for some major crops in 1978 combined with a
scenario of possible soil moisture patterns on a warmer earth
Source after Kellogg and Schware (1981)

reduce yields for winter wheat in Kansas and Oklahoma from 9 to 25 per
cent.

Contributing to this is the decline in the efficiency of fertilizer uptake,
with drier conditions and an increase in wind erosion potential. Since the
Soviet Union possesses similar bio-physical features for grain production,
the impact on wheat yields may also be expected to be similar. A study of
the sensitivity of spring wheat in the Cherdyn region of the Soviet Union
under conditions of a GISS 2 × CO_2 scenario tends to confirm this (Parry

and Carter, 1987). And Newman (1980) postulated a $179 \, km \, °C^{-1}$ shift in the American corn belt in a SSW or NNE direction, but a 2 per cent decline in corn yield with a $1 °C$ increase in temperature. This decline reflects an increase in the frequency of damaging temperatures as the average growing season temperature increases.

Canada, the Soviet Union and other boreal regions of the world have the most to gain from increases in temperature since length of growing season could expand ten to twenty days in the southern portion to as much as twenty to forty days in northern regions. As thermal conditions improve, the main limiting factor on the expansion of agriculture is the quality of soils. And these good quality soils are limited to a relatively few locals in Alaska, the Peace River region of British Columbia and Alberta, the Clay Belt in Northern Ontario and Quebec, and the alluvial soils of the Yakutian plain along the Lena River in the USSR.

Much of the rice grown today in the Middle East, South and South East Asia is in the dry region of production (see pp. 227–230 of this chapter for a discussion of this issue). The expected trend toward more moist conditions will benefit rice production, considerably reducing the risk of crop failure. The greater moisture availability in these regions, including North Africa, will also improve the prospects for grain production in existing areas and expand the range over which maize and wheat can be grown. The major limiting factor in the expansion of cultivated area is the quality of the land-resource base.

Biological effects

Against the great uncertainties of the climatological effects of increased CO_2 levels on agricultural production, stands more reliable evidence on the biological effects. This evidence points to a much more positive influence on agriculture – perhaps sufficient to offset the negative consequences of the climatological effects.

Carbon dioxide is important for crop production since it provides an essential raw material for the process of photosynthesis and hence plant growth. Numerous studies of increased atmospheric concentration of CO_2 have demonstrated an increase in photosynthetic rate, a reduction in transpiration and an overall improvement in water-use efficiency (Kimball and Idso, 1983). The growth in yields with higher ambient CO_2 has led some to suggest that the relatively low levels of CO_2 concentration could represent a limiting factor in global agricultural productivity (Wittwer, 1980). The corollary to this is that elevated levels of CO_2 act as a form of atmospheric fertilization (Rosenberg, 1981).

Calculation of yield responses to higher levels of atmospheric CO_2 are based primarily upon greenhouse experiments and generally controlled conditions. These experiments reveal a considerable range of increased growth by crop type and photosynthetic mechanisms – C_3 versus C_4 (See

Chapter 2 for a discussion of these terms.) Generally C_3 plants tend to respond better than C_4 plants to higher levels of CO_2 with legumes, roots and tubers in the upper range of average yield increases and grains and fruits in the lower range of average yield increases (Kimball and Idso, 1983). Yield response to higher levels of CO_2 is S-shaped, with plateauing occurring between 1000 to 1200 ppm. Since this represents approximately $3 \times$ current CO_2 atmospheric concentration and since it is estimated that photosynthesis increases by 0.5 per cent for every 1 per cent increase in CO_2, the growth in yield could more than double (Wittwer, 1980). Using a different yield gradient Kimball and Idso (1983) estimate average yield increases of 33 and 67 per cent for 660 ppm and 1000 ppm of CO_2 respectively.

Indications of an improvement in water-use efficiency with enriched levels of CO_2 also come from experimental setting. Higher levels of CO_2 decrease stomata openings and in turn reduce transpiration. The stomata and transpiration rates of C_4 plants are more sensitive to higher levels of CO_2 than C_3 plants. Given enhancement of photosynthetic production and a decline in transpiration, water-use efficiency should improve, which has great implications for those regions which are already arid or semi-arid and are threatened by changes to their water balance from higher levels of atmospheric CO_2.

The optimism expressed about the biological effects of rising CO_2 levels must be tempered against three weaknesses or shortcomings in the research to date. First, practically all of the tests conducted are small scale and within the confines of the greenhouse or the laboratory. Direct field evidence of change in net primary productivity as a result of higher levels of CO_2 is extremely difficult if not impossible to provide. Second, other trace gases associated with rising levels of CO_2 such as chlorofluorocarbons, nitrogen and sulphur dioxide, affect ozone levels and soil acidity, both of which can be damaging to plant growth. And third, some have argued that the prime limiting factors in the growth of many domesticated plants are water and nutrients and not CO_2 concentrations in the atmosphere (Rosenberg, 1981). Hence change in CO_2 will not bring forth dramatic change in net primary productivity as long as these factors remain limiting.

Adaptability of agricultural systems

The previous analysis suggests that over the short term climatic change will not be sufficient to overcome or exceed the resiliency of the agricultural system. The question of resiliency is an important one since numerous writers have argued that 'agriculture has already demonstrated a capacity to cope with changes of the sizes predicted' (Kimball and Idso 1983: 67), and the present geographical range of the major crops in North America indicates that 'making the Minnesota climate that of Texas, therefore, would not eliminate many important crops' (Wittwer, 1980: 117). There are a variety of 'adjustments' that can be made at the farm level to mitigate the effects of climatic variations. For example, Parry and Carter (1987) propose that adjustment can take the form of changes in crop varieties (e.g., spring to winter wheat to reduce losses to early summer moisture stress), changes in fertilizer application and drainage, and changes in capital expenditures and other inputs. While alternative cropping patterns and strategies exist, they may not be sufficient to allow humans to alter their agricultural systems over the long term, given prevailing levels of demand for food. There are three critical points to consider.

First, many crops are now grown on or near the margin of production (measured physically and/or economically). There is every reason to believe that not only are these areas highly sensitive to small changes in climate but also solid evidence indicates that lost production will not be compensated by other regions because of poor soils or 'crowding out' from other land uses. There are really three marginal areas of crop production particularly sensitive to short- or long-term changes in climatic resources: the high-altitude areas of the Andes and Himalayas; the high-latitude farming regions of the USSR, Canada and Northern Europe; and the semi-arid areas of the tropics and sub-tropics where famine has been a consistent reminder of the degree to which those regions are both economically and socially marginal (Parry and Carter, 1984).

Second, climate change does not impact the agricultural system in isolation, in that there are numerous interactive effects which may compound the difficulties. Change in climate will affect water availability, energy needs, forestry and the availability of alternative food sources (e.g., fish). Concerning the latter, it will affect what Borgstrum (1980) has termed 'ghost acreage' which will provide important non-land sources of food. Moreover, it has been argued that increases in temperature create a more favourable environment for pests which, given their already deleterious effects on agriculture, could make the situation worse (Parry and Carter, 1987).

Third, and perhaps most important, there is the problem of how farmers and societies react to and are affected by climatic hazards. Kates (1979) estimated that about three-quarters of the $40 billion a year natural hazard costs to society have a climatic origin and that, proportionately, the burden is heaviest in developing countries. Many developed countries have successfully adopted technological solutions to the problem of climatic hazards in the form of flood control, carry-over stocks of food, irrigation systems, soil conservation measures and weather modification. It can be argued that technological solutions or the growing modernization of Sahelian countries mitigated the effects of the severe drought through access to international relief medical aid, improved infrastructure, irrigation and better transportation. Still, others argue that the increasing dependency of the Sahelian countries on export markets and the internationalization of agriculture, capital, technology and terms of trade have actually reduced self-sufficiency and the ability to adapt to drought (Warnock, 1987). There is certainly evidence to support this underdevelopment thesis when one considers that international aid for the development of tub wells and veterinary services (as discussed by Sinclair and Fryxell) was a chief factor contributing to population and livestock concentrations. Moreover, throughout the drought in Ethiopia and Sudan the countries continued their cultivation of export crops.

It could be argued that a society's ability to respond to climatic hazards – either short-term variability or long-term change – is a function of where it is on the development continuum (Fig. 8.16). Those least developed are self-sufficient, highly adaptable, with a variety of traditional risk-averse strategies to avoid significant impacts. Similarly developed societies have the economic, technological and infrastructural bases to minimize the agricultural impacts. By far the most vulnerable are the relatively simple primary economies, largely agriculturally based, which are dependent upon the export market for revenue and international aid to develop the cash-crop sector.

Given the uncertainty regarding climate change and its implications for agriculture there are strategies available to humans to ensure that the future in terms of food and other resources will not be dramatically different from the past. Kellogg and Schware (1981) identify three classes of long-range strategies with short-term benefits. These include strategies that increase resilience to climate change, such as protecting arable land, improving water management and maintaining global food reserves; strategies which lower CO_2 emissions through conservation, reforestation and increased reliance on renewable energy resources; and strategies that improve choices through improvements in climate data, the use of environmental monitoring and the transfer of appropriate technology to developing countries. Added to this is the need for innovative agricultural policy at

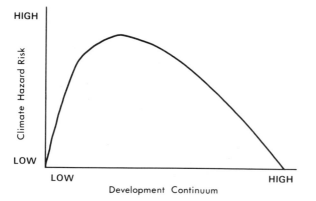

Fig. 8.16 Variations in climate hazard risk with changes of economic development

the regional and national level. Policies shaped by good 'intelligence' about climatic variations and their impact on food production can be used to match cropping patterns with changes in the spatial patterns of agricultural potential, to change land use, minimize environmental damage from wind and water erosion, improve food security and compensate the farmers for their declining fortunes (Parry and Carter, 1987).

Summary

Implicit in the notion of climatic variations are changes in the availability of heat and water resources for crop production. The sensitivity of cereals and other food crops to these changes within the context of demographic, technological and institutional conditions has been the theme of this chapter. While no definitive evidence exists to suggest that there is an increase in year-to-year variability in climate, the failure of the monsoons over India and drought in the Sahel drive home the unpredictability of climate and the vulnerability of people to the whims of nature and their own social organizations.

While the diffusion and adoption of various forms of agricultural technology have provided the underlying basis for an impressive growth in yields and production, it cannot be said to have reduced yield instability. In situations where optimal combinations of nutrients, moisture and heat are combined with new high-yielding seed varieties, yields are both high and stable about a trend. But all too often these optimal combinations are missing in developing countries because of climate anomalies/variability, expansion of production onto hazard-prone lands and failure to apply the 'correct' resource inputs. Given the narrowing of the crop genetic base with new high-yielding variety grains, crop tolerances to changes in weather/climate have declined relative to more traditional varieties.

On a regional level, the interaction of climate and agricultural technology produces dramatic differences in production stability. Tropical regions with irrigation systems have low-yield variability for rice. Arid and semi-arid regions without guaranteed access to irrigation but with the use of new seed varieties are prone to a high level of yield variability. The risks of growing grain in Canada and the Soviet Union are considerably higher than for the United States, reflecting both moisture and temperature constraints. The net effect of the risks for global grain production depends upon the similarity of crop failures and successes in different regions of the world.

The question of the sustainability of agriculture under certain agricultural production practices during periodic drought was examined for the Sahel and India. The failure of the monsoons to move as far north during the twenty years following 1968, compared to the preceding twenty years, was a necessary but not sufficient condition for the failure of crop and livestock systems and the resulting famine in the Sahel. The interaction of lower than average rainfall and increased grazing/cropping pressures contributed to a collapse in the carrying capacity of the land. Increased grazing/cropping pressures could be traced to lack of access to alternative, less hazard-prone lands, certain forms of international aid and high population/livestock growth rates.

Unlike the discussion of climate variability, and its influence on crop production, the discussion of climate change focused primarily on the long-term implications for food production. It was acknowledged that over the next twenty years the effects of inter-annual variability on crop production would be greater than the effects of climate change. Nevertheless, rising levels of CO_2 and other long-wave absorbing gases in the atmosphere have the potential to raise average global temperature and moisture availability.

Numerical and analogue models of temperature and moisture changes with increased (doubling/tripling) levels of CO_2 provided the basis for anticipating the agricultural effects. While the principal grain growing areas of the northern hemisphere will benefit from longer growing seasons, the quality of additional agricultural lands plus a decline in moisture availability could act as serious yield- and area-expanding constraints. Conversely, the environment for rice and wheat production in semi-arid tropics and humid tropics is expected to improve. Pitted against these climatological effects of climate change are biological effects. Since CO_2 is a necessary ingredient for photosynthesis, higher concentrations of CO_2 could act as a form of atmospheric fertilizer and thereby improve growth performance.

Finally, there is the question of the resilience of the agricultural system to the changes anticipated in the various modelling efforts. The marginal nature of many agricultural systems, the interactive and cumulative effects of climate change on food supply and the uncertain response of farmers to changes in climatic hazards are sufficiently real and of such importance to society to justify the development of a variety of long-range strategies which deal with both cause and effect of the problem.

CHAPTER 9

Role of energy in agricultural development

Energy relations

Agriculture is both a producer and a consumer of energy (see Fig. 9.1). As a producer of chemical energy, farming systems create food, fibre and other products. These products vary greatly in their caloric/protein output, their consumable proportion of energy, their contribution to nutritional needs of populations and in their contribution to net energy supplies through biogas and fuel alcohol production. As a consumer of solar, electrical, fossil and other chemical forms of energy, agricultural systems vary significantly in their share of energy forms, in their efficiency, input mix and impact upon the environment.

Although all agricultural systems are energy-dependent it is important to differentiate these systems according to their reliance on external, largely non-renewable inputs, their propensity to recycle material and their energy intensities. If we imagine a continuum of energy use, one end would be occupied by traditional/subsistence farming systems, which produce much if not all of their inputs, and consume most if not all of their outputs. The other end would be occupied by complex energy exchange systems in which the purchase of inputs and the marketing of outputs are all external to the system. The actual throughput of commercial energy on this continuum measured in giga-joules (GJ) per ha of arable area (if measured in relation to cropland the values become much higher) would be extremely low or non-existent for subsistence/traditional agricultural systems, between 2–6 GJ/ha for transitional agricultural systems such as India, Pakistan, Kenya, and the Philippines and generally from 7 GJ/ha to 40 GJ/ha for developed countries, such as the United States and France (low values) and Britain and Germany (high values). Japan has by far the highest energy intensities of close to 90 GJ/ha (Leach et al., 1986), (see Fig. 9.2).

The shift to the right of the energy continuum by the farming systems of developed countries has brought with it tremendous gains in productivity.

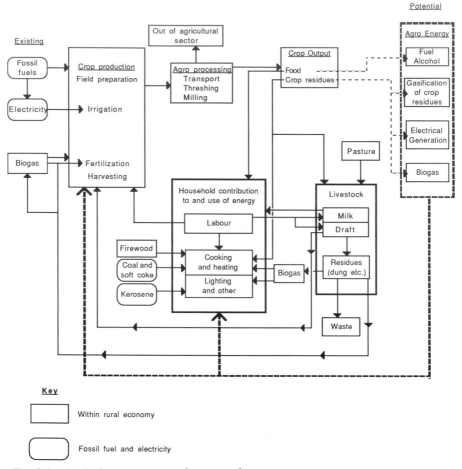

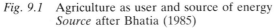

Fig. 9.1　Agriculture as user and source of energy
　　　　　Source after Bhatia (1985)

Concomitant with the increase in the productivity of land from the use of fertilizers, pesticides, herbicides, irrigation, machinery and storage facilities, the increased use of energy has increased the productivity of labour and other inputs, reduced the risk of crop failure, and reduced the dependence on animate sources of human and animal labour. High-energy input, in the form of fossil fuel subsidies and electricity, has been a hallmark feature and a cornerstone of richly productive farming systems which are noted for their surplus production capabilities. Despite the success of energy-intensive agriculture, numerous authors (Pimentel, 1979; Douglass, 1984; and Rifkin, 1980) have questioned the efficiency and sustainability of these systems, because of a perceived imbalance between the value of production and the value of inputs, measured in energy terms, the increasing dependence of agriculture on a depletable energy source and

256

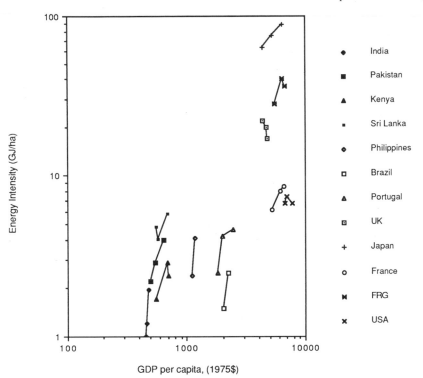

Fig. 9.2 Energy consumption of agriculture per unit of arable area, 1971–81
Source after Leach et al. (1986)

environmental effects of intensive agriculture.

In this chapter we examine a number of energy relations in agriculture. It is particularly important to understand the energy requirements, intensities and efficiencies in different agricultural systems, the role of supply and price in energy use in agriculture, the environmental effects of certain practices and alternatives to our present external commercial energy intensive system.

Components of energy use

Improvements in living standards and calorie/protein diets worldwide have been achieved by energy use increasing at a faster rate than population growth. World population doubled between 1950 and 1980, but it required only a third as long for energy use to multiply by an equivalent amount in the 1970s. Total primary energy consumption per capita, while higher for developed than developing countries, is either relatively stable or actually decreasing. Energy/GDP ratios for developing countries are still rising and must continue to rise if the caloric and living standard gap is to close between rich and poor nations. As agriculture has become more energy-intensive and dependent upon external/commercial sources of energy inputs, its share of the total commercial energy budget has increased for most regions of the world. Moreover, improvements in growth rates in the use of commercial energy in agriculture has dramatically increased developing countries' share of total commercial energy inputs in agriculture.

Table 9.1 illustrates these and other trends by energy input and region for 1972 and 1982. Total energy for agricultural production (includes energy for machinery/fertilizer production and application) grew at a faster rate than total commercial energy. The end result was that by 1982 agriculture in developed countries was consuming 4.6 per cent of the commercial energy for those countries, and in developing countries the proportion was 6.5 per cent. Generally equivalent proportions of the commercial energy budget went to food-processing (5 per cent) and distribution and preparation (5 per cent) in the United States. In the UK between 15 and 16 per cent of the primary energy budget is devoted to food production to the retail stage.

Developing countries more than doubled their consumption of commercial energy in agriculture, with the Far East and Asian centrally-planned economies experiencing the greatest net change. In India and the Philippines agriculture's share of total fossil fuel consumption between 1971 and 1979 increased from 3.6 to 7.4 and 1.5 to 6.5 per cent respectively (Leach et al., 1986). The higher growth rates in commercial energy inputs for agriculture in the developing world improved their share of global energy inputs for agriculture from 17 to 27 per cent. Developed countries conversely saw their share decline from 83 to 73 per cent. Despite the imbalance in energy expenditures between developed and developing countries, the latter are still able to produce close to half of the world's share of the cereals and over 60 per cent of its roots and tubers (Faidley, 1987), reaffirming the critical importance of labour and other forms of non-commercial energy in sustaining food output in these countries.

The consumption of energy in the rest of the economy can have a significant influence on the size of the shares of commercial energy used in agriculture. In the Near East, agriculture's share of total commercial energy use declined, even though in absolute terms energy use in agriculture expanded almost threefold.

The composition of energy inputs in agriculture shows a distinct bias for farm machinery in developed countries and for mineral fertilizer in developing countries. A major exception to this is in heavily-irrigated countries, such as India and Pakistan, where in the late 1970s electricity for pumping consumed 48 and 26 per cent (respectively) of energy used in agriculture. Over two-thirds of the developing world's energy inputs were derived from mineral fertilizers in 1982, with Asian centrally-planned economies reaching levels in excess of three-quarters. Although annual growth in pesticide/herbicide use has been high (1.8 per cent from 1972 to

Table 9.1 Commercial energy used in agricultural production and share of input in each region, 1972 and 1982

Regions	Commercial energy in agriculture (× 1000 tons) 1972	1982	As percentage of total commercial energy (%) 1972	1982	Each region's share of commercial energy in agriculture (%) 1972	1982	Components Farm machinery (%) 1972	1982	Pump irrigation (%) 1972	1982	Mineral fertilizer (%) 1972	1982	Chemical pesticides (%) 1972	1982
North America	67,973	66,161	3.9	4.0	33.6	23.1	71.9	66.8	1.1	1.4	25.2	29.7	1.9	2.1
Western Europe	51,654	67,912	5.4	6.8	25.5	23.7	65.7	66.4	0.6	0.6	32.0	31.6	1.6	1.3
Oceania	3,479	3,582	6.5	4.4	1.7	1.2	73.8	72.2	0.9	1.0	24.9	26.4	0.5	0.4
Other developed countries	6,104	16,204	2.1	4.6	3.0	5.6	59.5	82.3	1.4	0.5	38.9	17.1	0.3	0.1
Total developed market economies	129,211	153,859	4.2	4.9	63.8	53.6	68.9	68.4	0.9	1.0	28.5	29.1	1.7	1.5
Eastern Europe, USSR	39,574	56,510	3.7	3.8	19.6	19.7	47.6	44.9	0.8	0.8	49.5	52.7	2.1	1.6
Total developed countries	168,786	210,369	4.1	4.6	83.4	73.3	63.9	62.1	0.9	0.9	33.4	35.5	1.8	1.5
Africa	1,783	2,774	5.0	5.4	0.9	1.0	46.4	41.0	4.9	4.2	47.2	49.2	1.5	5.5
Latin America	7,158	11,203	3.8	3.8	3.5	3.9	46.2	40.3	1.7	1.4	50.4	56.2	1.7	2.1
Far East	8,789	20,738	6.5	14.1	4.3	7.2	17.4	21.9	7.1	6.9	75.0	71.4	0.4	0.7
Near East	3,989	9,946	7.4	4.3	2.0	3.5	34.6	42.9	13.2	6.8	51.4	49.1	0.8	1.1
Other developing countries	38	57	3.8	2.0	0.0	0	49.6	41.6	0.1	0.1	48.9	50.0	1.4	8.3
Total developing market economies	21,757	44,718	5.3	6.1	10.8	15.6	32.5	32.4	6.3	4.9	60.3	61.3	1.0	1.4
Asian centrally-planned economies	11,743	31,844	4.3	7.2	5.8	11.1	17.5	15.7	7.1	3.0	70.9	79.3	4.5	2.0
Total developing countries	33,500	76,561	4.9	6.5	16.6	26.7	27.2	25.5	6.6	4.1	64.0	68.8	2.2	1.7
Total	202,285	286,931	4.2	5.0	100.0	100.0	57.8	52.3	1.8	1.8	38.5	44.3	1.9	1.6

Source adapted from Faidley (1987)

259

1982), their share declined overall.

The choice of fertilizers as the main target for agriculture investment over farm machinery or irrigation equipment reflects the constraints of foreign exchange, uncertainties of shifting to more sophisticated equipment, relatively high interest rates of foreign capital, and the continued relative advantages of relying on labour as opposed to capital-intensive systems. In short, the use of fertilizers in developing countries offers a relatively high pay-off with a minimum of risk. Reliance upon energy-intensive technology in isolated rural areas with poor distribution facilities can be hazardous at best, even when national fuel supplies are adequate. In Somalia, fuel shortages during 1984 created 40–60 per cent yield reductions in irrigated crops (Faidley, 1987).

The continued importance of energy-intensive inputs in developed countries, such as machinery, fertilizer and pesticides/herbicides, reflects the desire to improve the productivity of labour through capital substitution. These inputs are also meant to enhance the productivity of larger and larger producing units through complementary inputs of pesticides.

Horsepower availability per hectare highlights the dichotomy in levels of mechanization between developed and developing countries. Horsepower-hour is a measure of the rate at which work is done. One horsepower-hour of work is equal to about ten manpower-hours of work (Pimentel, 1984). Whereas the average for Europe during the 1970s was approximately 0.93 hp/ha, much higher levels are found in Britain (1.8 hp/ha) and Japan (2.2 hp/ha). In sharp contrast, Latin America has 0.27, Asia 0.19 and Africa 0.05 hp/ha (Biswas, 1979). It has been argued that to achieve acceptable grain yields (2500 kg/ha) minimum power availability of 0.5 to 0.8 hp/ha is required (Biswas, 1979). This range reflects the use of machinery for which there is no efficient labour substitute, such as deep-water pumping and threshing which is non-continuous and periodic. Seen in this context the judicious use of machinery can expand the productivity of labour without necessarily reducing its requirements in agriculture.

Energy intensities

Given differences in energy growth rates and composition of energy inputs between developed and developing world, what is the impact on energy intensities? Earlier, energy intensity was expressed in terms of energy use per hectare of land. A rough relationship existed among the sample countries in Figure 9.2 between the scarcity of land and energy inputs, although many factors intervened to cloud this relationship, such as capital availability, effects of climate, importance of irrigation and farm price structures (Leach et al., 1986).

Other measures of energy intensity include energy use per person, energy output–input ratios and the energy consumption of agriculture per unit of agriculture GDP. In a comparison of energy use per person in the

United States and UK, Fluck and Baird (1980) note that when the US figures are adjusted for surplus production, which goes into the export market, and when the UK figures are adjusted for low self-sufficiency in food, the energy intensities are 4.5 GJ × yr^{-1}/person for the United States and 9.4 GJ × yr^{-1}/person for the UK – almost a reversal of estimates from an earlier study by Green (1978).

Energy intensities, using energy consumption of agriculture per unit of GDP, indicate that although industrialized countries use two to three times the energy compared to their developing counterparts, some developing countries such as India, Philippines and Brazil are rapidly increasing their energy intensities (see Fig. 9.3). This is due in part to modernization and the spread of machinery and pumping equipment for irrigation, but also to increased use of fertilizers. The fact that Kenya and Sri Lanka show little change suggests a major slowdown in modernization. Hence changes in GDP per capita have induced disproportionately large energy inputs into the agricultural sector for some countries. In contrast, countries such as the UK and the United States had from 1971 to 1981 experienced actual decreases in intensities. The decrease in the UK has been explained in terms of change in cropping methods, such as high tillage operations.

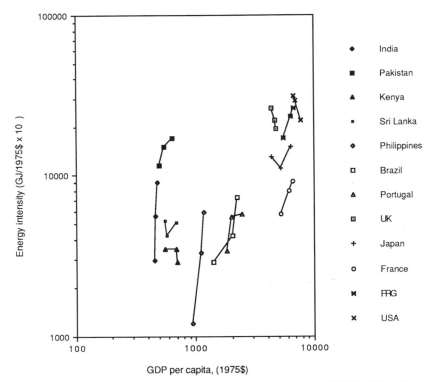

Fig. 9.3 Agricultural fossil energy per unit of agricultural GDP, 1971–81
      Source after Leach et al. (1986)

In summary, measures of energy efficiency must be used with great caution. While the United States is not among the most energy-intensive countries in terms of energy use per hectare and per person it joins the league of most energy-intensive nations when measured in terms of commercial energy inputs per 1975 US dollar of agricultural GDP. The United States also had the largest throughput of commercial energy at 12.23 million GJ in 1981, compared to 11 million GJ for the UK.

Productivity/efficiency issues

Underlying the differences in the intensities and shares of energy in agriculture between developed and developing countries are important differences in the productivity and energy efficiencies of farm operations. Developed countries tend to be highly productive in relation to developing countries in terms of energy output per unit of land or labour. But this occurs by sacrificing energy efficiency measured as energy output per energy input or yields per energy input (FAO, 1979a). Energy efficiency tends to be higher in developing countries. Some of these differences reflect the role and influence of a number of interwoven factors: agricultural operations in most Western industrialized countries are experiencing diminishing marginal returns to energy inputs, unlike their developing counterparts; type of crop and its energy conversion efficiency, end use for crop (food or feed) and degree of processing differ greatly among regions; and differences in relative pricing of factor inputs have favoured different production strategies and use of technology. Not to be ignored is the manner in which energy efficiency is measured. By excluding measures of non-commercial energy and/or labour energy, efficiency measures, as we shall see shortly, can be seriously overestimated.

Diet

An important factor affecting the efficiency and cost of food production is the choice of food to be produced and the length of the food chain. Traditional grains and rice yield approximately three to four times the energy yield per unit area, as does milk and many times that for beef production. The gross energy recovery from animal products such as milk, beef and eggs averages 15, 4 and 7 per cent respectively (see Table 9.2). The conversion efficiencies of vegetable protein to animal protein are also low. These figures would be considerably higher for milk production in a developing country such as India if that country were able to achieve the yearly North American production average of 6750 litres per animal instead of average production of only about 250 litres.

Given these relationships, Rao and Singh (1977a) have argued that in India, where land is scarce and where a relatively high proportion of average income is spent on food, more effort should be devoted to the

Table 9.2 Energy yield, recovery and conversion for major food items

Food	Energy yield (kcal × 10⁶/A)	Average gross energy recovery	Average conversion of vegetable to animal protein
Animal Products			
Milk	4.5	15	38
Butter	2.0	–	–
Eggs	1.25	7	31
Beef	1.0	4	6
Crops			
Sugar	62.5	–	–
Potatoes	29.0	–	–
Rice	16.5	–	–
Grain	13.25	–	–

Source adapted from Rao and Singh (1977a)

production of food such as grains and pulses, instead of attempting to lengthen the food chain through the production of animal products. Insufficient land exists in India at current yield levels to provide the diversified diet recommended by the Indian Council of Medical Research. Total land requirements for this diet for non-vegetarians was 0.48 ha/person. Per capita cultivable land in India during the 1970s was 0.27 ha. This is very low, even allowing for double cropping. A major unanswered question is whether these recommended diets could be met by a considerable input in commercial energy which would not only enhance yield but allow for more persons to be supported per unit area.

Measuring efficiency

In a comparison of the efficiency of different crop-production systems, Pimentel (1979, 1984) found enormous variation in the ratio of energy output to energy input. For corn production in Mexico where manual labour, ox, hoe and seeds were the only inputs, yield was approximately 1.94 tonnes or 6,842,880 kcal of food energy. The output–input ratio (which includes only fossil-fuel inputs and excludes labour) was 128.2 or approximately 50 times the US average. Similarly high output to input ratios were found for cassava (1164.8) and sorghum (37.5) production in Africa. However, when draft animals were introduced into the energy equation for these and other regimes the ratio drops to less than four. Table 9.3 provides further examples of output/input ratios for different crops and production systems and includes not only energy expenditures from fossil fuels but also from human labour.

Table 9.3 Ratio of energy output to input for crops

| | Inputs per hectare | | | | Crop yield (kg) | Outputs per hectare | | Energy output/input ratio |
	Fossil fuels (10⁶ kcal)	Labour (man-hours)	Human energy (10⁶ kcal)	Total energy (10⁶ kcal)		Crop energy (10⁶ kcal)	10³ kcal per man-hour	
Wheat (United States)	3.770	7	0.002	3.772	2,284	7.5	1,071.42	1.98
Wheat (India)	0.256	615	0.185	0.441	821	2.7	4.39	6.13
Rice (United States)	15.536	30	0.009	15.545	5,796	21.0	700.00	1.35
Rice (Philippines)	0.582	576	0.173	0.755	1,655	6.0	10.42	7.94
Corn (United States)	6.644	22	0.007	6.651	5,080	17.9	813.64	2.69
Corn (Mexico)	0.053	1,444	0.343	0.396	1,944	6.8	4.71	17.16
Sorghum (Sudan)	0.079	240	0.072	0.151	900	3.0	12.50	19.86
Potatoes (United States)	8.907	60	0.018	8.925	26,208	20.2	336.67	2.26
Cassava (Tanga)	0.016	1,284	0.385	0.401	5,824 (dry)	19.2	14.95	47.85

Source adapted from Rao and Singh (1977b)

A more thorough approach at measuring energy inputs for Third World agriculture was undertaken by Makhijani and Poole (1975). The energy characteristics of six villages (subsistence and export-oriented) were examined by incorporating human, animal, wood, dung and fossil fuel sources of energy (see Table 9.4). With all energy forms included, the energy efficiency ratios for these systems are considerably below those estimated by Pimentel (1979) or by Leach (1976) where, for the latter, energy ratios for subsistence and shifting agriculture in Africa varied from 12 to 37.

These findings prompted Makhijani and Poole to conclude that energy usage is neither small nor particularly efficient in Third World countries when consideration is given to the use of wood and dung in heating and cooking and the useful energy (or work) that can be derived from these sources. Useful energy is defined as the amount of energy developed at the plough or shaft of the pump. Moreover, Third World farms may be more energy-intensive per unit area than those of industrialized countries because of the use of draft animals and their feed requirements. Increased use of commercial energy and less reliance on draft animals will normally boost productivity. In the United States between 1945 and 1975, although primary energy input in maize production increased from 19 to 30 GJ/ha per year, yield increased from 2 to 5 tonnes. Hence energy inputs declined from 9.5 to 6 GJ/tonne of maize and land requirements for maize production fell by 60 per cent (Leach et al., 1986).

While developing countries may be more efficient in their use of fossil-fuel energy, their systems are not very productive. The average farm worker in Western agriculture can produce far more surplus production than his/her counterpart in Mexico or the Philippines. By extension the traditional subsistence system could, with more 'useful' energy inputs, raise output per unit area and the standard of living of those associated with the production of food, without necessarily sacrificing manpower – as we saw

Table 9.4 Energy characteristics of six villages

Location	Size	Total energy consumption $(MJ \cdot caput^{-1}d^{-1})$	Food production $(MJ \cdot caput^{-1}d^{-1})$	Energy efficiency ratio
Mangaon, India	1,000	30.8	11.1	0.36
Peopan, China	1,000	33.2	23.3	0.70
Kilombbero, Tanzania	100	8.7	15.3	1.76
Batagaware, Nigeria	1,400	10.5	11.9	1.13
Anango, Mexico	420	130.1	94.6	0.73
Quebrada, Bolivia	6	38.5	7.4	0.19

Source based on Makhijani and Poole (1975) and adapted by Fluck and Baird (1980)

for China in Chapter 6. The most efficient food systems then, measured in kilocalories of output to kilocalories of food input, would not have sufficient energy resources to meet the nutritional needs of the earth's population today or in the future with current technology. Figure 9.4 provides a graphic illustration of this where highest energy efficiency does not match the greatest yield per unit area in the case of nitrogen fertilizer (FAO, 1979a).

There is a danger therefore in evaluating the performance of agricultural systems along strictly energy dimensions or using energy as the major currency. For not only is a kilocalorie of oil not equivalent to a kilocalorie of food (some form of conversion must take place), but this approach ignores the role of other inputs and the values and costs of both inputs and outputs. Surely an important criterion is the degree to which agricultural systems balance the cost of energy and other inputs against the value of production (Hall, 1984b). The United States has pursued this path in its increasingly energy-intensive agricultural operations. From 1950 to 1978 there were convincing economic reasons for greater use of energy and energy-related inputs. Cost for land and labour increased in relative terms by 651 and 383 per cent, whereas for energy and fertilizer by 150 and 84 per cent. As Doering (1980: 199) argued 'There has been an increasing incentive over the long-term to use low-cost resources to improve the

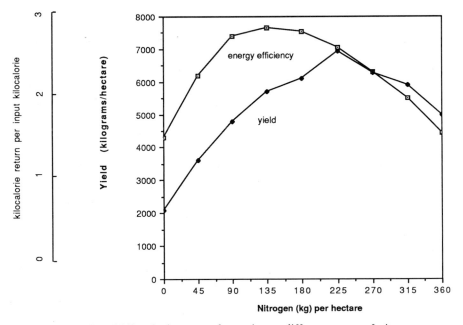

Fig. 9.4   Yield and kilocalorie return for maize at different rates of nitrogen
fertilizer application
Source FAO (1979a)

productivity of high cost resources or substitute for them.' Energy prices have remained lower than other OECD countries because the United States has not relied on the taxing of petroleum fuels to raise revenue. Moreover, the price of natural gas has been kept artificially low and electricity was provided to farms on a favourable basis through the Rural Electrical Act.

Doering also points out that the impetus to adopt new technology came from government-funded research and extension institutions and programmes that improved the income performance of the farmer. Aside from direct subsidies, the encouragement to idle farmland during periods of surplus production favoured the use of more energy-intensive inputs on the remaining land in order to offset production losses. The net effect of these programmes was to increase the value of the land, since increased returns were capitalized into the value of the farmland, while holding down the relative cost of energy inputs.

A non-economic incentive to adopt energy-intensive technology, such as larger equipment and the use of insecticides and herbicides, was the greater control and 'timeliness' that that technology allowed over the environment. Greater harvesting and planting capacity, along with reduced risk of insect and other pathogen damage, allowed for a greater security, real and perceived, in the agricultural industry.

Supply/demand relations

The need for improvements in the protein calorie diets of those living in the developing world is unquestioned, as is the need for more energy to sustain if not expand per capita production of food. But what of the physical and economic constraints in providing these important energy resources? Are there sufficient energy resources to supply the demands of a Western-style diet for the five billion persons living today, or the six billion expected by the year 2000? In attempting to answer these questions we must consider a few important variables, to some of which we have already alluded. In their simplest form they include population size (structure and growth), the recommended diet and the length of the food chain to produce it, the energy efficiency ratio of meeting the diet and the arable land base required under the above conditions.

Impact of fossil fuels

In the United States, it is estimated that 17 per cent of the total per capita energy budget is devoted to food production, processing, packaging and distribution, or about 1900 litres per person of gasoline equivalents a year (Pimentel, 1984). This represents an energy efficiency of about 9 kcal input per kcal of food output (see Fig. 9.5 for an example of energy flows using a 7:1 ratio) and occurs on a per capita arable land base (after adjusting for

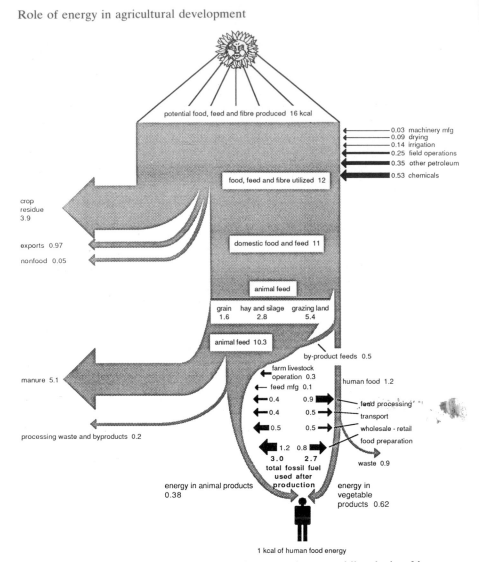

Fig. 9.5 Energy flow in the US food chain to produce one kilocalorie of human food energy.
Source after Stickler et al. (1975)

export area) of around 0.52 ha. If this per capita energy expenditure on food were extended to the global population of five billion persons, it would require 9500 billion litres of gasoline equivalents per year to sustain a US-style diet which is between 8–10 per cent of known usable petroleum reserves. An analysis of the energy implications of extending the energy efficiency of the UK diet (5:1 efficiency ratio) to the rest of the world indicated that for 1972, 40 per cent of global fuel consumption would have been needed (FAO, 1979a).

Alternative and perhaps more realistic measures of the adequacy of energy resources for higher caloric/protein diets have incorporated known reserves of all fossil fuels into the calculations. Hall (1975) examined the energy requirements of agricultural systems in meeting the food needs of a growing population using input/output ratios of 9:5 to 1 (high), 5:1 (intermediate) and 1:1 (low). By the year 2040 the high-input scenario consumed close to 100 per cent of fossil fuels, the intermediate input about 30 per cent, and the low approximately 8 per cent. Notwithstanding the problems of the cost of supporting ever-increasing proportions of total energy use devoted to agriculture, energy like water is essential for other sectors of the economy. Rising proportions of energy use would therefore not be tenable.

While the above estimates incorporated energy needs of fertilizer production, it must be recognized that the reserves for inorganic fertilizers such as phosphates, potash and sulphur, although large are being depleted. In the absence of major changes in energy-pricing and technology, both higher average costs and higher environmental costs will occur (FAO, 1979a).

It has also been argued, particularly by Pimentel (1979), that the global land resource base of 1.5 billion hectares is insufficient in size to support a US-style diet, even if the energy were available. Global per capita arable land availability is about 0.3 ha per person, or around half the US average. Arable land supplies per person would have to expand before parity in diets could be achieved. In most countries arable land supplies per person are shrinking, requiring growth in energy inputs such as fertilizer. In an historical analysis of the interrelationship between fertilizer use and land supplies per person, Weber (1977) demonstrated for Germany and Kenya the importance of expanding nutrient use with increasing land scarcity.

Economics of energy use

If the US or UK diet and energy efficiency to achieve that diet are used as standards for the rest of the world's population, current known energy reserves would be either insufficient or, along with the environment generally, placed under enormous strain. Although we shall discuss alternatives to this situation later in the chapter, it should be emphasized that few people are advocating that a solution to the food problems of today can be found in the energy production strategies of the United States or other Western countries. Nor are they advocating a continuation of the status quo. For not only is there tremendous scope for altering energy efficiencies by shortening the food chain and alleviating wasteful processing and packaging procedures, but many other energy-saving options exist. These include multiple cropping, improved uses of labour and technology, agricultural energy production, as well as reduction in the shortfall between planted and harvested area.

269

The use of energy in agricultural production to sustain existing diets in Western countries or to expand the quality of diets in developing countries is determined over the short to intermediate term far more by economics of energy supply than by ultimate physical energy supply. Energy price increases affect the agricultural system directly through changes in the relative cost advantages of fertilizer, irrigation and other energy inputs, and indirectly in the transportation and processing of food. Both effects in turn have great implications for the structure of agriculture (small versus large, irrigation versus rainfed, and location of production). Agricultural production is also affected by chronic and acute short-term interruptions in supply, such as the oil embargoes in the 1970s to OECD countries and supply bottlenecks in remote and poorly accessible regions of the developing world.

The production response of agriculture to energy price changes and supply shortages was a subject of considerable controversy during the 1970s. In energy-intensive systems, such as Western Europe and North America, energy inputs represented between 30–40 per cent of the value of production. In the United States, perhaps the most documented country when it comes to agriculture–energy relations, the direct energy costs for corn production during the early 1970s was between 5 and 15 per cent. Indirect costs for the manufacture of machinery, seed and fertilizer represented 20–30 per cent. Energy costs for other crops tend to be lower. Energy costs for soybeans were about 20 per cent of total costs (Crosson, 1979).

In developing countries the assessment of the relative contribution of energy costs to the total costs is clouded by the absence of a wage economy, unreliable farm statistics and the difficulty of attaching value to other inputs. The shift to the use of more energy-intensive inputs in the form of fertilizers, pumping equipment in irrigation, and herbicides and pesticides in recent years would, in the absence of changes to other inputs, increase both costs of production and energy share of those costs. This means that in relative terms energy and land probably contribute more to the cost of production in developing compared to developed countries.

The argument has been made for Western countries that since the direct cost of energy is a small proportion of total costs the demand for energy resources over the short term will be relatively inelastic (Crosson, 1979). In other words, farmers can afford to be insensitive to rapid price increases. Doering (1982) argued that even with a doubling in fertilizer costs resulting from increases in the price of natural gas, nitrogen use would not be greatly affected so long as commodity prices follow current trends. To better understand this argument we need to compare the yield response of corn to fertilizer inputs and the associated value and costs in this relationship. The largest incremental changes in yields occur during initial applications of fertilizer, becoming progressively smaller and eventually plateauing at 228 kg/ha of nitrogen (see Fig. 9.6). Table 9.5 provides two

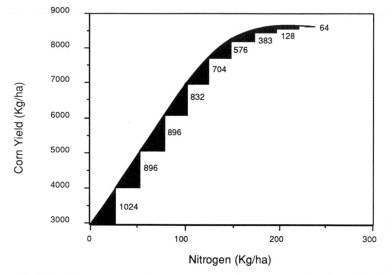

Fig. 9.6 Corn response to nitrogen on odell silt loam in Central Indiana 1967–69
Source adapted from Doering (1982)

Table 9.5 Comparative returns with different fertilizer/corn price ratios

		N @ 2¢/kg; corn @ $10/100 kg		N @ 52¢/kg; corn @ $13.50/100 kg	
N Application (kg/ha)	Yield (kg/ha)	Added N cost ($)	Added corn returns ($)	Added N cost ($)	Added corn returns ($)
67	5,785	–	–	–	–
90	6,602	6.00	81.70	12.00	110.30
113	7,293	6.00	69.10	12.00	93.30
136	7,860	6.00	56.70	12.00	76.50
159	8,237	6.00	37.70	12.00	50.80
182	8,361	6.00	12.40	12.00	16.74
205	8,425	6.00	6.40	12.00	8.64
228	8,487	6.00	6.20	12.00	8.37

Source after Doering (1982)

separate price/cost estimates for corn and fertilizers. The balance between cost and returns is approximately 228 kg/ha of nitrogen at the low cost scenario and 195 kg/ha of nitrogen at the high cost scenario. If we combine the low price of corn with the high cost of fertilizer, the new equilibrium is around 185 kg/ha.

Another study of crop–energy relations in the United States found that a doubling of energy prices led to a 5 per cent reduction in total energy use in agricultural production (Dvoskin and Heady, 1977). More dramatic

271

effects on agriculture were to be found by reduction in energy supply. A 10 per cent decline in energy supply led to sharp increases in food prices by way of considerably more expensive inputs of fertilizers and pumping costs. It was inferred that food cost increases would be even higher if allowance in the study had been made for increased transportation and processing costs. It should also be added that while agriculture may be relatively insensitive to price changes over the short term, if high energy prices prevailed over the long term, more dramatic changes would occur in the composition of farming and structure of the enterprise.

Since energy inputs in developing countries can represent a higher proportion of total costs, in the absence of major price increases for their products farmers tend to be more sensitive to price increases for energy. Given the fact that most developing countries are located on the steepest sections of the fertilizer crop-response curve, small changes in the application of fertilizer, particularly nitrogen, can have disproportionate effects on yields. In a study of energy use in India, Revelle (1976) concluded that if India tripled its fossil fuel energy inputs in agriculture it would add $3.2 billion (in 1976 dollars) to the cost of food production but add $35 billion to the value of agricultural output. Not surprisingly, India embarked on ambitious nitrogen-manufacturing schemes and price subsidies to the farmer in order to alleviate supply/price variations and the cost to the farmer.

Since the sharp decline in world energy prices in 1985, energy inputs regained their relative competitiveness *vis à vis* other inputs in the production process. While the change is an incentive for greater intensification, this will not occur unless prices for food and incomes rise. The income elasticity of agricultural energy intensity tends to be high for many developing countries. In Fig. 9.3 it was clear that small changes in income in India, Philippines and Brazil precipitated relatively large increases in energy use. Conversely, most developed countries have low if not negative income elasticities of agricultural energy intensities.

The issue of changes in energy costs, and their influence on the competitiveness of different inputs in agricultural production, is central to an understanding of the changes, past and potential, in the structure of farming and the geography of production. Much of the work on this subject has been done for the United States. Perhaps the most dramatic effects on energy price increases is the change in the importance of land, crops grown and production strategy (rainfed versus irrigated). In the United States between 1972 and 1975 fertilizer application per hectare declined by 12 per cent, yet harvested area increased by 18 million hectares or 15 per cent (Crosson, 1979). Part of this process may have been in response to higher commodity prices, but most likely it is linked to fertilizer and gasoline costs which rose at a faster rate than farmland or farm wages. This supports Dvoskin and Heady's (1977) contention that energy price increases tend to favour more land-extensive production strategies as farmers substitute less expensive inputs for energy. On the other hand, bringing more land into production can also require considerable energy for drainage, irrigation and clearing. The fact that land under production increased during the early 1970s does not negate this point since much if not all of it had already been cleared and used previously for production. Hence while the supply curve may be elastic for the existing reserve of land in the United States, it may be very inelastic in cases of poor quality land with high reclamation costs. In these situations conservation may become a much more favoured option. In this regard Buttel et al. (1980) have argued that since Dvoskin and Heady's and similar studies do not consider new conservation-induced production functions which produce the same amount with fewer inputs, the studies may overstate impacts of changing energy conditions.

Less contentious is the fact that rising energy prices have a devastating impact upon irrigated area. In the Dvoskin and Heady study (1977) it was calculated that a doubling of energy prices would lead to a 22 per cent decline in irrigated area. With a 10 per cent decline in energy supply, irrigated area would decline by 41 per cent. Only if exports were considerably higher than present levels could the negative impact of higher energy prices be offset. In the absence of these higher export prices rainfed farming would expand by 1.86 hectares for every hectare decrease in irrigated area. This retrenchment in irrigated area would affect numerous communities in the western United States.

Choice of crops would also be affected by higher energy prices because of the variation in the importance of certain other energy-intensive practices. With corn, the most energy-intensive and largest crop grown in the United States, energy price increases would affect negatively field-shelled and artificially-dried systems which consume 20 to 30 per cent of the direct energy budget. This may be sufficient to encourage more wheat production.

The structure of farming could also be affected by supply interruptions and/or price increases in energy. Over the short term, price escalations will influence the cost of direct energy costs, such as fertilizers, fuels and pesticides. Over the long term, machinery costs will rise. The fact that some farms are more energy-intensive means that they are more vulnerable to price/supply changes, as with irrigated farming. If energy-intensive operations are scale-dependent, it would follow that size of operation would be affected. There is conflicting evidence that a direct relationship exists between farm size and energy intensity (Buttel et al., 1980). Assuming for the moment that such a direct relationship exists, there is no indication that large farms were more affected by energy price increases than their smaller counterparts during the energy price increases of the 1970s. It has been argued that large farms benefit from scale economies, better access to capital and government subsidy schemes. Smaller farms have definite advantages, however, over larger ones in their ability to substitute labour for energy inputs and, generally, in their lower overhead costs; but these may not be sufficient to make these operations relatively more competitive as producing units.

Yield response and productivity

It was demonstrated earlier that the agricultural sectors of most developed countries are more commercial, energy-intensive and higher yielding than the majority of their counterparts in developing countries. Implicit in this observation is that energy or the lack thereof is a major constraint to expanded production. But exactly how sensitive is production and productivity to increases in energy inputs? One study tracing the historical change in farm output and energy input for the period 1920–70 for the United States found the relationship conformed to a classic S-shape growth curve (FAO, 1979). The steepest slope of the curve occurred during the late 1950s and early 1960s after which diminishing marginal returns to increase energy inputs set in. Another time series analysis undertaken in the Global 2000 study (Barney, 1980) for a number of leading food producers in the developed world indicates a trend to diminishing returns to energy inputs, especially towards the latter part of the fifteen-year study period (see Fig. 9.7). When cross-sectional energy-use data were plotted against crop and livestock yields for the largest food-producing countries, a similar trend emerged.

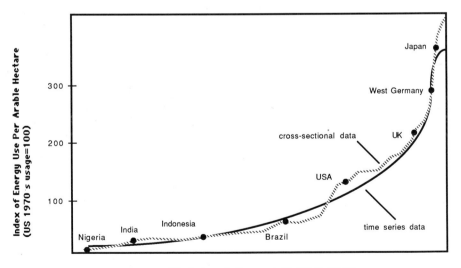

Fig. 9.7   Energy intensity data. Cross-sectional energy use data plotted against crop and livestock yields for the thirty largest food-producing countries; fifteen-year historical series plotted against time for United States and several major European producers
Source after Barney (1980)

274

The above findings highlight a number of important principles in the contribution of energy to enhancing food production. First, increasing energy intensity expands food production, but at a decreasing rate. Second, technology interacts with the energy inputs to determine the rate of yield growth. Third, developing countries stand to expand production far more than their developed counterparts per unit increase in energy use. Countries such as Nigeria, India and Indonesia have much higher marginal productivities per energy input than the Canadian, US or European countries (see Fig. 9.7). Fourth, the contribution to enhancing production of each energy input (fertilizer, machinery, pesticides) will vary greatly. This has implications for choosing the most appropriate energy-intensive strategy in attempts to expand productivity and production. And it is to this issue that we now turn.

The growth of yields due to energy inputs represents the individual or combined effects of four key energy-dependent sources: fertilizers, pesticides/herbicides, machinery and irrigation. We can define for each of these inputs a yield-response curve. For each curve we can define a partial energy productivity which is simply the tangent of a line drawn from the intercept to the point of the output curve associated with a given level of energy input (Fluck and Baird, 1980). Where the line is tangent to the curve is the point of maximum or highest (partial) energy productivity. By combining the optimal input levels for each energy input it is possible to maximize the yield response from the energy sector.

Figure 9.8 illustrates yield response curves for the four major energy inputs hypothesized by Fluck and Baird (1980). With fertilizer input, the highest marginal productivities are to be found at low rates of application. This indicates that by providing a more uniform application of fertilizer at both the farm, national and indeed global level, yields will be higher than with any other combination of a given quantity of a resource. For developing countries with relatively limited supplies of fertilizers the potential gains from a more uniform distribution of nutrients are enormous.

Unlike fertilizers, the highest marginal yield response to pesticides is delayed until sufficiently large quantities of the input are capable of reducing pest infestations. This assumes that the pesticides/herbicides are applied under the proper soil moisture and temperature conditions as well as the correct timing.

While it is recognized that the adoption of mechanized forms of agricultural production has the potential to displace labour and increase labour productivity, mechanized production also has the potential to greatly enhance yields by acting as a complementary as opposed to a substitutable input. We have already made reference to this fact, but it bears repeating since the timing (or timeliness) of numerous farm operations is critical. Harvesting, planting and irrigation-pumping all require peak energy requirements, whether they are from animate or inanimate

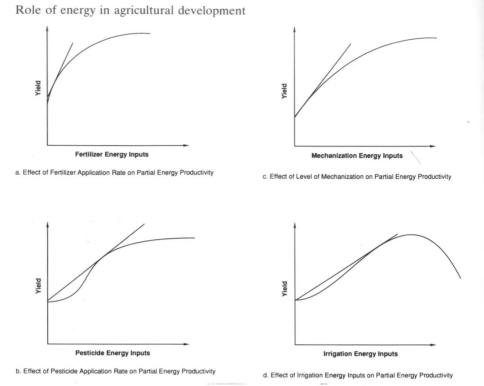

a. Effect of Fertilizer Application Rate on Partial Energy Productivity

c. Effect of Level of Mechanization on Partial Energy Productivity

b. Effect of Pesticide Application Rate on Partial Energy Productivity

d. Effect of Irrigation Energy Inputs on Partial Energy Productivity

Fig. 9.8   Yield response curves to changes in input factors
Source after Fluck and Baird (1980)

sources. The earlier discussion of research on the contribution of mechanization to yield growth suggested that shifts in average horsepower use from less than 0.25 hp/ha to 0.5 hp/ha created dramatic results. For this and other reasons, Fluck and Baird hypothesized a relationship between yield and power availability not unlike the one for yield and fertilizer. The highest partial energy productivity is at the point of minimal mechanization. Further mechanized inputs increase yield at a decreasing rate.

The relationship between yield and irrigation energy inputs is less clear simply because of the variation in the importance of irrigation systems in providing the water needs of plants. Some irrigation systems provide practically all the water needs of crops, whereas others only a small percentage. The yield response curve in Fig. 9.8 suggests, at least for systems not totally dependent on irrigation for their only source of water, that substantial energy subsidies are involved before maximum partial productivities are achieved. The lack of yield response in the lower reaches of the curve is indicative of the amount of energy required to make the system operational, whereas the decline in yield with high irrigation energy inputs is indicative of excess water applications. In situations where irrigation provides the only or most of the water, the curve would probably

276

rise more rapidly, since small additions of water and energy would create rapid gains in yield.

Environmental effects

The increasing energy intensification of agriculture worldwide and the shift to commercial supplies for that energy has conferred unchallengeable benefits for society at large. The source of these benefits, as emphasized in this chapter, has been in the adoption and use of yield-augmenting and labour/land-saving technologies. Perhaps insufficiently emphasized is that the growth in demand for food and fibre can be accommodated on a relatively stable land base, without the need to extend cultivation onto marginal and hazard-prone lands. In the absence of the availability/adoption of this technology, population pressures have forced expansion of food production onto these lands with predictable social and environmental costs. Costs can also be identified in the intensification process, but it can be argued that the net benefits of this process are still substantial. Although the above trade-off is seen as a necessary evil, the extent and long-term implications of environmental costs from intensification require the recognition of more remedial action. In this section we examine some of the major environmental effects of growing energy use in agriculture. The subject of remedial action will be dealt with in the following section on alternatives to increasing energy intensity.

Energy intensive agricultural systems have the potential to transform significantly their internal and external environments. The actual on-site and off-site effects are, however, as much a function of the information and management context within which the operation occurs as they are of the magnitude of the energy inputs themselves. We have already considered (in Chapter 7) some environmental effects of intensification – namely soil erosion and salinization, which are linked in some regions to the growth in mechanized and irrigated agriculture. To these examples can be added numerous environmental effects arising from the expansion in the use of fertilizers and pesticides. It is to these sources we now turn.

Fertilizers

The growth in global fertilizer use from approximately 15 million tonnes per year in 1950 to 120 in 1985 represents an eight-fold increase in consumption. Regionally, most of this fertilizer is consumed in the developed world (see Fig. 3.5), with nitrogen representing the largest share of total tonnage consumed, followed by phosphate and potash. The prospects for greatly expanded consumption in the developing world suggests that the problems experienced today in the developed world in the use of fertilizers will be shared in other regions in the not too distant future.

The concerns over the environmental effects of fertilizer use relate to the impacts on aquatic, edaphic and atmospheric systems. Perhaps the most important of these are changes in the quality of drinking water for humans and animals alike from high concentrations of nitrates in surface and groundwater systems and changes in nutrient levels in lakes, rivers and reservoirs leading to eutrophication. Nitrogen is by far the most easily of the three fertilizers to be leached out of the soil. Since nitrogen uptake by plants rarely exceeds 60 per cent, the potential exists for large quantities to be deposited into the aquatic system from erosion and run-off, particularly in regions with heavy applications of nitrogen fertilizer. Having said this and recognizing the potential impact on humans and aquatic systems, there is little empirical evidence isolating the non-point sources of the contamination. It is notoriously difficult to determine the source of nitrate contamination of water systems since, in addition to fertilizer, it may come from urban and industrial wastes.

A review of the health effects of nitrogen fertilizers in the United States concluded that the agricultural system is a relatively small contributor to nitrate in ground- and surface-waters (Crosson and Brubaker, 1982). With the exception of local 'hotspots' in the Mid-West, certain river basins in California and the sandhills region of Nebraska, where groundwater nitrate concentrations have exceeded 20 ppm,* most regions of the United States are experiencing declines in water quality from industrial and urban wastes. For eutrophication, the same study cites sources which argue that phosphorous and nitrogen nutrient loads again are generated primarily from non-agricultural sources. Information on other world regions is relatively scarce as to the origin and extent of the problem. But, given the already high rates of soil erosion and areas affected by irrigation and reliance on groundwater supplies in developing countries, the increased use of fertilizers will, in combination with urban and industrial contaminants, create increased health risks and environmental costs.

Even less well understood is the impact on the atmosphere from the release of oxides from denitrification. The production of nitrogen fertilizer from synthetic nitrogen fixation is approaching the quantity produced through natural or terrestrial fixation (Barney, 1980). The alteration of the nitrogen nutrient cycle through expanded use of artificial fertilizers has the potential to deplete the earth's ozone layer as do chlorofluorocarbons. This layer is responsible for reducing the amount of ultra-violet radiation which is the prime cause of skin cancer. Recent evidence suggests that the ozone layer is deteriorating in certain regions of the world, but the source of the decline has yet to be firmly established.

The chemical properties of soils and in turn their productive potential can be altered by applications of ammonium-based nitrogen fertilizer (see

---

*Maximum acceptable levels for human consumption are 10 ppm of nitrogen in the United States.

Chapter 8 for a general discussion of acidification). The acidification of soils, a naturally-occurring process responsible for the weathering of soils and release of nutrients, can be accelerated by the application of nitrogen fertilizer in humid regions where soils are low in neutralizing minerals such as limestone. Soils in dry regions or soils with a high calcium or magnesium content usually experience much lower rates of acidity (Coote, 1983). Other factors contributing to increases in acidity are sulphate in the fertilizer and the presence in the atmosphere of sulphur and nitrogen oxides from the combustion of fossil fuels.

Table 9.6 and Figure 9.9 provide regional breakdowns of the fertilizer and atmospheric sources of soil acidity and the relative risk of acidification for Canada. The soils of the eastern region of the country, which already receive the highest applications of nitrogen fertilizer, also possess the highest risk of acidification because of higher rainfall and lack of natural soil-buffering agents. Similarly, large areas of the tropics and sub-tropics with their oxisols and ultisols are sensitive to the risks of soil-acidification. Expansion of cultivation in these regions, along with increased use of fertilizers, must be done in conjunction with neutralizing agents such as calcium (lime) and magnesium.

Other edaphic impacts from increased fertilizer use include a decline in soil organic matter. Higher levels of soil nitrogen accelerate the decomposition of organic matter. Not only does this affect the natural fertility of soils but it adds to the carbon dioxide content of the atmosphere.

Table 9.6 Representative annual contribution to soil acidity by atmospheric deposition (1977–79) and fertilizer use (1974–79)

Location	$CaCO_3$ equivalents required annually for neutralization (kg/ha)		
	Atmospheric[a]	Fertilizer[b]	Total
Atlantic Provinces	30	84	114
Quebec	35	51	86
Ontario	33	90	123
Manitoba	5	72	77
Saskatchewan	0	12	12
Alberta	2	51	53
British Columbia	5	66	71

[a]Based on estimated contribution of long-range transported acidity from precipitation
[b]Based on fertilizer sales data. Canadian Fertilizer Institute, assuming an average requirement at a ratio of 3 : 1 (calcium carbonate to nitrate)
Source after Coote (1983)

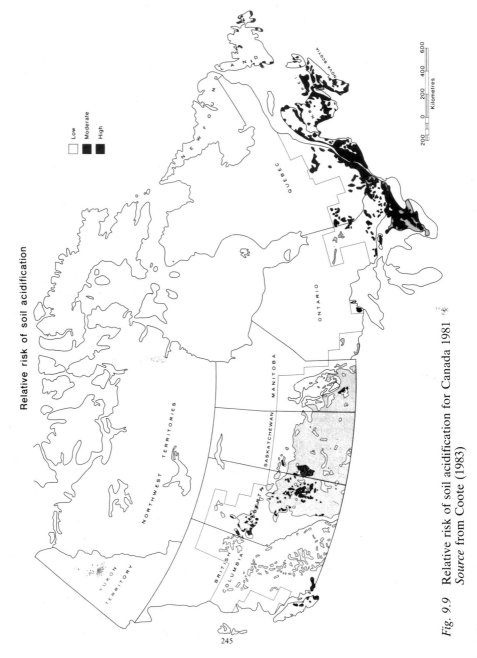

Fig. 9.9 Relative risk of soil acidification for Canada 1981
Source from Coote (1983)

Pesticides

Agro-ecosystems, both traditional and modern, lose anywhere from 20 to 40 per cent of production to pests. Weeds, insects, nematodes, bacteria, fungi, birds, rodents, viruses and other plant pathogens are the sources of significant costs to society and constraints to production. Elimination of pests in developed countries has been a somewhat elusive goal. Nearly 30 per cent of US food production is lost to pests. Pest control cannot be separated from the environment which nurtures those pests. Associated with energy-intensive agriculture are farm management practices that, if anything, have been conducive to the spread of pests. These practices include increased specialization in agriculture with fewer crop varieties and a trend towards monoculture, the spread of irrigation, abandonment of traditional crop rotation schemes, and the rise in importance of conservation tillage.

Of the four main means of pest control – crop rotation, plant breeding for resistance, development of natural enemies and the application of insecticides and herbicides – the last group has been the most popular and extensively used (Holdgate et al., 1982). The experience of developed countries suggests that while these chemicals are vital to sustain specialized forms of agricultural production, they have created an unanticipated array of problems such as pest-strain resistance to chemicals, destruction of natural predators, the growth of populations not originally regarded as pests and a variety of toxic residues and undesirable environmental impacts such as biological amplification and concentration in predators and humans (FAO, 1978). Many of these environmental effects extend far beyond the farm unit and the life-cycle of the plant or organism that they are supposed to control. For example, the potential for surface and groundwater contamination is very real. In a review of recent research on the topic, Crosson and Ostov (1988) report that at least seventeen pesticides have been found in the groundwater of twenty-three states as a result of routine agricultural use. And that some 12.6 million people live in areas of high or medium potential for pesticide contamination of groundwater. Potential is defined according to the use of pesticides, their solubility and leachability of soils. These consequences indicate a need for more careful use of insecticides/herbicides and a more sophisticated and integrated pest-management strategy.

The development and use of pesticides can be broken down into two periods (Holdgate et al., 1982). The first, beginning in the 1940s and extending into the 1960s, saw the introduction in developed and developing countries of persistent organochlorine insecticides such as DDT, dieldrin, aldrin and endrin and systemic herbicides, such as 2,4-D and 2,4,5-T. Evidence that the organochlorine compounds were bio-accumulative in the environment, with potential carcinogenic and/or teratogenic effects on humans and wildlife, prompted their general removal from use in the developed countries. The US Environmental Protection Agency banned the use of DDT in 1972 and most West European countries followed suit shortly after. However, their use in many developing countries has not subsided since in the case of DDT it is an inexpensive and effective means for the control of malaria. The bio-accumulative effects of DDT are therefore expected to increase. Although the previously-mentioned herbicides have been associated with a variety of unwelcomed side effects including the destruction of desirable but non-targeted vegetation, phytotoxic residues in the soil and the creation of a compound similar to dioxin, a teratogen for humans and livestock alike, it is argued that some of these problems are largely the result of misapplication (Holdgate et al., 1982).

The second period in pesticide use is distinguished by the increasing substitution of organophosphate and carbumate insecticides. In the UK between 1965–75 the number of organophosphate insecticides increased seven-fold, whereas the number of organochlorine decreased by 16 per cent (Holdgate et al., 1982). The environmental effects of organophosphates differ from their chloride counterparts. While they are neither persistent nor bio-accumulative, they are toxic to humans and to non-target organisms. Crosson and Brubaker (1982: 120) have argued in this regard that 'organophosphorus and carbumate compounds typically are sharp, localized and short-term'. This implies that the problem and environmental effects stemming from the use of these compounds are more easily identified.

The environmental cost of pesticide use in the United States has been estimated to be $839 million annually (Crosson and Brubaker, 1982). Among the contributing factors to this cost are human pesticide poisoning ($284 million or $1 million for every death), a decline in natural enemies and increased genetic resistance ($287 million). Total costs of pesticide use equal an estimated $3.5 billion annually. Against these costs are estimated total benefits of $10.9 billion. The ratio of benefits to costs therefore is three to one.

Herbicide use plays an equal if not greater role than the use of insecticides in most developed countries. In developing countries, herbicide use represents a small proportion of total pesticide use. With the spread in importance of high-yielding variety grains herbicide use nevertheless is growing rapidly. While such chemicals as paraquat, common in conservation tillage, are toxic to humans, one of the main environmental concerns over extended use of herbicides is potential damage to soil microorganisms (Crosson and Brubaker, 1982).

Energy alternatives

The preceding discussion of the role of energy inputs in agricultural development highlighted their actual and potential importance in enhancing the environment for food production. Although 'optimal' standards of use for energy inputs defied easy definition, it was clear that there was great scope for change and improvement, qualitatively and quantitatively, in the use of these resources to permit the maintenance and growth of productive capacity. In this section we examine alternative scenarios or patterns of energy use which address the need to improve the efficiency and productivity of energy through conservation and management approaches, as well as technological change; to minimize the environmental costs of increasing energy intensification; and to augment the supply/availability of energy in regions with traditional agricultural systems. These issues will be discussed within the context of three broad categories for the solution of energy-related problems: conservation of inputs; organic farming and the use of intermediate technology; and agriculture as a potential producer of energy.

Conservation of inputs

Expanding energy productivity can be accomplished on either the input or output side. We have already examined productivity and efficiency differences as the length of the food chain increases. Food energy yield per hectare is higher for crops than it is for animal products (see Table 9.2). This fact alone implies that small changes in dietary habits and/or improved conversion of grain/forage to animal products can on both input and output sides produce significant changes in energy productivity. Our main concern is with improving the use of energy inputs. Although the following observations apply particularly to developed or modern agricultural systems where there is perhaps not greater need but certainly greater potential for conservation, they also apply to more traditional systems where, as we saw in Chapter 6, irrigation efficiencies are notoriously low. Table 9.7 provides a summary of some of the main technological approaches to the reduction of energy inputs. A discussion follows of some of these approaches.

Fertilizers

It was shown earlier that with increasing fertilizer applications yields increased, but at a decreasing rate. This process of diminishing returns underlines the natural limits in the food system to absorb and mineralize nitrogen, phosphorous and phosphates, and demonstrates the excess quantities which become available for leaching and oxidation. Improvements in the uptake and efficiency of fertilizer use can be achieved by careful timing in the application of the nutrients, reduction in water erosion through certain tillage and irrigation practices, testing of mineral and nutrient composition of the soil and a knowledge of crop nutrient requirements.

The low and in some cases declining price of fertilizer has discouraged more efficient use and experimentation with alternative sources of nutrients. Nevertheless, fertilizer represents the single largest energy input and

Table 9.7 Some agricultural technology approaches to reduce energy inputs into food production systems

---

Enhancement of photosynthetic efficiency
  Improvement of plant architecture for better light interception (i.e. leaves with vertical orientation)
    Genetic selection of varieties with greater efficiency (i.e. high leaf-area index)
    Reduction or inhibition of photo-respiratory and/or night respiration
    Use of varieties of a more prolonged growth period
    Artificial enrichment with CO_2
    Hormonal stimulation of net photosynthesis
    Hormonal stimulation of crop senescence
    Genetic incorporation of C_4 or CAM mechanisms into C_3 crops
    Efficient planting patterns (orientation of rows N–S)
    Use of plastic mulches that reflect light back to underside of leaves

Environmental modification
  Wind modification with windbreaks and shelterbelts
  Frost control with windbreaks, heaters, fans, and irrigation
  Control of soil temperatures through mulching or application of black charcoal and asphalt

Soil management
  Genetic selection of crops tolerant to nutritional differences or toxicities
  Application of fertilizers at lower rates and increasing the efficiency of applied fertilizers
  Minimum or reduced tillage
  Use of manure, compost, cover crops, and green manures
  Enhancement of biological N_2 fixation, and selection of bacteria able to fix N_2 in the rizosphere of non-legume crops
  Direct use of primary fertilizer sources (i.e. phosphoric rock)

Water management
  Drip irrigation
  Mulching, reduced tillage
  Control of stomata aperture with chemicals (i.e. PMA)
  Cover management for shade control
  Windbreaks
  Application of 'required amounts' of water based on real soil water content

Insect pest management
  Preventive action: resistant varieties, manipulation of crop-planting date, tillage and row-spacing, crop rotation, improved field hygiene, use of attractants, pheromone traps, crop diversification, etc.
  Suppressive action: sterile male technique, sex-attractant pheromones, introduction, augmentation, and conservation of parasites and predators, microbial and botanical insecticides, use of mechanical or fire removal, induction of behavioural changes, pesticidal controls when economic threshold is reached, etc.

Disease management
  Resistant varieties, crop rotations, use of sub-optimal fungicide doses, multilines or variety mixtures, biological control with antagonists, multiple cropping and reduced tillage

Weed management
Design of competitive crop mixtures, rapid transplant of vigorous crop seedlings to weed-free bed, use of cover crops, narrow row spacings, crop rotation, keeping crop weed-free during critical competition period, mulching, cultivation regimes and allelopathy

Agronomic systems
Multiple cropping systems: inter-cropping, strip-cropping, ratoon-cropping, relay-cropping, mixed cropping, etc.
Use of cover crops in orchard and vineyards
Agro-forestry systems
Cropping systems analogous to the natural secondary succession of the area.

Source Altieri et al. (1984), based upon Wittwer (1975)

cost in American grain production (Doering, 1980). Small improvements in efficiency and use under these circumstances have the potential to achieve significant energy economies and reduction in environmental pressures. These economies can be achieved by recourse to some of the previously-discussed efficiency measures or by means of alternative sources of nutrients.

One such source is through symbiotic nitrogen fixation in the use of legume-based crop rotation systems. Pastures of white clover, alfalfa and ryegrass, commonly found in temperate regions, can fix the equivalent of 250–400 kg/ha of nitrogen yearly. Soybeans are capable of fixing between 25–50 per cent of their total nitrogen needs. Other sources of nitrogen can be derived from blue-green algae in combination with the water fern azolla in rice paddies. As much as 60 kg/ha of nitrogen can be taken up by a rice crop (FAO, 1978b).

Reliance on direct food crops or forage crops to fix nitrogen is not new. Until the 1940s most agricultural systems relied on crop rotation systems to restore needed nutrients and enhance productivity. Studies have demonstrated the superiority in energy and protein terms of legume systems compared to continuous-cropping corn and corn, wheat, soybean systems. It has been found that seeding recently-harvested corn-land with winter vetch, and ploughing the vetch under for green manure in April, produced about 150 kg of nitrogen/ha. Pimentel (1979) argued that if an equivalent quantity of nitrogen is to be applied to corn production, 2.28 million kcal/ha are required for artificial fertilizer compared to 222,300 kcal/ha for the planting of vetch. The vetch also contributes to a decline in wind and water erosion and adds organic material to soil. Yet continuous cropping is far more productive in absolute terms than the former (Doering, 1980).

The failure of many farmers to continue with or adopt the legume rotation system rests on a number of interrelated economic factors.

Markets tend to be weak for such nitrogen-fixing crops as alfalfa. A smaller proportion of the arable land base can be cropped annually under fallow systems. And inorganic fertilizers are still a competitively-priced source of nutrients. These considerations ignore the long-term environmental implications of cropping practices which deplete the natural organic and nutrient levels of the soil.

Yet another source of natural nutrients is livestock manure. One tonne of manure contains approximately 5.6 kg of nitrogen, 1.5 kg of phosphorus and 3 kg of potassium. Given these proportions, it would require a minimum of 25 wet tonnes of manure per hectare to satisfy the nitrogen requirements of corn. Pimentel (1979) argued that this quantity of manure and nutrients are produced from either three cows, twenty-two hogs or 207 chickens annually. In terms of energy equivalents the same author (1984) calculates that the hauling and spreading of manure with tractor and spreader in close proximity to the farm (1.6 km radius) would consume about 750,000 kcal compared to 2.3 million kcal for artificial fertilizers (including the energy in manufacture). An additional labour input of 6.4 hr is required for the loading, transport and application of the manure (Pimentel, 1984).

Despite this 3:1 energy advantage, the great weight, volume and storage problems and labour requirements associated with the use of manure have limited its usefulness. As the structure of farming has changed in favour of specialized monoculture operations and against diversified crop–livestock operations, the gap between manure production and potential consumption has widened. Still there is enormous scope for better integration of these operations and for expansion in the use of manures as a nutrient supplement. Pimentel (1984) has suggested that with better storage and application of manure to prevent nitrification, manure could supply double the nitrogen that it now supplies to US agriculture (about 8 per cent of requirements).

Field Operations

Field operations include field preparation, planting, spraying, harvesting and other routine mechanized operations such as crop-drying. Direct and indirect conservation methods have been applied to reduce energy expenditures. These can be as simple as ensuring proper maintenance and tuning of equipment, to much more complex approaches which require changes in machinery (gasoline to diesel) and cultivation practices such as conventional tillage to conservation tillage. Conservation tillage has expanded rapidly in the United States from approximately 14 per cent of harvested cropland in 1973 to 27.4 per cent in 1981 (Crosson and Brubaker, 1982). The shift to conservation tillage indicates considerable economic and environmental advantages in the form of reduced energy expenditures in field preparation and cultivation, and a decline in soil erosion and soil compaction from greater crop residues and less mechanical trampling of the soil. Crosson (1981) indicated that the cost per hectare of conservation tillage is about 5–10 per cent less than under conventional tillage. This estimate incorporates the increased cost of using herbicide and insecticides to control weeds and pests.

Conservation tillage is by no means a universal solution to greater energy efficiency since the energy savings are greater for some crops (wheat) than for others (corn). There is also the suggestion that conservation tillage may increase groundwater loads of nitrates through greater percolation rates of water (Crosson and Brubaker, 1982). Some regions would be more susceptible than others which would limit their suitability for this type of cultivation. The general benefits, however, cannot be denied from increased crop residues.

Crop residues enhance the level of nutrients and organic matter in the soil, reduce soil erosion and the seasonal fluctuations in soil temperature, and increase soil water (Larson et al., 1982). These are all-important properties and/or conditions for sustained productivity of the land. By extension, their absence requires increased energy expenditures to redress the balance. It has been estimated that between 10 and 15 per cent of the productive potential of US cropland has been lost to erosion. Pimentel et al. (1976) argued that to offset this loss the system requires an additional 494,200 kilocalories/ha or 7.9 billion litres of fuel equivalents annually, which in 1970 represented 4 per cent of the nation's total oil imports.

These losses can be redressed with better soil management. In Larson et al.'s (1982) study of the loss of nitrogen and phosphorus from soil erosion under two different residue management systems (with residues and without) in the US Corn Belt, the value of increased crop residue was firmly supported. Nitrogen and phosphorus levels in eroded sediments from fields with residues returned were only a third or less the levels of unprotected fields.

Irrigation

In Chapter 6 we explored the importance of irrigation systems in the agricultural development of Third World countries. Cost of installation, operation and maintenance represented formidable barriers to the adoption and use of this technology. It has been estimated that since 1973 there has been a 55 per cent increase in energy consumption by the irrigation sector (Faidley, 1987). By 1982 it consumed directly and indirectly the equivalent of 27 million barrels of oil per year most of which is used for pumping purposes.

There is a difference in energy requirements between surface and groundwater systems, with the former requiring an average energy investment of 748 MJ/ha/yr and the latter 1727 MJ/ha/yr. Table 9.8 provides comparative data on the energy requirements of these two systems broken

Table 9.8 Annual energy required for irrigation

Irrigation System Type ((%) efficiency)	Surface-water supply				Groundwater–50 m lift			Groundwater–100 m lift		
	Installation energy	Energy for supply	Pumping energy	Total energy	Energy for supply	Pumping energy	Total energy	Energy for supply	Pumping energy	Total energy
Surface (50)	0.47	0.75	4.7	5.9	1.29	83.3	85.0	1.72	161.8	164.0
Surface (70)	0.47	0.75	3.4	4.6	1.29	59.5	61.2	1.72	115.6	117.8
Surface (85)	1.22	0.75	4.6	6.6	1.29	50.8	53.3	1.72	97.0	99.9
Sprinkler (75)	0.81	0.75	55.5	57.1	1.29	107.9	110.0	1.72	160.1	162.6
Trickle (90)	4.22	0.75	30.6	35.6	1.29	74.3	79.8	1.72	117.8	123.7
LEPA (90)	1.20	0.75	14.3	16.2	1.29	58.0	60.5	1.72	101.6	104.5

Note All figures are in gigajoules per hectare per year.
Source Smerdon and Hiler (1987)

down by field application type. Because of the significant differences in the efficiencies of these various techniques, there are significant variations in energy requirements. Aside from shifting to these more efficient techniques, especially from high- to low-pressure irrigation systems, according to Smerdon and Hiler (1986) energy savings can be realized through a variety of approaches: improvements in net pumping efficiencies (thermal to mechanical energy) which stand at 12.5 per cent, improved crop varieties with lower water arequirements, levelling of fields, insulating distribution systems and better design/maintenance of existing systems. The authors estimate that as much as three-quarters of present energy use can be saved through the pursuit of these energy-saving approaches.

Pesticides

From both an environmental and energy efficiency/cost perspective, the concept of integrated pest management (IPM) has received increased support and application in most developed countries in recent years. Earlier it was noted that there were four major means or mechanisms for the control of pests. IPM involves selective use of all four and, in the process, abandons the sole dependence on persistent pesticides used so commonly until the early 1970s. Although not easy to define, since IPM will vary by crop and region, it encompasses a set of principles which include selective application of pesticides according to need, development of pest-resistant crop varieties, biological control through natural predators and sexual sterilization of pests, improved forecasting of pest infestations and changes in agricultural practices (FAO, 1978b). In 1966 FAO established a Panel of Experts on Integrated Pest Control, and in 1975, in combination with UNEP, created the Co-operative Global Programme for the Development and Application of Integrated Pest Control in Agriculture.

One practice was to introduce a corn/soybean rotation system for the control of rootworm in the US Corn Belt. Another was the shift in location of crop production from areas of high incidence of pests and pathogens to low-incidence areas. The High Plains area of Texas is a relatively hostile environment for most cotton pests and represents about 45 per cent of the state's cropland in cotton. Short-season varieties of cotton have been introduced, allowing for accelerated growth through the period that the crop is most vulnerable to pests. Insecticide use has declined as much as 50 per cent in major crop-growing regions. Throughout the United States, insecticide use per hectare declined from an average of 3 kg/hectare in 1971 to 2.5 in 1976. Herbicides have not shown a similar decline in part because of the growth in conservation tillage, although Crosson and Brubaker (1982) noted that whereas conservation tillage doubled between 1972 and 1976, total pesticide use (including herbicides) increased by only 6 per cent.

The success of IPM, and in turn the energy savings from reduced use of pesticides, depend on knowledge of the environment for pests and the risk they pose for crop development. Much of this will favour developed countries with a long tradition in research and development in pest control. But even developed countries are faced with basic obstacles to the adoption of IPM. Whereas wheat is more resistant to pests than corn, it is not always a viable economic or cultural substitute. Moreover, the use of scouts to assess the risk of crop damage from insects requires skilled and available personnel. It appears however that the advantages of scouting and IPM are low so long as insecticide prices remain low (Crosson and Brubaker, 1982).

Organic farming and intermediate technology

Intermediate or appropriate technology are terms coined to describe a system of agriculture or a means of production which is generally less energy-intensive and smaller-scale, but more labour-intensive than conventional agriculture. Closely allied, but not necessarily the same, is organic farming. It is based upon the notion that plant nutrients are to be supplied from organic wastes (as opposed to synthetic sources) in the form of livestock and leguminous green manures, in turn supplied from livestock and crop rotation systems, and that the control of weeds and pests is limited to mechanical cultivation, crop sequences, biological control mechanisms and other non-insecticide/herbicide IPM approaches.

While examples of intermediate technology can be found in numerous developed and developing countries in the form of wind-driven pumps, solar heating–drying facilities, hand cultivators, and *in situ* energy production, organic farming is an isolated phenomenon at least in Western countries. No more than 1 per cent of the farms in Britain and the United States can be classed as organic. Other European countries such as France and West Germany are estimated to have far higher but unspecified proportions (*The Economist*, 1987c).

Organic farming has been viewed since 1960 as a potential but not necessarily viable alternative to conventional farming. Most farming in developed countries until the 1940s and still to this day, in many developing countries of Africa, Central America and parts of South-East Asia, could be classed as organic. In the latter case it is largely by necessity not choice. The Amish and Mennonites in North America have a long tradition of organic farming. Comparative studies of Amish and non-Amish agriculture in Pennsylvania and Illinois have found that the Amish are normally medium scale diversified operations with high energy output–input ratios, but lower yields than non-Amish (Johnson et al., 1977). Some of the differences in yield can be attributed to physical or site conditions. The Amish system of agriculture performed better than modern systems where large-scale economies were not possible because of limitations in field size and difficult terrain for highly-mechanized agriculture. Differential advantages can also arise from superior soil and climatic conditions which can favour the viability of small producing units.

Other comparisons of organic and conventional farming in the United States suggest that whereas the yields in organic farming may be lower than conventional agriculture, the net return is generally as high on a per-unit basis. The energy savings are not to be found in the consumption of less fuel, which is generally the same regardless of the operation, but in the basic absence of inorganic fertilizers, insecticides and herbicides (Lockeretz et al., 1977).

Yield differences, however, appear to be greater between organic and inorganic farming in Western Europe than in North America. One report suggests that because North American farms are generally large operations with relatively low inputs, compared to their European counterparts, yield deficits are only 5–15 per cent whereas in Europe they are around 35 per cent (*The Economist*, 1987c). The viability of these lower-yielding operations in Europe is based upon a high-income elasticity of demand for organically-grown food, but also the already high food prices established under the EEC Common Agricultural Policy. In the absence of these higher prices, as in many developing countries, organic farming is faced with difficult economic constraints. While general levels of food production would undoubtedly decline if farming became more energy-efficient but less energy-intensive, the potential is there for modern agricultural systems to adopt selectively some of the organic farming approaches and techniques.

In developing countries, elements of organic farming are now being pursued or, until recently, were being pursued. The use of and reliance on organic materials and crop-rotation systems has been the basis for sustaining soil nutrients and stable agricultural systems in numerous regions of Asia. It has been argued, however, that an even greater use of organic wastes could be made as a supplement to, and even substitute for, expensive and sometimes unreliably-supplied mineral fertilizers (Nagar, 1977). The potential nutrient supply from using organic wastes in developing countries in 1980 has been estimated to be as high as 60 million tonnes of nitrogen, 20 million tonnes of phosphorus and 48 million tonnes of potash. These quantities of nutrients have a market value of over $20 billion (1973 dollars).

Agriculture as a producer of energy

The transition from low-yielding subsistence agricultural systems to high-yielding surplus-producing agricultural systems has been dependent upon securing cheap and abundant supplies of energy. Revelle (1976) suggested that if Indian agriculture boosted its energy inputs by an additional 58×10^{14} kilocalories, US yield levels could be approached. The shortage of energy generally and fuels specifically in most developing countries is highlighted by the dependence on fuelwood supplies for cooking purposes of nearly two billion persons. Moreover, scarcities of fuelwood have diverted crop and livestock residues away from their traditional use as a source of nutrients for field application to a more recent use as a source of fuel.

Although the use of commercial energy has expanded significantly in recent years, cost, lack of foreign exchange, balance of payments problems, and inadequate infrastructure and distribution facilities limit the role that this energy source can play in the immediate future. The rapid rise of oil prices during the 1970s prompted numerous oil-importing countries, both developed and developing, to search for alternative sources of energy. One such source was biomass production which represents all plant and animal materials derived from biological growth and their wastes and residues.

As stored solar energy in the form of carbohydrates (starches, sugars and lignocellulose materials) and hydrocarbons (milkweed, species of eurphobia, rubber tree and guayute shrub), biomass resources are large but difficult to mobilize. They also possess high moisture content but low carbon content, which limits their usable energy. And, as discussed earlier, diversion of crop residues away from their use as a mulch can reduce land productivity and increase erosion (Hall, 1984a). Forest-land and shrub-land are the sources of the largest production of biomass (80×10^9 t/yr), followed by grasslands (19×10^9 t/yr), cultivated land (9.1×10^9 t/yr) and tundra desert and swamps ($8.8 \times 7\ 10^9$ t/yr) for a total of 117 billion tonnes per year. Stored biomass is estimated to be seventeen times annual production. The energy content of the annual production and stored biomass is equivalent to forty-one and 640 billion barrels of oil, respectively. Biomass production from cropland has an energy equivalent of 205 million barrels of oil, which is about 6 per cent of world's total commercial energy needs (Montalembert, 1983).

Biomass resources have a number of competing end uses such as food, feed, fibre, fertilizer and fuel. The production of carbohydrates for fuel can compete with the production of carbohydrates for food. Given that the conversion losses from entropy are the same whether food is converted directly into fuel or whether the potential biomass resource is used in a step-by-step fashion (food–feed–fuel), Hall (1984a) argued that the greatest utilization of the resource occurs when the latter approach is pursued. With biomass resources which are capable of producing hydrocarbons directly, the efficiency of conversion to fuel is much higher than with carbohydrates. Despite this fact, the use of land for direct energy–fuel production precludes the use of the land for food production.

The use of biomass food resources for the production of fuels (solid, liquid, gaseous) has a variety of social economic, environmental and land-use implications (Smil, 1984). Food resources can be used directly to produce fuels such as ethanol and methanol through fermentation and anaerobic digestion of carbohydrates from corn, sugar cane, sugar beet, sweet sorghum and cassava. The by-products such as bagasse from sugar cane, pulp from sugar beet and distiller's grain from corn can be used for feed or fertilizer.

Brazil is one of the leaders in the production of alcohol from sugar cane and produces approximately eight billion litres per year, which is used primarily as a direct fuel or as a mixture with gasoline for automobiles. Not only has the food for fuel strategy favoured large plantations and large-scale distilleries because of the need for scale economies, but evidence suggests that sugar cane production is in some regions displacing food crops, such as in Sao Paulo state. Nationally, alcohol production increases have been associated with a decline in per capita output of major food crops (Rovere, 1985).

The USDA is favourably disposed to the use of cropland for energy production. If energy prices rise, ethanol production could rise from around the present two billion litres to an upper limit of 18 billion litres per year (Sampson, 1982). Notwithstanding the fact that this could displace about five million hectares of productive land, it would also accelerate erosion because of increased area devoted to row crops and require increased use of fertilizers and pesticides.

Against this food for fuel strategy, which at best is minimally integrated into the production of food through the reuse of residues as foodstuffs and at worst is a direct competition for cropland for food, stand other strategies which attempt to integrate food and fuel production. Through the use of co-products (such as the growth of perennials for food/feed and fuel) and by-products or wastes (such as animal manure, crop residues, and pulp and bagasse from distillation) as inputs for fuel and fertilizer production, multiple goals can be accommodated.

Perhaps the greatest potential and pay-off of these strategies is to be realized in relatively small-scale and decentralized projects. In Brazil, evaluations of experimental projects involving the production of alcohol from micro-distilleries using sugar cane or sweet sorghum, biogas from anaerobic digestion of animal waste, and biological fertilizers suggest that these projects are only economically feasible when fully integrated and complementary with respect to each other. Surplus yields 'are guaranteed only if certain complementary activities are functional, such as the production of protein from water hyacinth and/or sugar cane or sorghum bagasse, to be used in cattle feed, or the delivery of such by-products as bagasse and biogas outside the system' (Rovere, 1985: 27). Moreover, the ultimate success of these integrated projects will depend upon careful adaptation and use of different energy technologies to individual community needs and avoidance of the use of complex and expensive equipment.

Studies of biogas production from manures in the United States also highlight the difficulty, at least in commercial agricultural systems, of making it economically feasible despite the relative abundance of inputs and technical know-how. It is estimated that approximately 4×10^{17} joules of energy, the equivalent of 60 million barrels of oil, could be recovered from livestock and poultry manures (Martin, 1982). And there are numerous tested examples of the production of methane from anaerobic digestion. Yet energy density of biogas containing about 60 per cent methane is less than most other fuels (particularly liquid fuels), making it an inappropriate fuel for trucks or tractors but a possible source of energy for boiler fuel and electricity generation. Unless the average cost of electricity is above \$12.50/GJ, producing biogas using electricity is marginal. On the positive side, however, anaerobic digestion of manures does not destroy their nitrogen, phosphate and potassium which allows for the by-product to be used as fertilizer.

In China there are approximately seven million bio-digesters, the overwhelming majority of which are to be found in Szechwan province. While providing energy for domestic energy purposes, the systems are also designed to integrate the organic waste product from the bio-digesters into the agricultural production process. Having said this, the extremely heavy reliance on agricultural residues for biogas production has diverted their use from field application, sometimes reducing soil fertility and increasing the erosivity of the land. It appears that India's experiment with biogas production has been less successful since the available technology requires a minimum of 6–10 head of cattle and ten to twelve hectares, which would automatically exclude access to alternative energy supplies by those who could benefit most (Rovere, 1985).

Other equally important sources of biomass for the production of methanol and solid fuels are a variety of fast-growing trees. By integrating the cultivation of these trees with the production of food staples it is possible to secure a source of solid fuel for burning, lignocellulose material for fermentation, and direct production of hydrocarbons. Not only does this relieve pressure on erosion-prone lands and reduce labour expenditure in collecting wood, but agroforestry can contribute valuable nutrients to the soil since some species are nitrogen-fixing. And lastly, it can reduce or prevent the diversion of crop residues to energy production, thereby ensuring they will remain on the land to sustain soil fertility (Montalembert, 1983).

In evaluating the contribution of biomass resources in supplementing energy supply for agriculture, their greatest potential is to be found in regimes with poorly-developed infrastructure and transportation facilities where existing energy subsidies are low. The scale and degree of specialization of technologies must be closely tailored to regional needs, including the necessity to integrate fuel and food production as much as possible. Although we have not examined other potential energy sources which would complement the use of biomass, they are numerous. The use of wind power for irrigation-pumping purposes, solar power to operate photo-voltaic cells and to assist in crop-drying and water-heating, and better-designed cooking stoves are just a few additional sources of energy production which when combined with biomass sources can make the generation of agricultural surpluses at low cost a reality for many regions of the world.

Summary

The use of inanimate sources of energy has played a vital role in transforming agriculture from a low-yielding subsistence status to a high-yielding surplus one. Developed countries have expanded their agricultural sectors through large energy subsidies for the manufacture and use of machinery, fertilizers and pesticides. In developing countries commercial energy subsidies are increasing with the largest share going to fertilizers. For these regions animate energy from labour and animal sources provides an equivalent form of mechanical power. The fact that cereal production between developed and developing countries is roughly the same underlines the continued importance of this labour to sustain production.

To increase yields in most developing countries will require greater reliance on mechanical technology for irrigation, harvesting and planting purposes, as well as greater use of fertilizers and pesticides. Unlike most industrialized countries, developing countries stand to realize large gains in yields, with relatively modest gains in energy-intensive inputs. Far from being labour-displacing, the use of small horsepower machinery and fertilizer promises to increase land and labour productivity substantially. The benefits from these higher yields would include improved diets and income potential as well as less demand for land resources which are hazard-prone.

The inter-relationship between energy use and productivity of agriculture is a close one. Most developed countries have high area and labour productivities but are experiencing diminishing returns to expanded energy inputs. Since the cost of energy inputs in these countries has represented a small proportion of total costs, particularly under subsidized price conditions, farmers can afford to continue to expand inputs as cost of inputs rise. However, the consensus is if increases in price or supply bottlenecks in energy persist they will discourage the growth in irrigated area and encourage the substitution of land for non-land inputs in rainfed agriculture.

Despite the benefits to modern agricultural systems of energy subsidies, the source of that energy is largely non-renewable. Hence continued dependence on a depletable resource undermines the long-term sustainability of agricultural operations. Not only is more research required into alternative energy sources, but changes in the practice of agriculture are required in order to anticipate the inevitable limitations inherent in the use of fossil fuels. Closely linked to the energy-intensive agricultural systems are a variety of environmental effects. Excessive applications of fertilizer threaten surface and groundwater quality, insecticide and herbicide use threatens non-target populations and soil micro-organisms, heavy machinery compacts soil, and over-pumping of groundwater and poor irrigation design diminish the long-term viability of numerous agricultural regions. There are also numerous hazards to human health from contamination of surface and groundwater systems. While many of these problems are shared among developed and developing countries, those which are related to fertilizer/pesticide use and heavy machinery are particularly germane to developed countries. In this regard, alternative approaches to the use of energy-intensive inputs, offer many real and significant benefits to humans and their environment.

To meet the future agricultural energy needs of both developed and developing countries, while minimizing environmental cost, will require a variety of concerted initiatives on the demand and supply side of the energy equation. More judicious and selective use of fertilizer and the operation of machinery has the potential for sharp increases in energy efficiency, regardless of the measurement used. Further efficiencies can be realized through the use of integrated pest-management strategies, greater reliance on livestock and animal manures and a shift to nitrogen-fixing crops where possible.

On the supply side agriculture itself has the potential to become a producer of energy. This potential ranges from direct combustion of animal and crop biomass and the growth of crops for direct conversion of fuel to more sophisticated integrated schemes of food and fuel production. While the economics of these alternative sources and their associated conversion technologies are not generally favourable *vis à vis* conventional sources in developed countries, they nevertheless hold promise in numerous remote rural areas of the developing world. Poor transportation facilities, bottlenecks in supply, as well as lack of income to purchase imported fuel, make these alternative systems important supplements to, if not substitutes for, energy supply.

CHAPTER 10

Sustainable food systems

Challenges of the food problem

The social and economic viability of countries has depended upon their ability to generate food surpluses and to provide adequate nutrition for their populations. These requirements are no less important today and will continue to be important in the future. The challenges of meeting these requirements and ensuring an element of food security are formidable, both economically and environmentally. By the end of this century the earth will have to support an additional 1.3 billion persons with an average purchasing power well above 1980 levels.

To satisfy this growth in economic and physiological demand for food will require two major initiatives. First, global food output will have to expand by as much as 40–50 per cent. The majority of this growth must take place on the existing land base by narrowing the yield gap without sacrificing the environmental basis for food production. One study has noted that to meet anticipated growth in food demand of 1.8 per cent per annum to the year 2000 only 0.3 per cent will come from an expansion in area. The remaining 1.5 per cent will come from increases in yield – primarily based on new technologies (US Office of Technology Assessment, 1986). Moreover, the growth of food production ideally should serve goals other than nutritional ones. Expanding the productive capacities of the food system can allow for expanded employment opportunities, particularly in developing countries. If these opportunities translate into higher real incomes, rural population growth and migration to cities can be reduced and savings rate and local economic development improved.

A second challenge facing agriculture is to provide for a more equitable access not only to food but to the resources required for its production. Highly-skewed income distributions, the dominance of cash crops, and insecure or non-existent land tenure are but a few major obstacles to achieving this access. This second challenge highlights a central canon of the food problem. While increases in food output and production per

297

capita are a necessary condition for alleviating hunger, they are not a sufficient condition. The means not only to produce but also to purchase the food must be present.

Against the broader issues of the food problem, this book has attempted to develop a better understanding of the relationship between agriculture and the global environment. It has done this through an examination of major physical factors, defined in resource and environmental terms, which affect the productive capabilities of the food system. Influencing these physical factors were both human/institutional constraints and natural constraints. The analysis has indicated that the failure to maintain and expand productive capacity was due as much, if not more, to institutional than natural constraints.

This statement does not deny the importance and significance of natural limits to the growth in the food system. Parenthetically, these limits will have more influence on food development options in the future, as societies make increased demands on the ecosystem and use up the surplus capacity now available for development. The fact that at most 25 per cent of the earth's surface can sustain viable cropping systems attests to the importance of natural limitations in the form of soil, water and climate resources. Within this 25 per cent, pursuing long-term production is dependent on preserving the delicate physical and biological balance which sustains life systems. The necessity to preserve that balance in combination with the natural resources available for food production determines the ultimate flow of goods from the land and, of course, its carrying capacity. And perhaps the ultimate limit is energy supply. Agriculture is becoming increasingly dependent on finite fossil fuels.

Although difficult to isolate those physical factors which are the product of natural versus human constraints, much of the preceding analysis has pointed to institutional factors as being chiefly responsible for failure to expand productive capacity adequately. The enormous yield gap which exists among countries with similar ecological conditions supports this interpretation.

To conclude this section, and in preparation for the next section on strategies for the growth and maintenance of productive capacity, it is useful to synthesize some of the previously-discussed demand and supply issues in food systems. This will be based on physical and economic parameters.

A synthesis of demand and supply relations

Food production capacity can be conceptualized as the product of a number of driving forces which are at the same time limiting factors. The quantity and quality of resources and the availability of technology/capital/labour provide the impetus for growth or constraint within the food system. In Figure 10.1 the strengths or lengths of the

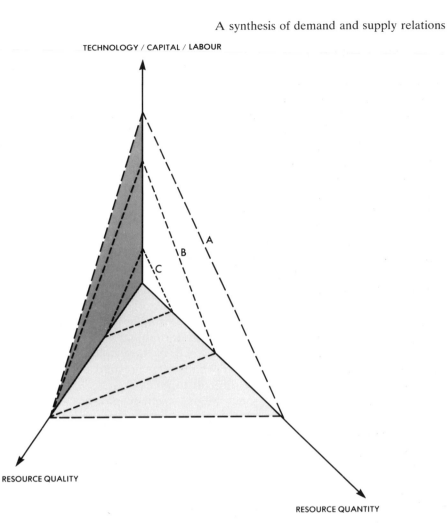

Fig. 10.1   Three principal dimensions affecting food production capacity.

individual dimensions produce different levels of possible food output, as defined by the size of shaded triangles (A, B, C,). Production capacity can expand, level off or decline over time, as we saw in Figure 1.1.

Quantity of resources is affected by the supply and efficiency in use of land, water, energy and climate resources. The quality of the resource, that is, the food production environment, is influenced by factors such as land fertility and degradation, mineral content of water, type of energy source and climatic suitability for crops. That quality can improve or decline through human intervention in the environment. Lastly, the factor which defines the scope and utility of these resources is the supply (including distribution) and efficiency of use of capital, labour and technology. This composite factor can offset or compensate for limitations in either the quantity or quality of resources available for agricultural production. And, as we have seen in a number of instances, this factor can have adverse effects on production as well. Of the three dimensions defining productive capacity, technology and capital supply are the most difficult to define, particularly in terms of the degree to which the process of substitution of 'man-made' capital for 'natural' capital can continue. The interdependencies among factors of production ensure that substitution is not perfectly elastic. The ecological law of the minimum is still very much in existence, imposing constraints on the use of technical fixes to override environmental realities.

Agricultural systems can therefore be categorized according to the strengths and relative balance among the dimensions and in turn the size of the resulting productive capacities. Agriculture within most developed countries has been characterized by growth in two of the three dimensions – technology/capital and quantity of resources. Not only has capital and technology been substituted for land-based inputs, but these same factors have been used to offset the productivity effects of various forms of land degradation. The degree to which these compensating processes can continue will depend upon the growth of technology, the rate of factor substitution this permits and the existence of threshold effects. These effects imply sudden or non-linear changes in resource–product relationships which once exceeded are difficult to reverse.

In contrast to these highly capital-intensive and science-based modes of production, agricultural operations in developing countries are more labour-intensive, with fewer technological and energy resources to enhance the productivity of the land or labour. The need to sustain the quality of the environment in these resource-based systems is critical. In those systems with traditional methods of cultivation and relatively high population pressures, declines in the quality of the environment for food production have been widespread. Often this reflects reduced access to less hazard-prone lands as export-oriented farming replaces traditional subsistence farming. Without the benefit of technology/capital or additional resources, production capacity has grown relatively slowly and has even declined in some regions.

Where Green Revolution technology, inputs and methods of cultivation are available, productive capacity has been enlarged significantly. Yet a large yield gap remains in most Third World countries, despite their shift to more energy-intensive and science-based inputs. In arid and semi-arid regions various forms of land degradation, inefficiencies in the use of irrigation water and lack of energy-intensive inputs have slowed growth in yields. In more humid regions water-based soil erosion and loss of nutrients, land fragmentation, inefficiencies in the use of energy-intensive inputs, disease and lack of research relating to the indigenous food sector are some of the major stumbling blocks towards narrowing the gap.

Where productive capacity represents what is feasible or capable of being produced within a region according to the previously-defined factors it may not, despite its size, fulfil basic food needs of a society. To better understand this feature of the food system let us turn to Figure 10.2. The upper half of the diagram reflects physiological demand as determined by population size and minimum caloric/protein requirements. Effective demand, on the other hand is defined by population and income or purchasing power. In Figure 10.2 effective demand is clearly smaller than physiological demand. Although not illustrated, effective demand may exceed physiological demand, as is the situation in most developed countries.

The lower half of the diagram represents the productive capacity of the system, as defined by the quantity and quality of resources and available technology/capital/labour. That capacity may be smaller or larger than the food required to meet effective and/or physiological demand. In Figure 10.2 it is illustrated as being considerably larger. Subsets of productive capacity are represented by economic, subsistence and export supply. Economic supply is a function of the quantity of food output available for national consumption, given prevailing prices and economic conditions. Subsistence supply, which exists only where peasant/traditional agriculture is practised, represents actual food produced, given resources/labour available within the context of physiological demand. And export supply

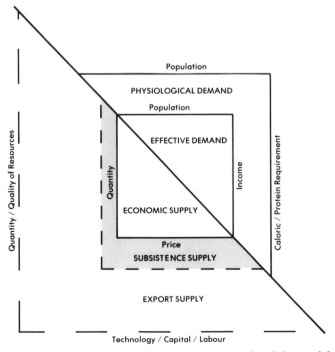

Fig. 10.2   Inter-relationships of the supply of and demand for food

(which is also a form of economic supply) represents quantity of food or agricultural products available for the international market, given international prices, terms of trade and economic conditions.

Many of the same factors which govern the productive capacity of the system, such as research and development, energy prices and supply, seed varieties, land capability, land degradation and government policy, will also influence economic, subsistence or export supply. In traditional or subsistence systems with minimal access to agricultural technology, declines in the quantity or quality of the resource base will have a devastating effect upon output. Desertification in the Sahel, soil erosion in high-altitude tropical regions and salinization in arid regions have all undermined the productive capabilities of the local/regional food systems.

Economic supply which is driven by effective demand, nationally and internationally, is also influenced by cost-increasing or decreasing factors, such as biological or mechanical technology, price of energy and water inputs, subsidies and infrastructure. For export supply, government policy relating to land tenure, export policy and the need for foreign exchange, and foreign investment are critical factors affecting its importance relative to the other components of food supply.

In North America and Western Europe effective demand for food exceeds physiological demand. At the same time productive capacity is sufficiently large to satisfy the indigenous demands for food as well as to meet a large number of international export commitments. The productive capacity of the agricultural system of Japan is such that economic supply is unable to match effective demand. Consequently, Japan is a net importer of food from fisheries and agricultural exporting countries.

In contrast to the developed world, a high percentage of low-income developing countries throughout Africa and South and South East Asia have effective demand levels below physiological demand. Lack of income prevents the expansion of effective demand. Since much of the agriculture in these countries is still traditional or subsistence despite the use of Green Revolution technology, lack of access to additional land, seed, water and fertilizer resources prevents capacity from being expanded farther. The existence of an export supply sector, in which use of land for non-indigenous food purposes intensifies the competition for land and reduces net food supply, can lead to fragmentation and increasing inequity and inefficiency in the agricultural system.

Strategies for sustainable development

Perspectives on the need for sustainable development

A consensus is emerging that new strategies are required in society's quest for a more secure food environment. The search for sustainable development strategies implies that our present course of action in developed and developing countries is non-supportable over the long term. In many ways the strategies are not new, but reflect an extension of thinking on environmental conservation and social equity.

The call for sustainable development in agriculture is based upon the recognition of a set of interrelated problems or issues facing agriculture which reflect three themes – resource stewardship, food sufficiency and agricultural community (Douglass, 1984). Unifying these themes is a fourth – the interconnection theme. Let us examine these in turn. First, as we have demonstrated in the preceding chapters, although agriculture is a renewable resource-based activity it is also a depletable resource-based activity. This resource base in practically all countries is undergoing retrenchment, quantitatively and qualitatively. The decline in soil fertility from land degradation, loss of agricultural land and water resources, the contamination of water, the loss of genetic stocks of plants and animals and the depletion of fossil fuels are all manifestations of this process. While this depletion implies environmental costs, it also implies economic costs in terms of lost or forgone opportunities and the need for additional offsetting inputs.

Second, there is a need, as discussed earlier in this chapter, for the growth and maintenance of food productive capacity. Not only will agriculture have to serve a larger and more affluent population in the developing world, but it will have to satisfy over the long term more stable demands for food and fibre in developed countries.

A third issue or theme is the recognition that within agriculture there are enormous variations in income, access to agricultural resources, nutritional levels and production per capita. While these concerns have been in-creasingly expressed within the context of development prospects for developing countries, they also apply to developed countries. The margina-lization of farmers and their declining economic fortunes in Western countries bears witness to the cross-national character of this problem.

And fourth there is increasing recognition of the complex linkages and interconnection among physical, biological and social systems. Relatively small changes in one system can induce often large and negative impacts on another. Agriculture, like all economic activity, is dependent on and not independent of the bio-physical resource base. Norgaard (1984) argued that for sustainable development to occur it must be 'coevolutionary' or in tandem with the evolution of the environmental system. As the competi-tion for space and use of land intensifies with growth, so will the complexities of these interconnections.

In preceding chapters we have seen numerous examples of changes both external and internal to agriculture which have on-site and off-site effects environmentally, socially and economically. Climate change, the product of the use of fossil fuels, the accelerated release of carbon from deforestation and decline in organic matter from fertilizer use, has potentially enormous implications for the inputs and outputs from agriculture and ultimately

303

Sustainable food systems

agriculture's viability. Climate change will affect energy use, the availability of water, the efficiency of plant growth, the type of plant that can be grown, the environmental effects of production practices, the spread of disease and the health of communities.

On a smaller scale, and perhaps more immediately comprehensible, are the interconnections between deforestation, agriculture and hydraulic-dependent activities. Figure 10.3 traces some of the impacts on a region following deforestation. Not only are the environmental costs significant,

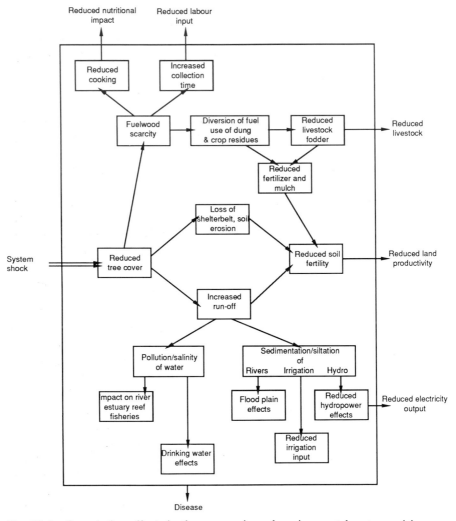

Fig. 10.3   Cumulative effects in the economic and enviromental system arising from deforestation
Source after Pearce and Markandya (1987)

but economically agriculture is faced with increasing costs as soil fertility declines and the cost of conservation measures rise.

Clearly agricultural development cannot be separated from its environment. Development has consequences for stewardship of the land and other resources, for sufficiency in meeting food needs and for community in terms of the economic and social well-being of a region or nation.

Defining sustainable development

If there is agreement on the need for more environmentally-positive agriculture which meets the nutritional and economic needs of the population, there is no single definition or goal for its achievement. In 1980 the World Conservation Strategy (1980) defined sustainable development by example. Three strategies or objectives were advocated: (1) to maintain essential ecological processes and life-support systems; (2) to preserve genetic diversity; and (3) to ensure the sustainable utilization of species and ecosystems.

Against this ecologically-based view of sustainability stand a number of other attempts to define and elaborate on the meaning of this difficult concept. Perhaps the best known of these is the Brundtland Report, *Our Common Future* (World Commission on Environment and Development, 1987). In its 'global agenda for change' sustainable development is defined as development 'that meets the needs of the present without compromising the ability of future generations to meet their own needs' (p. 43). The concept of needs is an important one in the Report. Considerable emphasis is placed on meeting the essential needs of the world's poor. Others have adopted similar criteria for the achievement of sustainable economic development. Barbier (1987: 103), for example, has argued that 'the primary objective is reducing the absolute poverty of the world's poor through providing lasting and secure livelihoods that minimize resource depletion, environmental degradation, cultural disruption, and social instability.'

The notion that today's growth should be based upon the dividends from a country's asset base and should not foreclose the future well-being of society is central to most definitions of sustainable development. Douglass (1984: 25) argued that 'agriculture will be found to be sustainable when ways are discovered to meet future demands for foodstuffs without imposing on society real increases in the social costs of production and without causing the distribution of opportunities or incomes to worsen.' And Repetto (1986: 15) viewed sustainable development as a 'development strategy that manages all assets, natural resources and human resources as well as financial and physical assets, for increasing long-term wealth and well being'.

The preceding definitions and goals of sustainable development highlight the importance of conservation of the delicate physical and biological

305

balance which sustains life systems, but it is much more than this. While we have seen that there is no unified definition of sustainable development, the concept embraces equity issues (within and between generations), integrated resource management, economic development and the interrelations of natural and social systems in addition to conservation issues. In summary, sustainable development is about balancing the need for agricultural development against the limitations of the environment, while ensuring the nutritional and economic well-being of society now and in the future.

Prospects

What are the prospects for achieving sustainable development? To answer that question we must consider the major obstacles to sustainable development. It has been argued in previous chapters that many of the resource and environmental constraints to expanded food production have an important underlying institutional dimension (see Fig. 1.2). There is nothing inevitable about these constraints, since they are the product of human actions. Thus the prospects for achieving sustainable development are closely tied to improvements in the management of agricultural resources and also, from a broader perspective, changes in the institutional frameworks – legal, political, financial, economic and cultural – which determine the efficiency and equity in the use of those resources.

It has been suggested that the development of Western societies during the past 200 years has been premised on the adoption of a mechanical world paradigm (Rifkin, 1980). Progress is measured in terms of increasing order, material abundance and control over nature. The scientific method, the abundance of fossil fuels and technology have provided the impetus for the scientific and industrial revolutions which are still with us today. Generally these systems make no distinction between natural and man-made capital. Not surprisingly, as Daly (1977: 110) noted 'our present economic institutions and theories are more attuned to maximizing throughput than to minimizing it.' The surplus conditions which characterized Western agriculture are based upon enormous energy subsidies of commercial non-renewable energy. Hence, while the earth is a closed system subject to the laws of thermodynamics, individual regions/countries are open systems capable of artificially expanding their land's carrying capacity through the regional transfer of energy, materials and information. Outputs or pollution from the process are often external to the region.

While the benefits from this process have been enormous, in nutritional and economic terms, there are of course limits to the ultimate availability of fossil fuels and the environment's ability to absorb the pollution. The dependence on fossil fuels in agriculture is therefore not sustainable over the long term. Fossil fuel dependence, without the development of alternative energy supplies, is a major obstacle to sustainable development. Practically all the research budgets and new technologies in recent years have been designed and executed within the context of a continued dependence on fossil fuels and on those technologies which provide a rapid return on investment. In this regard it has been observed that 'the current socio-economic structure of corporate agriculture and the organization of agricultural research prevents the incorporation of ecological research recommendations into agricultural management systems. Agricultural enterprises will not invest in sustainable technologies for which the profits cannot be immediately captured' (Altieri et al., 1984: 186).

One of the central and disturbing questions related to the use of fossil fuels is the degree to which Third World countries, with rapidly expanding populations and in some cases incomes, will be able to make the transition to a sustainable system. Can the future demands for food and fibre in these regions be supported on relatively low-energy subsidies of through-puts? Is the growth objective compatible with the sustainable objective? Although similar questions can be raised with respect to developed countries, they are much more able to withstand the price shocks to the system as energy prices rise. They are also, by virtue of their technological and capital superiority, able to make the transition more easily if there is a concerted effort to anticipate the need for change.

Other concerns have been raised about the present ability of capitalist systems to recognize environmental realities. The properties of ecological systems are often at odds with the atomistic–mechanical world view of neo-classical economics. Redclift (1987: 40) has pointed to the fact that 'market mechanisms fail to allocate environmental goods and services efficiently precisely because environmental systems are not divisible, frequently do not reach equilibrium positions and incur changes which are not reversible.' The non-divisibility principle is an important one since it ultimately governs or limits factor substitution. The substitution process (discussed in Chapter 3) has permitted the growth in food production and productivity by means of substituting less scarce for more scarce factors of production and by substituting more productive for less productive factors. While labour, land, capital and energy are divisible in a theoretical sense, in practice their availability and use are highly interdependent. Moreover, the continued inability of all industrial systems, socialist and capitalist alike, to attach value to environmental goods such as air and water is also a stumbling block to sustainable systems.

How resources are valued is an important ingredient affecting their efficient use. We have seen numerous instances where price distortions in the form of depressed prices for farmers in the Third World countries or subsidized prices in First World countries can lead to severe imbalances between supply and demand and numerous negative environmental consequences. Excessive rates of use of water are a direct result of low or non-existent cost to the user. An unregulated or non-priced use of other basic resources such as land has also been detrimental to the preservation of agricultural assets. The common property character of both land and water resources is a major obstacle to sustainable development, requiring political/regulatory action.

While most developed countries have relatively small and stable agricultural populations, the reverse obtains in many developing countries. Demands for fertile land resources within the context of insecure land tenure and limited access to the arable land base because of government and international support for export/cash crops have created numerous non-sustainable development patterns, including land fragmentation, deforestation and agriculture in steep slopes and other hazard-prone land.

The dependence of Third World farmers on Western nations for inputs to the production process and for marketing of their produce has contributed to what Redclift (1987) referred to as the internationalization of the environment for food production. Prices, terms of trade, research, government policy and debt are external driving forces that influence and impact the choices available in agriculture for many Third World countries. While some farmers have benefited from this arrangement, there is a whole class of farmers which is becoming marginalized economically and environmentally. The growing integration of traditional agriculture and the small farmer into the international economic system makes it extremely difficult to isolate the source or major cause responsible for non-sustainable development. Myers (1987) argued that although the slash-and-burn farmer has been blamed for destructive land-management practices, this is only the proximate and not the ultimate cause of deforestation. Instead, the ultimate source of the problem, as in Brazil, is the land-tenure system, foreign debt and international commodity markets.

Obstacles to sustainable development are not all supply-related. While nutritional levels and living standards in lesser-developed countries need to improve, is this to occur independent of a change in standards in developed countries? To what degree is the achievement of sustainable development in agriculture in developing countries contingent on modifying demand in developed countries? The culture of excess and waste so endemic to the food consumption habits of Western nations is, in energy terms, non-sustainable. The continued diversion of a vast quantity of resources to a small percentage of the earth's population ignores the very real possibilities, with little or no sacrifice in standards of living, of a change in the demands society makes to fulfil its food needs. In this respect Hardin (1984) has maintained that invariably we speak of a *shortage* of supply but never of a *longage* of demand. There is an important psychological dimension to demand independent of the physical requirements for food. How a society changes those demands or streamlines them will in no small way determine the success or failure of sustainable development.

While there are many today who adhere to the principle of sustainable development in agriculture, this does not ensure its practice for many of the reasons outlined above. The division between theory and practice highlights the enormous difficulty and challenges facing individuals and society in making the transition. To conclude this section we examine some of the requirements and pathways to sustainable agricultural systems.

Requirements

There is no high-output sustainable agriculture system operating at a large regional or national level. In developed and developing countries alike agriculture is based upon depletable resources which, given current rates of use, cannot sustain present consumption levels over the long term. For this reason there is no clear basis or strategy for sustainable development that allows for the achievement and integration of the numerous objectives which address ecological, economic, nutritional and equity concerns within agriculture itself and between agriculture and other sectors of society and the economy. Moreover, it has been argued that, given the environmental complexity of farming systems, sustainable agricultural technologies will have to be site-specific (Altieri et al., 1984).

While our practical knowledge of sustainable development is relatively weak and untested within the context of high demands, there is no need for a grand design or blueprint to guide society. We do have sufficient information on requirements which are likely to move us *closer* to a sustainable system. This transition from our current system to a sustainable one in agriculture will depend heavily on the achievement of a number of other transitions. Repetto (1986) outlined five critical transitions required before we can approach sustainable development. In their simplest form they represent: a demographic transition; an energy transition to high efficiency; a resource transition in which we rely on nature's income not capital; an economic transition which permits a broader sharing of benefits; and a political transition based on fostering complementary interests between North and South and East and West.

If agriculture is to meet the economic, social and nutritional requirements of people today and in the future, and to be at the same time 'environmentally rational', it will be necessary for there to be a close alliance between development and management of human and natural resources (Barbier, 1987). We have seen the critical role energy from fossil fuels plays in expanding productive capacity. Future development will also depend on large energy subsidies or throughputs, but this must be seen as a means to an end – the end being a system based on renewable energy sources which is in harmony with the annual solar energy budget. In short we must shift our dependence from stock to flow resources. This will require publicly-funded research and extension programmes, aimed at improving and expanding efficiency with which we use energy based inputs such as irrigation, fertilizers and pesticides. It will also require the development of appropriate technology – in both site and culture terms.

There appears to be enormous scope or potential for farmers to realize the gains from agricultural research. We saw in Chapter 3 that the tremendous growth in Western agriculture was based in no small way on induced technical change in agriculture. Ruttan (1984: 130) has suggested that 'The production of the new knowledge leading to technical change is the result of a process of institutional development.' Public-sector research or the socialization of agricultural research is the driving force underlying these changes.

This research in recent years has led to enhancement of photosynthetic efficiency, reduced respiration and hence the water needs of plants, increased the range of plants capable of biological nitrogen fixation, improved pest resistance of plants, development of agro-forestry and significant gains in livestock/poultry efficiency (Office of Technology Assessment, 1986). For these scientific advances to continue to benefit farmers and consumers and improve agricultural development prospects they must contain the following ingredients. First, they must be *accessible* to farmers on a regular basis and be manageable. Second, they must be *affordable* or economically viable. And third, they must be *acceptable* within the context of the social fabric of a community, the impact on risk and the current scale of operations. While Third World countries still rely on imported research and technology, the emergence in post-war years of a system of international crop and animal research institutes should help redress the balance. In Ruttan's (1984) view, the disparities in productivity between developed and developing countries of the world are directly attributable to lags in knowledge and lags in the shift from a resource-based to science-based system of agriculture. These lags are a measure of technical and scientific backwardness.

Despite a greater emphasis on science-based agriculture, the outcomes environmentally and socially are not necessarily favourable. Productivity has expanded through the adoption of bio-technology but this technology is still highly resource-based, particularly in its dependence on fossil fuels. It is also inequitable in its access, favouring large farms over smaller ones, and often is labour-displacing. Lastly, the technology has a reputation for being ecologically/environmentally questionable in terms of its narrowing of the genetic base and discouragement of traditional crop-rotation schemes in favour of mono-culture operations. A good example of the ambiguities surrounding the relative benefits of bio-technology can be found in the development of bovine somatotropin (BST). This is a mass-produced hormone, analogous to one found in cows which promises to boost milk production by 30 per cent (*The Economist* 1988b). While the drug promises to improve efficiency since it will require fewer cows to produce the same quantity of milk with no increase in feed, the benefits are likely to be realized by large farming enterprises capable of buying the drug and administering it. It is estimated that 'it could put half of

America's dairy farmers out of business in a decade' (*The Economist*, 1988b).

While research is essential, it must be attuned to the needs of farmers and society. Future research developments should not be viewed as supporting a simple extension of our current practices. There is a growing consensus that research should move us away from our dependence on a depletable asset such as fossil fuel and attempt to mimic or coexist with nature (Repetto, 1986; and Altieri et al., 1984).

Maintaining the asset base for agricultural production through resource management is one of the main instruments for coexisting with nature. Despite a clear need to halt desertification, reduce soil erosion, limit the loss of agricultural land and plant diversity, protect watersheds and improve the efficiency of irrigation, how is this to be accomplished, given the diverse contexts and sources of the problem? There are some basic principles that pave the way for a more efficient and ecologically-sound use of resources for agriculture.

Although there are imperfections in our competitive markets, they provide important sources of information through price about the relative scarcity of resources. Allocation of resources becomes increasingly wasteful and inefficient as prices paid for the use diverge from the marginal cost of supplying those resources. One of the major sources of inefficiencies in the use of water in developed and developing countries alike is the failure to attach a price to the use of water which reflects its marginal cost of supply.

Just as price distortions for water and in the use of other inputs such as pesticides in Third World countries lead to inefficient use of the resource base, so do subsidies in commodity markets. Subsidies paid to grain and livestock farmers in OECD countries are responsible for a legacy of over-supply and misuse of land. These outcomes are the direct product of government policies and represent the failure of public institutions to allocate resources efficiently.

While competitive markets have an important role to play in encouraging the efficient use of resources, their own imperfections regarding the absence of competitive markets for environmental goods require various forms of direct and indirect regulation and incentives ranging from taxing to limits on use and outputs. An important notion here is that prices or the cost to individuals in their own production and consumption activities should reflect their total cost to society. In this way society comes closer in its activities to reflecting the inherent materials and flows balance that exists. The wastes and by-products of our consumption represent a cost which must be reflected in the price.

Planning for better resource use has both efficiency (improved resource use) and equity goals (improved distribution of resources for current and future generations). There are three major obstacles to achieving these goals in resource conservation. First, information on land capabilities and possibilities for various types of development in Third World countries is limited. Second, lack of information including the nature of technological change and how it will affect resource use and productivity makes it difficult to assess the trade-offs which inevitably must be made in any plan. And third, the different emphasis politicians and planners attach to public versus private interests, the present versus the future and quality versus quantity of goods can compromise the achievement of the efficiency and equity goals.

Within the context of planning for better resource use these problems must be addressed. As our knowledge of land capabilities and consequences of various development options improve, it will at least be possible to make more informed choices. The choice which ultimately will be made will reflect a variety of exigencies in any society. Western Europe and North America have an enormous range of choices and alternatives in terms of the use of land for agriculture. Land can be retired from production. Conservation reserves can be created. Increased prices can be attached to the use of water. Restrictions can be placed on the use of agricultural land without at the same time dramatically affecting production potential or creating undue hardship for farmers. In many Third World countries no such flexibility exists because of real natural constraints, inadequate income and nutrition, or because of government policy on the use of lands. This has led to the use of hazard-prone lands which cannot sustain production over the long term. Poverty in itself is one of the major forces militating against resource conservation.

A basic requirement for resource conservation in these areas is to restrict use of some (hazard-prone) lands and intensify use on more resilient and productive lands. To do this will require changing or challenging the organizational framework which determines the choices available to planners and farmers. This framework and its linkages may include the World Bank, International Monetary Fund, agro-business, international market for commodities and various aid organizations. It will also require additional financial resources, the power to regulate common property resources, and incentives. There is an important necessity for incentives – both economic and social. There must be incentives to improve the efficiency with which we use resources either in terms of greater output or decreased costs. Conservation must be seen to pay. In situations where the pay-off is too long into the future to justify individual investment then society will have to take responsibility for investment, so that the costs, as the benefits, are more broadly borne.

Conclusion

Sustainable development is a radical concept or principle requiring dramatic changes to the social, economic, institutional and behavioural fabric of societies. It is no mere window-dressing which can be achieved by cosmetic planning strategies. Sustainable development over the long term is not a choice but an imperative for society. If we fail to make the conscious transition, the choice will be made for us – for sustainable development is a self-enforcing process capable of achieving its own equilibrium. We have the means to shape that equilibrium (high or low), to anticipate the necessary changes, but only if we are prepared collectively to reconsider, rethink and restructure our present modes of agricultural development. Above all else sustainable development will require relearning. The writer Tom Wolfe (1988) has argued that we are now in a great relearning period 'a prelude to the 21st century' in which the excesses of the past serve to inform and temper our approaches to and expectations of the future. There are limits to human actions, but enormous possibilities within those limits, which relearning will help us to achieve.

References

Aceves-Navarro, E. (1987) 'Salinity problems in food production of the Mexican irrigation districts,' in W. R. Jordan (ed.), *Water and Water Policy in World Food Supplies*, College Station: Texas A and M University Press, pp. 129–34.

Agriculture Canada (1983) *Selected Agricultural Statistics*. Ottawa: Supply and Services Canada.

Ahmad, M. (1987) 'Water as a constraint to world food supplies', in W. R. Jordan (ed.), *Water and Water Policy in World Food Supplies*, College Station, Texas: Texas A and M University, pp. 23–8.

Altieri, M. A., Letourneau, D. K. and Davis J. R. (1984) 'The requirements of sustainable agroecosystems', in G. K. Douglass (ed.), *Agricultural Sustainability in a Changing World Order*. Boulder, Colorado: Westview Press, pp. 175–89.

Ambroggi, R. P. (1980) 'Water,' *Scientific American* **243** (3): 100–17.

Aston, A. R. (1987) 'Salinity and food production in Australia,' in W. R. Jordan (ed.), *Water and Water Policy in World Food Supplies*, College Station, Texas: Texas A and M University Press, pp. 123–8.

Barbier, E. B. (1987) 'The concept of sustainable economic development', *Environmental Conservation* **14** (2): 101–10.

Barney, G. O. (ed.) (1980) *Global 2000. Report to the President Vol. II, Technical Report*, Oxford: Pergamon Press.

Barr, Terry N. (1981) 'The world food situation and global grain prospects', *Science* **214** (4 Dec): 1087–95.

Barrada, Y. (1987) 'Salinity management in Nile Delta food production', in W. R. Jordan, (ed.), *Water and Water Policy in World Food Supplies*, College Station, Texas: Texas A and M University Press, pp. 115–20.

Baumgartner, A. and Reichel, E. (1975) *The World Water Balance – Mean Annual Global, Continental and Maritime Precipitation, Evaporation and Runoff*, Amsterdam: Elsevier.

Baver, L. K., Gardner, W. H. and Gardner, W. R. (1972) *Soil Physics*, New York: John Wiley.

Bayliss-Smith, T. P., (1982) *The Ecology of Agricultural Systems*, Cambridge: Cambridge University Press.

Bennet, J. (1987) *The Hunger Machine*, Oxford: Basil Blackwell.

Berry B. J. L. (1980) 'The urban problem', in A. M. Woodruff (ed.), *The Farm and the City: Rivals or Allies?* Englewood Cliffs N J: Prentice-Hall, pp. 37–59.

Berry, B. J. L., Conkling, E. C. and Ray, D. M. (1987) *Economic Geography*, Englewood Cliffs, N J: Prentice-Hall.

Best, R. H. (1981) *Land Use and Living Space*, London: Methuen.

Bhatia, R. (1985) 'Energy and agriculture in developing countries', *Energy Policy* **13**, Aug: 330–4.

Bhuiyan, S. I. (1987) 'Irrigation technology for food production: expectations and realities in South and Southeast Asia', in W. R. Jordan (ed.), *Water and Water Policy in World Food Supplies*, College Station, Texas: Texas A and M University Press, pp. 325–34.

Biswas, A. K. (ed.) (1978) *United Nations Water Conference: Summary and Main Documents*, London: Pergamon Press.

Biswas, M. R. (1979) 'Energy and food production', in M. R. Biswas and A. K. Biswas (eds), *Food, Climate and Man*, New York: John Wiley, pp. 107–23.

Borgstrom, G. (1980) 'Ecological constraints of global food production', in N. Polunin (ed.), *Growth Without Eco-Disasters?* London: MacMillan Press, pp. 293–323.

Boyd, R. (1972) 'World dynamics: a note', *Science* **177**, 11 Aug: 516–19.

Boyer, J. S., (1982) 'Plant productivity and environment', *Science* **218**: 443–8.

Boyer, J. S. (1987) 'Water and plant productivity,' in W. R. Jordan (ed.), *Water and Water Policy in World Food Supplies*, College Station, Texas: Texas A and M University Press, pp. 23–8.

Brown, L. R. (1978) *The Worldwide Loss of Cropland*, Worldwatch Paper No. 24, Washington, DC: Worldwatch Institute.

Brown, L. R. (1981a) *Building a Sustainable Society*, New York: W. W. Norton and Co.

Brown, L. R. (1981b) 'Eroding the base of civilization,' *Journal of Soil and Water Conservation*, **36** (5): 255–60.

Brown, L. R. (1984a) 'A crisis of many dimensions. Putting food on the world's table', *Environment*, **26** (4): 15–43.

Brown, L. R. (1984b) 'The global loss of topsoil, *Journal of Soil and Water Conservation*, **39** (3): 162–5.

Bryant, C. R. (1976) *Farm-Generated Determinants of Land Use Change in the Rural–Urban Fringe in Canada, 1961–1975*, Technical Report, Lands Directorate, Ottawa: Environment Canada.

Bryant, C. R. (1981) 'Agriculture in an urbanizing environment: a case study from the Paris region, 1968–76', *The Canadian Geographer*, **21** (1): 27–45.

Bryant, C. R., Russwurm, L. H. and McLellan, A. G. (1982) *The City's Countryside: Land and its Management in the Rural–Urban Fringe*, Longman: London.

Bryson, R. A. and Murray, T. J. (1977) *Climates of Hunger*, Madison, Wisconsin: University of Wisconsin Press.

Bunting, A. H., Dennett, M. D., Elston, J. and Speed, C. (1982) 'Climate and crop distribution', in K. Baxter and L. Fowden (eds), *Food, Nutrition and Climate*, London: Applied Science Publishers, pp. 43–73

Buringh, P. (1977) 'Food production potential of the world,' *World Development* **5**: 477–85.

Buringh, P. (1981) *An Assessment of Losses and Degradation of Productive Agricultural Land In the World*, a paper prepared for the second meeting of the 'Working Group on Soils Policy', Rome, Feb 1981.

Buringh, P., Van Heemst, H. D. J. and Staring, G. J. (1979) 'Potential world food production', in H. Linneman (ed.), *Model of International Relations in Agriculture*, Amsterdam: North Holland, pp. 19–88.

Butler, J. H. (1980) *Economic Geography, Spatial and Environmental Aspects of Economic Activity*, New York: John Wiley.

Buttel, F. H., Lockeretz, W., Strange, M. and Terhune, E. C. (1980) *Energy and*

Small Farms: Paper II of the National Rural Centre Small Farms Project, Washington: National Rural Centre.

Butzer, K. (1980) 'Adaptation to global environmental change', *Professional Geographer*, **32** (3): 269–78.

Campbell, K. O. (1979) *Food for the Future*, Lincoln, Nebraska: University of Nebraska Press.

Castle, E. N. (1982) 'Agricultural and natural resources adequacy', *American Journal of Agricultural Economics* **64** (5): 811–20.

Centre for Science and Environment (1982) *The State of India's Environment. A Citizen's Report*, New Delhi (publisher unknown).

Chambers, R. (1983) *Rural Development*, London: Longman.

Chisholm, M. (1980) 'The wealth of nations', *Transactions, Institute of British Geographers*, (NS) **5**: 255–75.

Clark, C. (1967) *Population Growth and Land Use*, New York: St Martin's.

Conservation Foundation (1982) *State of the Environment 1982*, Washington, DC,: Conservation Foundation.

Cooper, C. F. (1981) 'Climatic variability and sustainability of xcrop yields in the moist tropics', in W. Bach, J. Pankrath and S. H. Schneider (eds), *Food–Climate Interactions*, Dordrecht, Holland: D. Reidel Co., pp. 167–86.

Coote, D. R. (1983) 'Stresses on land under intensive agricultural use,' in W. Simpson-Lewis, R. McKechnie and V. Neimanis (eds), *Stress on Land in Canada*, Environment Canada, Ottawa: Supply and Services Canada, pp. 227–58.

Cox, G. W. and Atkins, M. D. (1979) *Agricultural Ecology – An Analysis of World Food Production Systems*, San Francisco: W. H. Freeman and Co.

Crosson, P. (1979) 'Agricultural land use: a technological and energy perspective', in M. Schempf (ed.), *Farmland, Food and the Future*, Ankeny, Iowa: Soil Conservation Society of America, pp. 99–111.

Crosson, P. (1981a) *Conservation Tillage and Conventional Tillage: A Comparative Assessment*, Ankeny, Iowa: Soil Conservation Society.

Crosson, P. (1981b) 'Future economic and environmental costs of agricultural land', in P. Crosson (ed.), *The Cropland Crisis: Myth or Reality*, Baltimore: Johns Hopkins University Press, pp. 165–96.

Crosson, P. (1983) *Soil Erosion in Developing Countries: Amounts, Consequences and Policies*, Working Paper No. 21, Madison, Wisconsin: Centre for Resources Policy Studies, University of Wisconsin.

Crosson, P. and Brubaker, S. (1982) *Resource and Environmental Effects of U.S. Agriculture*, Baltimore: Johns Hopkins University Press.

Crosson, P. and Frederick, K. D. (1977) *The World Food Situation*, Baltimore: Johns Hopkins University Press.

Crosson, P. R. and Ostov, J. E. (1988) 'Alternative agriculture: sorting out its environmental benefits', *Resources*, No. 92 (Summer): 13–16.

Crosson, P. and Stout, A. T. (1983) *Productivity Effects of Cropland Erosion in the United States*, Baltimore: Johns Hopkins University Press.

Dahlberg, K. A. (1986) 'The changing nature of natural resources'. In K. A. Dahlberg and J. W. Bennett (eds), *Natural Resources and People*, Boulder: Westview Press, pp. 11–36.

Daly, H. E. (1977) 'The steady state economy: what, why, and how', in D. C. Pirages (ed.), *The Sustainable Society*, New York: Praeger, pp. 107–30.

David, L. *Vizugyi Muszaki Gazdasagi Tajeckztato*, Budapest (publisher unknown)

Deevey, E. S. (1960) 'The human population,' *Scientific American*, **203** Sept: 104–205.

Desjardin, R. L. and Ouellet, C. E. (1977) 'Influence of climate on wheat yield. Components during development stages'. in *Climatic Variability in Relation to*

Agricultural Productivity and Practices, Canada Commission on Agrometeorology, Ottawa: Agriculture Canada.

Doering, O. C. (1980) 'Energy dependence and the future of American agriculture,' in S. S. Batie and R. G. Healy (eds), *The Future of American Agriculture as a Strategic Resource*, Washington: The Conservation Foundation, pp. 191–223.

Doering, O. C. (1982) 'The effects of rising energy prices on agricultural production systems', in W. Lockeretz (ed.), *Agriculture and Energy*, New York: Academic Press, pp. 9–24.

Douglass, G. K. (1984) 'The meanings of agricultural sustainability,' in G. K. Douglass (ed.), *Agricultural Sustainability in a Changing World Order*, Boulder, Colorado: Westview, pp. 3–30.

Dregne, H. E. (1978) 'Desertification: man's abuse of the land', *Journal of Soil and Water Conservation*, 33 (1): 11–14.

Dregne, H. E. (1985) 'Aridity and land degradation', *Environment*, **27** (8): 16–33.

Dubos, R. (1981) *Celebrations of Life*, New York: McGraw-Hill.

Dudal, R. (1976) 'Inventory of the major soils of the world with special reference to mineral stress hazards', in M. J. Wright (ed.), *Plant Adaption to Mineral Stress in Problem Soils*, Ithaca, NY: Cornell University, pp. 3–14.

Dudal, R. (1982) 'Land degradation in a world perspective', *Journal of Soil and Water Conservation*, **37** (5): 245–9.

Dunne, T. (1977) 'Studying patterns of soil erosion in Kenya', in *Soil Conservation and Management in Developing Countries*, FAO Soils Bulletin No. 33, Rome: FAO, pp. 109–123.

Dunne, T., Dietrich, W. E. and Brunengo, M. J. (1978) 'Recent and past erosion rates in semi-arid Kenya', *Zeitschrift für Geomorphologie Supplementband*, **29**: 130–40.

Dvoskin, D. and Heady, E. O. (1977) 'Economic and environmental impacts of the energy crisis on agricultural production', in W. Lockeretz (ed.), *Agriculture and Energy*, New York: Academic Press, pp. 1–18.

Eckholm, E. P. (1976) *Losing Ground: Environmental Stress and the World Food Prospects*, New York: W. W. Norton and Co.

The Economist (1983) 'American survey: water in the west', **287**, 14 May: 41–50

The Economist (1987a) 'China's economy', **304** 1 Aug: 3–22.

The Economist (1987b) 'As prediction improves, the monsoon is less predictable', **304**, 22 Aug: 77.

The Economist (1987c) 'Does nature know best?', **304**, 22 Aug: 70–1.

The Economist (1987d) 'World population', **304**, 13 June: 51–4.

The Economist (1988a) 'Muddling through', **306**, 6 Feb: 80.

The Economist (1988b) 'As lakes become oceans', **307**, 16 Apr.: 19–20.

Edwards, A. M. and Wibberley, G. P. (1971) *An Agricultural Land Budget for Britain, 1965–2000*, Ashford, Kent: Wye College School of Rural Economics and Related Studies.

Ehlers, E. (1977) 'Social and economic consequences of large-scale irrigation developments – the Dez irrigation project, Khuzestan, Iran', in E. G Worthington (ed.), *Arid Land Irrigation in Developing Countries – Environmental Problems and Effects*, Oxford: Pergamon Press, pp. 85–98.

El-Gabaly, M. M. (1977) 'Problems and effects of irrigation in the Near East Region', in E. G. Worthington (ed.), *Arid Land Irrigation in Developing Countries – Environmental Problems and Effects*, London: Pergamon Press, pp. 239–49.

El-Swaify, S. A., Dangler, E. W., and Armstrong, C. L. (1982a) *Soil Erosion by Water in the Tropics*, Honolulu: University of Hawaii.

El-Swaify, S. A. and Dangler, E. W. (1982b) 'Rainfall erosion in the Tropics: a state-of-the-art', *Proceedings, symposium sponsored by American Society of Agronomy and Soil Science Society of America*, pp. 1–37, Madison, ASA and SSSA.

Espenshade, Jr, E. B., (ed.). *Goodes World Atlas* (15th edn), Chicago: Rand.

Faidley, L. W. (1987) 'Energy for world agriculture: water implications', in W. J. Jordan (ed.), *Water and Water Policy in World Food Supplies*, College Station, Texas: Texas A and M University Press, pp. 263–7.

Falkenmark, M. (1980) 'Water and land–independent but manipulated resources', in C. Widstrand (ed.), *Water Conflicts and Research Priorities*, London: Pergamon Press, pp. 11–61.

FAO (1950–75) *Production Yearbook*, FAO: Rome.

FAO (1977a) *Assessing Soil Degradation*, (FAO Soils Bulletin No. 34), Rome: FAO.

FAO (1977b) *The Fourth World Food Survey*, Rome: FAO.

FAO (1977c) *Soil Conservation and Management in Developing Countries*. (FAO Soils Bulletin No. 33), Rome: FAO.

FAO (1978a) *Report on the Agro-ecological Zones Project. Vol. 2: Methodology and Results for Africa*, World Soil Resources Report No. 48/1, Rome: FAO.

FAO (1978b) *State of Food and Agriculture*, Rome: FAO.

FAO (1979a) *Energy for World Agriculture*, Rome: FAO.

FAO (1979b) *A Provisional Methodology for Soil Degradation Assessment*, Rome: FAO.

FAO (1982a) *Agriculture Toward 2000*, Rome: FAO.

FAO (1982b) *State of Food and Agriculture*, Rome: FAO.

FAO (1983a) *Agriculture From the Perspective of Population Growth, Some Results from 'Agriculture: Toward 2000'*, Rome: FAO.

FAO (1983b) *FAO Production Yearbook*, Rome: FAO.

FAO (1983c) *State of Food and Agriculture*, Rome: FAO.

FAO (1984a) *Land, Food and People*, Rome: FAO.

FAO (1984b) *FAO Production Yearbook*, Rome: FAO.

FAO (1985a) *FAO Production Yearbook*, Rome: FAO.

FAO (1985b) *Fertilizer Yearbook*, Rome: FAO.

FAO (1986) *Food Outlook* (Statistical Supplement), FAO: Rome.

FAO/IIASA (1982) '*Potential Population Supporting Capacities of Lands in the Developing World*', Technical Report of Project FPA/INT 1513, Rome: FAO.

FAO/UNFPA (1979) *Land Resources for Populations of the Future*, Rome: FAO.

Fenster, C. R. (1977) 'Conservation tillage in the Northern Plains', *Journal of Soil and Water Conservation*, **32** (Jan–Feb): 37–42.

Field, N. (1968) 'Environmental quality and land productivity. A comparison of the agricultural land base of the USSR and North America.' *Canadian Geographer*, **12** (1): 1–14.

Finch, V. C., Trewartha, G. T., Robinson, A. H. and Hammond, E. H. (1957) *Elements of Geography*, Toronto: McGraw Hill.

Fitzhugh, H. A., Hodgson, H. J., Scoville, O. J., Nguyen, T. D. and Byerly, T. C. (1978) *The Role of Ruminants in Support of Man*, Morrilton, Ark.: Winrock International Livestock Research and Training Centre.

Flohn, H. (1979) 'A scenario of possible future climates – natural and man-made', in *Proceedings of the World Climate Conference* (WMO No. 537), Geneva: World Meterological Organization, pp. 426–74.

Fluck, R. C. and Baird, C. D. (1980) *Agricultural Energetics*, Westport, Conn.: AVI Publishing Co.

Forrester, J. W. (1971) *World Dynamics*, Cambridge: Wright-Allen.

Fournier, F. (1962) *Map of Erosion Danger in Africa South of the Sahara*, Paris: EEC, Commission for Technical Cooperation in Africa.

Frederick, K. D. and Hanson, J. C. (1982) *Water for Western Agriculture*, Washington: Resources for the Future.

Fukui, Hayao (1979) 'Climatic variability and agriculture in tropical moist regions', in *Proceedings of the World Climate Conference* (WMO No. 537), Geneva: World Meteorological Organization, pp. 426–74.

Furuseth, O. J. and Pierce, J. T. (1982) *Agricultural Land in an Urban Society*, Washington DC: Association of American Geographers.

Gardner, R. L. and Young, R. A. (1985) 'Assessing salinity control programs on the Colorado River', *Resources*, **80**: 10–13.

Gasser, R. W. (1981) *Survey of Irrigation in Eight Asian Nations*, Foreign Agricultural Economic Report No. 165, Economics and Statistics Service, USDA, Washington: USDA.

Gates, W. L. (1985) 'Modelling as a means of studying the climate system, in M. C. MacCracken and F. M. Luther (eds), *The Potential Climatic Effects of Increasing Carbon Dioxide.*, Washington: US Department of Energy, pp. 57–80.

Georgescu-Roegen, N. (1981) 'Energy, matter, and economic valuation: where do we stand?' in H. E. Daly and A. F. Umana, (eds), *Energy, Economics and the Environment*, Boulder, Colorado: Westview, pp. 43–80.

Golubev, G. N. (1980) *Agriculture and Water Erosion of Soils: A Global Outlook*, Laxenburg, Austria: International Institute for Applied Systems Analysis.

Green, M. G. (1978) *Eating Oil – Energy Use in Food Production*, Boulder, Colorado: Westview.

Grigg, D., (1985) *The World Food Problem 1950–1980*, Oxford: Basil Blackwell.

Gustavson, T. (1979) 'Environment conflict in the USSR', in D. Nelkin (ed.), *Controversy, Politics of Technical Decisions*, London: Sagi, pp. 69–83.

Haigh, P. A. (1977) *Separating the Effects of Weather and Management on Crop Production*, C. F. Kettering Foundation, ST 77–4.

Hall, C. W. (1975) 'The biosphere, the industriosphere and their interactions', *Bulletin Atomic Scientists* **31** (3): 11–21

Hall, C. W. (1984a) 'Energy sciences and conversions relating to food', in D. Pimentel and C. W. Hall (eds), *Food and Energy Resources*, New York: Academic Press, pp. 25–42.

Hall, C. W. (1984b) 'The role of energy in world agriculture and food availability', in D. Pimentel and C.W. Hall (eds), *Food and Energy Resources* New York: Academic Press, pp. 43–63.

Hansen, John A. G. (1982) 'Land use in North America and Britain, circa 1950 to 1970', *The Journal of Soil and Water Conservation*, **37** (3): 172–8.

Hardin, G. (1968) 'The tragedy of the commons', *Science*, **162**, 13 Dec.: 1243–8.

Hardin, G. (1984) 'Ending the squanderarchy', in H. E. Daly and A. F. Umana (eds), *Energy, Economics and the Environment*, Boulder, Colorado: Westview, pp. 147–64.

Hare, K. F. (1977) 'Climate and desertification', in *Desertification: Its Causes and Consequences*, UN Conference on Desertification, Oxford: Pergamon Press, pp. 63–120.

Hare, K. F. (1979) 'Climatic variation and variability: empirial evidence from meteorological and other sources', in *Proceedings of the World Climate Conference* (WMO No. 537), Geneva: World Meterological Organization, pp. 51–87.

Hart, John Fraser (1976) 'Urban encroachment on rural areas', *The Geographical Review* **66** (1): 3–17.

Hazell, P. B. R. (1982) *Instability in Indian Foodgrain Production.*, Research Report 30, Washington, DC: International Food Policy Reserach Institute.

Hazell, P. B. R. (1984) 'Increased instability in world foodgrain production – implications for agricultural research', *International Food Policy Research Institute*, **6** (1): 1–4.

References

Heathcote, R. L. (1983) *Arid Lands. Their Use and Abuse*, London: Longman.

Heimlich, R. E. and Anderson, W. D. (1987) 'Dynamics of land use change in urbanizing areas: experience in the economic research service', in W. Lockeretz (ed.), *Sustaining Agriculture Near Cities*, Ankeny, Iowa: Soil Conservation Society of America, pp. 135–54.

Herdt, R. W. and Barker, R. (1979) 'Sources of growth in Asian food production and an approach to identification of constraining factors', in *U.N. Univ. and the IRRI, Interfaces Between Agriculture, Nutrition and Food Science*, London: Macmillan, pp. 21–49.

Holdgate, M. W., Kassas, M. and White, G. F. (1982) *The World Environment 1972–1982*, Dublin: Tycooly Intenational Publishing Ltd.

Holy, M. (1971) *Water and the Environment*, Irrigation and Drainage Paper No. 8, Rome: FAO.

Hrabovszky, J. P. (1985) 'Agriculture the land base', in R. Repetto (ed.), *The Global Possible*, Newhaven, Conn.: Yale University Press, pp. 211–54.

Huat, T. E. (1974) *Effects of Simulated Erosion on Performance of Maize grown on Serdang Colluvium, Soil Conservation and Reclamation Report No. 1*, Kuala Lumpur, Ministry of Agriculture and Fisheries.

Huffman, Benjamin (1981) 'Agricultural land in national and regional economies', in *Agricultural Land Availability*, Committee on Agriculture, Nutrition and Forestry, United States Senate, Washington: US Government Printing Office, pp. 11–77.

Idso, S. B. (1985) 'The search for global CO_2 etc. "greenhouse effects" ', *Environmental Conservation* **12** (1): 29–33.

Ilbery, B. W. (1985) *Agricultural Geography*, Oxford: Oxford University Press.

Intenational Union for Conservation of Nature and Natural Resources (1980) *World Conservation Strategy*, IUCN.

Jayal, N. D. (1985) 'Destruction of water resources – the most critical ecological crisis of East Asia', *Ambio*, **14** (2): 92–8

Jenning, P. R. (1976) 'The amplification of agricultural production', in *Food and Agriculture. A Scientific American Book*, San Francisco: W. H. Freeman and Co., pp. 125–37.

Jensen, N. F. (1978) 'Limits to growth in world food production,' *Science* **201** 28 July: 317–20

Johnson, D. (1984) 'World food and agriculture', in J. L. Simon, and H. Kahn. (eds), *The Resourceful Earth. A Response to Global 2000*, New York: Basil Blackwell, pp. 67–113.

Johnson, S. (1983) *World Grain Economy and Climate Change to the Year 2000*, Washington: National Defense University.

Johnson, W., Stoltzfus, V. and Craumer, P. (1977) 'Energy conservation in Amish agriculture', *Science* **198** 28 Oct: 373–8.

Jones, P. D., Wigley, T. M. L. and Wright, P. B. (1986) 'Global temperature variations between 1961 and 1984', *Nature* **332** 31 July: 430–4.

Joseph, A. E., Keddie, P. D. and Smit, B. (1988) 'Unravelling the population turnaround in rural Canada', *Canadian Geographer* **32** (1): 17–30.

Judson, S. (1968) 'Erosion of the land, or what's happening to our continents', *American Scientist*, **56** (4): 356–76.

Kassas, M. (1982) 'Food and resources', in J. Faaland (ed.), *Population and the World Economy in the 21st Century*, Oxford: Basil Blackwell, pp. 78–95.

Kates, R. W. (1979) 'Climate and society: lessons from recent events', in *Proceedings of the World Climate Conference (WMO No. 537)*, Geneva: World Meterological Society, pp. 682–92.

Keating, M. (1985) 'The march of the Sahara. Much worse than a food crisis,' *The Globe and Mail*, Tuesday 14 May: 7.

Kellogg, W. W. (1977) *Effects of Human Activities on Global Climate. (WMO Technical Note No. 156)*, Geneva: World Meterological Organization.

Kellogg, W. W. (1978) 'Global influences of mankind on climate', in J. Gribbin (ed.), *Climatic Change*, Cambridge: Cambridge University Press, pp. 205–27.

Kellogg, W. W. and Schware, R. (1981) *Climate Change and Society: Consequences of Increasing Atmospheric Carbon Dioxide*, Boulder, Colorado: Westview Press.

Kerr, R. A. (1985) 'Fifteen years of African drought', *Science*, **227** 22 Mar.: 1453–4.

Kimball, B. A. and Idso, S. B. (1983) 'Increasing atmospheric CO_2: effects on crop yield, water use and climate', *Agricultural Water Management*, **7** (1): 55–72.

Kogan, F. N. (1981) 'Geographical aspects of climate and weather limitations for cereal production in the USSR', in *15th Conference on Agriculture and Forest Meteorology and 5th Conference on Biometeorology*, Boston, Mass., American Meteorological Society, pp. 128–30.

Kogan, F. N. (1983) 'Soviet grain production: resources and prospects', *Soviet Geography*, **24** (9): 631–61.

Kogan, Felix (1985) 'Climate – technology interaction index as an early indicator of changes in long term yield trend', in *17th Conference, Agricultural and Forest Meteorology and 7th Conference, Biometeorology and Aerobiology*, Scottsdale, Arizona, American Meteorological Society, pp. 209–12.

Kovda, V. A. (1977) 'Arid land irrigation and soil fertility problems of salinity, alkalinity, compaction', in E. B. Worthington (ed.), *Arid Land Irrigation in Developing Countries – Environmental Problems and Effects*, London: Pergamon Press, pp. 211–35.

Kovda, V. A. (1979) 'Soil reclamation and food production', in M. R. Biswas and A. K. Biswas (eds), *Food, Climate and Man*, New York: Wiley and Sons, pp. 159–86.

Krueger, R. R. (1959) 'Changing land use patterns in the Niagara Fruit Belt', *Transactions of the Royal Canadian Institute*, **32** (2), No. 67.

Kumar, S. (1988) 'The Third World toils to feed the west', *The Globe and Mail*, 15 April: A7.

L'vovich M. I. (trans. and ed. R. L. Nace) (1979) *World Water Resources and the Future*, American Geophysical Union.

Lal, R. (1976) 'Soil erosion problems on an alfisol in Western Nigeria and their control', *IITA*, Monograph 1.

Larson, W. E., Pierce, F. J. and Dowdy, R. H. (1983) 'The threat of soil erosion to long term crop production', *Science*, **219** 4 Feb.: 458–65.

Larson, W. E., Swan, J. B., and Pierce, F. J. (1982) 'Agronomic implications of using crop residues for energy', in W. Lockeretz (ed.) *Agriculture as a Producer and Consumer of Energy*. Boulder Col.: Westview Press, pp. 91–122.

Leach, G. (1976) *Energy and Food Production*, Guildford, England: IPC Science and Technology Press.

Leach, G., Jarass, L., Obermain, G., and Hoffman, L. (1986) *Energy and Growth: A Comparison of 13 Industrial and Developing Countries*, London: Butterworth.

Leontief, W. (1977) *The Future of the World Economy*, New York: Oxford.

Lieth H. (1987), 'Ecological aspects of irrigation', in W. R. Jordan (ed.), *Water and Water Policy in World Food Supplies*, College Station, Texas: Texas A and M University Press, pp. 215–24.

Lilley, J. (1982) *Dryland Salinity in Alberta*, ECA82–17/1B13, Edmonton: Environmental Council of Alberta.

Lindh, G. (1979) 'Water and food production', in M. R. Biswas and A. K. Biswas (eds), *Food, Climate and Man*, New York: John Wiley, pp. 52–72.

Linneman, H. (ed.) (1979) *Model of International Relations in Agriculture*, Amsterdam: North Holland.

References

Lockeretz, W., Klepper, R., Commoner, B., Gertler, M., Fast, S., O'Leary, D., and Blobaum, R. (1977) 'Economic and energy comparisons of crop production on organic and conventional corn belt farms', in W. Lockeretz (ed.), *Agriculture and Energy*, New York: Academic Press, pp. 85–101.

Luther, F. M. (1985) 'Projecting the climatic effects of increasing carbon dioxide: volume summary', in M. C. MacCracken and F. M. Luther (eds), *The Potential Climatic Effects of Increasing Carbon Dioxide*, Washington: US Department of Energy, pp. 259–72.

Lyles, L. (1975) 'Possible effects of wind erosion on soil productivity', *Journal of Soil and Water Conservation* **30** (Nov – Dec): 279–83.

Mabbutt, J. A. (1978) 'Desertification of Australia in its global context', *Search*, **9** (7): 252–6.

Mabbutt, J. A. (1984) 'A global assessment of the status and trends of desertification', *Environmental Conservation*, **11** (2): 103–13.

MacKey, J. (1981) 'Cereal production', in Y. Pomeranz and Lars Munck (eds), *Cereals: A Renewable Resource; Theory and Practice*, St Paul: The American Association of Cereal Chemists, pp. 5–23.

Makhijani, A., and Poole, A. (1975) *Energy and Agriculture in the Third World*, Cambridge, Mass.: Ballinger

Martin, J. H. (1982) 'Biogas production from manures: a realistic assessment', in W. Lockeretz (ed.), *Agriculture as a Producer and Consumer of Energy*, Boulder, Col.: Westview, pp. 123–34.

Mattei, F. (1979) 'Climatic variability and agriculture in the semi-arid tropics', in *Proceedings of the World Climate Conference*, (WMO No. 537), Geneva: World Meteorological Organization, pp. 475–509.

McQuigg, J. D. (1979) 'Climatic variability and agriculture in the temperate regions', in *Proceedings of the World Climate Conference* (WMO No. 537), Geneva: World Meteorological Organization, pp. 406–25.

McQuigg, J. D. (1981) 'Climatic variability and crop yield in high and low temperate regions', in *Food–Climate Interactions*, Dordrecht, Holland: D. Reidel Co., pp. 121–38.

McWilliam, J. R. (1981) 'Research and development to service a sustainable agriculture', *Search* **12** (1–2): 15–21.

Meadows, D., Richardson, J. and Bruckman, G. (1982) *Groping in the Dark*, New York: John Wiley.

Meadows, D. H., Meadows, D. L., Randers, J. and Behrens, W. W. III (1972) *Limits to Growth*, New York: Universe Books.

Meadows, D. L., Behrens, W. W. III, Meadows, D. H., Naill, R. F., Randers, J. and Zahn, E. K. O. (1974) *Dynamics of Growth in a Finite World*. Cambridge Mass: Wright-Allen Press Inc.

Medawar, P. (1969) 'On the effecting of all things possible', *Technology Review* **72** (2): 30–5.

Mellor, J. W. and Johnston, B. F. (1984) 'The world food equation: interrelations among development, employment, and food consumption', *Journal of Economic Literature*, **22** (June): 531–74.

Mesarovic, M. and Pestel, E. (1974) *Mankind at the Turning Point. The Second Report to the Club of Rome*, New York: E. P. Dutton & Co. Inc., New York: Wiley.

Mitchell, R. (1984) 'The ecological basis for comparative primary production', in R. Lawrence, B. R. Stimmer and G. J. House (eds), *Agricultural Ecosystems: Unifying Concepts*, New York: J. Wiley and Sons, pp. 13–55.

Montalembert, M. R. de (1983) 'Biomass resources for energy: the critical issues', *Ceres* **16** (1): 40–4.

Myers, N. (1987) 'The environmental basis of sustainable development', *The*

Annals of Regional Science, **21** (3): 33–43.

Nagar, B. R. (1977) 'Alternatives to energy intensive fertilizers. Organic materials as fertilizers', in W. Lockeretz (ed.), *Agriculture and Energy*, New York: Academic Press, pp. 657–68.

Newman, J. E. (1980) 'Climate change impacts on the growing season of the North American Corn Belt', *Biometeorology* **7**: 128–42.

Norgaard, R. (1984) 'Coevolutionary development potential', *Land Economics* **60** (2): 160–73.

Norse, D. (1979) 'Natural resources, development strategies and the world food problem', in M. R. Biswas and A. K. Biswas (eds), *Food, Climate and Man*, New York: Wiley and Sons, pp. 12–51.

OECD (1985) *The State of the Environment*, Paris: OECD.

Ophuls, W. (1977) *Ecology and the Politics of Scarcity*, San Francisco: Freeman.

Oram, P. A. (1982) 'Economic cost of climatic variation', in K. Blaxter and L. Fowden (eds), *Food, Nutrition and Climate*, London: Applied Science Publishers, pp. 355–92.

Oram, P. A. (1985) 'Sensitivity of agricultural production to climatic change', *Climatic Change*, **7** (1): 129–52.

Organization for Economic Cooperation and Development, *Study of Trends in World Supply and Demand of Major Agricultural Commodities*, Paris: OECD.

Parry, M. L. and Carter, T. R. (eds) (1984) *Assessing the Impact of Climatic Change in Cold Regions*, Summary Report, Laxenburg, Austria: IIASA.

Parry, M. L. and Carter, T. R. (1987) 'The assessment of effects of climatic variations on agriculture: aims, methods and summary of results', reprinted from M. L. Parry, T. R. Carter and N. T. Konijn (eds), *Assessment of Climatic Variations on Agriculture. Vol. 1 Assessments in Cool Temperate and Cold Regions*, Dordrecht, Netherlands: Reidel.

Pearce, D. and Markandya, A. (1987) 'Marginal opportunity cost as a planning concept in natural resource management', *The Annals of Regional Science*, **21** (3): 18–31.

Pels, Simon (1978) 'Waterlogging and salinization in irrigated semi-arid regions of NSW', *Search* **9** (7): 272–80.

PFRA (1983) *Land Degradation and Soil Consumption Issues on the Canadian Prairies*, Regina: Agriculture Canada.

Pierce, F. J., Larson, W. E., Dowdy, R. H. and Graham, W. A. P. (1983) 'Productivity of soils: assessing long-term changes due to erosion', *Journal of Water and Soil Conservation*, **38** (1): 39–44.

Pierce, J. T. and Furuseth, O. J. (1986) 'Constraints to expanded food production: a North American perspective', *Natural Resources Journal*, **26** (1): 15–39.

Pierce, J. T. and Stathers, R. J. (1988) 'Environmental impacts on cereal grain production in the Canadian Prairie provinces: a growth constraint model', *Agriculture, Ecosystems and Environment*, **21**: 225–43.

Pimentel, D. (1979) 'Energy and agricultural', in M. R. Biswas and A. K. Biswas (eds), *Food, Climate and Man*, New York: John Wiley and Sons, pp. 73–103.

Pimentel, D. (1984) 'Energy flow and the food system', in D. Pimentel and C. W. Hall (eds), *Food and Energy Resources*, New York: Academic Press, pp. 1–24.

Pimentel, D. and Pimentel, M. (1979) *Food, Energy and Society*, New York: John Wiley and Sons.

Pimentel, D., Terhune, E. C., Dyson-Hudson, R., RocLereau, S., Samris, R., Smith, E. A., Denman, D., Reifschneider, D., and Shepard, M. (1976) 'Land degradation: effects on food and energy resources', *Science*, **194**, 8 Oct: 149–55.

Pirie, N. W. (1976) 'The world food supply: physical limitations', in *Futures*, **8** (6): 509–16.

Plaut, T. R. (1980) 'Urban expansion and the loss of farmland in the United States:

References

implications for the future', *American Journal of Agricultural Economics*, **62** (3): 537–42.

Population Reference Bureau (1985) *1985 World Population Data Sheet*, Washington: Population Reference Bureau.

Posner, J. L. and McPherson, M. F. (1982) 'Agriculture on the steep slopes of Tropical America: current situation and prospects for the year 2000', *World Development*, **10** (5): 341–53.

Preston, R. E. and Russwurm, L. H. (1977) 'The developing Canadian urban pattern: an analysis of population change, 1971–1976', in R. E. Preston and L. H. Russwurm (eds), *Essays on Canadian Urbanization*, Waterloo: University of Waterloo, pp. 1–30.

Rangeley, W. R. (1987) 'Irrigation and drainage in the world', in W. R. Jordan (ed.), *Water and Water Policy in World Food Supplies*, College Station, Texas: Texas A and M University Press, pp. 29–36.

Rao, A. R. and Singh, I. J. (1977a), 'Choice of foods to shorten food chains in India, In W. Lockeretz (ed.) *Agriculture and Energy*, New York: Academic Press pp. 581–595.

Rao, A. R. and Singh, I. J. (1977b) 'Bullocks – the mainstay of farm power in India, In W. Lockeretz (ed.) *Agriculture and Energy*, New York: Academic Press pp. 597–606.

Rapp, A. (1974) *A Review of Desertification in Africa – Water, Vegetation and Man*, Stockholm, Sweden: Report No. 1, Secretariat for International Ecology.

Raup, Phillip M. (1980) 'Competition for land and the future of American agriculture', in S. Batie and R Healy (eds), *The Future of American Agriculture as a Strategic Resource*. Ann Arbor, Michigan: The Conservation Foundation, Edwards Brothers, pp. 41–7.

Redclift, M. R. (1987) *Sustainable Development: Exploring the Contradictions*. London: Methuen.

Rennie, D. A. Beaton, J. D. and Hedlin, R. A. (1980) *The Role of Fertilizer Nutrients in Western Canadian Development*, Calgary: Canada West Foundation.

Repetto, R. (1986) *World Enough and Time*, New Haven, Conn.: Yale University Press.

Revelle, R. (1976a) 'Energy use in rural India', *Science*, **192**, 4 June: 969–75.

Revelle, R. (1976b) 'The resources available for agriculture', in *Food and Agriculture a Scientific American Book*, San Francisco: W. H. Freeman and Co., pp. 113–125.

Revelle, R. (1982) 'Carbon dioxide and world climate', *Scientific American*, **247** (2): 38–43.

Revelle, R. (1984) 'The world supply of agricultural land', in J. L. Simon and H. Kahn (eds), *The Resourceful Earth*, Oxford: Basil Blackwell, pp. 184–201.

Richards, J. F. (1984) 'Global patterns of land conservation', *Environment*, **26** (9): 6–38.

Ridley, A. O. and Hedlin, R. A. (1980) 'Crop yields and soil management on the Canadian Prairies, past and present', *Canadian Journal of Soil Science*. **60** (3): 393–402.

Rifkin, J. (1980) *Entropy*, New York: Bantam.

Riquier, J. (1977) 'Philosophy of the world assessment of soil degradation and items for discussion', in *Assessing Soil Degradation*, FAO Soils Bulletin No. 34, pp. 36–48, Rome: FAO.

Riquier, J. (1982) 'World assessment of soil degradation', *Nature and Resources,* **18** (2): 18–21.

Robinson, A. R. (1981) 'Erosion and sediment control in China's Yellow River basin', *Journal of Soil and Water Conservation*, **36** (3): 125–7.

Rogers, P. P. (1985) 'Fresh water', in R. Repetto (ed.), *The Global Possible:*

Resources, Development and the New Century, New Haven, Conn.: Yale University Press, pp. 255–98.

Rosegrant, M. W. (1986) 'Commentary: irrigation with equity in Southeast Asia', *International Food Policy Research Institute*, **8** (1): 1–4.

Rosenberg, N. J. (1981) 'The increasing CO_2 concentration in the atmosphere and its implication on agricultural productivity', *Climatic Change*, **3** (3): 265–79.

Rosenzweig, C. (1985) 'Potential CO_2-induced climate effects of North American wheat-producing regions', *Climatic Change* **7** (4): 367–89.

Rovere, E. L. La. (1985) 'A South–South assault on the food/energy problem', *Ceres*, **18** (1): 25–8.

Ruttan, V. W., (1980) 'Agricultural research and the future of American agriculture', in S. Batie and R. Healy (eds), *The Future of American Agriculture as a Strategic Resource*, Ankeny, Iowa: The Conservation Foundation pp. 117–55.

Ruttan, V. W. (1984) 'Induced innovation and agricultural development', In G. K. Douglass (ed.), *Agricultural Sustainability in a Changing World Order*, Boulder, Colorado: Westview Press, pp. 107–34.

Sampson, R. N. (1982) 'Land for energy or land for food?', *Ecologist*, **12** (2): 67–79

Sanchez, P. A. and Buol, S. W. (1975) 'Soils of the Tropics and the world food crisis', *Science* **188**, 9 May: 598–603.

Sandford, S. (1983) *Management of Pastoral Development in the Third World*, New York: John Wiley and Sons.

Santer, B. (1985) 'The use of general circulation models in climate impact analysis – a preliminary study of the impacts of a CO_2-induced climatic change on West European agriculture', *Climatic Change*, **7** (1): 71–95.

Schaffer, G. (1980) 'Ensuring man's food supplies by developing new land and preserving cultivated land', *Applied Geography and Development*, **16**: 7–24.

Schlesinger, M. E. and Mitchell, J. F. B. (1985) 'Model projections of the equilibrium climatic response to increased carbon dioxide', in M. C. MacCracken and F. M. Luther (eds), *The Potential Climatic Effects of Increasing Carbon Dioxide*, Washington, DC: US Department of Energy, pp. 81–148.

Schneider, S. (1976) *The Genesis Strategy Climate and Global Survival*, New York: Plenum Press.

Scrimshaw, N. S. and Taylor, L. (1980) 'Food', *Scientific American* **243** (3): 78–100.

Secretariat of the United Nations Conference on Desertification (1977) *Desertification: Its Causes and Consequences*, Oxford: Pergamon Press.

Sheridan, D. (1981) 'The desert blooms – at a price', *Environment* **23** (3): 7–41.

Silliman, J. and Lenton, R. (1987) 'Irrigation and the land poor, in W. R. Jordan (ed.), *Water and Water Policy in World Food Supplies*, College Station, Texas: Texas A and M University Press pp. 161–72.

Simon, J. L. (1981) *The Ultimate Resource*, Princeton, NJ: Princeton University Press.

Sinclair, A. R. E. and Fryxell, J. M. (1985) 'The Sahel of Africa: ecology of a disaster', *Canadian Journal of Zoology*, **63**: 987–94.

Sinclair, R. J. (1967) 'Von Thunen and urban sprawl', *Annals of the Association of American Geographers*, **57**: 72–87.

Slogget, G. R. and Mapp, H. P. (1984) 'Analysis of rising irrigation costs in the Great Plains', *Water Resources Bulletin* **20** (2): 229–33.

Smerdon, E. T. and Hiler, E. A. (1987) 'Energy in irrigation in developing countries', in W. R. Jordan (ed.), *Water and Water Policy in World Food Supplies*, College Station, Texas: Texas A and M University Press, pp. 279–84.

Smil, V. (1981) 'Land use management in the People's Republic of China', *Environmental Management*, **5**(4): 301–11.

Smil, V. (1984) 'On energy and land', *American Scientist*, **72** (1): 15–21.

Smil, V. (1984) *The Bad Earth: Environmental Degradation in China*, London: Zed Press.

Smit, B. and Flaherty, M. (1984) 'Assessing land use options for future food needs', paper presented at the *Association of American Geographers' annual Meeting*, Washington, DC.

Snead, R. E. (1980) *World Atlas of Geomorphic Features*, Huntington, NY: Kreiger.

Statistics Canada, (1975) *Handbook of Agricultural Statistics*, Ottawa: Supply and Services Canada.

Stickler, F. C., Burrows, W. C. and Nelson, L. F. (1975) *Energy from Sun, to Plant, to Man*, Moline, Ill.: Deere Co.

Swindale, L. D. et al (1981) 'Climatic variability and crop yields in the semi-arid Tropics', in W. Bach, J. Pankrath and S. H. Schneider (eds), *Food-Climate Interactions*, Dordrecht, Holland: D. Reidel Co. pp. 139–66.

Szabolcs, I. (1979) *Review of Research on Salt Affected Soils*, Paris: UNESCO, Natural Resources Research Series xv.

Takaya, Y. (1971) 'Physiography of rice land in the Chao Phraya basin of Thailand', *Southeast Asian Studies*, **9** (3): 375–97.

Tarrant, J. R. (1980) *Food Policies*, Chichester: John Wiley.

Tarrant, J. R. (1987) 'Variability in world cereal yields', *Transactions of the Institute of British Geographers*, NS 12: 315–26.

Thompson, L. M. (1975) 'Weather variability, climatic change and grain production, *Science*, **188**, 8 May: 534–41.

Todaro, M. (1985) *Economic Development in the Third World*, 3rd edn, New York: Longman.

Tomlin, E. W. F. (1978) (ed.) *Arnold Toynbee – A Selection from His Works*, Oxford: Oxford University Press.

UN (1966) 'A compendium of major international rivers in the Ecafe region', *Water Resources Series*, No. 29.

UN (1980) *Patterns of Urban and Rural Population Growth*, New York: Department of International Economic and Social Affairs, Population Study No. 68.

UN (1985) *UN Compendium of Human Settlement Statistics*, New York: UN Press.

UN Department of Economic and Social Affairs (1976) *The Demand For Water*, New York: United Nations.

US President's Advisory Committee (1967) *The World Food Problem*, Vol. ii Washington: The White House.

UN Water Conference (1977) *Water for Agriculture*, Annex 1, New York.

US Environmental Protection Agency (1971) *The Mineral Water Quality Problem in the Colorado River Basin*, San Francisco: EPA.

US Office of Technology Assessment (1986) 'New technologies and agricultural productivity', *Economic Impact*, **53**: 14–21.

USDA (1957 and 1983) *Agricultural Statistics*, Washington DC: US Printing Office.

USDA (1976) *Eygpt – Major Constraints to Increasing Agricultural Productivity*, Foreign Agricultural Report No. 120, Economics and Statistics Service, USDA, Washington: USDA.

USDA (1980) *America's Soil and Water: Conditions and Trends*, Washington: USDA Soil Conservation Service.

USDA (1981) *World Indices of Agricultural and Food Production, Statistical Bulletin No. 669*, Washington: Economic Research Service, USDA.

USDA (1987) *The Second RCA Appraisal. (Draft Copy)*, Washington: Soil Conservation Service, USDA.

Virgo, K. J. and Munro, R. N. (1978) 'Soil erosion features of the Central Plateau region of Tigrai Ethiopia', *Geoderma*, **20** (2): 131–57.

Voskrensky, K. P. (1978) 'Water balance of land. Distribution of external and internal run-off areas', in V. I. Korzum (ed.), *World Water Balance and Water Resources of the Earth*, Paris: Unesco Press, pp. 489–91.

Walker, L. D. (1980) 'An assessment of water resources in the United States, 1975–2000, in *Resource Constrained Economics: The North American Dilemma* (Proceedings of the 34th Annual Meeting of the Soil Conservation Society of America), Ankeny, Iowa: Soil Conservation Society of America, pp. 73–95.

Wang, W. C., Weubbles, D. J. and Washington, W. M. (1985) 'Potential climatic effects of perturbations other than carbon dioxide', in M. C. MacCracken and F. M. Luther (eds), *The Potential Climatic Effects of Increasing Carbon Dioxide*, Washington: US Department of Energy, pp. 191–236.

Warnock, J. W. (1987) *The Politics of Hunger*, Toronto: Methuen.

Weber, A. (1977) 'Perspectives on population growth, food supply and energy use in agricultural development by historical and cross-sectional graphical analysis', *Eastern Africa Journal of Rural Development*, 10: 1–21.

Wellhausen, E. J. (1976) 'The agriculture of Mexico', in *Food and Agriculture, a Scientific American Book*, San Francisco: W. H. Freeman, pp. 87–101.

White, G. (1983) 'Water resource adequacy: illusion and reality', *Natural Resources Forum*, 7 (1): 12–21.

Widstrand, C. (ed.) (1980) *Water Conflicts and Research Priorities*, Oxford: Pergamon Press.

Wigley, T. M. L., Jones, P. D. and Kelly, P. M. (1980) 'Scenarios for a warm, high-CO_2 World', *Nature*, 283, 3 Jan: 17–21.

Willet, J. W. (ed.), 1976. *The World Food Situation Problems and Prospects to 1985*, Washington: Oceania.

Williams, G. D. V., Pocock, N. J. and Russwurm, L. H. (1978) 'The spatial association of agroclimatic resources and urban population in Canada', In R. M. Irving (ed.), *Readings in Canadian Geography*, Toronto: Holt, Rinehart and Winston, pp. 165–79.

Williams, J. (1979) 'Anomalies in temperature and rainfall during warm Arctic seasons as a guide to the formulation of climate scenarios', *Climatic Change* 2 (3): 249–66.

Wittfogel, K. A. (1970) *Oriental Despotism: A Comparative Study of Total Power*, New Haven Conn.: Yale University Press (1st edn, 1957).

Wittwer, S. H. (1975) 'Food production: technology and the resource base', *Science*, 185 9 May: 579–84.

— Wittwer, S. H. (1980) 'Carbon dioxide and climatic change: an agricultural perspective', *Journal of Soil and Water Conservation*, 35 May–June: 116–20.

Wolfe, T. (1988) 'Brave new world bites the dust', *The Globe and Mail*, 14 Jan: A7.

World Bank (1980) *World Development Report*, New York: Oxford University Press.

World Bank (1982) *World Development Report*, Oxford: Oxford University Press.

World Bank (1984) *World Development Report*, New York: Oxford University Press.

World Bank (1985) *World Development Report*, New York: Oxford University Press.

World Bank (1986) *World Development Report*, Oxford: Oxford University Press.

World Commission on Environment and Development (1987) *Our Common Future*, Oxford: Oxford University Press.

World Meteorological Organization (1986) *Monthly Climatic Data for the World*. Washington: Department of Commerce.

Worthington, E. B. (ed.), (1977) *Arid Land Irrigation in Developing Countries – Environmental Problems and Effects*, Oxford: Pergamon Press.

Environmental Problems and Effects, Oxford: Pergamon Press.

Yeates, M. (1985) *Land in Canada's Urban Heartland*, Land Use in Canada, Series No. 27, Ottawa: Environment Canada.

Yeh, C. J., Tweeten, L. G. and Quance, C. L. (1977) 'U.S. Agricultural Production Capacity', *American Journal of Agricultural Economics*, **59** (1): 37–48.

Yotopoulos, P. A. (1980) 'A strategy for irrigated agricultural development', in S. S. Johl (ed.), *Irrigation and Agricultural Development*, Oxford: Pergamon Press, pp. 31–40.

Zeimetz, K. A., Dillon, E., Hardy, E. E. and Otte, R. C. (1976) *Dynamics of Land Use in Fast Growth Areas*, Washington, DC: USDA Economic Research Service Report No. 325.

Index

Index

Index